WITHDRAWN

D0205473

327.0956
P872r

The
POWERS
in the
MIDDLE EAST

THE ULTIMATE STRATEGIC ARENA

Edited by

BERNARD REICH

PRAEGER

New York
Westport, Connecticut
London

Library of Congress Cataloging-in-Publication Data

The Powers in the Middle East.

Bibliography: p.
Includes index.
1. Near East – Politics and government – 1945–
2. Near East – Foreign relations. I. Reich, Bernard.
DS63.1.P7 1986   327′.0956   86-21266
ISBN 0-275-92304-5 (alk. paper)

Copyright © 1987 by Praeger Publishers

All rights reserved. No portion of this book may be
reproduced, by any process or technique, without the
express written consent of the publisher.

Library of Congress Catalog Card Number: 86-21266
ISBN: 0-275-92304-5

First published in 1987

Praeger Publishers, 521 Fifth Avenue, New York, NY 10175
A division of Greenwood Press, Inc.

Printed in the United States of America

The paper used in this book complies with the Permanent
Paper Standard issued by the National Information Standards
Organization (Z39.48-1984).

10 9 8 7 6 5 4 3 2 1

Contents

CA [May23 o6

ALLEGHENY COLLEGE LIBRARY

87-5944

Preface

The Middle East has been a major focal point of international concern for centuries, and that attention has increased since World War II. Numerous powers—some regional and some from beyond, some of the rank of global superpower and others much smaller—have sought gain and glory in the area. In recent decades the danger of superpower confrontation has added to other interests and increased the strategic significance of the region.

Our purpose is to examine systematically the interests, objectives, and policies of the major external actors in the Middle East as they have evolved to the present. The introductory chapter considers the strategic nature of the region, focusing on its significance in the latter part of the twentieth century, and explains the reasons it became a major arena of competition among the powers. The analysis of the policies of the United States and the Soviet Union considers the central contemporary powers and their rivalry in the region and the context in which the other powers function. The section on Europe examines the roles of Britain and France, the traditional European actors in the Middle East, but also the European Community as a new actor seeking to develop a pan-European approach. The Asian section looks at the primarily economic roles of Japan and Korea, as well as the special case of China. Each chapter explores the interests, objectives, policies, and achievements of the powers as well as the competition and cooperation among them. The authors have elaborated on past activities and assessed the prospects for future achievements.

The book derives from the experience of its authors in studying and teaching the international relations of the Middle East, especially the role that external powers play in the region. Although the identified authors wrote the specified sections, all shared in its research and writing and reviewed the manuscript to assure accuracy and consistency as part of a team effort. In addition to this collaborative effort, the volume has benefited from a number of outside readers who made useful and important suggestions for its revision. Matthew Freund and Sally Ann Baynard were particularly helpful in this regard, and Seth Perlman provided valuable assistance in the early stages of the work. Joseph Helman helped in the preparation of the index. Professor Hugh L. LeBlanc, long-time chairman of the Department of Political Science at George Washington University, provided encouragement and support for the effort throughout its gestation.

I
INTRODUCTION

1

The Strategic Arena

John H. McFadden

No region of the world has figured so prominently in the policies of so many states as has the Middle East. The region is strewn with battlefields that chronicle the rise and fall of empires built upon the wealth of trade between the Indian Ocean and the Mediterranean Sea. Three great monotheistic religions had their origins there, each spreading its influence globally. Today, the Middle East continues to be the focus of great power interests. In the place of empires, independent and strongly nationalistic states have emerged, some aligned with one or the other of the superpowers. Together, they form a crucial bridge connecting Europe with African and Asian Third World nations. Most importantly, Middle Eastern states are the largest single source of petroleum for the noncommunist world.

This chapter examines three aspects of the Middle East that form the core issues of great power international policies: the role of oil as it pertains to international stability, the geopolitical importance of the region in relation to the great power rivalry, and the impact of Middle Eastern regional conflicts on international politics.

OIL AND THE INTERNATIONAL POLITICAL ARENA

To a significant degree, the policies of Western states toward the Middle East are aimed at securing access to oil in order to maintain domestic economies and national security. The states of the industrialized world, with their large energy requirements, generally have very little oil while Middle Eastern states, with minimal energy needs, are endowed with most of the world's proven oil reserves.

TABLE 1.1: **Estimated Reserves of Crude Oil, 1986 (thousands of barrels)**

State	Reserves
Saudi Arabia	168,800,000
Kuwait	89,774,000
USSR	61,000,000
Iran	49,300,000
Mexico	47,876,000
Iraq	44,110,000
Abu Dhabi	31,500,000
United States	28,000,300
Venezuela	25,591,000
Libya	21,300,000
China	18,420,000
Nigeria	16,600,000
United Kingdom	13,000,000
Norway	10,900,000
Algeria	8,820,000
Indonesia	8,500,000
Canada	6,500,000
Oman	4,000,000
Egypt	3,850,000
India	3,736,000
Noncommunist World Total	618,770,000
World Total	700,140,560

Source: *Basic Petroleum Data Book* 6, No. 2 (May 1986) (American Petroleum Institute, Washington, D.C.).

The distribution of the world's petroleum reserves, seen in Table 1.1, and the recent trends in crude oil production, seen in Table 1.2, emphasize the degree to which states of the Middle East dominate the international petroleum market. Because more oil was produced in 1979 than in any other year, those data have been included in Table 1.2.

Some states of the industrialized world are more dependent on Middle Eastern oil than others. Table 1.3 shows that while the United States is the largest single consumer of energy in the world, oil provides only 40 percent of U.S. energy requirements. In mid 1985 the largest single supplier of oil to the United States was Saudi Arabia, which provided less than 3 percent of the total energy requirement. Other close allies of the United States, however, are totally dependent on Middle Eastern sources for their energy.

TABLE 1.2: World Crude Oil Production (thousands of barrels)

Producer	1979	Producer	1984
USSR	4,187,280	USSR	4,344,420
Saudi Arabia	3,376,615	United States	3,249,696
United States	3,114,545	Saudi Arabia	1,626,504
Iraq	1,269,105	Mexico	1,005,036
Iran	1,156,320	United Kingdom	927,890
Venezuela	859,940	China	834,480
Nigeria	840,230	Iran	800,442
Kuwait	807,745	Venezuela	633,558
China	774,530	Indonesia	536,556
Libya	763,580	Canada	516,426
United Arab Emirates (UAE)	668,315	Nigeria	509,838
Indonesia	580,715	Iraq	440,298
United Kingdom	572,320	UAE	401,502
Canada	546,040	Libya	392,718
Mexico	533,265	Kuwait	333,792
Algeria	415,005	Egypt	302,682
Neutral Zone*	207,320	Norway	256,200
Egypt	191,625	Algeria	233,508
Brunei/Malaysia	187,925	India	173,248
Qatar	185,420	Australia	180,072
Totals:			
Middle East	7,868,670	Middle East	5,459,253
Noncommunist	17,825,515	Noncommunist	14,420,748
World	22,970,545	World	19,753,368

*Exploited jointly by Saudi Arabia and Kuwait.
Source: Basic Petroleum Data Book 5, No. 3 (Sept. 1985) (American Petroleum Institute, Washington, D.C.).

TABLE 1.3: Middle East Oil as an Energy Source, 1985

Country	Percent of Energy Consumption Worldwide	Percent of Energy Derived from Oil	Percent of Oil from Middle East
United States	25.0	40.2	17.6
OECD (Europe)	17.3	47.3	48.1
France	2.3	46.1	47.3
United Kingdom	2.6	46.2	28.0
Germany	3.6	42.5	37.8
Italy	2.0	60.4	66.9
Japan	5.9	59.2	70.8

Sources: BP Statistical Yearbook, June 1985, and Oil and Gas Statistics (1985/No. 3), Organization for Economic Cooperation and Development (hereafter OECD), International Energy Agency, Second Quarter, 1985.

The policy implications of this are clear. States dependent on the Middle East for oil tend to view events in that region from a different perspective than do the United States and Great Britain. Greater economic dependence means that the political costs of losing economic partners in the Middle East are also high and this denies the more dependent states room to maneuver diplomatically. These differences often create tensions that threaten to place allies on opposing sides of political and economic disputes.

There is evidence to suggest that this dependence will continue in the foreseeable future. Some studies suggest that consumption rates are expected to continue to rise, and that for some industrial states, dependence on oil will actually increase (see Table 1.4).

The oil industry has created great wealth for many Middle Eastern states and, simultaneously, stimulated great demand for advanced technology and consumer items produced by industrialized states. Despite the mutual advantage this situation offers to both consumer and producer, their relationship has been that of adversaries. On several occasions, Middle Eastern governments have attempted to use their domination of the oil market to their advantage by restricting or embargoing oil for political reasons. To understand better the nature of these relationships between producer and consumer, it is necessary to review the history of the petroleum industry in the Middle East.

The Struggle for National Control

For most Middle Easterners, the history of the petroleum industry is one of imperialism. In 1901 a team of British explorers obtained a concession to search for oil in Persia (Iran). They made their first strike in January 1908 and in 1909 formed the Anglo-

TABLE 1.4: World Oil Consumption, History and Projection (millions of barrels per day)

Consumer	1980	1985	1990	1995
United States	17.5	16.1	16.9	17.7
Canada	1.9	1.6	1.6	1.6
Japan	5.0	4.5	5.0	5.1
OECD Europe	13.5	12.5	13.1	12.6
Other Countries	9.0	9.1	10.0	11.1
Total	49.6	47.0	50.9	53.2

Source: Basic Petroleum Data Book 6, No. 2 (May 1986).

Persian Oil Company, which eventually evolved into British Petroleum (BP). British success encouraged other states to explore for oil in the region and between the two World Wars, major oil fields were discovered in Iraq (1927), Bahrain (1931), Saudi Arabia (1933), and Kuwait (1938)—all by non-Middle Easterners, the latter two by American corporations.

Until the early 1970s, most of the decisions concerning the production, shipping, marketing, and sale of Middle Eastern oil were made by a group of Western oil companies known as the Seven Sisters: Exxon, Royal Dutch Shell, Texaco, Gulf, Mobil, British Petroleum, and Socal. These companies enjoyed special exemptions from local laws and occasionally interfered in local political affairs.

Several factors made such an unusual arrangement possible. First, the demand for petroleum existed principally in the industrialized West. Second, the West possessed the technological knowledge and skills needed to extract the oil, convert it to usable forms, and manage the complex international petroleum market. Finally, there was an historic precedent for granting special status to foreign private enterprise in the Middle East, set by the Ottoman sultans. From the standpoint of local governments, as long as the oil companies were willing to reimburse the producing states for the oil they pumped, their presence was regarded as a minor inconvenience.

In the 1950s and 1960s, however, a spirit of nationalism became predominant in the states of the Middle East and the governments of the oil-rich countries demanded changes in the status of foreign oil companies. At first, the oil companies successfully resisted major changes in these arrangements; but then in 1959 and 1960 the major oil companies unilaterally reduced the price of oil on the international market. The oil producing states, which had come to plan their budgets around the taxes paid by the oil companies, were faced with a sudden loss of revenue. In 1960, to defend themselves from future price reductions and to gain a better financial grip on their own resources, Iran, Iraq, Kuwait, Saudi Arabia, and Venezuela formed the Organization of Petroleum Exporting Countries (OPEC). For the first five years of its existence OPEC made its headquarters in Geneva, Switzerland, thereafter moving to Vienna, Austria. The day-to-day business of OPEC is conducted by a permanent staff headed by a secretary general appointed by the members. Today, OPEC includes the original five members plus Algeria, Ecuador, Gabon, Indonesia, Libya, Nigeria, Qatar, the United Arab Emirates (the UAE), and Venezuela. It has no formal, internationally recognized status nor does it have the power to compel any of its members to comply with its resolutions. The political diversity of its members is such that the only unifying feature of the organization is the common desire to maintain a high price for their oil. The history of the organization has proven this to be a poor foundation upon which to base cooperation.

OPEC first attempted to use oil as a foreign policy instrument in June 1967, after the outbreak of hostilities between Egypt, Syria, Jordan, and Israel. The Arab states in OPEC attempted to impose an embargo on the shipment of oil to the United States, Great Britain, and West Germany, hoping to force these governments to end their support for Israel. The attempted embargo failed because oil was so abundant that the targeted states were able to obtain sufficient supplies from non-Arab sources. It created minor dislocations in the market and had a temporary adverse effect on such international currencies as the British pound. Most important, members of OPEC did not act in unity. Venezuela, a charter member of OPEC, was a major source of oil to the United States and Europe during the embargo.

In 1973, the Arab oil producers made a second attempt at an embargo, this one more successful. It should be noted, however, that the success of the 1973 embargo required an unusual set of circumstances, bringing together an intricate mixture of international politics, economics, and the nationalistic pride of the oil producing states. To begin with, between 1967 and 1973, the surfeit of oil on the international market had disappeared. Politically, the disunity among the members of OPEC had given way to a general agreement that the time had come to gain a better handle on their oil assets. In October 1973, representatives of OPEC requested that the major oil companies negotiate a new set of pricing agreements. The two sides met in Vienna on October 8, 1973—soon after that the 1973 Arab-Israeli war began.

On October 16, negotiations broke down and OPEC launched a double assault on the Seven Sisters. First, it announced a unilateral price increase from $2.25 to $5.12 per barrel. The following day, the Arab members of OPEC declared that they were reducing oil production by 5 percent and would continue to do so every month until Israel relinquished control over occupied Arab territories and the rights of the Palestinians were restored. Most of the Arab states suspended shipment of oil to the United States and Holland because of their pro-Israel stands. On December 23, Iran announced a unilateral increase in the price of its oil to $11.65 per barrel or nearly four times the previous rate. The other oil producing states raised their prices accordingly.

The combined price increase and reduced production caused spot shortages of certain fuels in North America, Western Europe, and Japan. As could be expected, the price of all commodities associated with petroleum rose, exacerbating a world recession that had started a few years earlier. Because the transportation and distribution of oil was still controlled by the international oil companies, the attempt to direct the oil weapon against specific consumers—the core of the embargo strategy—failed, and after some brief interruptions oil was available to all states. But the effects of reduced production on a market already short of supply were sufficient for OPEC members to achieve their broader objective, the attainment of control over their individual oil resources. The Seven Sisters, under great international pressure, agreed to renegotiate their price-setting policies with OPEC and the days of cheap petroleum came to an end.

Although the OPEC price rise and the embargo of oil to selected states came together, their joining was coincidental. The price hike must be seen primarily as an economic issue. Iran, the driving force behind the fourfold increase in price, was motivated by a desire to obtain the funds necessary to finance development programs including plans for a major increase in the size and quality of the state's armed forces. The embargo was not a matter of concern to Iran since it was not involved in the Arab-Israeli dispute. In fact, Iran supplied oil to Israel, the United States, and the Netherlands throughout the embargo. To be sure, the reduction in the amount of oil available on the open market that resulted from the embargo added strength to demands for higher prices. But it took the combination of economic and political circumstances to create the necessary pressure to force the Seven Sisters into meeting OPEC's demands.

The oil embargo was lifted in 1974 after Arab governments were assured that reasonable progress toward settlement of the Arab-Israeli dispute was being made. Thereafter, individual state imperatives took over. The oil producing countries began separate negotiations with the oil companies that were to lead to their full participation in the production of oil and the complete control over their petroleum assets. The oil companies retained their position as international managers of petroleum markets but from then on performed more as service contractors to the oil producing states than as policymakers.

The Counter-Strategies of the Oil Consuming States

When management of the international petroleum market shifted from the oil companies to the governments of the oil producing countries, both the political and commercial relationships between the members of the Organization for Economic Cooperation and Development (OECD) and the Middle Eastern oil producers changed. Until 1973, the industrialized states had relied heavily on the oil companies to provide them with a continuous flow of oil. It was not until the oil companies lost control over the industry that the oil consuming states began to devise strategies to deal with another embargo. Measures adopted or considered by the West European states and Japan to reduce the effects of a future oil embargo fell into three categories.

First, all of the developed states undertook extensive measures to reduce their dependence on oil as a source of energy. These efforts were initially successful. Returning to Table 1.4, note that oil consumption rates began to drop after 1980 as a consequence of new energy policies adopted by OECD members in 1974 that were starting to come into full operation. It is worth noting, however, that a ten-year progress study conducted in 1984 by the European Economic Community (EEC) revealed that around a third of the energy savings had occurred as a result of reduced residential consumption. The study determined that oil was still the most important source of energy in the industrial and transportation sectors critical to national security. Energy usage in the transportation sector had actually increased.[1]

After conservation, two other options were considered: military occupation of Middle East oil fields, and the formation of an international organization—the International Energy Agency (IEA)—to improve cooperation and to manage world oil resources in the event of crisis.

The military option, which proved to be the least viable of the three options, grew out of a U.S. concern that the Soviet Union might be encouraged to threaten Western Europe militarily if it appeared that a shortage of oil had weakened NATO defenses. A quick solution to the oil shortage would be needed and the thinking was that the rapid deployment of Western military forces to the oil fields would provide a reasonable means of assuring the flow of oil. In 1975, however, a study for the U.S. Congress (*Oil Fields as Military Objectives: A Feasibility Study*) concluded that the use of military force to occupy oil fields in the Middle East would probably not succeed. Among other things, the study determined that a military operation was not feasible because the oil producing states would have sufficient warning time to sabotage the oil fields, temporarily leaving the world with less oil than if the embargo continued. Further, such an operation was deemed politically undesirable because U.S. military aggression would alienate otherwise pro-Western states in the region, thereby strengthening the Soviet position. The fact that military intervention was considered, however, may have induced a measure of caution in the policies of the oil producing states, bringing them to the conclusion that another embargo could jeopardize them as much as the oil consumers. As a viable counterstrategy to another oil embargo, however, the military option was set aside.

Attempts at international cooperation among the major industrial states led to the establishment of the IEA under the auspices of the OECD to coordinate sharing of oil assets. In November 1974, states participating in the agency agreed that in the event of another supply disruption they would jointly share fuel supplies among themselves when available supplies fell below a predetermined level by at least 7 percent. Like OPEC, however, the IEA has no power to compel any of the members to comply. Its only international standing is that which is voluntarily accorded to it by its members and because of this, the range of situations under which the provisions of cooperation would come into effect was kept narrow.

For the reasons discussed above, when another energy crisis occurred in 1978 the IEA proved to be of little value in compensating for changes in the international petroleum market. Civil conflict in Iran caused a temporary shutdown of Iranian oil facilities. At about the same time, major oil companies abrogated their third-party sales agreements and a number of smaller companies lost their sources of supply. Combined with an unusually hard winter in Europe and North America, these factors created an international shortage of oil of over 3 million barrels per day (mbd). Starting from a base of about $12 a barrel, prices began to rise in early February 1979 and continued to do so even after Iran resumed producing oil in early March, thus reducing the international shortage to an estimated 1.5 mbd. On March 27, concerned about the effect of increased oil prices on the world economy and its ability to import Western technology, OPEC set a ceiling price of $14.50 a barrel in the hope of stabilizing the market. Only 30 days later, OPEC had to set a new ceiling of $18–20 a barrel because several members continued to sell oil at any price the market would bear. Prices continued to soar and by December 1979, oil was selling for $26.27 a barrel.

The provisions for cooperation agreed upon by the IEA membership were never implemented. When prices began to rise in early 1979, the European states paid them, luring Latin American fuel oil away from the United States. Concerned about delays in replenishing fuel stocks after the hard winter, U.S. buyers announced they would pay a subsidy of $5 per barrel for heating oil. The European governments countered by raising the price they were willing to pay, resulting in an oil price panic. By 1981 the price of oil had risen to as high as $40.08 per barrel on the spot market. On average, the price of a barrel of oil in 1979 was $18.67. The rise peaked in 1981 at an average price of $35.50 and then began to drop slowly. By April 1986 prices had dropped to less than $11.00 per barrel for some types of crude.[2]

The Impact on the International Economy

The changing relationships between the petroleum producers and the Western oil companies, and the accompanying rise in the price of oil, had separate effects on the international community. The new relationships were heralded by states in the Third World as a victory over the forces of imperialism. Initially there was some expectation, largely among the developing states, that the producers of other raw materials, such as bauxite, copper, and aluminum, could be organized into international cartels. The hopes of forming OPEC-like cartels soon proved to be illusory, however, because unlike oil, other strategic materials are found in many countries as opposed to just a handful, and because there was no unity among the developing countries that possessed the resources.

On the other hand, the sharp increase in the price of oil caused concern among Western economists that a new international economic system was in the making. Because oil is a primary ingredient in many consumer items such as plastics and synthetic fabrics and in basic commodities such as fertilizer, the economies of the noncommunist world experienced inflation. In 1974 the annual inflation rate in the United States was 10 percent, in France it was 19 percent, and in Japan it reached 26 percent. Analysts with the Chase Manhattan Bank estimated that the combined effects of inflation and foreign trade deficits slowed the usually active Japanese economy to a 2 percent growth rate in 1974. Great Britain, with a $4.3 billion trade deficit to OPEC states, experienced a negative GNP growth that year.[3]

It was the economies of the developing states, however, that suffered most from the inflation. Many Third World countries had had extensive trade deficits prior to the financial chaos that followed the 1973 oil embargo. Whereas industrial states could export more to offset internal financial problems, most of the developing countries were net importers and were far more dependent on basic economic ingredients such as fertilizer, much of which has a petroleum base. Some states went to the brink of bankruptcy, and indeed for some economies the effects of the "oil shock" price rise can still be seen today.

Eventually, however, all states were able to adjust to the new price structures and inflation rates began to stabilize in the second half of the 1970s. Of longer range concern, however, were the huge trade deficits to OPEC countries. The industrialized states were forced to deal with a sudden flow of capital out of their treasuries in amounts that had previously been considered unthinkable. Oil producing states were accumulating capital at the rate of $50–60 billion per year. Furthermore there seemed to be no way to achieve a trade balance. In the first half of 1974, the United States imported $11.8 billion from oil producing countries and exported less than $2.4 billion back to them. The dilemma was that for the first several years after the oil boom, the OPEC countries had so much money that there was no economically sound way for them to spend it.

International economists expressed widespread concern that the world economy would suffer severe shock unless the oil consuming countries were able to recycle some of the petrodollars into the industrialized world's economies. This occurred when the oil producing states began transferring their profits to international banks, which in turn channeled the money into a wide range of investments and purchases. In addition, OPEC states took steps to improve their domestic economic infrastructures by building transportation and communication systems, hospitals, schools and hotels, and investing heavily in services required by businessmen and tourists. Most of this money was spent in industrialized countries. For example, in 1970 the four wealthiest Persian Gulf states—Iran, Iraq, Kuwait and Saudi Arabia—imported less than $7.8 billion worth of goods, of which 47 percent was from developed countries. In 1975 they imported more than $31 billion worth of goods, 78 percent from the industrialized West and Japan, and in 1980, $63 billion in goods and services were imported, more than 82 percent from noncommunist industrialized states.[4]

In 1979 the second oil price rise occurred, but it was different from the earlier one. The private banking system was not in a position to act as an international investor the way it had six years earlier. To make matters worse, the civil war that broke out in Lebanon in 1975 destroyed the international financial network that had served the Middle East, and Western investors were forced to enter regional markets piecemeal. While for the Arab oil producers

ALLEGHENY COLLEGE LIBRARY

the most efficient use of their petrodollars was to continue to place them into capital investments such as steel mills, cement factories, and the production of tools and industrial machinery, with but few exceptions this was impossible, for two reasons. First, many of the oil producing states were still adjusting to the social and economic dislocations that had resulted from the first spate of massive investments. Second, most of the Middle Eastern oil producers lacked the population, the natural resources, and the human skills to absorb further infrastructure projects. As Table 1.5 shows, this situation was reflected in the rapidly growing foreign currency reserves held by the oil rich states of the Middle East.

TABLE 1.5: Total Reserves* (millions of U.S. dollars)

Year	Algeria	Iran	Iraq	Kuwait	Libya	Saudi Arabia	UAE
1972	285	818	626	269	2,832	2,383	—
1973	912	1,078	1,380	381	2,024	3,747	92
1974	1,454	8,223	3,097	1,249	3,511	14,153	453
1975	1,128	8,744	2,559	1,491	2,095	23,193	988
1976	1,765	8,681	4,434	1,702	3,106	26,900	1,906
1977	1,684	12,106	6,811	2,883	4,786	29,903	800
1978	1,981	11,977	—	2,506	4,105	19,200	812
1979	2,655	15,210	—	2,870	6,344	19,273	1,432
1980	3,773	—	—	3,928	13,091	23,437	2,041
1981	3,695	—	—	4,067	9,003	32,236	3,202
1982	2,422	—	—	5,913	7,059	29,549	2,215
1983	1,880	—	—	5,192	5,129	27,287	2,072
1984	1,464	—	—	4,590	3,634	24,748	—

*Gold reserves have not been included.
Source: *International Financial Yearbook,* The International Monetary Fund (Washington, D.C. 1985).

By 1980, the oil producers had invested so much in the Western and Japanese economies that many of them were forced to borrow in order to maintain a constant level of domestic development and meet the demands of their own people. While none of the producers was considered a financial risk by international investors, a large amount of their recycled oil money had gone into nonproductive sectors of their economy: roads, schools, and, most significantly, the military. As shown in Table 1.5 above, by 1981 the financial reserves of even the wealthiest Middle Eastern oil producing states had begun to fall.

The Decline of OPEC

The decline of OPEC as a dominant force in the international oil market was the result of a combination of factors. First, starting around the end of 1981 and throughout 1982, the shortage of oil that had allowed OPEC to dictate prices had changed to a surplus and the price of oil began to fall. This increase in the international supply of oil had come about for several reasons: a) Efforts to shift energy sources away from oil, which were begun in the 1970s, came into operation. For example, in 1973 Western Europe had virtually no nuclear energy plants but by 1984 nuclear sources were producing energy equivalent to 104.6 million tons of oil or 8.4 percent of the energy consumed that year. By way of comparison, the United States used nuclear generation to produce the energy equivalent of 89.4 million tons of oil or slightly less than 5 percent of the total energy consumed.[5] b) More importantly, recently discovered oil fields in Mexico, Alaska and the North Sea began producing at full capacity. The combined effects created a surplus of oil, putting downward pressure on international prices.

The second reason for OPEC's decline was the lack of internal unity. A fundamental concern of any cartel is the probability that when prices begin to fall, individual members will attempt to compensate by selling more of their product in order to maintain a steady level of income. OPEC faced just such a problem in 1983. In March, they agreed to reduce their production rates to reduce the amount of oil on the market. Initially a production ceiling of 17.5 mbd was set, but when prices began to fall in 1984 the ceiling was lowered to 16 mbd, less than half of the 1979 rate. Saudi Arabia voluntarily assumed the role of "swing" producer, adjusting its rates downward whenever necessary to counter the effects of excess oil and to keep prices high. In mid 1984, Saudi Arabia, with a capacity to pump in excess of 10 million barrels of oil per day, was averaging 5.2 mbd. Kuwait, with a capacity of 2.9 mbd, was pumping less than 1 million.[6]

The data in Table 1.6 show the impact of the combination of declining demand, increasing noncartel production, and OPEC's efforts to make oil a scarce commodity by reducing production. Part of the reason for the decrease in OPEC's control over the market was that OPEC's constraint was not matched by oil producers outside the cartel. Non-OPEC production rose from 21 mbd in 1979 to 26.4 mbd by early 1985. Although Middle Eastern states continued to pump a majority of the oil produced by OPEC, they no longer dominated either the international oil market or OPEC.

TABLE 1.6: OPEC States' Contribution to Worldwide Production of Crude, 1960–1984 (thousands of barrels per day)

Year	Middle East Members of OPEC	Middle East Percentage of OPEC	OPEC Percentage Free World	Middle East OPEC Percentage Free World
1960	5,028	64	44	28
1965	7,996	61	53	32
1970	13,229	60	58	35
1975	18,904	70	65	45
1976	21,309	70	67	47
1977	21,805	69	67	47
1978	21,013	69	64	45
1979	21,016	68	64	43
1980	17,913	67	59	40
1981	15,221	67	55	37
1982	12,137	64	49	31
1983	10,965	62	46	29
1984	10,755	63	43	27
1985	9,890	60	30	25

Sources: Middle East Oil and Gas (Exxon Corp. Dec. 1984) and *Oil and Gas Journal* (March 11, 1985, and June 9, 1986).

Only a few members, such as Saudi Arabia, Kuwait, and Libya, had sufficient foreign exchange reserves to absorb the loss of revenues that would result from an additional drop in production—a necessary tactic in any attempt to regain control of the market and maintain prices. Most producers had borrowed heavily against their future oil revenues in order to acquire Western technology. Even the wealthiest producers needed a constant supply of oil revenues to meet financial obligations. By the end of 1985, OPEC members were producing up to 1 million barrels of oil a day over the agreed-upon levels.[7]

Having failed to establish a viable production ceiling, OPEC, led by Saudi Arabia, attempted to create a price floor, but given the condition of the market the move never obtained the wholehearted cooperation of OPEC's members. On January 30, 1985, after three days of tense discussions, OPEC agreed to set a market price for Saudi Arabian light crude oil of $28 per barrel. Within hours after the close of the meeting it was clear that some of the members would not abide by the agreement. Iran, for example, was reported to be selling oil in the Persian Gulf at $23 per barrel while other members continued to sell oil on the open market in Rotterdam at the agreed price.

Price chiseling was only one manifestation of OPEC disunity. In mid 1985 an increasing number of OPEC members were shipping oil to the Soviet Union as payment for arms—oil that they were not charging against their production ceiling quotas. In turn, the Soviet Union was re-exporting the oil on the open market in order to earn hard currency needed for the purchase of Western technology. By late 1985, Moscow was obtaining 60 percent of its hard currency from such transactions. Moreover, because of the weak international petroleum market, the Soviets were offering selected contract customers a subsidy that priced their oil $1 below the market price.[8]

In July 1985 the daily output of OPEC members dropped to a 20-year low. At a meeting held on July 22 the Saudi Arabian oil minister, Ahmad Zaki Yamani, announced that Saudi Arabia would no longer serve as "swing" producer and in September Saudi Arabia began producing as much oil as it could sell. By the end of 1985 it became clear that the issues of production ceilings and price floors were dead. Complaining that the North Sea producers and Mexico were competing for its customers, OPEC announced that it would fight for its "fair share" of the market, which led analysts to forecast a competition for sales that could force oil prices to $18.00 per barrel.[9] By mid-1986, through their own disunity, OPEC had lost control of the international petroleum market.

GEOGRAPHIC FACTORS

The geographic location of the Middle East contributes to its strategic importance. The Middle East's historical location astride the world's most lucrative trade routes brought great international powers in contact with the region. Oil and the confrontation between the Soviet Union and the United States have magnified that importance. From the Western perspective, the barrier formed by the Caucasus, the Elburz, and the Himalaya Mountains provides a major obstacle to a Soviet ground invasion of the area. Equally sensitive are the Persian Gulf and the Red Sea, which are vital to the flow of oil to noncommunist countries, and the Turkish Straits, which limit Soviet access to the region by sea.

The Persian Gulf

The Persian Gulf is approximately 500 miles long and 230 miles wide. The littoral populations comprising Oman, the United Arab

Emirates (the UAE), Qatar, Saudi Arabia, Kuwait, and Bahrain are Arabic speaking and predominantly Sunni Muslim. Iraq is also Arab but probably more than half of its population are Shia Muslim. (These states choose to call the area the Arabian Gulf.) Iran is largely Persian and Shia Muslim and has always called the waterway the Persian Gulf.

With few exceptions the states in the region have economies that depend largely on the production and export of oil. The Gulf region is the center of the world petroleum industry. The shores are dotted with oil rigs and refineries, and once-barren islands have been converted to massive loading terminals. If the oil facilities of all the Gulf states were to operate at full capacity, they could produce more than 22 million barrels of oil a day. Most of this oil passes through the Strait of Hormuz, which separates the Gulf from the Arabian Sea and the Indian Ocean. In the late 1970s, as much as 19 million barrels of oil a day passed through the Strait. Even taking into consideration the Gulf states' reduced production, in 1985 an average of 8.5 million barrels of oil passed through the Strait of Hormuz daily.

Lying at the southern end of the Gulf, the Strait of Hormuz is a passage approximately 125 miles long that provides the Gulf states their only outlet to the high seas. The navigable portion is 12 miles wide and has two shipping lanes, each 2 miles wide. The Musandam Peninsula, which forms the western promontory of the Strait, is part of Oman and is located on the coast of the Arabian Peninsula. Iran is on the other side of the strait.

Occasionally, there has been concern that some power might blockade the Strait of Hormuz in an effort to halt the flow of oil to the West. For the present, that possibility seems remote. The Strait of Hormuz is too wide to be closed by simply sinking a vessel or two and the alternative, a naval blockade, would be difficult against the combined naval and air power of the Western states, which would probably be brought to bear against any embargo. Such an operation would require a significant naval force combined with massive air cover. Only Iran, with three destroyers and four frigates, has significant naval capability, and none of the military establishments on the Gulf presently possesses an air force large enough to establish air superiority over the entire Persian Gulf.[10]

At the other end of the Gulf is the Shatt al-Arab, a 100-mile long waterway formed by the confluence of the Tigris and Euphrates rivers. The Shatt al-Arab serves as the link between the Persian Gulf and the most important oil terminals of Iraq and Iran, located at the cities of Basra and Abadan, respectively. At one time or another, both Iran and Iraq have claimed control over the Shatt al-Arab. The waterway is especially vital to Iraq, which has only 80 miles of coastline on the Persian Gulf and only one port, Umm Qasr, with direct access to international waters. Conflict over the use of the waterway dates back to well before the twentieth century.

The Red Sea

The Red Sea is approximately 1,500 miles long and 200 miles across at its widest point. Ships entering from the south must pass through the Bab el-Mandeb, "the Gate of Lamentation." At this point the island of Perim divides the channel into two passages, both within the territorial waters of the People's Democratic Republic of Yemen. The eastern channel is 2 miles wide and the western channel is 10. There are no legal constraints imposed by the states on the Bab el-Mandeb to the freedom of innocent passage.

The Suez Canal, located at the north end of the Red Sea, links the Indian Ocean (via the Red Sea) to the Mediterranean Sea. It is approximately 100 miles long, extending from Port Said on the Mediterranean Sea through three small lakes on the Isthmus of Suez, emptying into the Gulf of Suez. Because there is little difference in elevation between the Mediterranean Sea and the Red Sea, the Suez Canal requires no locks. It has a surface width of 390 feet but heavy silting reduces the width of the canal's bottom to an average of 120 feet. Consequently the canal can handle only single-lane traffic. The Egyptian Suez Canal Authority, which is charged with operating the Canal, organizes convoys of ships—two north-bound and one south-bound—every 24 hours.

The Suez Canal can be easily blockaded. As a result of war between Israel and Egypt, the Canal was blocked and closed to all shipping between June 1967 and October 1975. Before that time it served as the major sea route for oil from the Middle East to Western Europe. While the Canal was closed, shippers transporting oil to Europe were forced to send their tankers around the Cape of Good Hope at the southern tip of Africa, which added 4–6 thousand miles to the trip. To reduce the costs of transportation, oil companies and private shippers built fleets of supertankers: enormous ships that could carry up to half a million dead weight tons of oil. By 1975 when the Canal reopened, supertankers were carrying more than half of all the oil shipped by sea. Because of their deep draft, however, they are unable to use the Suez Canal. Table 1.7 shows how the shift to supertankers has influenced the oil trade through the Suez Canal.

TABLE 1.7: Suez Canal Traffic (thousands of tons)

| Year | Northbound | | Southbound | |
	Total	Petroleum Products	Total	Petroleum Products
1964	172,463	144,661	38,518	6,136
1965	183,441	155,086	42,001	7,908
1966	194,168	166,718	47,725	9,935
1975*	18,480	5,309	19,140	2,012
1976	72,020	29,855	45,633	3,969
1977	72,630	30,878	56,063	4,068
1978	69,597	28,363	80,182	4,316
1979	78,730	27,284	81,919	8,970
1980	86,547	28,474	39,729	13,994
1981	93,896	36,566	102,532	18,211
1982	124,805	63,139	106,588	20,312
1983	141,002	81,223	115,703	17,010
1984	154,237	86,628	109,491	11,056

*210 normal transit days.
Sources: The Suez Canal Yearly Report: 1982 (Cairo: Suez Canal Authority, 1982) and JPRS–NEA–85–026–L, p.4.

The Suez Canal is of great strategic significance despite its reduced importance in the movement of oil from the Middle East to Europe. It is the major trade route between the Middle East, East Africa, the Far East, and Western Europe. Most importantly it is the principal line of communications between Western Europe and U.S. naval forces in the Indian Ocean.

The importance of the Red Sea to the international petroleum market has increased in recent years. In 1981, Saudi Arabia built two parallel pipelines, called the "Petroline," that move oil and natural gas liquids from oil fields on the east coast to the Port of Yanbu on the Red Sea. Iraq and Saudi Arabia have jointly built a spur line from oil fields in southern Iraq tying into the Petroline. Called Saudi I, the line can move between 300 to 500 thousand barrels of Iraqi oil a day. A second pipeline called Saudi II, is under negotiation between Baghdad and Riyadh. If completed, Saudi II would give Iraq the capacity to pipe an additional 1.1 mbd to the Red Sea. The Petroline can carry 1.8 mbd. If all planned pipelines are completed, the Red Sea would become a source of approximately 3 mbd. Additionally, in the mid-1970s Saudi Arabia began construction of petrochemical facilities at Yanbu and Rabigh on the Red Sea. These centers, consisting of several petrochemical plants, fertilizer factories, and export refineries, are expected to go into operation in 1986 and will be capable of producing 5.3 million tons of petrochemicals, a million tons of fertilizer, and 850,000 barrels of refined oil products a day.[11]

The Turkish Straits

The state that controls the shores of the Turkish Straits controls shipping between the Black Sea and the Mediterranean. The Straits consist of two waterways linked by the Sea of Marmara: the Bosphorus in the North and the Dardanelles in the South. The Bosphorus is 19 miles long and 2 miles wide at its maximum, but narrows to half a mile. The Dardanelles is 37 miles long, averaging more than 3 miles across, but narrows to a mile at one point. The Straits range from 200 to 300 feet in depth. Together they form two long, narrow, easily defended naval choke points.

Because of their historical and strategic importance to the major powers, access to the Turkish Straits is governed by international law. The Montreaux Convention, which came into force in July 1936, governs the passage of both military and commercial vessels. The Convention bestows on Turkey full sovereign rights over the Straits. Article 25 states that "Nothing in the present Convention shall prejudice the rights and obligations of Turkey, or any of the other High Contracting Parties members of the League of Nations, arising out of the Covenant of the League of Nations." In peacetime, commercial ships under any flag can pass without restriction but the Convention imposes limits on the passage of warships. The operative sections regarding the peacetime passage of warships are articles 10 and 11 of the Convention.

Article 10. In time of peace, light surface vessels, minor war vessels and auxiliary vessels, whether belonging to Black Sea or non-Black Sea powers, and whatever their flag, shall enjoy freedom of passage through the Straits without any taxes or charges whatever, provided such transit is begun during daylight hours and subject to the conditions laid down in Article 13 and the articles following thereafter.

Article 11. Black Sea Powers may send through the Straits capital ships of a tonnage greater than that laid down in the first paragraph of Article 14 on the condition that these vessels pass through the Straits singly, escorted by not more than two destroyers.

Article 13 prescribes that the transit of warships through the Straits requires eight days advance notice be given to the Turkish government through diplomatic channels. Article 14 stipulates,

> The maximum aggregate tonnage of all foreign naval forces which may be in course of transit through the Straits shall not exceed 15,000 tons, except in the cases provided for in Article 11 and in Annex III to the present Convention.
>
> The forces specified in the preceding paragraph shall not, however, comprise more than nine vessels.

The effect of these provisions is that the peacetime passage of NATO (other than Turkey's) ships is limited to vessels no larger than a cruiser. Submarines can pass only during the daylight hours and on the surface. Aircraft carriers of any flag are denied passage because the Montreaux Convention makes no mention of them. This places Soviet forces in the Mediterranean Sea at a disadvantage. In modern warfare, a naval force without effective air cover is vulnerable to enemy air and submarine attack. This interpretation of the Convention denies Soviet forces in the Mediterranean (called the Fifth Escadra or squadron, a task force of the Soviet Black Sea Fleet) the kind of effective air protection available to the NATO states, which have both land and carrier-based combat aircraft available to them.

Most importantly, Articles 19 through 21 of the Montreaux Convention make it clear that in time of war, Turkish rights become predominant.

> Article 19. In time of war, Turkey not being a belligerent, warships shall enjoy complete freedom of transit and navigation through the Straits under the same conditions laid down in Articles 10 to 18.
>
> Vessels of war belonging to belligerent powers, however, shall not pass through the Straits except in cases arising under Article 25 of the present Convention and in cases of assistance rendered to a state victim of aggression in virtue of a treaty of mutual assistance binding Turkey, concluded within the framework of the Covenant of the League of Nations...
>
> Article 20. In time of war, Turkey being a belligerent, the provisions of Articles 10 to 18 shall not be applicable; the passage of warships shall be left entirely to the discretion of the Turkish government.

Article 21. Should Turkey consider herself to be threatened with imminent danger of war she shall have the right to apply the provisions of Article 20 of the present Convention.

Articles 19 through 21 make it possible for the government of Turkey to influence the balance of naval power in the Mediterranean Sea. To the countries of the West, the Turkish Straits are important as the first line of defense against the Soviet navy. To the USSR, for its navy to conduct effective naval warfare in the Mediterranean, control over the Straits is essential. In the event of war with the West, the Soviet Union would most likely seek to gain control over the Turkish Straits either by occupying them militarily or permanently blocking them. For this reason, their importance to the strategic interests of the world's great powers must be weighed equally in the international balance with the Suez Canal.

THE MIDDLE EAST AND THE EASTERN MEDITERRANEAN SEA

The ability of the Western states to control the Mediterranean Sea is of direct relevance to European security for three reasons. First, naval domination of the Mediterranean is necessary for NATO to protect what Churchill once referred to as Europe's "soft underbelly"—Italy and the southern coast of France. Second, West European and U.S. strategists have been concerned about the Soviet Union promoting instability in countries along Mediterranean sea lanes. The concern was that the Soviet Union would attempt to weaken European economies by gaining control over oil-rich states in the Middle East and encouraging them to close their oil terminals to European customers. Also, in time of war the Soviet Union could use its naval forces in the Mediterranean to interdict the flow of oil. Even in the era of the supertanker, a significant amount of Western European oil flows through the Suez Canal, while France, Italy, and the Federal Republic of Germany import a large percentage of their oil from Libya and Algeria. The West's control over the Mediterranean is related to the degree of its influence over the Turkish Straits.

Turkey and the International Balance of Power

There is little disagreement among military strategists about the importance of Turkey to the regional military balance. It is the only NATO state that shares a border with the Soviet Union. In peacetime, Turkey provides airfields for the forward basing of NATO tactical aircraft, contingency storage facilities for strategic war materials, such as fuel for the U.S. Sixth Fleet, and air defense warning systems. Turkey hosts and even jointly operates military installations devoted to monitoring a wide range of military activities in the Soviet Union that are considered essential to NATO's early warning system. More than a dozen NATO Air Defense Ground Environment (NADGE) sites and a number of U.S. communications systems provide an estimated 25 percent of NATO's current intelligence on military activities in southern USSR.[12]

In the long term, Turkey's importance to the West lies in its control of the Turkish Straits. In time of war, Turkey will play a critical role in determining Soviet naval strength in the Mediterranean. Without Turkish cooperation, NATO's naval "choke point" would shift to a line running from the Peloponnesus through Crete to the Greek islands just off the Turkish southern coast, an area far more difficult to defend. If circumstances were to result in the loss of both Greece and Turkey from the Western alliance, the hypothetical choke point would move west to the Straits of Messina and the gap between Sicily and Tunisia. This would jeopardize the Suez Canal and NATO naval facilities at Souda Bay in Crete.

The Soviet view is the mirror image of this. The Turkish Straits are the only sea passage linking its Black Sea commercial ports with the Mediterranean Sea. It is estimated that nearly half of the Soviet Union's sea-borne trade passes through the Straits.[13] Equally important, they provide the Soviet Union with the ability to establish a naval presence in the Mediterranean Sea. In times of crisis in the Middle East, the Soviet Union usually increases the size of the Soviet naval forces in the Mediterranean to give the impression that it is willing to back its allies in the region militarily. For example, during the 1973 Arab-Israeli War, the Cyprus crisis in 1974, and the 1978 crisis in Lebanon, the Fifth Escadra was augmented by surface combatants from the Baltic Sea Fleet. At one point, the size of the Fifth Escadra was estimated to be over 100 vessels—more than double the normal number. Finally, the southern flank of the Soviet defensive perimeter is much more difficult to defend if Turkey is aligned with NATO. As long as Turkey is potentially a belligerent, Moscow must commit forces to protect its vitally important oil fields near Baku.

For these reasons, the Soviet Union has made relations with Turkey an important focus of its Middle Eastern foreign policy. Following the end of World War II, the Soviet Union sent a formal note to the Turkish government in which it demanded rectifications in their joint border in Eastern Turkey and renegotiation of the Montreaux Convention that would have included joint Soviet-Turkish authority to regulate traffic in the Straits and the establishment of Soviet military bases on Turkish soil.[14] Taken together with a reported Soviet troop buildup in the Balkans, the United States perceived Soviet demands as a prelude to attack. In 1946, the U.S. State, War, and Navy Departments sent a memorandum to President Truman outlining for the first time a domino theory of Soviet control over Greece, Turkey, and eventually the entire Middle East. It concluded with one of the first clear statements of what was to become the U.S. policy of containment: "The only thing that will deter the Russians will be the conviction that the United States is prepared, if necessary, to meet aggression with force of arms."[15] To signal this to the Soviet Union, the United States sent the battleship *Missouri* into the Sea of Marmara. This began a period of close relations between the United States and Turkey.

In the early 1950s, Soviet acts of provocation in Turkey and Iran continued to be of concern to the Western powers but reaction from them was slow in coming. Elsewhere in the world the policy of containment, as explicated in a 1950 policy paper that came to be known as NSC 68, was accompanied by concrete policy actions such as the establishment of the North Atlantic Treaty Organization (NATO), the Marshall Plan, and the U.S. military involvement in Korea. In the Middle East, evidence of a firm U.S. commitment was harder to find. While Washington had made it clear that Turkey and Greece were vital to U.S. interests, neither was to receive immediate benefits from the Marshall Plan.

By the time of the Korean War, the West's strategy to counter the perceived Soviet threat to the Middle East began to crystallize. Greece and Turkey were admitted into NATO in 1952. In early 1953 Secretary of State John Foster Dulles found states located along the "northern tier" (Turkey, Iran, Pakistan, and Iraq), which were in close proximity to the Soviet Union, were willing to participate in a regional alliance with Western backing. The alliance, known as the Baghdad Pact, was initiated through a bilateral agreement between Iraq and Turkey, and subsequently joined by Iran, Pakistan, and Britain in early 1955. Although the United States was the motivating force behind the alliance and maintained a military representation within its headquarters, it was not formally a member. Iraq eventually withdrew from the organization after the 1958 revolution. The organization then moved its headquarters to Ankara, Turkey, and changed its name to the Central Treaty Organization or CENTO.

Changing world views, the arrival of new leadership within the states represented in the organization, and differing perceptions of the threat from the Soviet Union wore away at the unity of CENTO. The fall of the Shah of Iran sealed the alliance's fate and in March 1979 the pact was dissolved. Until that time, however, Turkey regarded its membership in the alliance as a sign of its commitment to Western opposition to the Soviet Union.

Over the years, particularly since the revolution in Iran, the importance of this commitment to Western control of the Mediterranean Sea has increased. Greece's role in NATO, meanwhile, has changed in the last several years, particularly under the government of Andreas Papandreau's Socialist party, which has threatened to end Greece's military participation in NATO and has taken steps to reduce U.S. military presence in Greece. In January 1982 Papandreau granted Soviet naval supply ships access to repair facilities on Spyros Island.

Despite Turkey's growing importance to the West, three events have caused Turkey to reevaluate its reliance on military support from the United States. First, Turkey felt abandoned by the United States when, as part of the resolution of the Cuban Missile Crisis, President Kennedy ordered U.S. Jupiter missiles removed from Turkey without adequate prior consultation with the Turkish government. Second, in 1964 when violence erupted between Greek and Turkish ethnic groups on Cyprus, Turkey was told it could not expect any NATO support after the USSR warned Ankara that it would view any move by Turkey to intervene as an act of aggression. In a secret letter dated June 5, 1964, President Lyndon Johnson warned Ankara that help would not necessarily be forthcoming because Turkey's allies had not had a chance to consider whether the NATO charter obliged them to intervene under such circumstances. Third, after the overthrow of the government of Archbishop Makarios in 1974, and the landing of Turkish troops on Cyprus, the U.S. Congress suspended all military sales and assistance to Turkey. The embargo remained in effect until June 1978.

The arms embargo had a profound effect on Turkish military capabilities. In 1975, the majority of Turkey's military equipment was of U.S. manufacture and the most important of these items (trucks, tanks, artillery pieces, aircraft, and warships) were approaching obsolescence. Nearly all of Turkey's tanks and aircraft were over 20 years old; its naval combat vessels were over 30 years old. In 1983, the U.S. Department of Defense estimated that to bring Turkish armed forces to minimum NATO standards would require $18 billion over 13 years.[16]

Doubts about the reliability of the United States as an ally brought Turkey to a more realistic assessment of its position within NATO and its relations with Washington. Ankara began a prolonged effort to improve its ties with Moscow. State visits from Soviet President Podgorny (January 1965) and Soviet Premier Kosygin (December 1966) and a number of important economic commitments reflected Ankara's new foreign policy focus. During the October 1973 Arab-Israeli war and the conflict between Somalia and Ethiopia in 1977–1978 Soviet aircraft carrying military equipment overflew Turkey. Although the Turkish government moved to stop it, such actions on the part of the Soviets would have been impossible ten years earlier. In 1976, the Turkish government allowed the Soviet warship *Kiev* to pass through the Turkish Straits. NATO classified the vessel as an aircraft carrier but the Turkish government accepted Moscow's designation and allowed it to pass as an "antisubmarine cruiser," thereby circumventing restrictions imposed by the Montreaux Convention. In 1978, the Turks and Soviets signed a document called "Principles of Good-Neighborly and Friendly Cooperation." Although the memorandum was hardly more than a protocol gesture and in no way modified Turkey's formal position in NATO, it signaled Turkey's revised view of their relationships with the West.

Since the arrival of a moderately pro-U.S. government in 1983, Turkey once again has increased the distance between itself and the Soviet Union and has improved its relations with the United States. Ankara has expanded its military and economic ties with the Western European states and broadened relations with countries of the Middle East.

Soviet Military Presence in the Middle East

Until the mid 1950s, the Western powers were successful in limiting Soviet gains in the Middle East. In an effort to prevent an arms race between the Arab states and Israel, on May 25, 1952, the United States, France, and Great Britain jointly issued a Tripartite Declaration by which each power pledged to restrict the provision of arms to Middle Eastern states to amounts sufficient for internal security and self-defense. However, on July 23, 1952, Gamal Abdul Nasser seized control of the government of Egypt and within a few years had moved to the front of an Arab nationalist movement that focused on the independence of Arab states from Western European control and the military defeat of Israel.

In early 1955 a minor flare-up along Egypt's border with Israel brought Egypt's military weakness into sharp focus. Nasser had initially sought arms from the United States but the Eisenhower administration refused to make a commitment. When Nasser vehemently opposed the Baghdad Pact, the Soviet Union perceived that his opposition to the Western military presence in the Middle East provided a common ground between them and offered to sell him the arms he needed in exchange for Egyptian commodities. In late 1955, the USSR, through Czechoslovakia, began delivering tanks, armored personnel carriers, naval vessels (including destroyers and submarines), and tactical aircraft to Egypt. The arms race began in earnest after France agreed to supply arms to Israel in reaction to Nasser's support for anti-French rebels in Algeria.

The Czechoslovakian arms deal gave the Soviet Union access to an important Middle Eastern state, and the Soviet Union parlayed this into political access elsewhere. The transaction turned Nasser into a regional hero and he used his new-found influence to dissuade Syria and Jordan from entering the Baghdad Pact. In March 1956, Syria's positive view of Nasser and growing antagonism toward the West encouraged Damascus to enter into an arms agreement with the Soviet Union similar to that of Egypt. In 1958 a violent revolution in Iraq brought to power a strongly nationalistic group of officers who signed an arms agreement with Moscow within weeks of the takeover. Shortly thereafter, Algeria began receiving sizable arms shipments from the Soviet Union and, upon its independence from Great Britain in 1967, the People's Democratic Republic of Yemen began buying arms from the Soviet Union. In 1969, new regimes in the Sudan and Libya (that of Muammar Qaddafi) followed suit.

Establishing a network of states that were, to one degree or another, dependent on the Soviet Union for arms was only one aspect of Moscow's strategy to obtain a role in Middle Eastern affairs. The USSR also has exerted a great deal of effort to establish regional support facilities to maintain its naval presence in the Mediterranean Sea, securing the use of maintenance facilities in Syria, Tunisia, Algeria, Yugoslavia, and, as already mentioned, Greece.

The largest Soviet gain in the area came after the 1967 Arab-Israeli war. The defeat of Egypt at the hands of Israel provided the Soviet Union with an opportunity to deepen Cairo's dependence. Within four months after the war, all of Egypt's military equipment war losses were replaced. In return, Nasser agreed to allow the Fifth Escadra the use of Egyptian ports as naval support installations. Starting in March 1968, existing facilities at Matruh and Sollum near Alexandria were expanded by Soviet naval experts. In

October 1970 there were an estimated 14,000 Soviet military personnel in Egypt—a large percentage of whom were involved in support of the Fifth Escadra. In 1971 and 1972, air fields in the area of Matruh were being used almost exclusively by Soviet transport aircraft delivering spare parts and equipment for Soviet naval vessels.

The death of Nasser in 1970 and the arrival of Anwar Sadat changed the complexion of Egyptian-Soviet relations. Sadat's first move to reduce his dependence on the Soviet Union was to expel 15,000 Soviet advisors from Egypt, effective July 17, 1972. After the 1973 war, while the negotiations for the Sinai disengagement agreements were being conducted, Sadat began to reduce his dependence on the Soviet Union for weapons. After some skillful diplomacy on his part, in early 1974, Egypt obtained $100 million from Saudi Arabia to purchase arms from France and Britain to replace equipment lost in the 1973 war. In May 1975, Sadat curtailed Soviet access to the facilities at Matruh and Sollum and in March 1976, the final clauses of a 1971 Soviet-Egyptian Friendship Treaty were abrogated by Sadat and he gave the Fifth Escadra one month to close down its facilities outside Alexandria.

At the same time, the United States and Egypt broadened their ties and the new relationship has proved to be a beneficial one for Egypt. In 1985, for example, Egypt was to receive $2.2 billion in economic aid from the United States and an additional $3.14 billion in 1986. On more than one occasion, the United States has sent Airborne Warning and Control Systems to Egypt in response to increased tensions with Libya. More importantly, the United States has provided Egypt with arms; by 1985, Egypt had 20 F-16 aircraft, more than 200 M-60 tanks, and 300 U.S. armored personnel carriers.

The loss of Egyptian facilities was a serious blow to the Soviet Union and subsequent arrangements with other Middle Eastern states have not replaced them. The Fifth Escadra customarily maintains a level of 30–40 ships in the Mediterranean Sea. Around 12 of these are surface combatants, usually including one ship capable of carrying a limited number of aircraft such as *Kiev* class vessels. The lack of support and maintenance facilities reduces their average stay time in the Mediterranean to around 80 days. Even accepting the fact that data on naval strength are always approximate because of the mobility of the forces, Table 1.8 shows that the balance is decidedly in favor of NATO and other Western European navies.

Lacking major port facilities such as those offered by Egypt, the Soviet naval presence in the region is likely to remain symbolic. The only way the Soviet Union can add to its strength is to bring in ships from its Baltic Fleet. These must pass through the Danish Straits

TABLE 1.8: The Balance of Forces in the Mediterranean

Type of Vessel	USSR[a]	U.S.	France	Italy	Spain	Greece	Turkey
Carriers	1	1–2	2	2	1	—	—
Submarines	8–10	NA	9	10	7	10	16
Nuclear submarines	—	6	2	—	—	—	—
Combatants[b]	8	12–16	14	22	22	21	18
Total	17	20–24	27	34	29	31	34

[a]Ships from the Black Sea and Northern Fleets. Average strengths are shown above.

[b]For the purposes of this study, only battleships, cruisers, destroyers, and frigates are classified as surface combatants.

Source: *The Military Balance: 1985–1986* (London: Institute for International and Strategic Studies).

and the North Sea, both of which are controlled by NATO forces. Ships of the Soviet Pacific Fleet, which are based out of Petrovpanlovsk and Vladivostok, could be added but these must pass through the Japanese and Korean Straits before making the long passage through the Indian Ocean. From a Soviet point of view, neither solution is a satisfactory replacement for a major support facility in the Mediterranean Sea.

As to Moscow's relations with Cairo, Soviet hopes for restoring close ties with Egypt to their previous high levels are dim. Since Anwar Sadat's assassination on October 6, 1981 Egypt's new president, Hosni Mubarak, has attempted to improve his relations with the Soviet Union but has had to be careful not to move too close to Moscow. For the immediate future at least, Moscow must remain content to negotiate arrangements with other Mediterranean littoral states for use of their naval support facilities and remain on good terms with Turkey.

REGIONAL INSTABILITY

Historically, the Middle East has been entangled in great power politics. A principal reason for this of late has been the rapid improvement of Middle Eastern economic fortunes brought about by the oil boom, which has earned states such as Saudi Arabia a degree of international influence unimaginable prior to the 1960s. The economic and geopolitical features of the area are so critical to the interests of the great powers that they have become party to a wide range of regional issues. Among these are tensions between Iran and the Arab states over hegemony in the Gulf, and the conflict between Israel and neighboring Arab states, which has been the prime cause of the arms race in the Middle East.

The Great Powers, Iran and the Gulf Region

Iran's common borders with the Soviet Union have given the Soviets a special interest in the country's political, military, and economic affairs. At the beginning of World War II, Iran proclaimed its neutrality, although ruling circles were known to be pro-German. Hitler's invasion of the Soviet Union in 1941 made allies of the noncommunist powers and Moscow and the only way the Western allies could ship military supplies to the Soviet army was through Iran. In 1941, when Iran refused to expel German technicians, British and Soviet forces occupied the country—the Soviets the five northern provinces and the British the south. Faced with their combined military might, a young Reza Shah Pahlavi agreed to facilitate the transshipment of military supplies to the Soviet Union and in return the occupying powers agreed to withdraw their forces within six months after the end of the war.

During the occupation, the Soviet Union gave every indication that it intended to remain in Iran. Soviet representatives were responsible for freeing Iranian members of the communist Tudeh party who had been jailed by Reza Shah, supported communist newspapers, and encouraged Kurdish and Armenian separatist movements. As soon as the war ended, antiregime riots broke out among the Azerbaijanis, a Turkic-speaking group living principally in the Soviet occupied zone, resulting in the overthrow of the Iranian governor of Tabriz. Backed by the Soviet military, the rebels proclaimed the Autonomous Republic of Azerbaijan and forced Iranian government officials to leave. Shortly thereafter, Moscow supported the formation of an independent Kurdish republic in Mahabad, which immediately concluded a treaty of alliance with the Azarbaijanis. The government in Teheran was finally able to secure the departure of Soviet troops from the country only after it agreed to Moscow's request for an oil concession, included members of the Soviet-backed communist Tudeh party in the cabinet, and withdrew complaints of Soviet behavior lodged with the United Nations. On May 9, 1946, two months after the deadline, the Soviet Union pulled its forces out of Iran.

In February 1947, the Shah outlawed the Tudeh party after one of its members attempted to assassinate him. During the government crackdown the USSR openly supported the Tudeh party, and Soviet armored divisions made several raids across the northern borders of Iran. Fearing an all-out Soviet invasion, the Shah appealed to the United States for support. Responding to these and other perceived threats of Soviet expansion in Greece and Turkey, on March 12, 1947 President Truman announced the "Truman Doctrine," which proclaimed the U.S. policy to contain the spread of communism. The policy declaration was followed by the delivery of $10 million worth of surplus U.S. military equipment to Iran. As long as the Shah ruled, the provision of military equipment was the centerpiece of U.S. relations with Iran.

Moscow continued to back dissident groups seeking to overthrow the government. In 1951, factions within the Iranian *Majlis* (parliament) led by Mohammad Mossadeq began pressing for nationalization of the oil industry. They were joined by fundamentalist Islamic groups opposed to the presence of foreigners in Iran. In March 1951, a member of a fundamentalist organization assassinated the pro-Western prime minister, General Ali Razmara, and subsequently the Majlis unanimously passed a law nationalizing the oil industry. In September, Iranian soldiers took over the Abadan refinery, locked out the British technicians, and cancelled the resident permits of British employees of the Anglo-Iranian Oil Company. Major importers of oil retaliated for the nationalization of the oil industry by boycotting Iranian crude, bringing the flow of petroleum from Iran to a near halt.

Six weeks after the oil industry was nationalized, Mohammad Mossadeq was made prime minister. Backed by a loose coalition of religious groups, socialists, communists, and nationalists, Mossadeq obtained full control over the government by August 1952. To do so, however, he purged the army of officers he feared would oppose him and in the process, sowed the seeds of his own destruction. The Shah, stripped of most of his power, left the country in August 1953. Soon, however, violent disagreement over the direction in which Iran was to proceed broke out between ultra-nationalist and Moscow-backed communist groups. Deteriorating economic conditions caused by the lack of oil revenues sparked protests from moderate elements in Iranian society. The unrest spread to the army where a strong residue of opposition to Mossadeq persisted. On August 18 and 19, assisted by the U.S. Central Intelligence Agency, the military deposed Mossadeq, scattering his forces. The Shah returned and set Iran on a consistently pro-Western course, which it maintained until 1979 when he fell from power.

Iran's dispute with Iraq over the use of Shatt al-Arab has also contributed to superpower interest in the Middle East. The centuries-old dispute over the boundary between Iran and Iraq was placed before the League of Nations in 1937, which resolved that between Abadan and the Gulf the boundary line would be the thalweg line—the midpoint of the navigation channel. Iran abrogated the 1937 treaty in 1969 when the Shah sent warships into the waterway to take control of it. In the face of Iranian military superiority, Iraq was forced to accept the fait accompli, but it caused a rift between the two states that never healed. Nonetheless, Iraqi and Iranian officials met in Algiers in 1975 and agreed on joint use of the waterway, establishing the thalweg as the international border.

Iraq's close relationship with the Soviet Union and Iran's alignment with the West contributed to tensions between the two countries. In 1972, Baghdad signed a treaty of friendship with Moscow, and shortly thereafter the Soviet navy began making ship visits to Umm Qasr, which became a source of concern to Teheran. After the 1973 oil crisis, Iran embarked on a massive program to build the most powerful military establishment in the Gulf region, with the assistance of the United States and Great Britain. Until the collapse of his regime in January 1979, the Shah became the self-appointed military guarantor of stability in the Persian Gulf to ensure the unimpeded passage of oil through the Strait of Hormuz. He did this with the tacit agreement of the United States and Britain.

With the otherthrow of the Shah in 1979, Iraq's president, Saddam Hussain, viewed the establishment of a radical Shia Moslem state on his borders as a threat to his rule. Differences between Shia and Sunni Muslims have been an important feature of the friction between the Arabs of Iraq and the Persians of Iran since the seventh century AD. Shia Muslims, who comprise approximately half of Iraq's population, make up the majority of those in the lower economic classes and are underrepresented in the Sunni-dominated government. In the past, Iraq's Shia Muslims responded positively to Iranian efforts to get them to oppose the state's Sunni Muslim regimes.

Perhaps because he was convinced that conflict with the Islamic fundamentalist government of the Ayatollah Khomeini was inevitable and hoping to take advantage of the political confusion and civil unrest in Iran to assert Iraqi leadership in the Gulf, on September 18, 1980, Saddam Hussain ordered his army to attack across the Shatt al-Arab into Iran. After some initial gains the Iraqi invasion ground to a halt. Starting in April 1982, Iraqi forces suffered a series of reversals and by mid June they were forced to retreat. The Shatt al-Arab and Umm Qasr were closed to shipping and as oil revenues fell to a trickle, Iraq's economy began to suffer. In June 1982, Saddam Hussain withdrew his forces to his own borders, unilaterally declared a ceasefire, and offered to negotiate with Iran. Tehran rejected the proposals to negotiate and on July 14, Iranian troops attacked across the Iraqi border toward Basra. On December 15, 1982, Saddam Hussain again announced his willingness to end the war if Iran would recognize Iraq's borders but the offer was ignored.

Iran threatened other Gulf states as well. On September 30, 1981, Iranian fighters attacked Kuwait, striking the oil refinery at Umm al-Ayish, to punish Kuwait for providing financial assistance to Iraq. In December 1981, internal security agents of Bahrain and Saudi Arabia uncovered Iranian-backed plots to overthrow their respective governments. They found evidence to indicate that the plotters had been trained by an organization connected to the Supreme Propagation Council of Iran's Ministry of Foreign Affairs.

By the beginning of 1984, the war between Iran and Iraq had degenerated to a state of mutual siege characterized by desultory air and artillery engagements. In April 1984, Iraq began attacking oil tankers of neutral states bound for Iranian ports in the hope that the threat to international shipping would force the West to intervene in the conflict or that the damage to the Iranian economy would force the Ayatollah to sue for peace. Iran retaliated by conducting air strikes against tankers of neutral countries bound for the ports of Arab states supporting Iraq including Saudi Arabia and Kuwait. In addition, Iran announced that if its oil exporting facilities were destroyed, it intended to close the Strait of Hormuz to all shipping and begin relocating combat aircraft to Bandar Abas.

In a show of force designed at keeping the Gulf combatants from closing the strategic Strait of Hormuz, the United States sent a two-carrier task force drawn from the U.S. Seventh Fleet in the Pacific to a point in the Indian Ocean outside the Strait. These were soon joined by warships from France and Great Britain. The presence of Western naval forces in the region put a halt to any Iranian plans to close the Strait of Hormuz but attacks on tankers continued. In the fall of 1985, Iraq began launching air assaults on Iran's oil refinery on Kharg Island, located 20 miles off the southern coast of Iran near the port of Bushehr. In early 1986, Iranian forces successfully occupied the city of Faw in Shatt al-Arab at the entrance to the Gulf, closing the waterway to any commercial traffic.

The Iran-Iraq war affected both regional alignments and the great powers. Starting around 1978, Iraq began a concerted effort to diversify its sources of military equipment. Even before the war, Iraq's relations with the Soviet Union were strained. Baghdad had refused a Soviet request for a naval facility at Umm Qasr, opposed the Soviet invasion of Afghanistan, and had cracked down on the pro-Soviet Iraqi Communist party. Conversely, when Iran broke off relations with the United States, Moscow perceived the possibility of improved relations with Iran, which was geopolitically more important than Iraq. When the war with Iran broke out in September 1980, the Soviet Union withheld an arms shipment to Iraq for which Baghdad had already paid. The equipment was delivered on September 28, 1983, only when it became apparent that the fundamentalist regime in Iran was not interested in improving ties between the two countries.

Relations between the United States and Iraq, severed by Baghdad in 1967 because of U.S. support for Israel, began improving in the 1970s. Baghdad sent moderating signals to Washington throughout the decade. With the onset of the war with Iran, Saddam Hussein stepped up his activities to establish a new set of relationships with the United States. The United States was more receptive than it might otherwise have been because of the lingering bitterness toward Iran over the 1980/81 hostage crisis. After holding several high-level meetings in 1984, the United States and Iraq resumed diplomatic relations on November 26, 1984.

The Iran-Iraq war created tensions within the Western alliance. Initially, French efforts to improve its position in Iraq ran counter to U.S. desires to stabilize the area. France had built Iraq's first nuclear reactor and, after it was damaged by an Israeli air attack in 1981, agreed to rebuild it. When the Soviet Union suspended weapons deliveries, France agreed to fill the gap and became a major supplier of military hardware to Iraq by 1982. Japan and West Germany walked a tightrope between their solidarity with the United States and the need to maintain their economic relations with Iraq and Iran. This was particularly true in the case of Japan since Tokyo had entered into oil import barter agreements with Iran and was building a multi-million dollar refinery there. Iraq was an important supplier of oil to Japan. Japan's interests in maintaining good relations with both Iran and Iraq even prompted it to consider acting as a go-between—a most unusual move for the Japanese who have made it a policy to stay out of local and regional political disputes.

The Gulf War affected regional relations as well. At the outbreak of the war, Syria, a long-time foe of Iraq, closed an existing pipeline that ran from Iraq's northern oil fields to the Syrian port of Banias on the Mediterranean Sea. To compensate for the loss of revenues, Iraq negotiated an agreement with Turkey to build a pipeline to the Mediterranean Sea, which went into operation in 1984. Known as Ceyhan I, the pipeline has a capacity of approximately 1 million barrels of oil a day. An expansion of this line (Ceyhan II) is expected to be in operation by the end of 1986 and will have a capacity of an additional 500 thousand barrels of oil a day. Together with existing pipeline arrangements with Saudi Arabia, Iraq has the capability of transporting a majority of its daily production to ports outside the Gulf.

Between the early 1960s and the mid 1970s, Iraq's policy toward conservative Arab states on its borders was aggressive. The threat to regional stability posed by Iran, however, brought increased solidarity among the Arab states and they began providing support to Baghdad in its war with Iran. In 1984, it was reported that Saudi Arabia and Kuwait were producing oil on Iraq's behalf—earmarking the production revenues from 300 barrels of oil per day for Iraq with repayment suspended until after the war. Jordan opened its port facilities on the Gulf of Aqaba to the transshipment of Iraqi consumer goods.

Finally, and perhaps most importantly, the war provided increased incentive for the Arab Gulf states to cooperate militarily. On August 31, 1981, shortly before Iran's attack on Kuwait's refinery at Umm al-Ayish, Saudi Arabia, Kuwait, the United Arab Emirates, Qatar, and Bahrain formed the Gulf Cooperation Council (GCC). As originally conceived, the Council was intended to coordinate regional industrial and economic policies and no provisions were made for military consultations. Iraq was excluded from the GCC, partially because the Gulf states wanted no linkage between membership in the Gulf Cooperation Council and the Gulf War. However, following the Iranian raid on Kuwait and the coup plots against Bahrain and Saudi Arabia six weeks later, the Gulf Cooperation Council incorporated military cooperation into its framework. On January 26, 1982, the Ministers of Defense from all member states met in Riyadh and agreed upon establishing a joint air defense system.

The GCC is not a military alliance in the usual sense. Thus far, only Bahrain and Saudi Arabia have signed the Council's defense pact, and even these two states have not agreed on the amount of military support that should be extended to Iraq in the war with Iran. Even if the GCC had been charged with Gulf security, differences in orientation prohibit the joint military planning and coordination necessary for the GCC to perform that function. To build the necessary military establishment for the GCC to effectively provide stability in the Gulf would take billions of dollars and years of training and organization.

The Arab-Israeli Wars

Nowhere in the Middle East is the potential for a superpower confrontation more likely than in the Arab-Israeli conflict. Since the late 1940s the confrontation between the Arab states and Israel has been a central feature of the Middle East. Tensions between the Jewish and Arab communities in Palestine began around World War I and by the end of World War II had become a permanent part of life in Palestine under the British mandate. Following World War II, British forces in the area attempted to maintain order and in the process became the target of terrorist attacks from both sides. Exhausted by World War II and unable to separate the warring factions, the British turned to the United Nations for a solution to the Palestine problem. The UN responded by sending an investigatory panel to Palestine for a firsthand assessment of the situation. The committee, known as the United Nations Special Committee on Palestine (UNSCOP), was composed of delegates from 11 nonregional states.

In the fall of 1947 UNSCOP presented two recommendations to the UN General Assembly. The majority of the committee proposed partitioning Palestine into separate Jewish and Arab states with Jerusalem, because of its importance to the region's religious communities, granted an international status. The minority recommended a loose federation of two locally autonomous Jewish and Arab states. Most of the Jewish population of Palestine accepted the majority plan. The Arabs opposed it, probably in part because this option gave 57 percent of the land in Palestine to the Jewish community, which made up only one-third of the area's population. On November 29, 1947 two-thirds of those voting in the General Assembly, including the United States, Great Britain, France, and the Soviet Union, supported the majority recommendation of the partition of Palestine. The two states were to be created sixty days after the British withdrawal from the region.

The Arab states challenged the United Nation's right to impose such a settlement upon the people of Palestine, the majority of whom were Arab. In February 1948, the Arab Higher Committee announced it would resist attempts to establish a Jewish state in Palestine and began to send organized military detachments into the area, which quickly raised existing levels of violence. The British, lacking the political will and military resources to restore order and seeing that political compromise was out of the question, changed their departure date from August to May 14, 1948 and preemptorily turned the matter over to the UN. On the day of the British departure, the Jewish National Council, which had acted as the representative of the Jewish population during the mandate period, declared the establishment of the Jewish state of Israel. The United States immediately announced de facto recognition of the new state and the Soviet Union extended full diplomatic recognition three days later.

The day following the announcement of the Jewish National Council, about 24,000 regular troops from Egypt, Syria, Iraq, Transjordan, and Lebanon entered Palestine, and the first Arab-Israeli war began. The Arab forces were met by a hastily organized Israeli army of around 30,000 troops. The first phase of the fighting lasted four weeks during which the Arab armies made limited gains. Both sides agreed to a truce, which began on June 11, 1948 and lasted only four weeks, but it provided the Israeli forces sufficient time to reorganize and to obtain new weapons, mostly from Eastern European states. Fighting began again on July 9, ending in a second truce on July 19 that lasted until October 15. From then until January 7, 1949, there was intermittent violence.

Armistice agreements were negotiated between Israel and Egypt in February 1949 under the auspices of the UN Mediator and the Palestine Conciliation Council. Israel reached similar agreements with Lebanon in March 1949, Transjordan in April and Syria in July. The territorial disposition that resulted from the war placed nearly 80 percent of the area under the Palestine Mandate under Israeli authority and extended Israel's de facto boundaries beyond the lines envisaged in the Partition Plan of 1947. Hundreds of thousands of Palestinian Arabs left their homes and fled to neighboring Arab territories.[17]

As a result of the UN negotiated armistice, Egypt assumed administrative control over the Gaza Strip. Jordan annexed a large enclave, including the old city of Jerusalem, from the Jordan River west to Israel's new borders—an area that is now referred to as the West Bank. Of the major powers, only Great Britain recognized this action. UN armistice commissions were set up to police the agreements.

The armistices of 1949 left open the question of Israel's boundaries and never evolved into peace talks. Partially for these reasons, the Arab states refused to reconcile themselves to the fact of Israel's existence. Equally important were the humiliating defeats they had suffered at the hands of the Israeli army. Unilateral actions on the part of all participants kept tension between the parties high. Border skirmishes involving Arab raids into Israel met with swift reprisals. It was this situation that led the major powers to conclude the Tripartite Agreement, which limited arms supply to Israel and its Arab opponents.

The proximate cause of the war in 1956 was Nasser's decision to nationalize the Suez Canal, which had been under British administration since 1882. Adding to French and British distress was the Czechoslovakian arms deal and Nasser's support of anti-French rebels in North Africa as well as his shrill anti-Western rhetoric. When a unified command was set up between the armies of Egypt, Syria, and Saudi Arabia, Israel expressed concern that the Arabs were preparing for an attack. Secretly working in concert with the French and British, Israel executed a preemptive strike against Egyptian troops in the Sinai Peninsula on October 26, 1956 and within days, Egyptian forces were driven back to the Suez Canal. Ostensibly to separate the two armies and to protect the Canal, the British and French launched an airborne assault along the Suez Canal on November 5, occupying Port Said. Egypt's Arab allies, on the other hand, made no move to provide military support and Egyptian forces suffered a humiliating defeat.

It took the combined efforts of the United States and the Soviet Union to end the conflict and force France and Britain to withdraw. On November 7, 1956, the United States and the USSR introduced a joint resolution in the UN General Assembly calling for the evacuation of the British and French forces and the creation of a United Nations Emergency Force (UNEF) composed of forces from several small- and medium-sized states, to police the border areas. The British withdrew their last troops in December 1956 and Israel completed its withdrawal in February 1957. Meanwhile, the UNEF troops took up positions in Egyptian territory along the southern tip of the Sinai Peninsula on the Gulf of Aqaba and between Egyptian and Israeli forces along the Gaza frontier. As part of the terms of the ceasefire, Israeli shipping was guaranteed safe passage through the Gulf of Aqaba.

No peace treaty was negotiated and although the frontier remained quiet until the spring of 1967, no progress was made toward solving the underlying problems between Israel and the Arabs. By virtue of the 1955 Czechoslovakian arms deal with Egypt, the Soviet Union established a presence in the region for the first time since the fall of the Ottoman Empire. Through its diplomatic dealings alongside the United States on behalf of Egypt, Moscow gained added credibility as an alternative source of international political support among Arab states opposed to Israel.

From 1957 to 1967, there was no lessening of tensions between Israel and the Arab states. The Palestine Liberation Organization (PLO) was established at a summit meeting of Arab leaders in 1964. The organization and its military arm, the Palestinian Liberation Army (PLA), was created to organize Palestinian refugees into regular army and guerrilla units with the objective of driving the Israeli government from lands that were once Palestinian and to restore Arab authority there. The PLO began to conduct raids into Israel from Jordan and the Gaza Strip, and in response Israel retaliated against Jordanian and Egyptian troops. At the same time, Arab governments began accumulating large stockpiles of weapons. The combination of terrorist attacks and the arms buildup created such international tensions that by May 1967, a relatively minor terrorist raid on a military vehicle north of Galilee was sufficient to trigger a sequence of events that resulted in the third Arab-Israeli war.

Israel's prime minister, Levi Eshkol, announced that Israel reserved the right to retaliate for the Arab raid. Syria reacted by putting its military units on alert, moved troops to the Israeli border, and called for the activation of the Cairo-Damascus defense pact signed in November 1966. On May 17, Egypt and Syria announced that they had reached a high state of military readiness and charged that Israel had begun a major military buildup along its borders. The charges were supported by the Soviet Union.

On May 18, the Egyptian government requested that UNEF withdraw from its positions along the Gaza Strip and in the Sinai and on May 22, announced that the Strait of Tiran, at the southern end of the Gulf of Aqaba, was closed to Israeli shipping and that the Strait had been mined. Subsequently, Jordan and Egypt signed a mutual defense pact. All international efforts to defuse the situation failed and on June 5, 1967, Israel launched preemptive air and ground attacks against Egypt.

In four days, Israel had overrun Egyptian troops and occupied the Sinai as far as the Suez Canal. When Jordanian and Syrian forces began a bombardment of Israeli positions on June 5, Israel counterattacked, gaining control of the important Hebron-Jerusalem road. By June 8 Israel had occupied all the territory from its eastern borders to the west bank of the Jordan River and by June 9 had seized the Golan Heights. A ceasefire resolution passed by the UN was accepted by Jordan on June 7, by Egypt on June 8, and by Syria on June 9. Israel refused to agree to the resolution and continued to apply military pressure on the Golan front, taking Kuneitra on June 9. Concerned that Israel intended an assault into Damascus, Soviet Premier Aleksei Kosygin warned U.S. president Lyndon Johnson on June 10 that if Israel did not immediately accept a ceasefire, the Soviet Union might intervene. Johnson conveyed the Soviet message to Israel and at the same time took the precaution of ordering the U.S. Sixth Fleet to move closer to Syria. Israel accepted the ceasefire on the evening of June 11.

The 1967 war radically altered the geopolitical realities in the Arab-Israeli sector of the Middle East. The war left Israel in possession of substantial amounts of Arab territory including the Sinai Peninsula, the west bank of the Jordan River, and the Golan Heights. From a military standpoint, Israel's borders had never been more secure and conversely, the Arabs borders never less so. When the Arab states demanded that Israel withdraw to the borders that existed prior to June 1967, Israel felt no compelling pressure to comply and declared its intention to remain in occupation of the captured territories until direct negotiations with Arab states resulted in a peace settlement. Partly because of the defeat they had suffered, none of the Arab states was inclined to agree to such terms. Instead, Syria and Egypt appealed to the Soviet Union for replacement of their lost equipment. To counter these Soviet moves the United States began to ship military hardware to Israel.

In the face of what appeared to be a military and diplomatic standoff, several efforts were made to provide a solution to the problem. The most important of these occurred on November 22, 1967 when the United Nations Security Council unanimously adopted a resolution known as UNSC Resolution 242, which called for:

   i. Withdrawal of Israeli armed forces from territories occupied in the recent conflict;
   ii. Termination of all claims or states of belligerency and respect for and acknowledgment of the sovereignty, territorial integrity and political independence of every state in the area and their right to live in peace within secure and recognized boundaries free from threats or acts of force;
   iii. Guaranteed freedom of navigation through international waterways in the area;
   iv. Achieving a just settlement of the refugee problem;
   v. Guaranteeing the territorial inviolability and political independence of every state in the area, through measures including the establishment of demilitarized zones;
   vi. Requested the Secretary General to designate a Special Representative to proceed to the Middle East to establish and

> maintain contacts with the states concerned in order to promote agreement and assist efforts to achieve a peaceful and accepted settlement in accordance with the provisions and principles in the resolution.

UNSC Resolution 242 has been the basis for most subsequent negotiations to end the Arab-Israeli dispute. At the time, however, it had no immediate effect on the situation and both sides remained adamant in their respective positions.

Between 1967 and 1969, the Arab states and Israel began intensive efforts to rebuild their armed forces. The arms race escalated in terms of the quantity and the sophistication of weapons provided, and the destructive capability afforded to the antagonists. In March 1969, Egypt began shelling Israeli positions along the east bank of the Suez Canal. The stated purpose of the bombardment was to wear Israel down, forcing it to bear the economic burden of maintaining a high level of military preparedness, forcing Israel to reconsider its decision to occupy the territory won in 1967. Israel retaliated with its own artillery in an attempt to put Egypt on the defensive and make the bombardment of Israeli positions too costly to continue. In January 1970, Israel began deep penetration air attacks into Egypt, striking military installations just outside Cairo. To put a stop to this, Nasser requested that Moscow supply Egypt with advanced air defense weapons systems. The Soviet Union agreed to provide MiG 21 interceptor aircraft, SAM 2 and SAM 3 anti-aircraft missile batteries, and even Soviet pilots and crews for the air defense weapons. In April 1970, Soviet pilots began flying operational missions for Egypt.

The deteriorating conditions were of grave concern to the United States. As Israeli aircraft losses began to rise, the Soviet-manned defense systems began to edge closer to the Canal. In July 1970, the inevitable occurred and Israeli aircraft shot down Soviet piloted Egyptian fighters over the Suez Canal. The event shocked all the participants into action and U.S. Secretary of State Rogers negotiated a ceasefire that went into effect on August 7, 1970. Following the ceasefire, UN mediator Gunnar Jarring launched a round of talks with the Arab states and Israel. They stalled on the Arab insistence that Israel withdraw from the occupied territories and on Israel's refusal to do so before the Arab governments agreed to direct negotiations leading to a peace settlement.

The August 1970 ceasefire agreement along the Suez Canal and the activities of the Jarring mission was viewed by the PLO as a prelude to a negotiated settlement at the expense of the Palestinian cause. In an effort to maintain their cause at the forefront of world politics, radical elements within the PLO (the Popular Front for the Liberation of Palestine, led by George Habbash) hijacked three commercial airplanes, took them to a desert field in Jordan and destroyed them. Activities such as these and raids conducted by the PLO from Jordan into Israel resulted in Israeli retaliatory attacks on Jordanian soil, exacerbating long-standing animosities between Jordan's King Hussein and the PLO leadership. Hussein viewed such incidents as leading toward an attempt by the PLO to challenge his authority in Jordan. In September 1970, responding to pressure from within his own military to impose constraints on Palestinian military activity in Jordan, King Hussein authorized his army to move against the PLO. The PLO resisted and a brief but violent confrontation broke out, which came to be known as "Black September" by the Palestinians. The Jordanian forces soon overwhelmed the PLO and the more intransigent of them were forced to flee to Syria and Lebanon.

Nasser died in 1970. His successor, Anwar Sadat, warned that if necessary, Egypt would resort to force to alter Israel's position. In early 1973 he cautiously sounded out Western European and the U.S. governments to see if there were any new initiatives on the horizon. Finding none, on October 6, 1973, he launched a well planned and executed attack against Israeli positions along the Suez Canal. Israeli intelligence failed to perceive the threat in time and Israeli defenses along the Suez Canal, lightly manned because of the Jewish holiday of Yom Kippur, were quickly overrun. When the Israeli air force mounted an air attack against Egyptian airfields in order to gain air superiority over the Suez, it was turned back by an effective screen of air defense missiles. The Egyptian army, facing no threat from the air, repelled an Israeli ground counterattack, secured a bridgehead over the Canal, and advanced into the Sinai. At the end of the first day, Egyptian forces had penetrated several miles beyond the Canal and dug in.

Shortly after Egypt began its assault across the Suez Canal, Syria launched an attack in the Golan Heights. On October 7, after some initial gains, the drive was halted. A second offensive on October 9 gained nothing and the Israeli forces were left in good position in the field. On the 10th, feeling no pressure from the Egyptians in the Sinai, the Israeli army launched its counterattack on the Golan Heights, regaining its old positions by nightfall. In the following days, Israel began to push beyond the 1967 lines and conducted bombing raids around Damascus. Egypt attempted to take the pressure off Syria by reopening its offensive in the Sinai but the attack was repulsed.

Between October 10th and 13th, Israeli reconnaissance units discovered a gap between the Egyptian Second Army in the north and the Third Army in the south. When Egypt prepared to launch a new attack, a number of armored units that had been left on the west bank of the Canal as strategic reserves were moved to the east bank. This move left Egypt insufficient forces west of the Canal to prevent an Israeli crossing. After repulsing the Egyptian attack on October 15, Israel pierced the gap between the two Egyptian armies and on the 16th, crossed the canal. By the next day, the Egyptian Third Army was completely cut off from the other Egyptian forces. A single armored brigade was the only Egyptian unit between the Israeli army and Cairo.

On October 20, responding to an urgent request from the Soviet government, U.S. Secretary of State Henry Kissinger flew to Moscow to discuss how to deal with the new military situation on the Suez Canal. On October 21, at an emergency session of the UN Security Council, the United States and the USSR presented a joint ceasefire proposal that was passed as UN Resolution 338 on October 22. The proposal included in the resolution seemed more in the Arabs' interests than Israel's, because of a battlefield situation that benefitted Israel, and it broke down as Israeli units consolidated their position and began preparing for an all-out attack on the Egyptian Third Army. The Soviet Union saw that such an eventuality would damage its position with Egypt and, in a worst case situation, could open the way for an Israeli ground assault on Cairo. On the 24th of October, U.S. intelligence received reports of Soviet mobilization of airborne divisions. Concerned that Moscow was planning to insert regular combat units into Egypt the United States placed its forces worldwide on a higher state of alert as a signal that it would militarily oppose such a move. After a flurry of diplomatic activity between Washington and Moscow, the major powers exerted pressure on Israel and the Arabs and brought about another ceasefire—one that lasted.

Between the end of the October 1973 war and 1975, the United States expended considerable effort to arrange a settlement between Egypt and Israel. In January 1974, Secretary of State Kissinger's "shuttle diplomacy" achieved a military separation in the Sinai and in May the same year, a similar disengagement was negotiated between Israel and Syria. A more extensive set of agreements between Egypt and Israel was negotiated in September, 1975. Egyptian President Anwar Sadat's announcement in November 1977 that he was prepared to go to the Israeli Knesset to discuss the Arab-Israeli situation constituted a major change in the policy of the most populous Arab state and the major Arab participant in the wars with Israel. His visit to Jerusalem and the subsequent negotiations with Israel with U.S. assistance set in motion a peace process that led to the Camp David Accords of September 1978 and the Egypt-Israel Peace Treaty of March 1979 and that generated some hope that the effort could be broadened to include other participants and achieve other results. Autonomy talks to resolve the future of the West Bank and Gaza Strip were initiated but no major achievement resulted.

At the same time that Egypt and Israel were negotiating a settlement of their grievances, the situation in Lebanon was deteriorating. A civil war had broken out in 1975 and in 1976 Syrian units had moved into the country in a attempt to separate the warring factions. With no effective central government to impede it the PLO moved troops into southern Lebanon, turning it into a base of operations against Israel. In early 1978, a dramatic PLO seizure of an Israeli bus full of passengers south of Haifa highlighted Israel's vulnerability to attacks based from Southern Lebanon. In March 1978, Israel launched a massive operation (Operation Litani) to neutralize PLO strengths along its northern borders. Although it failed to resolve the problem completely, the number of raids was reduced and UN troops (the United Nations Interim Forces in Lebanon or UNIFIL) were inserted in the area.

In April 1981, as PLO raids and Israeli reprisals continued, Syria placed missiles in Lebanon in apparent violation of prior agreements. Emboldened by this the PLO increased the level of attacks on Israel. The problem of Syrian missiles remained unresolved and Israel was concerned that the PLO would launch a new "war of attrition" under the protection of the Syrian missile umbrella. Israel responded to a prolonged PLO artillery attack on northern Israeli villages with a bombing raid on PLO positions in Beirut. A ceasefire was arranged by U.S. Ambassador Philip Habib in July 1981 but it failed to alleviate either the underlying problem along the Israeli-Lebanese border or the problem of Syrian missiles in Lebanon.

Despite reduced levels of violence along the border, Israel's Prime Minister Menahem Begin was convinced that as long as the PLO remained entrenched in southern Lebanon, there would be no security for Israeli citizens in Galilee, or northern Israel. On June 6, 1982, Israel sent forces across the Lebanese border with the objective of removing the PLO threat to Israel. The operation, called "Peace for Galilee," was launched ostensibly to "place all the civilian population of Galilee beyond the range of the terrorists' fire from Lebanon where they, their bases, and their headquarters are concentrated." By June 8, however, it was obvious that the Israeli forces had far more ambitious goals—to destroy the PLO political and military position in Lebanon and thereby to reduce PLO influence over Lebanese political events. By June 12, Israeli forces were in control of the southern 40 percent of Lebanon and had Beirut under seige. U.S. ambassador Philip Habib secured a halt in the hostilities in early August 1982 but the Israeli forces continued to occupy positions around Beirut. One of the conditions for the Israeli agreement to lift the siege was that the PLO be required to leave Lebanon and in early August, PLO Chairman Yasser Arafat agreed. On August 21, as the evacuation of approximately 8,000 PLO fighters began, a multinational force consisting of U.S., French, and Italian troops began to arrive. On September 1, the evacuation was completed and starting September 11, 1982 the multinational forces withdrew as well.

Three days after the multinational forces were withdrawn from Lebanon, Beshir Gemayel, president-elect of Lebanon, was assassinated, presumably by Palestinian terrorists. His death augered renewed violence as various factions attempted to take advantage of the uncertain situation. Israeli authorities asked the Lebanese Army to take control of West Beirut until a new president could be elected but it refused, so the Israeli chief-of-staff, Rafael Eitan, ordered Israeli forces to move in.

In the area occupied by Israeli forces there were two large Palestinian refugee camps, called Sabra and Chatilla, which according to Israeli intelligence sheltered a large number of Palestinian terrorists. Prior to the departure of the PLO, Israeli military authorities had asked the Lebanese forces to clear them out but no action had been taken. Once Israeli forces were in position, the Israeli command asked troops from Gemayel's private militia, known as Kataeb, to take control of the two camps and round up the terrorists for expulsion. On September 16, Kataeb militiamen entered the camps and immediately came under fire. Kataeb struck back with a vengeance turning the mission into a 36-hour massacre in which perhaps as many as 700 or 800 Palestinians, died including some women and children. The event became a cause celebre for the Palestinian movement.

Israeli-Lebanese negotiations for a settlement of the tensions between Lebanon and Israel began in December 1982 and resulted in an agreement involving Israeli withdrawal on May 17, 1983. Almost immediately the agreement was denounced by Syria because it was tantamount to diplomatic recognition of Israel by

Lebanon and because the agreement would leave Syria almost alone among the Arab states confronting Israel. In July, Syria organized opponents of the weak Lebanese government into an umbrella organization called the National Salvation Front. Efforts to resolve differences between this group and the weakened Lebanese central government failed and in February 1984, the largest faction within the Front, the Shia Moslems, seized control of West Beirut and forced the Lebanese president, Amin Gemayel, a Maronite Christian, to dismiss his government and form a new one that included all his opponents, some of whom commanded militia forces as well trained and equipped as the Lebanese Army. On March 5, 1984, they forced Gemayel to abrogate the May 17 agreement with Israel.

Israel continued to hold out for a negotiated agreement with Lebanon that would provide for the withdrawal of its troops and ensure the security of its northern border. Lebanon, under Syrian pressure, demanded that Israel withdraw unconditionally. The Syrian government refused to moderate its stand, so in June 1985 Israel completed a unilateral withdrawal of its forces, leaving behind a security zone to be maintained by local Lebanese militia units favorably disposed toward Israel. While this arrangement was clearly less stable than either Israel or the central government of Lebanon would have liked, without Syrian cooperation there was no alternative.

The withdrawal of Israeli troops from Lebanon altered none of the differences existing between Israel and its Arab neighbors. As the Middle East entered the second half of the 1980s, the salient political and military feature of the region was the absence of peace.

The Arms Race

Throughout the Arab-Israeli conflict the great powers have played a significant role as suppliers of arms to the belligerents. One of the first arms shipments directly connected with the confrontation took place on April 1, 1948 when the Soviet Union arranged the delivery of Czechoslovakian rifles and light machine guns to the Israeli independence fighters. These were followed by aircraft and artillery pieces that were important to Israel's victory in the 1948/49 War of Independence.

Conflicts between Middle Eastern states have been the major element spurring the regional arms race. Each war between the Arabs and Israel brought greater numbers of weapons into the area and increased the number of suppliers as well. The Shah's determination to be the policeman of the Persian Gulf caused him to embark on the region's largest military buildup. The hositilities between Iran and Iraq have encouraged the states on the Gulf to improve their military capabilities and Syria's hostile intentions have been of concern to Jordan on more than one occasion. Turkey's strategic importance to NATO has resulted in the United States and other NATO members providing it with massive amounts of military aid to the point that the Turkish army is the second largest in the alliance.

The French and the British traditionally have been the suppliers of arms to their former Arab colonies. The entrance of the Soviet Union as a result of the Czechoslovakian arms deal to Egypt in 1955 was the first turning point as far as the two superpowers are concerned. After the Arab-Israeli war in 1967 the United States added its considerable production capacity to the arms trade of the Middle East. Since 1950, states in the Middle East have purchased more than half the total foreign military cash sales worldwide.[18]

Regional states have developed their own military industries. Prior to the fall of the Shah of Iran, Israel was an important arms exporter to Iran. The Shah also undertook agreements with the Northrop, Bell, and Vickers corporations to assemble military aircraft. Turkey has been producing light arms since the early 1970s and in 1980 signed agreements with West Germany to assemble submarines and patrol boats in Turkey. At about the same time, the Arab Organization for Industrialization provided Egypt with $1.4 billion to establish a defense industry as part of a plan to make Arab states less dependent on foreign arms suppliers. Within ten years, 30 arms factories with a labor force of over 100,000 were producing more than $500 million worth of arms each year. (The agreement was terminated by the Arab Organization for Industrialization after Sadat signed peace agreements with Israel.) In 1980 Turkey signed agreements with West Germany to assemble submarines and patrol boats in that country, and in 1982 Ankara contracted with Northrop and General Dynamics corporations for limited co-production and assembly of F-16 or F-18A fighter aircraft in Turkey.

Regional instability provides only part of the explanation for the arms race in the Middle East. As Table 1.9 shows, the comparison between arms transferred before and after 1970 is striking. The oil boom of the early 1970s provided great amounts of excess dollars that were used to purchase military hardware, and the imbalance of trade encouraged the producers of weapons to sell. Looking at the arms race from the point of view of the supplier presents the same picture. Table 1.10 clearly shows the sharp increase in the level of arms sales to Middle Eastern states that occurred after the 1973 oil

TABLE 1.9: Arms Imports and Suppliers, 1970–1979 (millions of U.S. dollars)

Country	Total Value	1970–1974 Percent Total of Regional	Largest Supplier	Percent of Country's Total
Middle East				
Syria	2,320	25	USSR	95
Egypt	2,181	23	USSR	98
Iran	2,053	22	USA	60
Israel	1,688	18	USA	97
Iraq	336	4	USSR	94
Saudi Arabia	324	3	USA	51
North Africa				
Libya	656	84	France	67
Morocco	64	8	USA	69
Tunisia	41	5	France	96
Algeria	23	3	France	52
		1975–1979		
Middle East				
Iran	6,229	31	USA	81
Saudi Arabia	2,806	14	USA	79
Jordan	2,615	13	USA	98
Iraq	2,418	12	USSR	93
Israel	2,008	10	USA	95
Syria	1,170	6	USSR	84
North Africa				
Libya	3,151	65	USSR	79
Morocco	863	20	France	81
Algeria	660	14	USSR	79
Tunisia	72	1	Italy	38

Source: SIPRI Yearbook (1980) Tables 3.6 and 3.7; MERIP Reports (February, 1983).

boom. The pattern has continued in the Middle East even though worldwide arms transfers declined between 1980 and 1983 and nearly every Middle Eastern state is suffering financially as a result of the drop in demand for petroleum. In 1974, the Middle East

TABLE 1.10: Arms Deliveries to the Middle East, 1973–1984 (billions of US dollars)

	1973–1976	1977–1980	1981–1984
Unites States	6.9	11.3	11.9
France	1.0	3.4	10.8
United Kingdom	1.0	2.8	4.1
West Germany	.5	1.2	1.3
Italy	.3	.6	1.5
Soviet Union	6.7	13.4	14.4
Other Warsaw Pact	.3	1.0	6.2
Total Middle East	16.7	33.7	50.2

Source: US Arms Control and Disarmament Agency, *World Military Expenditures and Arms Transfers 1985* (August, 1985).

imported 27.4 percent of all the weapons transferred worldwide. In 1984 the Middle East's share had risen to 42.6 percent.

STRATEGIC FOCUS

The combination of great oil wealth and the strategic value of its geographic location has made the Middle East a focal point of great power vital interests. The passage of time and the addition of petroleum as a strategic resource has intensified these interests and the dynamics of the intra-regional political milieu have become more complicated rather than less. For a number of reasons there are no intra-regional organizations strong enough to act as forums for the negotiation of differences as an alternative to armed conflict. As a result actors both within the area and without enter the political arena unencumbered by any restraining institutions.

Perhaps the most striking feature of the Middle East is the inability of any single actor, regional or international, to establish a dominant position. The diminished influence of the world's great powers has not created a "power vacuum" as has occasionally been asserted. On the contrary, the prevailing condition is one in which a number of regionally powerful Middle Eastern states are contending for positions of leadership.

Irreconcilable differences among progressive and traditional regimes, opposing ideological and religious orientations, the presence of unassimilated immigrants, and the absence of any viable regional institution to reconcile differences serve to keep tensions high. What separates the Middle East from other regions with similar difficulties is not the nature of the problems but their intensity. Social differences are magnified by the fact that the depth of Middle Eastern tradition is profound, stretching back to the dawn of civilization. The tensions created thereby have been given added impetus by bureaucracies geared to spending oil money on Western technology and foreign agencies eager to sell every imaginable type of goods and services from oil refineries to soft drinks. This combination is found nowhere else in the world. With no power able to establish domination over events in the Middle East and the costs of miscalculation as high as they are, the Middle East will remain an area of primary concern to all the major powers and a threat to international stability for some time to come.

NOTES

1. "Review of member state's energy policies," a report submitted to the Commission of the European Communities (1984).

2. Washington *Post* (April 12, 1986).

3. "The $100 billion oil bill," *Business Week* (July 6, 1974), pp. 70–72.

4. *Direction of Trade Statistics Yearbooks*; 1971, 1976, and 1981.

5. *BP Statistical Review of World Energy* (London: Dix Motive Press, 1985), p. 30.

6. *International Energy Statistical Review*, Organization of Economic Cooperation and Development, October 30, 1980.

7. Washington *Post* (December 10, 1985), p. A23.

8. *Middle East Economic Digest* (May 1985), p.12.

9. Washington *Post* (December 12, 1985), p. A19.

10. *The Military Balance 1984–1985* (London: Institute for Strategic Studies, 1985).

11. Washington *Post* (November 26, 1984).

12. Bruce C. Kunniholm, "Turkey and NATO: Past, present and future," *Orbis* 27 (Summer, 1983), pp. 437–38.

13. Malcolm Yapp, "Soviet relations with the countries of the Northern Tier" in Adeed Dawisha and Karen Dawisha (eds.), *The Soviet Union in the Middle East* (New York: Holmes and Meier Publishers, 1982), p. 31.

14. *Foreign Relations of the United States 1945* Vol. 8, p. 75 and the section entitled "Conference of Berlin" (Potsdam Conference) Vol. 1, pp. 1018ff.

15. *Foreign Relations of the United States 1947*, Vol. 7, pp. 827–29.

16. Kunniholm, "Turkey and NATO: past and present," p. 141.

17. The exact size of the refugee population and the reasons for their departure have been the subject of much debate.

18. U.S. General Accounting Office, *U.S. Security and Military Assistance Programs Related Activities*, Report Number ID–82–40, June 1, 1982.

II
THE SUPERPOWERS

2
The United States

Gershon R. Kieval and Bernard Reich

THE BACKGROUND OF U.S. POLICY

The interest of the United States in the Middle East was slow to develop and to be supported by policy and commitment. Although specialized interests and activities may be traced to the first decades after the founding of the United States, until World War II U.S. interests and activities in the Middle East were primarily private in nature, and the U.S. government made few decisions of consequence with regard to strategic or political developments in the region. U.S. interests were circumscribed in scope and limited to portions of the region rather than to its entirety.

During the nineteenth century U.S. activities were those of individuals or groups and did not concern the United States as a government. U.S. political and strategic interests were not identified, and the United States virtually abstained from official political involvement or policy in the area. Primary attention focused on religious, educational, cultural, and humanitarian pursuits. Commercial interests of a significant nature emerged only with the discovery of substantial oil fields in the region.

To a significant degree the United States relied on Great Britain, with its longstanding interest and involvement in the area, to advance the few U.S. interests that had developed. World War I and the Wilson presidency generated some thought about the future of the region, but the United States was not a central actor and had little detailed knowledge of and no direct role in the British and French decisions with respect to the dismemberment of the Ottoman Empire, particularly the crucial arrangements (such as the Sykes-Picot Agreement, the Hussein-McMahon Correspondence, and the Balfour Declaration) that were later to affect conflict and stability in much of the region. The U.S. role was limited largely to President Wilson's participation in the peace conferences after World War I—at which Wilson's idealism and such pronouncements as the Fourteen Points had little practical effect.

Between the world wars the United States had no specific Middle East policy; it deferred to and, on the whole, supported the British in the region, including in the Palestine Mandate. Nevertheless, President Wilson endorsed the British-issued Balfour Declaration (1917), as did the Congress, individual Senators and Congressmen, and numerous state governments and legislatures. Pious pronouncements in the form of vague expressions of support for the creation of a Jewish homeland as called for by the Balfour Declaration and endorsed by the Palestine Mandate were common but no official action of significance was taken by the U.S. government.

At the same time, U.S. corporations were beginning to get involved in the region's oil industry as a commercial and economic opportunity. The U.S. government promoted application of the "open door" principle to U.S. commercial interests and sought U.S. participation in commercial activity in the region without disadvantage.

World War II altered and enhanced U.S. interests in the region. Physical presence and strategic involvement in the area gave rise to concerns that ultimately led to the formation of a political and security policy for the area. Oil became a military/political concern, thus making the strategic value of the area more obvious. Soviet and Soviet-sponsored activity in the northern tier of the Middle East immediately after World War II contributed to U.S. concern and led to the formulation of policies designed to contain the Soviet threat. The Truman Doctrine, developed in response to the Soviet threat, became the first major political/strategic U.S. policy statement on the Middle East and presaged future policies.

World War II and the Holocaust, with their devastating effects for European and world Jewry and the shift of focus of the Zionist movement from Europe to the United States, helped lead to U.S. advocacy of expanded immigration of displaced European Jewry to Palestine, support for the partition of Palestine and the creation of a Jewish state, and the recognition of the new state of Israel upon its independence in May 1948. These developments, along with British weariness that led to reduction of the British presence and commitment in the Middle East, combined with greater U.S. awareness of the region, the Soviet threat, and the assumption by the United States of a new global role, set the stage for increased U.S. involvement in the Middle East, particularly in the Arab-Israeli zone. Nonetheless, the United States entered the postwar era with no specific policy for the Middle East or even for the more narrowly-defined Arab-Israeli sector.

Israel's declaration of independence was accompanied by the first of the Arab-Israeli wars, during which the United States adopted a position of neutrality and of support for United Nations' actions. It was hoped that the war and resultant armistice agreements would soon be replaced by a permanent peace, which would permit all the states of the region to initiate programs for economic and social development; but this did not materialize. The ongoing conflict has remained at the focus of U.S. Middle East policy, increasingly occupying its attention, concern, diplomacy, and resources. Underlying the importance of the conflict has been the recognition of its potential for superpower confrontation and the view that its peaceful resolution is the best means for promoting other U.S. interests in the region and elsewhere.

Within a few years after World War II the main principles of U.S. policy and official involvement had been established. U.S. policy initially sought to reduce the scope and level of regional violence by an embargo on arms shipments to the area in 1947 and by the support of UN armistice efforts. The Truman administration also provided economic assistance to Israel and some of the Arab states. Defense of the Middle East against the Soviet Union, termination of the Arab-Israeli conflict, and stability of the region complemented previously-devised policies in support of U.S. interests, which included the open-door policy for U.S. firms involved in oil and other commercial opportunities and the continued educational, cultural, and philanthropic activity of missionaries and other U.S. citizens. U.S. activities have continued to be guided by these broad concerns although the specific elements have varied in intensity and importance over time, as have the nature and extent of the U.S. role in attempts to resolve the Arab-Israeli conflict.

U.S. efforts to reach an accomodation among the various parties in the Middle East have taken several forms and involved a variety of programs. The United States has sought regional stability through such instruments as the proposed Allied Middle East Command. Assurances to Israel and the Arab states have also been offered in presidential statements that supported the political independence and territorial integrity of the states of the region. There were efforts to limit the arms race through programs of arms control which, at various times, included (with Britain and France) the Tripartite Declaration regarding security in the Middle East of May 1950, and a later (now superceded) self-imposed limitation made with the intention of not becoming a principal supplier of military equipment to the Middle East. Programs to foster economic and social development have involved technical and economic assistance to the states of the region.

Efforts to improve the Arab-Israeli situation often took the form of specific functional approaches dealing with only a portion of the overall problem, including such noteworthy efforts as Eric Johnston's plan for sharing the waters of the Jordan River among Israel and her neighbors (1953–1955) and Joseph Johnson's activities relating to the refugee problem (1961–1963).

These particular efforts and others, such as the broader approaches articulated by Secretary of State John Foster Dulles in 1955, had little real effect. By the mid 1960s the United States, and most other interested powers, had largely withdrawn from efforts to achieve long-term peace and appeared to concentrate on preventing an Arab-Israeli war while promoting regional security and stability and socioeconomic improvement.

The lower priority given to peace as an attainable objective of U.S. policy in the early 1960s was altered by the Six Day War of 1967. The war suggested the failure of the previous approach to the Arab-Israeli conflict and radically changed the political climate of the Middle East by creating new circumstances, initially thought to be more conducive to a settlement of the conflict.

U.S. Interests

The U.S. national interest lies in its continued independent existence, survival, and security, with its institutions and values safeguarded and with the welfare of its people enhanced. There is an "American ideology" that seeks democratic institutions, with morality and principles as guidelines of policy, and seeks to promote liberty and human rights for its own people and for others. "Making the world safe for democracy" is an operational imperative as the United States cannot maintain its existence in isolation; it requires a world conducive to its unique political experiment.

In the Middle East, U.S. core interests and concerns can be cataloged with substantial agreement, although debate surrounds their priority: Preventing Soviet dominance (and the expansion of its power and influence in the area); assuring the flow of oil at reasonable prices, particularly to U.S. friends and allies; assuring access to regional markets, as a means of recycling the petrodollars; and the security and well-being of Israel. The United States also has increasingly considered it to be "in its interest" to resolve the Arab-Israeli conflict.

The overriding U.S. strategic-political interest in the Middle East for more than four decades has been the avoidance of nuclear confrontation with the Soviet Union. Although this concern has been apparent since 1945, there also has been a contemporaneous and sometimes conflicting interest in ensuring the prevention of Soviet dominance, which is seen as a threat to the North Atlantic Treaty Organization (NATO) and ultimately to U.S. allies and the United States itself. Countering Soviet action was a factor in the U.S. policy concerning Iran in 1945/46, as well as in numerous activities subsequently designed to respond to the Soviet threat. Both the Truman and Eisenhower Doctrines were clear responses to this interpretation of U.S. interests.

The strategic significance of the region resulting from its geographic location has also generated U.S. interest. Located at the hub of Europe, Asia, and Africa, the Middle East is a crossroads and a bridge. Unimpeded transit utilizing the air and sea routes that cross the region and constitute significant global communications links is an interest of the United States.

These communications links include the maritime passage through the Suez Canal, which is the shortest shipping route between Western Europe and Asia and a primary route for the transit of Persian Gulf oil to Western Europe. It is also an important route for other goods between Europe and Indian-Pacific Ocean locations. Also of importance are the Turkish Straits, control of which strengthens any state interested in the Black Sea-Mediterranean area; the Mediterranean Sea because of its peacetime use for trade and its military value for warships and supply ships, which adds to the strategic significance of the states bordering it; the Gulf of Aqaba, connecting both the Israeli port of Eilat and the Jordanian port of Aqaba with the Red Sea and the Indian Ocean, because it has an intrinsic value to Israel and Jordan and because of the role it played in the 1956 and 1967 Arab-Israeli wars; the Bab al-Mandab at the southern end of the Red Sea because it separates southwestern Arabia from the Horn of Africa and is the gate to the southern approaches of the Suez Canal and the Gulf of Aqaba; and the Strait of Hormuz because it is the major transit route for Persian Gulf oil shipped to Europe and Japan. Middle East air routes provide direct flight paths from Europe to Asia and the Pacific and offer good climatic and geographic conditions. North-to-south air routes from

Europe and the Soviet Union also cross the Middle East. The importance of these communications links has grown with the increased participation of African and Asian states in world production, world trade, and international affairs. The geographic position of the Middle East has made it a logical area for bases and staging posts as it provides a convenient focal point for military activity on three continents and is proximate to the Soviet Union. This has long been recognized and forms part of the rationale for continued attempts at control of the region by outside powers.

Oil, the major natural resource of the Middle East, is of strategic interest, although its value has changed over time. Immediately following World War II, Middle East oil was seen as strategically and politically important to the United States and this was one of the arguments advanced, especially by the Defense Department, in determining U.S. policies toward the Palestine problem and Israel. This view eventually receded into the background, and much of the later discussion revolved around the commercial interest in oil. It was recognized, however, that oil had a far greater value for United States allies in Western Europe and Japan. There thus evolved an indirect U.S. strategic/political interest in Middle East oil resources, even though that resource was not significant for the United States itself, which imported virtually no oil from the region.

By 1973, with the growth of U.S. dependence on Middle East oil for its own use, the oil factor began to loom increasingly large. The October 1973 war provided the impetus that linked U.S. efforts on the Arab-Israeli problem with its concerns about the availability and price of Gulf oil for the United States and its allies. After the 1973 war, oil emerged from being essentially a commercial-financial interest of U.S. business and economic concerns to become a significant component of U.S. political and strategic interests and in calculations of policy.

Trade and investment have been important elements of the U.S. economic interest in the Middle East. The United States has long pursued an economic "open-door" policy in the Middle East (and elsewhere) that seeks freedom for private U.S. corporations to function in the area. In the commercial realm there has been the desire to explore, produce, and distribute oil resources and to participate in other profitable activities. The earnings on that investment have been important for the U.S. balance of trade and balance of payments. Oil has accounted for a large share of the earnings, in part by providing jobs for U.S. employees who remit substantial portions of their payrolls to the United States. There also is an interest in economic development as a means of expanding markets and increasing trade as well as promoting improved local conditions. Prior to the October War, this was seen as a commercial interest only of a segment of the U.S. economy rather than as a significant national interest of the United States. Tension often resulted from the differing interpretations of this interest by U.S. officials and representatives of business enterprises. The U.S. government saw its role as facilitating the efforts of private concerns rather than as officially involving itself directly in the economic/financial/commercial sector.

The Middle East has generated substantial interest for Western states because Judaism, Christianity, and Islam had their origins in the area and many of the holy places of these three monotheistic faiths are located there. The Judeo-Christian heritage of Western civilization provides a link between the United States and Western Europe and the Middle East that transcends the purely cultural.

More tangible cultural interests go back to the early nineteenth century and revolve around missionary/educational/philanthropic activities. Robert College, the American University of Beirut, and the American University of Cairo are prominent examples of long-standing cultural involvement which, in recent years, has had U.S. government financial support. Programs and activities within the United States for expanding and increasing cultural links with the region have flourished since World War II.

The Israel Interest

Israel has a special position in U.S. Middle East policy, unmatched by that of any other state and going beyond the role it plays in the Arab-Israeli conflict. The existence and security of Israel have been central themes of U.S. policy since the establishment of the state, and the United States has provided support throughout the period. The special relationship has grown closer over the years and reached significant new levels of political, economic, and military cooperation and parallelism in the period between the June 1967 War and the October 1973 War, despite occasional lapses and periods of coolness. This focus has been the subject of controversy, revolving not around support for the existence and security of Israel (which is beyond substantial debate or discussion) but around the exclusivity of the relationship, especially during the period 1967–1973. Former U.S. Ambassador to Egypt John Badeau, who expressed concern about the wisdom of the policy, has argued that Israel represented a priority:

> Israel represents our oldest direct interest in the area. Before the Truman Doctrine—indeed, before the emergence of the State of Israel—Congress went on record as being favorably inclined toward the plan envisioned by the Balfour Declaration. . . .The continuance of Israel as an independent state certainly represents a basic foreign policy commitment of the United States. . . .[1]

This view, expressed in the 1950s, indicates the constancy of the U.S. interest in the Arab-Israel zone as compared with the Persian/Arab Gulf/Arabian Peninsula zone. Unlike the latter, the U.S. approach to the Arab-Israeli conflict and its interest in Israel have remained essentially steadfast, despite some changes in the policy to achieve that interest and the addition of some new elements to the equation.

Recognition of the interest remains widespread, even by observers such as George Ball who are regarded by Israel as hostile:

> First of all, one of our interests in the Middle East is the carrying out of a rather deep emotional commitment to the Israeli people to permit them to achieve their objective of a national home. Now this goes back a long way . . . From a strictly strategic position, apart from the intellectual and emotional basis for our commitment, the fact that we had made it not formally and in treaty form, but in a dozen different ways, means that we should sustain it. It is not in the American interest to engage in a reversal of alliances, or to indicate that we abandon our friends. Israel is established as a friend of the United States.[2]

The U.S. interest in and commitment to the survival and security of Israel and termination of the Arab-Israeli conflict is deeply rooted in history and has been reaffirmed by every administration since Truman. A multitude of factors, including those that are political-security, economic, and cultural-religious (or "ideological") underlie this interest.

The ideological factor is based on the view that the United States seeks more than mere survival; it believes in the need to promote the existence of other free societies to reinforce the democratic ideal and to preserve the uniquely American way of life. Israel is seen as a like-image state whose survival is crucial to the ideological prospering of the United States and the prevention of the dominance of nondemocratic perspectives.

There is a broad affinity between the United States and Israel. There is in the United States widespread goodwill toward Israel that is not restricted to the Jewish community that favored the establishment and consolidation of a Jewish state in Palestine and the continued existence, integrity, and security of Israel. Israel is perceived to be a progressive state with a similar outlook to that of the United States and an example of the type of state the United States would like to see exist all over the world. There is an element of cultural identity that leads to the view that Israel is a "Western" state in a sea of feudal, oriental states and is a perpetuator of the Judeo-Christian heritage. Israel is perceived as a brave and gallant state—providing a model of courage and tenacity—and its people are praised for their sacrifice, dedication, and spirit. As a result Israel is seen as having achieved substantial progress and development during its brief existence and as worthy of emulation by developing states.

There is an historical affinity and similarity of national experience, which includes the immigrant and pioneering nature of the two states. There is also a religious factor. Some perceive Israel as fulfilling the biblical prophecy that the Jews would return to the "promised land." This perception, nurtured in America's Bible-belt fundamentalist Christian areas, is further reinforced by "Sunday-school stories" linking the Jews to the Holy Land. In response to the Holocaust and the destruction of large segments of world Jewry in Europe during World War II, there appears to be a "guilt" element that Israel's existence helps to assuage. There is a response to the historical persecution of the Jews and the effort to provide for the saving of the remnant of world Jewry through the maintenance of a sanctuary. This maintenance of a refuge for a persecuted people also helps relieve feelings of guilt associated with traditional Western anti-Semitism and thus provides for a form of atonement. There is also a feeling of moral responsibility for the preservation of Israel because of the U.S. effort that helped to establish the state. Often there is reference to the "natural" ties that have linked these two states, although there is little precision as to what these actually are. There is the sympathy for Israel that derives from the American concern for the weak against the strong (the "underdog" sympathy factor) and the few against the many.

The ideological/emotional interest is buttressed by a perspective that regards Israel as a political-strategic asset. Israel has been supportive of U.S. policy in the United Nations and in other world forums. Tangible national security advantages have included the view that Israel is a reliable bulwark against Soviet penetration and domination of the Middle East and against radical Arab expansion. The Reagan administration codified this perspective in the Memorandum of Understanding on Strategic Cooperation (1981), which focused on the Soviet threat, and has articulated this view in the statements of Secretary of Defense Weinberger and other administration officials.

Israel is seen as militarily the most powerful state in the region and as a reliable ally. Some have argued that U.S. military bases in, and logistical support provided by, Israel might be useful for action against the Soviet Union. Some have suggested that Israel can defend the oil wealth of the region. In the event of an oil embargo or related difficulty (which would threaten the United States or its allies in Europe and Japan or both), Israel is seen by some as a significant asset in the event of military action against the oil fields and the producing states.

There is a more direct U.S. concern with the Arab-Israeli conflict and Israel's survival. Israel's fall would most likely increase Soviet prestige and influence. It would weaken those moderate Arab states, such as Jordan and Saudi Arabia, whose overthrow has been a stated goal of various opposition groups within the Arab world and who would no longer be diverted from their aim by preoccupation with Israel. It would probably facilitate Arab radical pressures that have been destabilizing factors in the Persian Gulf. These achievements would, in turn, adversely affect the U.S. ability to maintain regional stability and peace, U.S. economic interests, and the flow of oil to the West. Israel's existence, as a democratic, energetic, and progressive force, thus tends to strengthen other states and regimes whose survival is important to the United States.

It has been suggested that the peace, stability, and security of the Middle East and U.S. interests in that region can best be preserved by a strong Israel supported by U.S. arms supply and financial assistance. It was argued, especially after the 1967 war, that support of Israel helped to deter Arab aggression that in turn might have led to a larger conflict affecting U.S. interests or involving the United States in a confrontation with the Soviet Union. In this view, Israel represents the only solid foothold for the West, and especially for the United States, in the region. It is, after all, a modern and developed state resembling U.S. allies in Western Europe. It has been argued that Israel acts as a proxy for U.S. interests as a countervailing factor to the Soviet presence in some of the Arab states (for example, in Egypt between 1967 and 1973 and in Syria in the post-1973 War period).

Israel's strategic value became a component of U.S. interest primarily after 1967, when specific Israeli contributions could be identified. Israel's position in Sinai and along the Suez Canal prevented Soviet use of the Canal to shorten its supply lines to the Indian Ocean and Southeast Asia. Israel provided the United States with valuable military information and intelligence, as captured Soviet equipment facilitated U.S. countermeasures against similar weaponry in Vietnam, and Israeli experience with U.S. equipment helped in modification of designs and tactics. Israeli military installations could prove valuable to the United States in various military situations. During the 1970 civil war in Jordan, Israel took actions that the United States could not because of political and military constraints; Israel thus acted on behalf of the United States in support of King Hussein to prevent Syrian intervention on behalf of the PLO.

President Reagan has articulated his perspective of Israel's value:

> ... our own position would be weaker without the political and military assets Israel provides.... The fall of Iran has increased Israel's value as perhaps the only remaining strategic asset in the region on which the United States can truly rely....Israel has the democratic will, national cohesion, technological capacity and military fiber to stand forth as America's trusted ally.[3]

U.S. credibility is at stake because Israel is perceived by the Arab world and much of the international community as benefitting from a U.S. security commitment. U.S. actions that might be interpreted as backing away from that obligation would undermine the credibility of the United States as an ally. If the United States were to "abandon" Israel, the U.S. role in other, lesser, relationships would be open to question.

In sum, the U.S. interest in Israel revolves around two distinct, though related, factors of an ideological and a political-strategic nature; and, generally, there is an interest in maintaining a like-image, democratic, and progressive state—a reliable ally that acts as a bulwark against Soviet penetration and domination and Arab radical expansion in the Middle East.

CONFLICTING INTERESTS AND POLICY CHOICES

The United States has substantial interests in the Middle East. Preventing confrontation with, and possible regional domination by, the Soviet Union remain salient. Israel retains its special position because of the values it espouses and the strategic functions it serves, and for these reasons the United States remains committed to Israel's survival and security. Resolution of the Arab-Israeli conflict—to prevent precipitation of superpower conflict, to reduce its adverse economic and military effects, and to allow regional capabilities to be channeled to more positive accomplishments—is a core policy objective. The assurance of the flow of oil from the Gulf and the Peninsula has taken on added significance (because of U.S. and Allied needs), as has the financial power of the producing states, which relates to the price of oil and to the vast sums of petrodollars that have been accumulated and that can affect the stability of the world economic order.

These interests are clearly interrelated. Commenting on U.S. policies in Lebanon in the wake of Israel's 1982 invasion, Robert C. McFarlane, President Reagan's national security adviser, wrote:

> ... what we do in Lebanon affects our policies in the rest of the Middle East and throughout the world. To withdraw [the multinational force] now would dim the prospects for a broader peace process between Israel and its neighbors. . . .Ultimately, a premature withdrawal could compromise Israeli security, which in turn could lead to another Israeli-Syrian war. This could easily trigger greater Soviet involvement and the attendant risk of escalation involving the superpowers. . . .A withdrawal of our forces could also diminish our hope for a negotiated settlement to end the war between Iran and Iraq in the Persian Gulf. Our Arab friends in the Gulf, otherwise disposed to take risks for peace, would have no choice but to conclude that the U.S. will not stand by its commitments. . . .If, on the other hand, our principal opponents are convinced we will not be driven out of Lebanon, they might well conclude that accommodation is better than confrontation.[4]

Since the October 1973 war, the link between the Arab-Israeli conflict and the promotion of U.S. interests in the Gulf has focused largely on the nature of the special relationship between the United States and Israel. The special relationship has been seen by various policymakers either as a liability or an asset in U.S. efforts to prevent another Arab-Israeli war—and the inherent risk of superpower confrontation and a new Arab oil embargo—and to improve ties with moderate Arab states. The extensive U.S. role as mediator in the Arab-Israeli conflict, which it assumed after the October 1973 war, has depended on exploiting Israel's special relationship with,—and dependence on, the United States, to "deliver" Israel at the negotiating table and give to the Arab states what they have been unable to accomplish on the battlefield.

Initial U.S. mediation efforts coincided with a reassessment of its interests and policies in the Persian Gulf. Concerns about the availability and price of Gulf oil for the United States and its allies in Western Europe and Japan became a significant component of U.S. strategic interests and policy calculations in the Middle East.[5] Nevertheless, the Persian Gulf did not become the focal point of U.S. attention until after the Soviet invasion of Afghanistan and the revolution in Iran. The watershed in U.S. policy in the Gulf was the enunciation of the Carter Doctrine, which for the first time acknowledged U.S. interests in the region and declared U.S. determination to respond to a Soviet threat to the area with military force.

The Carter Doctrine notwithstanding, U.S. policy in the Persian Gulf under Reagan has been dictated more by the course of events than any grand strategy to deal with potential Soviet threats to vital U.S. interests. The Reagan administration initially felt no sense of urgency to deal with the Arab-Israeli conflict and focused instead on the Gulf and the need for building a "strategic consensus" in the area to counter the Soviet Union. But the United States was forced to shift its attention to the Arab-Israel arena in the spring of 1981 in order to defuse a crisis caused by the movement of Syrian missiles into Lebanon's Bekaa Valley. Although the Reagan administration thereafter was preoccupied with Arab-Israeli problems, the Persian Gulf war remained a matter of concern. The achievement of U.S. policy goals—a comprehensive settlement of the Arab-Israeli conflict and restoration of stability to the Gulf—have remained elusive.

The Persian Gulf Arena

U.S. involvement in the Persian Gulf developed slowly and, as in the rest of the Middle East, the United States did not display any sustained political interest in that zone prior to World War II. The United States tended to see the area as a British preserve and limited its involvement to private and commercial dealings, supporting the preeminent position of the British and relying on Britain to protect Western interests.

U.S. interest in the Gulf increased in the 1950s, largely as a result of growing commercial activity involving oil and an evolving perception of the Soviet threat. The dramatic growth of oil production in Saudi Arabia and Kuwait impressed upon U.S. policymakers the area's strategic importance and this led to a modest military assistance program with Saudi Arabia.

In the 1960s the oil industry continued at the center of U.S. interests in the Gulf where some 20 U.S. oil firms were involved, accounting for more than half of the area's oil production. U.S. investment in the Middle East oil industry amounted to more than $1.5 billion and much of this was concentrated in the Gulf. Income from this investment was about $1 billion a year.

Shipment of oil for U.S. consumption at home and abroad was an important but not vital interest in the eyes of most U.S. policymakers. A former State Department official described the U.S. interest in Persian Gulf oil in the following terms:

> Experience has shown that the United States itself needs to import little oil from the Gulf. Less oil is imported now [1968] from this source than a decade ago. Nor were we seriously inconvenienced in 1967 when Arab oil was for several months embargoed for shipment to American, British and West German ports.
>
> Our Western European allies, of course, do depend substantially on Gulf crude. . . .while United States commercial interests in Persian Gulf oil remain extensive, our strategic interest thus lies primarily in assuring that Gulf oil remains available on a nondiscriminatory basis.[6]

Thus, although the United States itself was not dependent on Gulf oil, assuring the oil supply of U.S. allies in Western Europe and Japan was a U.S. interest.

Trade with the Gulf states expanded as their oil wealth grew. United States exports to Gulf states quadrupled between 1947 and 1967, which had a favorable effect on the U.S. balance of payments. U.S. officials expected the favorable trade balance to continue as long as the Gulf states' prosperity continued to grow and, along with it, the demand for goods and services.

Thus the United States has had a strong interest in ensuring a stable economic and political environment, deemed essential for ensuring the unimpeded flow of oil and protecting U.S. citizens and commercial interests in the Gulf area. The problem of protecting political and commercial interests became more acute in 1968 when Britain announced its decision to withdraw its military forces from the Gulf within three years. U.S. officials were concerned by the British decision, particularly in light of the perceived growth of Soviet activities in the Middle East, but the Nixon administration decided not to move to fill the vacuum created by the British departure.

To help maintain Persian Gulf security following the British withdrawal, the United States adopted what came to be known as the "twin pillar" policy. The United States urged two friendly states in the area—Iran and Saudi Arabia—to cooperate and settle their bilateral differences in order to minimize local threats to regional stability. The United States also supported Iran's plan to take the lead in the defense and preservation of Persian Gulf security after the British withdrawal. The Nixon administration pledged to assist Iran and the Gulf states in their economic development and in the development of their military capabilities by providing material and training for their armed forces. The reluctance to establish a military presence in the Gulf was in keeping with the Nixon Doctrine—a global policy of military and economic aid to regional surrogates in lieu of a U.S. military presence. Within the framework of this approach, the United States intended to reduce its military presence abroad, while helping U.S. partners to develop their own self-defense capabilities.

The October War of 1973 and the resultant Arab oil embargo and dramatic price increase provided the impetus for a reassessment of U.S. policy in the Persian Gulf zone. Whereas policymakers had heretofore been reluctant to adopt a more active diplomatic or military posture, the realization that the United States was becoming increasingly dependent on Middle East oil contributed to a new appreciation of the political and strategic importance of the Gulf. Policymakers were concerned that inadequate increases in regional oil production or denial of that oil to the United States would have a disruptive effect on the U.S. economy and security. The continued flow of Gulf oil and U.S. access to it at reasonable prices were important interests.

Concern that the Arab oil-producing nations could threaten the economic stability and security of the United States by withholding or limiting oil exports sparked media speculation about the possibility of military intervention to seize control of the oil fields in the event of another embargo or to prevent exhorbitant prices. Secretary of State Henry Kissinger refused to rule out U.S. recourse to military action should the oil situation threaten to "strangle" the Western states. In a highly publicized interview published in *Business Week* in early 1975 he said:

> I am not saying that there's no circumstance where we would not use force. But it is one thing to use it in the case of a dispute over price, it's another where there's some actual strangulation of the industrialized world.[7]

The vastly increased revenues from the sale of oil made the oil-producing Gulf states very attractive expanding markets for U.S. goods and services and the growing surplus of capital permitted investment abroad and economic development throughout the region. The market opportunities were enhanced by the fact that these states often imported most of what was consumed locally and also required capital goods for their ambitious development plans. The desire to improve military capabilities created a substantial market for military equipment, the provision of training, and infrastructure construction. In this the United States was often the primary and initial choice of the regional states. The capital surplus also created the potential for investment in the United States. In the mid 1970s the oil-producing states invested mainly in U.S. government securities and bank certificates of deposit. Estimates of the investment in the United States from these countries varied, but as early as 1974 it was estimated to be some \$10 billion.[8]

The goals of stability and economic development of the region and the enhancement of U.S. commercial and financial interests required the maintenance of close and cooperative relations with the Gulf states, and the United States made significant progress in the early 1970s in developing those ties. U.S. diplomatic recognition was extended to Bahrain, the United Arab Emirates (UAE), and Qatar in 1971, and the United States established small diplomatic missions in the UAE, Qatar, and Oman a year later. Visits to the Gulf area by President Nixon and Secretary of State Rogers reflected increased ties with the Gulf states.

Nixon's visit to Teheran in May 1972 underscored not only the importance ascribed to Iran because of its oil reserves and financial surpluses but also the critical role Iran played in safeguarding U.S. strategic and military interests in the Persian Gulf sector. In 1973, James Noyes, Deputy Assistant Secretary of Defense for Near Eastern, African and South Asian Affairs, described U.S. security concerns in the Gulf as: containment of Soviet military power within its present borders; access to Persian Gulf oil; and continued free movement of U.S. ships and aircraft into and out of the area and access to support facilities in Bahrain.[9] The United States supported the expansion and modernization of Iran's military forces in keeping with the Nixon Doctrine. The United States maintained only a modest military position in the Gulf area, primarily a small naval force operating out of Bahrain and a naval and air base at Diego Garcia in the Indian Ocean. United States officials publicly welcomed Iran's military development and its "cooperation" with regional defense efforts as an important element in "regional efforts to achieve stability and progress in the Persian Gulf area."[10]

The Arab-Israeli Arena

After the June 1967 war the United States modified its approach to the Arab-Israeli conflict—actively seeking a settlement—as it believed that the prospects for resolution were enhanced. Various factors combined to lead to an increasingly positive and active U.S. role. Between the June 1967 and October 1973 wars, under both the Johnson and Nixon administrations, the United States sought an effective and durable Arab-Israeli settlement arrived at by the parties themselves within an appropriate international environment created, in part, by the United States.

The process had its origins in President Lyndon Johnson's enunciated "five principles of peace" of June 1967 (the right to national life, justice for the refugees, innocent maritime passage, limits on the wasteful and destructive arms race, and respect for political independence and territorial integrity), which sought to establish the elements essential to the termination of the dispute and the attainment of a settlement. These principles, and UN Security Council Resolution 242 of November 22, 1967, which incorporated many of them, became the bases for U.S. and, subsequently, other international efforts to achieve a settlement.

The June 1967 war was also an important turning point in U.S. arms supply policy. Despite initial post-World War II efforts to control the arms race in the region, the United States soon found itself competing with the Soviet Union in the provision of arms. The United States sought to ensure a "military balance" and provided Israel with the equipment essential to balance Soviet arms supplies to the Arab states, especially Egypt and Syria. The provision of F-4 Phantom jets to Israel in 1968 established the U.S. role as a principal supplier of non-defensive, modern, sophisticated military equipment.

The June 1967 war also marked an important change in U.S. relations with the regional states as it became more closely identified with Israel—an identification fostered by Soviet pursuit of a policy of polarization, the rupture in 1967 of diplomatic relations between the United States and some of the Arab states, and the parallelism of Israeli and U.S. views on the central issues of the postwar situation. The congruence included the necessity of peace, the security of Israel, and the prevention of war, although there was divergence concerning techniques and discord on specific issues.

There were several significant efforts to achieve an Arab-Israeli peace settlement between the June 1967 and October 1973 wars. The Jarring Mission, the Nixon "new initiatives," the two-power (U.S. and USSR) and four-power (U.S., USSR, Britain, and France) talks, the Rogers' Plans (and interim settlement and proximity talks proposals), the mediation activities of the Organization of African Unity and of the Romanian President, and other efforts—all were unsuccessful at achieving peace and, ultimately, even in preventing war.

The October 1973 war was a major watershed in U.S. policy and led to an alteration in its approach to, and its role in, the Middle East. The conflict itself, the potential for U.S.-Soviet confrontation, the employment of the Arab "oil weapon," and the fourfold increase in oil prices contributed to a reassessment of U.S. interests and policies. The United States emerged as the central extra-regional power in the search for an Arab-Israeli peace settlement, coinciding with a changing regional and international environment and the strategic/economic role that oil would thereafter play.

The war that erupted on October 6, 1973 caught the United States by surprise. Once the war began, the United States launched a multifaceted effort to limit the extent of regional conflict, in order to avoid confrontation with the Soviet Union and to halt the fighting in such a way that the postwar environment would be more conducive to a settlement than that which preceded it.

Among the developments in the war, the United States undertook a massive airlift of military supplies to Israel to redress the imbalance brought about by heavy Israeli combat losses and by an ongoing shipment of Soviet military equipment to Syria and Egypt; and on October 25 the United States placed its troops on a worldwide precautionary alert (partly in response to a reported alert of Soviet airborne troops). After some two weeks of hostilities, and after the breakdown of an initial ceasefire and its subsequent restoration, a ceasefire/negotiations formula was developed with the heavy involvement of both the United States and the Soviet Union, and this formula was later adopted by the UN Security Council as Resolution 338. As U.S. postwar diplomacy emerged, Kissinger foreshadowed his future efforts in a statement on October 25:

> The United States is prepared to make a major effort to help speed a political solution which is just to all sides. The United States recognizes that the conditions that produced the war on October 6 cannot be permitted to continue. . . .[11]

This signaled the intensification of U.S. efforts to achieve an accommodation. Over the next two years, U.S. involvement in the Middle East increased, and the region assumed a high priority in the Nixon administration's foreign policy. Kissinger based his postwar efforts on the fact that only the United States could talk to both sides in the conflict, on the fact that there had been no victory (or a "double victory"), and on the "interim settlement" concept.

After the Security Council mandated ceasefire became effective on October 24, 1973, Kissinger concentrated on pragmatic first steps on the road to peace—the stabilization of the ceasefire and the disengagement of the hostile forces. Initially he focused on Egypt because of its important position in the Arab world and because of the unstable postwar military situation resulting from the unusual post-hostilities troop deployments along the Suez Canal. It was also believed that some form of accommodation might be developed more easily with Egyptian President Anwar Sadat than with the more mercurial and unpredictable Syrian president Hafez Assad. Israeli and Egyptian officers met at Kilometer 101 on the Cairo-Suez road on October 28, 1973 and agreed to permit relief for the encircled Egyptian Third Army. With Kissinger's aid, Egypt and Israel subsequently concluded a six-point agreement to implement resolution 338 and to stabilize the ceasefire, which was signed on November 11, 1973. Most of the provisions were implemented, but the question of disengagement and the separation of forces continued.

A Geneva Conference to discuss the Arab-Israeli conflict was convened on December 21, 1973, under U.S. and Soviet co-chairmanship and was followed by negotiations on disengagement that continued into January 1974 with little success. To break the deadlock, Kissinger inaugurated an Egypt-Israel shuttle that culminated in an agreement, announced on January 17, 1974, providing for the disengagement and the separation of military forces. Additional assurances and understandings made to and by Kissinger remained secret. The Syria-Israel disengagement of May 1974 further enhanced the United States' position in the region and the prestige of Kissinger and, by extension, Nixon. The agreement produced a euphoric public mood: the United States clearly regarded Kissinger's efforts as central to the settlement process and the parties seemed to concur in this view.

The agreement between Israel and Syria marked the end of the first phase of the U.S. postwar diplomacy and indicated some of the changing parameters of this policy. The disengagement agreements reduced the threat of war in part by restructuring the complex pattern of troop deployments and providing for United Nations Emergency Force (UNEF) buffer units between the respective parties. They also provided the basis for further efforts, but these were limited agreements dealing with pressing military problems and did not involve political concerns central to the positions of the parties.

The second stage proved more difficult. Kissinger's efforts to develop second-phase agreements began in the summer of 1974 with consultations in Washington, but these discussions, overshadowed by the Nixon-Brezhnev summit meeting, the Cyprus crisis, and Nixon's resignation, did not point clearly in the direction of an agreement. Kissinger visited the region in October, but his efforts were soon clouded by developments at the Arab summit meeting in Rabat and later at the United Nations. He returned to the Middle East in November to reassess his step-by-step diplomacy in light of the Rabat decision to recognize the Palestine Liberation Organization (PLO) as the sole legitimate representative of the Palestinian people. Kissinger's visit averted the collapse of efforts to achieve step-by-step agreements and reaffirmed the Egyptian-Israeli focus for discussions.

Kissinger visited the Middle East again in early February 1975 on an "exploratory trip" to determine the possibilities for an agreement; he was apparently sufficiently buoyed by his discussions to return in March. Kissinger subsequently made a number of trips between Egypt and Israel, with brief stops elsewhere. Egypt sought extensive Israeli territorial withdrawals while Israel sought substantial Egyptian political concessions. Although there were areas of agreement, the differences proved irreconcilable. The failure of the Kissinger shuttle ended a euphoric post-October War period in which two important but primarily technical—and critically apolitical—agreements had been reached.

The diplomatic failure led to a brief flirtation with the concept of utilizing the Geneva Conference to work for an overall settlement, but this was soon discarded in favor of a renewed effort to achieve an interim Egyptian—Israeli agreement. President Ford ordered a "reassessment" of U.S. policy to determine appropriate "next steps" in light of the disarray of the international environment, including the Communist victory in Cambodia and Vietnam. The reassessment also served to pressure Israel to move closer to Egypt, thus allowing a U.S. effort to bridge the gap. Following a cooling-off period, the United States reinstituted the step-by-step process with consultations in Washington and elsewhere, followed by another Kissinger shuttle in August. Finally, a complex of agreements was initialed on September 1 in Jerusalem and Alexandria and was signed in Geneva on September 4, 1975.

The Sinai II agreements of September 1975 provided for Israeli withdrawal from territory in Sinai (including the strategic Gidi and Mitla passes and oil fields) in exchange for Egyptian political concessions and pledges of U.S. support. Israel and Egypt agreed to observe the ceasefire on land, sea, and in the air, and to refrain from the threat or use of force or military blockade; they established a new buffer zone and agreed to extend the mandate of the UNEF annually. They also agreed to continue negotiations for a final peace agreement and Egypt promised that nonmilitary cargoes for or from Israel would be permitted to use the Suez Canal. An annex spelled out some details for the implementation of the agreement. There was also a U.S. proposal providing for an early warning system in which up to 200 U.S. volunteer civilians would participate and would report to both Israel and Egypt.

In addition to the formal agreement released by the U.S. Department of State, other agreements were subsequently made public by the U.S. Senate Committee on Foreign Relations. These incorporated U.S. assurances to Israel and to Egypt on various matters, including military and economic assistance, coordination between the United States and Israel on the reconvening of the Geneva Peace Conference, U.S. assurances of oil for Israel, and a U.S. pledge concerning the PLO: "The United States will continue to adhere to its present policy with respect to the Palestine Liberation Organization, whereby it will not recognize or negotiate with the Palestine Liberation Organization so long as the Palestine Liberation Organization does not recognize Israel's right to exist and does not accept Security Council Resolutions 242 and 338."[12]

Sinai II was a U.S. accomplishment that resulted from the extensive and intensive involvement of the U.S. government—the shuttles, the proposals, the pledges, and the commitments—for which the parties were not prepared to allow any other power or instrumentality to serve as substitute. Although substantial and complex issues remained, for the first time Israel and Egypt went beyond the previous ceasefire or armistice agreements—military in nature and content—and reached accord on matters with political and psychological overtones that moved them in the direction of an overall settlement. The direct, formal, and essentially irreversible U.S. involvement, foreshadowed by its policies in the post-June 1967 and post-October 1973 war periods, marked the inauguration of a new phase of policy in the Arab-Israeli zone.

The 1975 agreements established a period of relative tranquility and stability from which new efforts toward peace could be initiated, and in this quest for peace, the United States remained the central and indispensable power. As the major diplomatic actor in the search for peace, as Israel's primary military and economic provisioner, and as an emerging provider of assistance to Egypt (in addition to Jordan and Saudi Arabia), the United States remained the focal point of regional attention. There seemed to be recognition, shared by all the major actors, that without the United States there could be no significant movement toward a settlement.

Nonetheless, the agreements were not soon followed by any further significant movement. This was due, in part, to the disarray within the Arab world (symbolized most notably by the civil war in Lebanon), the forthcoming parliamentary election in Israel, and the quadrennial U.S. presidential election.

THE CARTER ADMINISTRATION

The Middle East policy of the Carter administration assumed a sharp focus on the Arab-Israeli conflict. Carter sought a comprehensive settlement and attempted to reconvene the Geneva Middle East Peace Conference as an appropriate mechanism to achieve that goal. In so doing, the Carter effort contrasted with Kissinger's preference for step-by-step techniques and a U.S. monopoly on the peace process, but the basic goal remained that of a settlement achieved through substantial U.S. effort.[13]

In the early days of the administration, the United States paid little attention to the Persian Gulf and the Arabian Peninsula, apparently believing that it was not of major strategic or political significance. At the same time, Carter believed that the changes in Lebanon, increased moderation in the Arab world, and the potential for change in Israel's leadership, all suggested the opportunity to make progress toward solving the Arab-Israeli conflict. Within weeks after the new administration took office, Secretary of State Cyrus Vance was sent to the Middle East—on his first overseas mission as secretary of state.

The administration's concept of a lasting peace emerged during the spring and summer of 1977. Carter articulated his views on three elements that he saw as central and indispensable: the definition and assurance of permanent peace, the delineation of territory and borders, and the Palestinian issue.

The definition of peace involved a comprehensive approach that went beyond the end of war. It was most fully expressed by Carter in Clinton, Massachusettes, in March 1977:

> . . . the first prerequisite of a lasting peace is the recognition of Israel by her neighbors, Israel's right to exist, Israel's right to exist permanently, Israel's right to exist in peace. That means that over a period of months or years that the borders between Israel and Jordan, Israel and Egypt must be opened up to travel, to tourism, to cultural exchange, to trade, so that no matter who the leaders might be in those countries the people themselves will have formed a mutual understanding and comprehension and a sense of a common purpose to avoid the repetitious wars and death that have afflicted that region so long.[14]

The United States did not specify where the future borders between Israel and the Arab states should lie, but the main elements of its approach were substantial Israeli withdrawal from occupied territories and negotiated minor adjustments or modifications in the pre-1967 armistice lines. Although the Carter administration believed that major changes in the 1967 lines were not consistent with UNSC Resolution 242, it suggested that Israel's defense capability might go beyond the legal borders.[15] Negotiations and agreement between Israel and the Arabs would have to decide border and security arrangements.

The Palestinian element increasingly emerged as the most significant and the most controversial component of the Carter framework. The traditional U.S. approach, which concentrated on the refugee and humanitarian aspects of the problem and, after the June War of 1967, also on terrorism, was given a political context by the Carter administration. The terrorism issue receded, and while refugees were still a concern, the issue was seen as broader in scope. The administration sought to include provisions for the legitimate interests of the Palestinian people in any settlement. The idea of a Palestinian homeland appeared publicly for the first time on March 16, 1977, in Clinton, Massachusetts, when Carter said that the solution required some form of homeland for the Palestinians:

> The third ultimate requirement for peace is to deal with the Palestinian problem. The Palestinians claim up till this moment that Israel has no right to be there, that the land belongs to the Palestinians, and they've never yet given up their publicly professed commitment to destroy Israel. That has to be overcome. There has to be a homeland provided for the Palestinian refugees who have suffered for many, many years.[16]

Carter believed that the boundaries, nature, and political status of the "homeland" would have to be negotiated, and his preference was that the Palestinian entity (not an independent country) be linked with Jordan.[17] To gain the benefits of such a settlement he felt the Palestinians should be expected to demonstrate their willingness to live in peace.

Seeking to move in the directions outlined by the President, the Carter administration believed that cooperation with the Soviet Union would help to achieve those goals. Carter saw the Soviet Union as a benign power, interested in promoting development in the region rather than in taking advantage of its difficulties. Cyrus Vance noted: "If they were prepared to play a constructive role, as I believe they were in 1977, then I feel it would be much better to include them, because they could become a spoiler if they are not included."[18] Cooperation with the Soviet Union reached its zenith on October 1, 1977, when the United States and the Soviet Union issued a joint communique stressing the need for "achieving as soon as possible, a just and lasting settlement of the Arab-Israeli conflict."[19] The statement was designed to accelerate the efforts toward reconvening the Geneva Conference by eliciting Soviet cooperation. Accordingly, it invited the Soviet Union back into the Arab-Israeli peace process for the first time since the termination of the October War. The Soviet Union had been a co-chairman at the December 1973 Geneva Conference and had aspired to return to a central role in the peace process but was excluded due to the efforts of Henry Kissinger, the preferences of Anwar Sadat, and the desires of the government of Israel. Jimmy Carter changed that on October 1, 1977. But the communique, which the Soviet Union had tried to have restored as the central factor in the Arab-Israeli peace process, was soon abandoned by the United States because of domestic protest, opposition from Israel and its supporters, and opposition from Egypt.

The Sadat initiative, which soon followed, in part as a reaction to the joint communique, reflected the desire of President Anwar Sadat of Egypt to move things forward in his own way. Sadat's visit to Jerusalem, his speech to the Knesset on November 20, 1977, and the negotiations that followed led the United States to focus its policies somewhat differently. The United States took an active role in the deliberations that followed Sadat's November 1977 initiative. Finally, in the summer of 1978 Carter invited Sadat and Israeli Prime Minister Menachem Begin to Camp David, Maryland, for a summit meeting to consider various suggestions for resolutions of the Arab-Israeli conflict. After thirteen days at the summit, the

United States, Egypt, and Israel reached agreement on two accords: "A Framework for Peace in the Middle East," which set forth general principles and some details for a comprehensive peace settlement between Israel and its Arab neighbors, and "Framework for the Conclusion of a Peace Treaty between Egypt and Israel," which provided for a peace treaty in which Israel would withdraw from the Sinai Peninsula and the two states would establish normal and peaceful relations.

After the signing of the accords, the goal of the Carter administration was to implement the Camp David Accords, to ensure that Egypt and Israel would achieve peace, and to encourage them to begin to deal with the question of autonomy for the Palestinians and, ultimately, a comprehensive peace for the Middle East.

Progress was made: an Egypt-Israel Peace Treaty was signed in March 1979 and the "autonomy talks" were begun involving Egypt, Israel, and the United States. Carter's approach, however, was altered by developments elsewhere in the Middle East. The sector that he had all but ignored, the Persian Gulf and the Arabian Peninsula, soon became the main focal point of U.S. policy.

The revolution in Iran dealt a severe blow to U.S. policy and its position in the Persian Gulf. The United States had relied on Iran, implicitly if not explicitly, to ensure the security and stability of the Persian Gulf sector and the flow of oil from the region to the West. Iran's role in assuring the stability of the Persian Gulf was reflected in U.S. decisions—initially made by the Nixon administration in 1972—to provide Iran substantial amounts of military equipment, including some of the most advanced and sophisticated in the U.S. inventory, and technicians and other advisors for the armed forces. The massive arms sales to Iran were justified on the grounds that on major international issues the policies of Iran and the United States were parallel. It was also argued that Iran was working for its own economic development and was prepared to make a significant contribution to its own defense.

The Carter administration was slow to react to the abrupt transformation of Iran from one of the major pillars of U.S. policy in the Gulf region to a determined adversary. To a large extent, this was because the ultimate outcome of the revolution and its impact on U.S. policies and interests in the region were still unclear by the time the taking of U.S. hostages overshadowed other aspects of the revolution. It was not until after the Soviet invasion of Afghanistan in December 1979 that the Carter administration focused on the problem created by the loss of Iran—assuring and protecting the uninterrupted flow of Persian Gulf oil in reasonable quantities and at reasonable prices to the United States and its allies and assuring the stability of the Gulf sector.

The U.S. view of Iran and Saudi Arabia as the "twin pillars" providing stability for the Persian/Arab Gulf sector proved illusory as the revolution in Iran changed the government from one friendly to the United States to one hostile to it. Iran's pro-U.S. government, which had provided a modicum of stability in the Gulf, was replaced by a regime whose policy was to promote instability and the overthrow of neighboring regimes. The efforts of the Khomeini regime to overthrow the government of Bahrain and to create difficulties for Saudi Arabia and other Gulf states soon reminded U.S. decision makers of the importance of this sector. The revolution, and the taking of U.S. hostages, dramatically altered U.S. policy. For the last fourteen months of the Carter administration the main effort of the President of the United States was not focused on the Arab-Israeli issue, nor even on the revolution in Iran and its regional and international consequences, but on securing the release of U.S. hostages held by the revolutionary government of Iran. No previous U.S. administration had concentrated that much attention and effort on one issue, but then no U.S. regime has been faced with the holding of so many U.S. diplomats as hostages for such an extended period of time.

At the same time, U.S. policy was faced with another dilemma: The Soviet Union's invasion of Afghanistan in December 1979, which was to prove a major watershed in U.S. policy.

Afghanistan had previously been all but ignored by U.S. administrations. Indeed, the failure of U.S. intelligence and the lack of U.S. credibility in Iran were believed to be among the factors that led the Soviet Union to believe that it could act decisively in Afghanistan. Jimmy Carter himself said publicly in January 1980 that he learned more about the Soviet Union in one week than he had in his previous years as president of the United States.[20] The Soviet action generated concern not only about the future of Afghanistan but also about the potential threat to the Gulf and to U.S. friends in the Arabian Peninsula. It shifted the administration's attention from the Arab-Israeli sector to a newly-identified "Southwest Asia" sector, the center of which was the Persian/Arab Gulf (with its oil and petrodollars). The invasion convinced Carter that the Soviet Union was not a benign power but a hostile one, a power that sought domination of the region and whose threat had to be countered by U.S. policy.

The Afghanistan invasion led to the Carter Doctrine. In his State of the Union message to Congress in January 1980 Carter declared:

> An attempt by any outside force to gain control of the Persian Gulf region will be regarded as an assault on the vital interests of the United States of America, and such an assault will be repelled by any means necessary, including military force.[21]

The Carter Doctrine represented a major shift in policy by identifying a potential Soviet threat to the region and affirming U.S. determination to take whatever steps necessary to protect its interests. The Doctrine was new in its statement, and in the area on which it focused, but it followed a long trend of U.S. policy opposing the Soviet Union in the Middle East. The first major post-World War II U.S. policy statement for the Middle East was the Truman Doctrine of 1947, which opposed Soviet/Communist activities in Greece and Turkey and by extension, also in Iran. The Truman Doctrine was followed ten years later by the Eisenhower Doctrine, which committed the use of U.S. forces to defend the Middle East from overt Soviet aggression and Communist subversion. The Nixon Doctrine sought to oppose Soviet activity worldwide, including the Middle East. The Carter Doctrine was the latest statement, but focused on the Gulf. Carter declared the Persian Gulf area to be of vital interest to the United States—something that no previous president had said.

Declaring the Gulf an area of vital significance and the U.S willingness to take military action, if necessary, to counter the Soviet Union, were important new dimensions of U.S. policy. The main difficulty was that the United States had little force to back up the President's rhetoric. The United States hoped to deploy to the region what it called the Rapid Deployment Force (RDF). But the common reaction in Washington was that there was no force that could be deployed rapidly to the Middle East. The U.S. nonetheless sought to reach agreements for limited access of U.S. forces and some prepositioning of equipment to facilities in Kenya, Oman, and Somalia. In addition, U.S. naval strength in the Indian Ocean was brought up to more than 30 vessels, including two aircraft carriers, by the end of the year. The potential for success remained in doubt as the Soviet leadership made clear its intention to continue its role until external interference in Afghanistan had ceased, and it showed no alteration in its position as a result of the Carter Doctrine.

Although the Carter Doctrine was applauded for recognizing the potential threat of Soviet control of the West's oil supply in the Persian Gulf, critics charged it had come too late and that it did not address threats to U.S. interests emanating from inside the Gulf, and thus it could not guarantee access to the region's oil supplies.

The outbreak of hostilities between Iraq and Iran less than a year after the enunciation of the Doctrine appeared to bear out the charge. The question for U.S. policy then became whether the Doctrine could or should be applied in response to internal threats to the flow of oil to the West.

The initial reaction of U.S. policymakers to the war between Iran and Iraq was that U.S. interests would not be served by a decisive victory by either side. The United States believed that an Iraqi victory that brought down the Khomeini regime could well pave the way for Soviet penetration of Iran. At the same time, an Iranian victory would increase the Islamic fundamentalist threat to the other oil-producing states in the Gulf. In either case, the victor might well become the preeminent power in the region, asserting its influence over the other Gulf states.

The United States was not in any position to influence the course of the conflict in any meaningful way. It had limited diplomatic leverage, and support for one side or the other would either have endangered the lives of U.S. hostages still in Teheran or angered the Arab states who sided with Iraq. Consequently, the United States adopted a policy of avoiding identification with either combatant while supporting the territorial integrity and independence of both Iran and Iraq, as well as the other states in the Gulf.[22] The United States was particularly concerned that Iran might take action against the smaller Gulf principalities because of their support for Iraq. The Carter administration sent four AWACS (Airborne Warning and Control Systems) aircraft to Saudi Arabia in a move intended to serve as a visible sign of the U.S. commitment to the Saudi kingdom as well as a means to detect hostile air incursions into the Gulf.

The war also prompted fears that the flow of oil to the West would be severely disrupted since the hostilities had produced an immediate drop in oil exports from the two combatants, estimated at between three and four million barrels a day, which affected the principal importers from Iraq and resulted in a surge in oil prices. Nevertheless, because of the critical role played by Saudi Arabia and the other Gulf states in the overall international oil market, a major disruption of world oil supplies never materialized. The United States remained concerned, however, about the possible spread of the fighting to the oilfields, pipelines, terminals, and shipping lanes of the Gulf, and it reaffirmed its commitment to freedom of navigation through the Strait of Hormuz and continued to build up its naval forces in the Indian Ocean.

The Carter administration concluded its tenure with a mixed legacy for the Reagan team. In the Arab-Israeli sector Carter left the Camp David Accords, progress on their implementation, and the precedent of extensive Presidential involvement in the Arab-Israeli peace process. But this was overshadowed by the Carter Doctrine, which focused on the "vital" Persian Gulf and required the building of appropriate forces, such as the RDF, and the securing of regional support and cooperation.

THE REAGAN ADMINISTRATION

The Reagan administration began its term in office with no precise plan or policy for the Middle East. It was faced with a problem in Afghanistan and with a potential threat in the Gulf; it was believed that the Arab-Israeli conflict was of lesser importance; and it was decided to ensure that U.S. policy was able to respond to the Soviet threat anywhere in the world. In the Middle East, therefore, the main focus of Ronald Reagan's attention was not the Arab-Israeli conflict. In fact, he all but ignored it during the first months of his administration as he concentrated on domestic economic issues and moved slowly on foreign policy issues.

In the spring of 1981, the administration identified a new policy concept called "strategic consensus"—Middle East regional cooperation focusing on the Soviet threat. In March 1981 Secretary of State Alexander Haig told the Senate Foreign Relations Committee there was a need "to establish a consensus in the strategic-regional sense among the states of the area, stretching from Pakistan in the east to Egypt in the west, including Turkey, Israel, and other threatened states."[23] These states and others in the area would, it was hoped, cooperate with the United States and with each other to oppose the perceived Soviet threat and would be supported to that end by the United States. The goal appeared to be the construction of a geopolitical grouping to contain the Soviet Union and oppose its threat to the region. The United States would seek to strengthen, through military, economic, and political cooperation and assistance, a number of regional states. To that end, the United States offered to sell additional equipment for F-15 aircraft and AWACS aircraft to Saudi Arabia and anti-aircraft missiles to Jordan, thereby enabling them to participate in the regional response to the Soviet threat.

The administration also sought increased capability for the Rapid Deployment Force, including facilities in the region and the prepositioning of military equipment. As part of this policy the two carrier task forces already stationed in the Indian Ocean were maintained in place. These actions were intended to demonstrate to the Soviets the seriousness of the U.S. commitment and readiness to act, as well as to convince its friends in the Middle East that the United States was prepared to stand by them. In the administration's first comprehensive policy statement on the Middle East, Secretary of State Alexander Haig stressed the need for "security cooperation" between the United States and the states in the region:

> The United States, working with its local friends, despite their sometimes conflicting concerns, can be a responsive partner in the achievement of greater security for all. . . .Greater cooperation in the field of security will increase measurably the confidence that our local friends repose in the United States. If properly managed, such cooperation reinforces American diplomacy.[24]

Regional support for these goals was not readily available; the administration had not taken appropriate cognizance of regional sensitivities and concerns when it sought to create this consensus. Although Pakistan and Turkey were both concerned about the Soviet Union, as were Egypt and Israel (although at different levels), the focus for Saudi Arabia and Jordan was elsewhere (they saw the major threat as Zionism, not Communism). It was inconceivable that Saudi Arabia and Jordan would cooperate with Egypt, with which they had broken diplomatic relations, or with Israel, with which they were officially at war. Yet there was hope in the administration that this policy might work.

The administration's interest in retaining assured access to the Persian Gulf's oil reserves was threatened not only by the Soviet Union's expansionism but also by the continuing Iran-Iraq war. Secretary of State Haig noted that the Iran-Iraq war was a cause of great concern to Saudi Arabia, Kuwait, and other oil-producing states of the Gulf, all of which were concerned that should Iran succeed in the overthrow of the regime in Baghdad this would be followed by Iran's seeking their overthrow as well. While elaborating on U.S. policy objectives in the Middle East, Haig sought to reassure U.S. friends in the region that the United States would stand by their side and cautioned them not to confuse U.S. neutrality in the war with indifference:

> We have friends and interests that are endangered by the continuation of hostilities. We are committed to defending our vital

interests in the area. These interests, and the interests of the world, are served by the territorial integrity and political independence of all countries in the Persian Gulf.[25]

Reagan agreed with his predecessor's assessment that the longer the Iran-Iraq war went on the greater the risk that either Iran or Iraq would escalate the fighting and interefere with freedom of navigation in the Persian Gulf or act in other ways that would restrict oil exports. The Reagan administration warned both belligerents "that the unrestricted flow of oil from the Gulf is vital to the entire international community. Our commitment to freedom of commerce and navigation in the international waters of the Gulf is firm ... we expect them [Iran and Iraq] to respect this principle."[26]

At the same time, the priority of the Arab-Israeli conflict was downgraded. Although the administration prodded Egypt and Israel to assure that the peace treaty would be implemented and that the autonomy talks would make progress, it expended no major effort on these issues. In part, this was a result of the view that the conflict did not require urgent action and that, in any event, there was no special opportunity for a renewed effort. There was also a view that the forthcoming Israeli elections might lead to the replacement of Menachem Begin as prime minister, thereby improving the prospects of moving toward a settlement.

In the spring of 1981 a new kind of diplomacy developed—an "episodic diplomacy"—which responded to episodes of crisis in the region and elsewhere but had no comprehensive dimension. In the Middle East this began in April 1981 when Syria moved anti-aircraft missiles into Lebanon, contrary to tacit arrangements with Israel that had been worked out in the mid 1970s. The United States seemed aware of the fact that Israel would seek to destroy these missiles if Syria did not remove them. To prevent that action and to defuse the crisis, the Reagan administration brought from retirement a distinguished U.S. diplomat of Lebanese-American background, Philip Habib, and he began his mission to try to prevent war in the Middle East.

Episodic diplomacy developed further with the Israeli bombing of the Baghdad nuclear reactor in June 1981 and the PLO headquarters in Beirut in July 1981 and continued with a series of events between the summer of 1981 and the war in Lebanon of 1982. In July 1981, Ambassador Habib arranged a ceasefire along the Israel-Lebanon border between the PLO and Israel with the good offices and assistance of the governments of Lebanon and Saudi Arabia. In

December 1981 Israel extended its civil law and administration to the Golan Heights, which further increased the tension in the region. The crucial factor was that Ambassador Habib continued to work not in the context of an overall policy but in response to specific episodes of difficulty in the region. The Reagan administration still had not formulated a comprehensive policy for the Arab-Israeli conflict.

The shift from episodic to comprehensive diplomacy—a diplomacy to deal with all facets of the Arab-Israeli conflict within a broad policy framework—occurred with the war in Lebanon in the summer of 1982.

On June 6, 1982 Israel launched a major military action against the PLO in Lebanon. It sought to remove the PLO military and terrorist threat to Israel and to reduce the PLO's political capability. The United States did not support the action but, aware of Israel's concerns about the situation, made no significant effort to discourage it; ambivalence characterized the administration's initial response to the war. Eventually, Ambassador Habib was instrumental in terminating the hostilities between Israel and the PLO, lifting the siege of Beirut, arranging ceasefires,and negotiating and arranging the withdrawal of the PLO from Beirut. A multinational force (MNF), composed initially of U.S., French, and Italian troops, began to arrive in Lebanon in late August 1982 to help assure the evacuation of the PLO from Beirut.

With the termination of hostilities the Reagan administration saw a new opportunity to move toward resolution of the broader Arab-Israeli conflict. In the U.S. perspective, the war not only highlighted the dangers inherent in the Arab-Israeli conflict but also created a lessened opportunity for future war given the clear military superiority of Israel, the difficulties faced by Syria during the conflict, and the disarray in the Arab world. The United States also believed that the prospects for PLO guerrilla or terrorist activity against Israel had been significantly reduced by the PLO's loss of its Lebanon base of operations and by the lack of alternative facilities in other countries bordering Israel. The administration believed this was an opportunity for movement toward an Arab-Israeli peace and saw the possibility that Lebanon could restore itself to a legitimate political existence and for terminating the civil war, which had lasted from 1975 until the 1982 hostilities. The United States was pleased that the Soviet role had been diminished with the destruction of Soviet military equipment and with the significant difficulties faced by Syria in using Soviet equipment, training, and doctrine. The United States was convinced that Soviet credibility had been affected and that the United States had regained its position as the central external power in the efforts at conflict resolution. The Arab delegations that came to Washington in the summer of 1982 seemed to reaffirm the U.S. role as the focal point of Arab attention and suggested that the United States should increase its efforts to achieve a settlement and to assist Lebanon.

The "fresh start" initiative for peace in the Middle East was outlined by President Reagan in a television address on September 1, 1982. It was a direct outcome of the strategic alterations in the region, and it sought to exploit them. It was not a plan with specific elements to be implemented through specific techniques within specific timetables. It was an initiative—an attempt to get the regional states to think in terms of a peace process and to help them with U.S. ideas. It sought to bring together Jordan, under King Hussein, and moderate Palestinians in negotiations directly with Israel to work out a solution for the future of the West Bank and Gaza. It was based on the perspective that the Arab world should recognize that the option of going to war to defeat Israel no longer existed; that guerrilla or terrorist activity would not serve the Arab purpose; and that, if the Palestinians hoped for any kind of future in the region, the most effective means was to negotiate for a settlement. The administration appeared to believe that if the Arabs and Israelis did not negotiate the result would be continued Israeli settlement in the West Bank and Gaza and, ultimately, Israeli annexation of that territory. Reagan believed that the Arabs needed to recognize reality.

Reagan set forth the position of the administration on some of the central elements of the Arab-Israeli conflict. He said that in the West Bank and Gaza neither alternative preferred by the parties would be acceptable. He opposed Israeli sovereignty in the West Bank, and he opposed an independent Palestinian state. Reagan believed that Israel should stop building settlements in the West Bank, and he suggested that there be a self-governing West Bank associated with Jordan under Palestinian control. He proposed that Jerusalem, a city important to all three major faiths, remain undivided but that its future be negotiated by the parties. Other specifics were outlined as well.

Reactions to the "fresh start" initiative varied. On September 2, 1982, the Israeli cabinet rejected the proposal on a number of grounds, the major objections being that it departed from the conceptual framework agreed to at Camp David and that it seemed prematurely to determine the outcome of negotiations on several points, including the status of Jerusalem as the capital of Israel and the future of the West Bank and Gaza.

The main and initial Arab response came at the Fez Arab Summit where the Arab leaders restated the designation of the PLO as the sole legitimate representative of the Palestinians. They refused to grant King Hussein the required mandate to negotiate on behalf of the Palestinians, which U.S. policy had assumed would be forthcoming on the basis of its earlier consultations with King Hussein and other Arab leaders.

Implementation of U.S. policy took two forms: the administration waited for Hussein to agree to join the process and it concentrated on the immediate problem of Lebanon. Ambassador Philip Habib was appointed the President's Special Representative for the Middle East with overall responsibility for implementing the initiative as well as for coordinating the negotiations concerning Lebanon. He was to be assisted by Ambassadors Morris Draper and Richard Fairbanks.

The administration's efforts were affected by developments in the region: the assassination of president-elect Beshir Gemayel of Lebanon; the massacres at the Shatila and Sabra refugee camps; the election of Amin Gemayel as president; the appointment in Israel of the Kahan commission, its investigation, and its report; and various acts of violence against the multinational force and against the American Embassy in Beirut.

Washington continued to wait for Hussein. It held the view that Jordan's participation was essential and that Hussein was prepared to participate, if given the appropriate mandate by the other Arabs, especially the PLO. After Hussein's failure to secure a mandate at the Fez Summit, he began to negotiate with Yasser Arafat to secure PLO support. By April 1983 it was apparent that the effort had failed. On April 10, 1983, Jordan's cabinet announced that Jordan would not participate in the peace process and could not and would not negotiate on behalf of the Palestinians because Arafat's apparent arrangement with Hussein had been vetoed by radical elements in the PLO. The Reagan administration was left with neither an Arab nor an Israeli negotiator, and it focused its attention on other issues.

U.S. policy sought the reconstitution of Lebanon as a sovereign entity and the withdrawal of all foreign forces from that country. A total of 35 negotiating sessions between Israel and Lebanon, with U.S. participation, failed to achieve agreement on withdrawal of Israeli troops. In May 1983 U.S. Secretary of State George Shultz went to the Middle East and secured an agreement that was signed by representatives of the governments of Israel and Lebanon. It was not a peace treaty, but it did call for the withdrawal of Israeli troops (and other foreign forces) from Lebanon, the delineation of the Lebanon-Israel border, and the termination of the state of war between them.

The next step was to arrange an agreement for the withdrawal of Syria and the PLO from Lebanon, but they opposed the Israel-Lebanon agreement. In this they had the strong backing of the Soviet Union. U.S. envoy Habib attempted to go to Damascus on May 18, 1983, but was told by Syrian officials that there was nothing to discuss. Subsequently Secretary of State Shultz held discussions with Syrian leaders in Damascus, but the Syrians continued to oppose any withdrawal agreement as long as Israel maintained a presence in southern Lebanon. The administration appeared frustrated by the Syrian refusal to withdraw or to negotiate seriously. At the same time Israel began a partial withdrawal. In a press conference on July 26, 1983, Reagan noted that the partial Israeli withdrawal in Lebanon "will give us a better case for breaking the roadblock that has been established by Syria and persuading them to keep their original promise that when others withdrew, they would withdraw."[27]

The first anniversary of the "fresh start" initiative was not particularly noteworthy. No negotiations had begun under its auspices. Hussein, after months of deliberation, had refused to participate, and no other Arab interlocutor was prepared to come forward. The problems of Lebanon, which had become a surrogate for the initiative, showed amelioration in some sectors and deterioration in others but no dramatic breakthrough. The Israel-Lebanon agreement was an important accomplishment, but it was virtually stillborn as a result of Syrian, PLO, and Soviet opposition. Limited progress was made on extending the authority of the Gemayel government beyond small sectors of Beirut, on rebuilding the Lebanese army to establish broader central government authority, and on the reconstruction of Lebanon, but even this was slow. United States-Israel relations, which had been seriously impaired by the war, the massacre at the Shatila and Sabra camps, the Israeli rejection of the Reagan initiative, and by a host of lesser events, returned to their former positive levels. There were no major issues of controversy in the United States-Israel relationship, given the absence of a substantive peace effort where the differing views of the two parties might clash.

Despite increasing concern with other issues, such as Central America, the Reagan administration remained committed to resolution of the problems of Lebanon and to the broader peace process. The United States continued to focus on these issues because the

President regarded them at that point as his most important foreign policy achievement, [28] because of the dangers involved, and because of the increased Soviet involvement (in the form of the transfer of sophisticated military equipment and advisors) which was seen in the administration as a major obstacle to peace and stability in that area and a factor contributing to the potential for conflict.

U.S. concern with the Persian Gulf receded in the face of U.S. preoccupation with the search for a comprehensive Arab-Israeli peace and the problems of Lebanon. The war in Afghanistan, and the continued Iran-Iraq conflict, motivated the United States to continue to support the rebels against the Soviet-backed regime and to begin giving encouragement, albeit circumscribed, to Iraq. The inability and/or unwillingness of the United States to affect significantly the course of either conflict became increasingly obvious. Continued warfare seemed likely in both venues and U.S. concern—or the lack thereof—did not presage consequential action.

Nevertheless, in mid 1983 U.S. concern about the war in the Persian Gulf increased as Iran began issuing warnings that it would close the Strait of Hormuz and prevent all oil exports from the Gulf if its own exporting capability were disrupted as a result of Iraqi attacks. These warnings had been precipitated by the French decision to deliver to Iraq five Super Etendard aircraft armed with highly sophisticated Exocet air-to-ground missiles, which would enable Iraq to attack Iran's main oil terminal at Kharg Island and seriously damage Teheran's oil industry. The United States adopted a dual-track approach in responding to the potentially deteriorating Gulf situation. Publicly, the United States reaffirmed its commitment to freedom of navigation in the Persian Gulf and moved a naval task force from Central America to the Indian Ocean. Behind the scenes, the Reagan administration explored the possibility of improving ties with Iraq.

The Reagan administration had a longstanding interest in improving relations with Iraq but had not been able to overcome Baghdad's apparent disinterest in improving ties with Washington. By the spring of 1983, however, Iraqi overtures to the United States and its public support of the Israel-Lebanon agreement suggested to the United States that Iraq might be amenable to improved ties. The United States agreed to several high-level meetings with Iraqi officials, including a meeting between U.S. Secretary of State Shultz and Iraq's Deputy Prime Minister Tariq Aziz in Paris in May 1983. The following September, Iraq's Deputy Foreign Minister Ismat Kittani met with several U.S. officials in Washington, among them Vice President George Bush and Under Secretary of State Lawrence

Eagleburger. Iraq's decision to moderate its attitude toward the United States probably was prompted in part by the war of economic attrition waged against it by Iran—because of the damage to its oil-exporting facilities at the head of the Persian Gulf and the closure of its pipeline in Syria by the Syrian government, Iraq's oil exports had declined dramatically. Moreover, annual subsidies to Baghdad from Saudi Arabia and other Arab oil-producing countries had been cut significantly because of their financial difficulties brought on by the world oil glut and sagging oil prices.

The United States, for its part, was responding to what it perceived as the growing threat to regional stability from the radical Islamic regime in Teheran. The administration believed that U.S. interests would suffer a major setback if Iran defeated Iraq and that there was little the United States could do directly to assist Iraq. It also believed that an Iranian victory would produce an extremist Islamic fundamentalist government in Baghdad that would become a threat to those Gulf states with ties to the United States. The Reagan administration decided to assist Iraq indirectly by urging Arab countries to increase their financial support to Baghdad and by urging other countries to limit their arms sales to Iran.

In the wake of what many U.S. officials believed to be Iranian-inspired and -supported attacks on U.S. forces in Lebanon, the "tilt" toward Iraq probably also was meant in part to send a message to Teheran that the United States was capable of abandoning strict neutrality in the Iran-Iraq war and of openly assisting Iraq if there were further attacks on U.S. interests in the Middle East. U.S. officials also viewed the improved relations with Iraq as playing a potentially useful role beyond the Gulf. Together with growing cooperation between Egypt and Iraq, they could provide necessary political support to Jordan's King Hussein and U.S. efforts to "reengage" him in the Arab-Israeli peace process. A Cairo-Baghdad axis was seen as a counterweight to Syrian influence in the region and allaying Hussein's fears about possible Syrian retaliation if he were to enter the peace process.[29]

By publicly reaffirming its determination to preserve freedom of navigation, particularly in the strategic Strait of Hormuz, the United States sought to raise the possibility of direct military intervention. Assistant Secretary of State Richard Murphy told Congressional leaders in January 1984 that while the United States was urging Iran and Iraq to seek a negotiated settlement to the war, "We have also put all parties on notice that we will not accept any attempt to interfere with freedom of navigation in the international waters of the Gulf and in the Strait of Hormuz and that we will take whatever measures are necessary to prevent this."[30]

U.S. officials nonetheless refused to spell out what action was contemplated if the shipping lanes were closed. Typical of the administration's position was President Reagan's response when asked if he would sanction the use of military force if Iran threatened to cut off Western access to the Gulf's oil supplies:

> ... I don't think it would be proper for me to talk about tactics or what ought be done, but I will say this: I do not believe the free world could stand by and allow anyone to close the Strait of Hormuz in the Persian Gulf to the oil traffic through those waterways.[31]

The U.S. tilt toward Iraq was intended at least in part to make the threat of U.S. intervention in the war credible in the eyes of the Khomeini regime. At the same time, the United States held out the prospect of better relations with Washington to discourage Iraq from going through with its threats to damage Iran's oil industry by attacking its main oil terminal at Kharg Island. This strategy included U.S. support for the proposed construction of an oil pipeline from Iran to the Jordanian port of Aqaba. The United States hoped that by actively encouraging Baghdad to increase its own oil exports—thereby helping to alleviate the impact of Iran's war of economic attrition—Iraq would not feel compelled to threaten Iran's oil exports.

The Reagan administration also began planning how to deal with the war's escalation—if it occurred—by seeking to expand security ties with Saudi Arabia and other states in the Gulf. Such efforts already had been undertaken to no avail in mid 1982 when Arab fears of an Iranian victory were most pronounced. Administration proponents of a renewed effort at joint contingency planning with Gulf states argued that their growing fear of Iran provided an opportunity for the United States to enhance its presence in the Gulf.

Despite local reluctance, the Reagan administration nonetheless continued to try to coax the Gulf states into some form of joint military planning. At the same time, the United States pursued a parallel strategy to get around the problem of Arab sensibilities about too closely associating with the United States by creating an Arab mobile strike force to aid Persian Gulf states faced with internal subversion. This effort—similar to one derailed by Congress in 1982—was known as the Joint Logistic Planning (JLP) program and involved supplying Jordan with an initial $220 million worth of military equipment for an 8,000-man "rapid deployment force" for use within a 1,500-mile radius of Jordan. As part of this program, the United States was to provide Jordan with three C-130 military transport aircraft, TOW antitank weapons, mobile medical stations, tank-supported bridge-laying equipment, self-propelled anti-aircraft weapons, and satellite communications equipment.[32]

In the spring of 1984, the Reagan administration's Jordanian strategy was dealt a setback by Congressional opposition to the JLP program in the wake of King Hussein's scathing criticism of the United States for being "too pro-Israeli," which he made in a newspaper interview in mid March. The administration also cancelled a separate deal to sell Jordan more than 1,500 "Stinger" anti-aircraft missiles.

At the time of the cancellation of the JLP program, the war between Iran and Iraq took a new turn as Iranian and Iraqi planes began attacking neutral shipping in the Gulf. The Reagan administration responded by trying to prevent further escalation and planning for dealing with escalation if it occurred. The U.S. response involved the reaffirmation of U.S. support for freedom of navigation in the Gulf and willingness to use military power to keep the waterways open. It was hoped that the credible threat of intervention would prevent a dangerous escalation of the fighting by Iran. A different strategy had to be pursued with Iraq, however, because of the administration's fear that Iraq deliberately escalated the war in order to compel the United States and other Western powers to intervene. With Baghdad, the United States continued to work to improve relations in order to moderate Iraq's conduct of the war and prevent the "internationalization" of the conflict. In its contingency planning, the Reagan administration contemplated escorting international shipping from Persian Gulf ports to an area south of the war zone in cooperation with the British, the French, and the Gulf countries.

Saudi Arabia and the Gulf states, however, remained wary of having the United States take a direct military role in the Gulf. As a stop-gap measure, the administration sent 400 "Stinger" anti-aircraft missiles to Saudi Arabia to be used in establishing a "protected" zone for shipping along the Western coast of the Persian Gulf.

The attacks on shipping in the Gulf eventually began to decline, and so too did the sense of urgency with which U.S. officials viewed the Persian Gulf war. The worst-case scenarios envisioned by policymakers did not materialize. U.S. military capability to respond quickly and effectively to external or internal threats in the region was untested and hampered by the refusal of the Gulf states to accept a direct U.S. presence. In the absence of access to land bases, the Reagan administration was left with little choice but to continue efforts to build up local military forces—particularly Saudi Arabia's—to protect U.S. interests in the region while publicly reaffirming its resolve to use military force, if necessary, to keep the strategic waterways open.

During the summer and fall of 1983 events drew U.S. attention back to the problems of Lebanon. The U.S. Marines stationed in Lebanon as a part of the multinational force came under fire and casualties were suffered. The President's resolve was clear and strengthened by the view that those who were acting against the government of Lebanon and the U.S. presence were assisted by Syria, the PLO, and the Soviet Union, which he identified as a "hostile influence."

Despite the talk of improving the situation in Lebanon, securing the withdrawal of foreign forces, and moving toward more comprehensive negotiations, by mid October 1983 the administration was unable to achieve any significant momentum in the situation. This stemmed in part from the increasing identification of the U.S. component of the multinational force with the government of President Amin Gemayel because of efforts to improve and support the Lebanese Army, in effect making the U.S. forces an additional warring faction in the Lebanese conflict. This new identification became obvious with the bombing of the U.S. Marine headquarters in Beirut, resulting in the death of more than 200 Marines. This incident brought forth increased U.S. domestic opposition to the U.S. presence in Lebanon and raised doubt about the administration's policy. At the same time it seemed to strengthen Reagan's resolve and to stiffen his determination to pursue his efforts in the Middle East. In comments to journalists on October 24, 1983, the day after the bombing incident, Reagan noted that the United States must keep its forces in Lebanon until the situation was under control because "we have vital interests in Lebanon and our actions in Lebanon are in the cause of world peace."[33] He defined the role of the Marines and the United States in these terms: "With our allies, England, France and Italy, we are part of a multinational peace force, seeking a withdrawal of all foreign forces from Lebanon and from the Beirut area while a new Lebanese government undertakes to restore sovereignty throughout that country."[34] By promoting peace in Lebanon the administration sought to strengthen peace throughout the Middle East. Reagan clearly attributed to Lebanon a strategic value of considerable importance, greater than any previous administration. Thus, he noted: "If Lebanon ends up under the tyranny of forces hostile to the West, not only will our strategic position in the eastern Mediterranean be threatened, but also the stability of the entire Middle East, including the vast resource areas of the Arabian peninsula."[35]

In a number of ways, the Reagan administration sought to link the continued presence of the Marines in Lebanon to an array of U.S. interests and policies in the region. Reagan also suggested a more specific connection between the situation in Lebanon and U.S. support of Israel. He linked the U.S. presence to the 1982 war and the subsequent "fresh start" peace initiative. He used terms that had been noted earlier: "the idea of us continuing to help, as we did at Camp David, in furthering that process bringing more nations into the kind of peaceful arrangement that occurred between Egypt and Israel, producing more Egypts, if you will."[36] At the same time, the administration recognized that before it could proceed with a peace plan, foreign forces (Syria, the PLO, and Israel) had to be withdrawn, a stabilizing force had to be introduced, then the Lebanese military could acquire the capability necessary for the government to institute control within its borders. That is why the multinational force was sent in—to provide stability so that when foreign forces were removed, order could be maintained. Yet, despite the bombing of the Marine barracks, no U.S. plans for altering their position or for modifying U.S. policy were put forward.[37]

The increase in U.S. firepower, through such measures as the stationing of the battleship "New Jersey" offshore at Beirut and a general increase in the offshore presence and capability of United States forces, marked an important milestone in the administration's approach. It reflected Reagan's willingness to stage a show of force to support his political actions—in this case support of the Gemayel government and its objectives in Lebanon. In the administration's view it marked a firmness in opposing Soviet-supported adventurism, and the blame for the deteriorating situation in Lebanon was placed by Reagan on Syria and the Soviet Union.

The Reagan administration entered the crucial 12-month period prior to the 1984 election with U.S. forces under siege in Beirut and with little progress toward improvement of the situation in Lebanon. The removal of foreign forces from Lebanon remained stymied by Syria's refusal to consider that objective and by the administration's apparent inability to persuade Syria to alter its policy, which was bolstered by strong Soviet support. The stability of Lebanon had not been attained and the power and authority of the Gemayel government and its army had not been extended beyond its original limits within a portion of Beirut. The prospect of U.S. Marines remaining under fire for an extended period raised doubts in the minds of some Americans about the wisdom of their presence in Beirut. The willingness of Congress to provide the administration with an 18-month mandate for those forces in Lebanon, under the terms of the War Powers Act, reflected more a Congressional desire not to have the issue raised to any significant degree during the forthcoming election year than Congressional support for the policy. The "fresh start" initiative showed no real progress, and negotiations between Israel and Jordan were no closer to starting than they had been at the time the initiative was first announced.

In sum, 1984 was a year of little progress and much frustration for the Reagan administration in the Middle East. In February the U.S. Marines were withdrawn from Lebanon where they had increasingly become targets for the various fighting factions. The United States retained its commitment to the reconstitution of the Lebanese polity, but there was a reluctance to become directly involved in negotiations unless some form of diplomatic success was assured. In part this reflected the administration's frustration after the Lebanese government unilaterally abrogated the May 1983 agreement with Israel that Secretary of State Shultz had helped to secure. Furthermore the Lebanese government remained incapable of restoring its authority throughout its territory; it could not secure the removal of foreign forces nor the requisite strengthening of its own military capability to monopolize violence within the country; and Syria continued to be the dominant force within the territory of Lebanon.

The United States continued to restate the September 1, 1982, initiative as the basis of its policy for resolution of the Arab-Israeli conflict, but there was a hiatus in the peace process as a result of the U.S. presidential election and a national election in Israel. Peace between Egypt and Israel was maintained but did not flourish and was not expanded to include other states, as President Reagan had hoped. The special relationship between the United States and Israel continued to be marked by a positive aura that reflected a fundamental congruence of U.S. and Israeli policies concerning the main issues affecting the region. The lack of progress toward a comprehensive Middle East peace and the close relations between the United States and Israel also reflected the reality that, in 1984, there was no clear and obvious mechanism for a breakthrough in the peace process. All parties seemed to await the beginning of Reagan's second term.

The Reagan administration's first term in office ended without major achievements in its Middle East policy despite various attempts at an activist approach to several of the problems facing the region. Reagan's policy in the Persian Gulf revealed a basic ambivalence about both ends and means. Whereas it was conceived primarily in response to the danger of the perceived Soviet threat and the need to contain Soviet expansionism, the Iran-Iraq war forced the administration to come to grips with dangers emanating from internal unrest and the threats they posed to U.S. interests. Whether U.S. policies are directed primarily against external or internal threats has implications for the selection of the instruments of those policies. A naval presence and small mobile force are intended to deter Soviet adventurism, but the success of this strategy depends on the receptivity of local governments to close security ties with the United States. The United States found out early, however, that a shared concern about Soviet intentions is not enough to draw key Persian Gulf states into a security framework with the United States.

The Reagan administration slowly adjusted its strategy in light of local political predilictions and resisted the temptation to establish a permanent presence in the Gulf to control access to the region's oil supplies. Rather, the United States adopted a more modest role in strengthening local military capabilities and promising more support if requested. It also supported local security initiatives, such as the Gulf Cooperation Council, which serve U.S. interests, and did not attempt a more formal regional security arrangement. This strategy may not have appealed to an administration that took office convinced that the United States had to beef up its military might in the region, but it seemed a more pragmatic approach—one that appeared to be in line with the realities of the Persian Gulf while still holding out the prospect of closer U.S. security ties in the region down the road.

The administration's record in the Arab-Israeli zone also had few successes. In Lebanon, the U.S.-mediated accord of May 17, 1983, which provided for the withdrawal of Israeli troops, was abrogated by Lebanon under Syrian pressure. Although Israel eventually withdrew the bulk of its forces, it was a unilateral decision that pointed to the failure of both Israeli and U.S. policy goals in Lebanon, and the success of Syria's. The United States remained committed to supporting the establishment of a stable government in Beirut, but given the costs already incurred, it probably would not expend much energy or resources to that end.

Frustrated in Lebanon, the Reagan administration in its second term turned most of its attention to resolving the Arab-Israeli conflict. Reagan's 1982 "fresh start" initiative remained the basis for efforts to achieve a comprehensive settlement. This policy ultimately is grounded in the administration's basic ideology, which focuses on the Soviet Union as a threat and the need for the United States to remain in an area that the President has designated as vitally important to the United States and its allies. In hopes of laying the groundwork for direct Arab-Israeli talks, the administration also has explored the possibility of holding preliminary discussions with a joint Jordanian-Palestinian delegation that would not include known members of the PLO, in keeping with the U.S. promise to Israel not to negotiate with the PLO until it first accepts UN Resolutions 242 and 338 and recognizes Israel.

The relationship with Israel has been the one constant of, and has served as a motive for and an asset to, U.S. involvement in the region. One of the reasons for the involvement of the United States, as Reagan has said, is that since 1948 the United States has recognized and accepted a moral obligation to assure the continued existence of Israel as a nation. Israel shares U.S. democratic values and is a formidable force with which an invader of the Middle East would have to reckon. This is both a commitment to and a rationale for U.S. involvement, and it comports with the view that Israel serves a positive purpose. Even Secretary of Defense Weinberger—who is widely regarded as less-than-sympathetic toward Israel—has called Israel an asset against possible Soviet intervention. Despite this, and the resuscitation of the concept of U.S.-Israeli strategic cooperation, the administration also sees Israel as an asset that has its limits, as was demonstrated by the U.S. decision not to use Israeli facilities for the evacuation of wounded Marines after the Beirut bombing, by the concept of a Jordanian rapid deployment force, and by efforts to build facilities at Ras Banas in Egypt rather than utilizing Israeli facilities that were offered.

MILITARY AND ECONOMIC ASSISTANCE

The U.S. approach to the Middle East has been multifaceted and has employed a wide variety of policy instruments to achieve its interests and implement its policies. The utilization of various diplomatic/political and strategic/military means has been considered in detail in the preceding discussion. The provision of U.S.

economic/technical aid and military assistance has become an increasingly prominent instrument of the United States in the Middle East (see Table 2.1A–C).

U.S. economic assistance consists basically of two categories: Economic Support Funds (ESF) and Development Assistance (DA). The stated primary objective of U.S. aid programs is to help resolve some of the economic problems faced by countries in the region and to help bring a just and lasting peace to the Middle East. The argument is that by supporting long-term social and economic development, as well as shorter term economic stabilization and reconstruction where required, the United States helps governments meet the reasonable expectations of their people that peace will bring greater prosperity and an improved quality of life. By contributing to the stability and longer term economic development of the region and meeting the basic human needs of the people, U.S. assistance seeks to strengthen the groundwork for the achievement of peace in the region.

Security assistance has increasingly been a major tool of U.S. policy in the Middle East, as it has been in other sectors of the world. Security assistance programs are believed to contribute to U.S. objectives by assisting allies and friends to meet their defense needs and by supporting collective security efforts. They are also seen as a means of building positive government-to-government relations. By strengthening U.S. allies and friends, security assistance programs allow the United States to concentrate its efforts in areas of particular need. As officially argued, the primary military objectives of security assistance are to assist countries to preserve their independence; to promote their regional security; to help obtain base rights, overseas facilities, and transit rights; to ensure access to critical raw materials; and to provide a means to expand U.S. influence.

Among the major components of U.S. security assistance programs are: the Foreign Military Sales (FMS) Program (including FMS Credit Program); Military Assistance Program (MAP); and International Military Education and Training Program (IMETP). The FMS program enables eligible governments to purchase defense equipment, services, and training from the United States on a cash or credit basis. The MAP program is a grant program that allows designated economically disadvantaged countries to obtain equipment and selected services. The IMETP provides training to foreign military and certain foreign government-sponsored civilians on a grant basis and generally consists of formal courses, orientation tours, and on-the-job training.

The fashioning of the economic and security assistance program has a direct relationship to the foreign policy goals identified by the administration. The fiscal year 1986 aid request, for example, reflected the Reagan administration's goals and priorities in the Middle East. The request included: $3,321 million in FMS Credit including $3,100 million in foreign credits for Israel and Egypt; $67 million in grant MAPs; $10.15 million in IMETP; $932 million in Economic Support Funds (not including ESF for Israel); $52.2 million in Development Assistance; and $276.5 million in PL480 food assistance.[38]

In recent years Egypt and Israel have been the main Middle Eastern recipients of U.S. aid. Assistant Secretary of State Richard W. Murphy has argued: "Israel and Egypt remain our principal partners in the quest for peace, and these two nations are the largest recipients of our proposed foreign assistance for fiscal year 1986. This assistance is aimed at ensuring their security and strengthening their economies, both essential to their continuing on the path to a broader peace settlement."[39] It was, of course, argued that small programs for other states (such as Lebanon and Jordan) were also designed to promote regional stability and progress toward peace.

In the case of Egypt the funds are primarily allocated to specific projects in various sectors of the economy. In the case of Israel the aid is general in nature and is used to support directly Israel's civilian economy and help restore economic stability.

The overall role of the United States in Middle Eastern arms supply changed in the period following the October 1973 war. The United States became more extensively involved, not only by the supply of equipment to Israel but also by the sale of increasingly sophisticated equipment to Arab clients and to new Arab customers such as Egypt. The overall scale of U.S. sales increased dramatically, and Saudi Arabia became the largest military customer. Military supply to Egypt developed in the wake of the 1974 disengagement agreements and the Sinai II accords. After signing the agreements Egypt requested military assistance and the United States supported the concept of an Egyptian shift from reliance on Soviet weaponry to reliance on Western supply. It began by providing jeeps and trucks and, in 1976, agreed to sell C-130 transport aircraft. Jordan and Saudi Arabia also secured additional U.S. equipment, including jet fighters. Jordan was able to secure tanks, antitank missiles, air-to-air missiles and Hawk surface-to-air missiles. Egypt became a major recipient of U.S. arms in the aftermath of Sadat's 1977 visit to Jerusalem, as part of the Egypt-Israel peace process.

A major watershed in U.S. military assistance programs was the 1978 "package deal" that approved the sale of F-5E aircraft to Egypt, F-15 aircraft to Saudi Arabia, and an increase in the number of F-15s previously pledged to Israel. This gave Egypt and Saudi Arabia access to the U.S. arsenal at sophisticated levels and in amounts that they did not previously have. This was soon overshadowed by the 1981 decision to allow Saudi Arabia to purchase AWACS aircraft and to enhance the capability of the previously sold F-15s. This multi-billion dollar deal was a major turning point in the U.S. role as arms provider in the Middle East, and indicates the dramatic alteration in U.S. policy on arms sales to the Arabs: The weapons systems were of increasing sophistication and a growing number of customers were involved.

The Special Case of Israel

Military and economic assistance to Israel has become a salient aspect of the U.S.-Israeli relationship, particularly since the October 1973 war. The rationale for U.S. assistance has been framed in terms of promoting peace through the commitment to the security and well-being of Israel, as well as to developing confidence, maintaining a friendly relationship, and helping to maintain Israel's military edge over its hostile neighbors. It has been argued that Israel must be sufficiently confident of its ability to defend itself if it is to take the risks necessary to make peace. From 1949 to 1983 U.S. aid totaled more than $25 billion, including more than $16.5 billion in military loans and grants; more than $6.5 billion in economic loans and grants under the Security Assistance Program; and more than $2 billion in other programs, including Food for Peace, housing guarantees, Export-Import Bank loans, and aid for resettling Soviet Jews.[40]

Aid for Israel has evolved from a rather modest, primarily economic effort to a substantial and multifaceted program. Between 1946 and 1971 the overwhelming portion of aid was economic, and most of that was loans. The military portion also was in the form of loans, although the United States was not Israel's major source of external military assistance until after the June 1967 war.

The program shifted in the 1970s, particularly after the October War of 1973, as Israel's need for both economic and military assistance began to grow considerably, primarily as a result of the growth of military expenditures, the rise in the price of oil and other essential imports, and the growing burden of external debt service. Since 1974 almost half of the military assistance has been grant aid; and since 1979 economic aid has been a cash transfer unlinked to specific projects or commodity imports, although it must be used for nonmilitary purposes. By 1983 U.S. military assistance to Israel exceeded assistance to any other country.

TABLE 2.1A: U.S. Overseas Loans and Grants, Obligations and Loan Authorizations (net of deobligations) Fiscal Years 1946–1984 (millions of dollars)

Country	Total	Economic Assistance Loans	Grants
Afghanistan	537.2	117.4	419.8
Bahrain	2.4	—	2.4
Cyprus	208.3	1.2	207.1
Egypt	10519.0	5290.0	5229.0
Greece	1910.3	351.4	1558.9
Iran	765.6	301.4	464.2
Iraq	45.5	14.4	31.1
Israel	8851.0	2079.6	6771.4
Jordan	1488.2	336.1	1152.1
Kuwait	—	—	—
Lebanon	279.5	33.0	246.5
Oman	54.0	30.0	24.0
Saudi Arabia	31.8	4.3	27.5
Syria	581.9	494.2	87.7
Turkey	3920.3	1972.1	1948.2
Yemen	228.2	9.4	218.8
Yemen, P.D.R.	4.5	—	4.5
Near East Regional	628.2	—	628.2
Algeria	203.3	11.6	191.7
Libya	212.5	7.0	205.5
Morocco	1276.7	668.0	608.7
Sudan	815.8	163.1	652.7
Tunisia	985.3	455.4	529.9
All Countries	174138	53170	120968

TABLE 2.1B: U.S. Overseas Loans and Grants, Obligations and Loan Authorizations (net of deobligations) Fiscal Years 1946–1984 (millions of dollars)

Country	Total	Military Assistance Loans	Grants
Afghanistan	5.6	—	5.6
Bahrain	—	—	—
Cyprus	—	—	—
Egypt	5648.1	4550.0	1098.1
Greece	4874.3	2234.1	2640.2
Iran	1404.8	496.4	908.4
Iraq	50.0	—	50.0
Israel	19104.2	11204.2	7900.0
Jordan	1265.7	706.3	559.4
Kuwait	—	—	—
Lebanon	263.8	243.7	20.1
Oman	150.3	150.0	0.3
Saudi Arabia	292.4	254.2	38.2
Syria	0.1	—	0.1
Turkey	7154.2	2455.9	4698.3
Yemen	27.5	14.0	13.5
Yemen, P.D.R.	—	—	—
Near East Regional	*	—	*
Algeria	—	—	—
Libya	17.6	—	17.6
Morocco	553.5	436.6	116.9
Sudan	257.3	111.3	146.0
Tunisia	501.8	411.5	90.3
All Countries	106995	31317	75678

*Less than $50,000.

TABLE 2.1C: U.S. Overseas Loans and Grants, Obligations and Loan Authorizations (net of deobligations) Fiscal Years 1946–1984 (millions of dollars)

Country	Total Economic and Military Assistance Total	Loans	Grants
Afghanistan	542.8	117.4	425.4
Bahrain	2.4	—	2.4
Cyprus	208.3	1.2	207.1
Egypt	16167.1	9840.0	6327.1
Greece	6784.6	2585.5	4199.1
Iran	2170.4	797.8	1372.6
Iraq	95.5	14.4	81.1
Israel	27955.2	13283.8	14671.4
Jordan	2753.9	1042.4	1711.5
Kuwait	—	—	—
Lebanon	543.3	276.7	266.6
Oman	204.3	180.0	24.3
Saudi Arabia	324.2	258.5	65.7
Syria	582.0	494.2	87.8
Turkey	11074.5	4428.0	6646.5
Yemen	255.7	23.4	232.3
Yemen, P.D.R.	4.5	—	4.5
Near East Regional	628.2	—	628.2
Algeria	203.3	11.6	191.7
Libya	230.1	7.0	223.1
Morocco	1830.2	1104.6	725.6
Sudan	1073.1	274.4	798.7
Tunisia	1487.1	866.9	620.2
All Countries	281133	84487	196646

Sources: United States, Agency for International Development, *U.S. Overseas Loans and Grants and Assistance from International Organizations, Obligations and Loan Authorizations, July 1, 1945 – September 30, 1984* (1985).

NOTES

1. John S. Badeau, "The Middle East: Conflict in priorities," *Foreign Affairs* 36 (January 1958, pp. 232–40), p. 235. He went on to suggest, however, that Israel was not a priority in the sense that the Arab-Israeli conflict was a barrier to U.S. influence in the area.

2. "American policy on trial: An interview with George Ball," *Journal of Palestine Studies* 7 (Spring 1978, pp. 17–30), p. 20. See also George W. Ball, "How to save Israel in spite of herself," *Foreign Affairs* 55 (April 1977), pp. 453–71.

3. Ronald Reagan, "Recognizing the Israeli asset," Washington *Post* (August 15, 1979). During the campaign for the presidency Reagan said, in a speech to B'nai B'rith on September 3, 1980: ". . . the touchstone of our relationship with Israel is that a secure, strong Israel is in America's self-interest. Israel is a major strategic asset to America." Text in New York *Times* (September 4, 1980).

4. Washington *Times* (January 26, 1984).

5. Secretary of Defense Harold Brown linked Persian Gulf oil to U.S. strategic interests in a speech to the Los Angeles World Affairs Council on February 20, 1978: "Because the area is the world's greatest source of oil, the security of the Middle East and the Persian Gulf cannot be separated from our security and that of NATO and our allies in Asia. Japan, for example, imports 80 percent of her oil from this area. We intend to safeguard the production of oil and its transportation to consumer nations without interference by hostile powers." Office of Assistant Secretary of Defense (Public Affairs), *News Release*, "Remarks Prepared for Delivery by the Honorable Harold Brown, Secretary of Defense, to the Los Angeles World Affairs Council, February 20, 1978," p. 3.

6. William D. Brewer, "United States interests in the Persian Gulf," in Princeton University Conference, *Middle East Focus: The Persian Gulf* (Princeton, NJ: Princeton University Conference, n.d. [1968]), p. 177–78. The U.S. oil community did not share the view that Persian Gulf oil did not constitute a vital U.S. interest, citing the potential decline of U.S. oil reserves and resulting need for Persian Gulf oil as the basis for its concern. In early 1969, U.S. oil companies launched a major campaign to impress upon the Nixon administration and the public that because of the vital importance of Arab oil for the United States, U.S. policy in the Arab-Israeli conflict should be more sympathetic toward the Arabs.

7. Interview with *Business Week*, January 2, 1975; quoted in *The Middle East: U.S. Policy, Israel, Oil and the Arabs*, 2nd ed., (Washington, D.C.: Congressional Quarterly, 1975), p. 28.

8. *The Middle East: U.S. Policy, Israel, Oil and the Arabs*, 2nd ed. (Washington, D.C.: Congressional Quarterly, 1975), p. 34.

9. United States, Congress, House of Representatives, Committee on Foreign Affairs, *Hearings, New Perspectives on the Persian Gulf*, 93rd. Cong., 1st. sess., 1973, p. 39.

10. William P. Rogers, *United States Foreign Policy, 1972* (Washington, D.C.: U.S. Government Printing Office, 1973), p. 386.

11. Kissinger press conference, October 25, 1973, Department of State, Press Release No. 390, p. 11.

12. "Memorandum of Agreement Between the Governments of Israel and the United States on the Geneva Peace Conference," in United States, House of Representatives, Committee on Foreign Affairs, *The Search for Peace in the Middle East: Documents and Statements, 1967–79* (Washington, D.C.: U.S. Government Printing Office, 1979), pp. 15–16.

13. For details of the initial Carter administration policy see Bernard Reich, "The continued quest for peace: The United States and the Middle East," in Colin Legum and Haim Shaked (eds.), *Middle East Contemporary Survey*, Vol. 1, 1976–77 (New York and London: Holmes and Meier, 1978), pp. 21–33.

14. *Weekly Compilation of Presidential Documents* (March 21, 1977), p. 361.

15. See Carter's press conference on March 9, 1977 and Vice President Walter F. Mondale's speech to the World Affairs Council of Northern California, June 17, 1977.

16. *Weekly Compilation of Presidential Documents* (March 21, 1977), p. 361.

17. In an interview on September 16, 1977 Carter noted: "I've never called for an independent Palestinian country. We have used the word 'entity.' And my own preference . . . is that we think that if there is a Palestinian entity established on the West Bank, that it ought to be associated with Jordan, for instance." *Weekly Compilation of Presidential Documents*, September 26, 1977, p. 137B.

18. Vance interview, Washington *Times*, June 8, 1983. See also Cyrus Vance, *Hard Choices: Critical Years in America's Foreign Policy* (New York: Simon and Schuster, 1983), p. 191.

19. For the text of the joint United States-Soviet statement see *Department of State Bulletin* (November 7, 1977), pp. 639–40.

20. In an interview with Frank Reynolds of ABC News, President Carter, in response to a question concerning his changed perceptions of the Russians, noted: "My opinion of the Russians has changed most drastically in the last week than even the previous two and a half years before that. It's only now dawning on the world the magnitude of the action that the Soviets undertook in invading Afghanistan. . . . But to repeat myself, this action of the Soviets has made a more dramatic change in my own opinion of what the Soviets' ultimate goals are than anything they've done in the previous time I've been in office." Text in New York *Times* (January 1, 1980).

21. New York *Times* (January 24, 1980).

22. This policy was reaffirmed periodically after the outbreak of hostilities by both the Carter and the Reagan administrations. For example, Assistant Secretary of State Nicholas Veliotes told a Senate subcommittee in March 1983: "We continue to emphasize our support, publicly and privately, for a peaceful, early resolution of the devastating war between Iraq and Iran on a basis which preserves the independence and territorial integrity of both countries. Continuation of the war endangers the peace and security of all nations in the Gulf region and in our view serves neither the interests of Iraq nor Iran, nor does it serve any U.S. interest or those of our allies." Statement before the Subcommittee on Near Eastern and South Asian Affairs of the Senate Foreign Relations Committee on March 2, 1983 in *Department of State Bulletin* 83:2074 (May 1983), pp. 57–61.

23. New York *Times*, March 20, 1981.

24. New York *Times*, May 25, 1982. Assistant Secretary of State Veliotes told a Senate subcommittee in June 1983 that the Reagan administration was committed to helping nations to defend themselves by means of "economic and military assistance to friendly nations of the region to enable them to defend themselves and deter threats from the Soviet Union and its proxies, as well as arrangements for strategic cooperation for access in times of threats. . . ." *Department of State Bulletin* 83:2076 (July 1983), p. 87.

25. New York *Times* (May 25, 1982).

26. Statement of Deputy Assistant Secretary of State Robert H. Pelletreau before the Subcommittee on Europe and the Middle East of the House Foreign Affairs Committee on September 26, 1983, in *Department of State Bulletin* 83:2080 (November 1983), p. 55.

27. Text in New York *Times* (July 27, 1983).

28. When asked by reporters on December 23, 1982 what he considered his greatest foreign policy accomplishment, Reagan responded: "I think that the initiative that we've taken in the Middle East is probably the greatest accomplishment, and I have great hopes for that. If we can bring peace to that very troubled area, I think we will have made a very great accomplishment." *Weekly Compilation of Presidential Documents* (December 27, 1982), p. 1658. In the 1983 State of the Union address Reagan said: "All the people of the Middle East should know that, in the year ahead, we will not flag in our efforts to build on that [Camp David] foundation to bring them the blessings of peace." New York *Times* (January 26, 1983).

29. On January 26, 1984, Assistant Secretary of State Richard Murphy praised Iraq's "positive" contribution, together with Jordan, to promote the reintegration of Egypt into the Arab world. In a statement to the Subcommittee on Europe and the Middle East of the House Foreign Affairs Committee, Murphy said this is one example where Iraq "has taken constructive positions on issues of concern to the United States."

30. Statement before the Subcommittee on Europe and the Middle East of the House Foreign Affairs Committee on January 26, 1984.

31. News conference of President Reagan on October 19, 1983, cited in *Department of State Bulletin* 83:2081 (December 1983). p. 8.

32. New York *Times* (January 27, 1984). In explaining the Jordanian "rapid deployment force" to Congress, Deputy Assistant Secretary of State Pelletreau commented that ". . . Jordan shares with us an interest in the stability of the area [Persian Gulf] and has actively aided other moderate countries in their defense." (Statement before the Subcommittee on Europe and the Middle East of the House Foreign Affairs Committee on September 26, 1983, cited in *Department of State Bulletin* 83:2080 [November 1983]).

33. Reagan's comments to visiting journalists. Transcript in Washington *Post* (October 25, 1983).

34. *Ibid.*

35. *Ibid.*

36. *Ibid.*

37. In a nationwide television address on October 26, 1983, during which he discussed the Beirut bombing and the U.S. invasion of Grenada, Reagan reiterated previous U.S. policies and restated his resolve to maintain existing approaches and gave no indication of new initiatives. He restated his determination to support the Gemayel administration in Lebanon.

38. United States, House of Representatives, Committee on Appropriations, *Hearings, Foreign Assistance and Related Programs, Appropriations for 1986*, part 4 (Washington, D.C.: U.S. Government Printing Office, 1985), p. 17.

39. *Ibid.*, p. 18.

40. Bernard Reich, *The United States and Israel: Influence in the Special Relationship* (New York: Praeger, 1984), pp. 145–75.

3

The Soviet Union

Alexander J. Bennett

The Soviet Union—and previously, Russia—has had long-term interests in the Middle East although it is primarily since World War II that Soviet involvement has become both intensive and extensive. Part of the explanation for this is the Soviet Union's recently acquired superpower role, permitting a more aggressive pursuit of traditionally held goals in the region. The USSR has long sought to be a Middle East power and believes that its geographic proximity justifies this aspiration. Soviet President (formerly Foreign Minister) Andrei Gromyko has been involved in Middle Eastern issues since the 1940s, the longest continuing participation of any of the senior actors, and he has consistently asserted that the Soviet Union has a right to such interest.

Russian involvement in the Middle East dates to the ninth century,[1] with the founding of the Kievan state, and to a significant extent can be explained in terms of location, commercial significance, and security interests. To the early rulers of Kiev, trade with the Middle East was a natural outgrowth of the state's strategic situation on the trade route "from the Varangians to the Greeks" (running from the Baltic region to Constantinople). Trade, especially with Byzantium, formed one of the cornerstones of the Kievan economy, providing an outlet for the export of raw materials and a source of finished goods, including military hardware. During this period, Kiev was preoccupied with the protection of trade routes, the expansion of markets in the south, and the alleviation of the threat of foreign aggression.

Following a time of general decline and foreign domination a new, centralized and expansionist state centered around the principality of Moscow rose to prominence in the fourteenth and fifteenth centuries. Moscow turned its attention to the southeast where it viewed the khanates of Astrakhan and Kazan and the Crimea as threats to the security of its border areas. Several campaigns were fought, resulting in the annexations and colonization of Astrakhan and Kazan in the middle of the sixteenth century. Ottoman-backed Crimea remained independent until the end of the eighteenth century. These conquests served as an outlet for Czarist imperial ambitions, which encountered few major impediments until the frontiers of the Ottoman Empire were approached. Russian interests in the areas controlled by the Ottomans included securing a natural southern border on the Black Sea, recovering productive lands lost during the two and a half centuries of the Mongol occupation of Russia (1237–1480), and gaining access to Turkish-controlled waterways, particularly the Straits.[2] Over several centuries Russia and Turkey engaged in a series of protracted and inconclusive conflicts, reaching a climax with Russian victories in the First (1768–1774) and Second (1787–1792) Turkish wars. The treaties of Kuchuk Kainarji (1774) and Jassy (1792) granted Russia, among other provisions, direct access to the Black Sea, special commercial privileges for Russian traders in the Ottoman Empire, Turkish recognition of the annexation of the Crimea, and certain religious rights. In essence, Russia obtained important advantages and territorial gains that facilitated the expansion of its influence in the Ottoman Empire while neutralizing a long-standing threat on its southern frontiers.[3]

The Black Sea stood as Russia's natural southern boundary and as it gained access to it, Russian attention focused on Persia and Afghanistan. Russian interest in Transcaucasia and Central Asia took form under the reign of Peter the Great, who envisaged large-scale trade with India by way of Central Asia and Persia. In 1722/23 a war was fought against Persia and won for Russia short-lived access to the Caspian Sea. However a more serious challenge to Persia erupted when Russia annexed Georgia, resulting in a Russo-Persian war (1804–1813), following which a vanquished Persia agreed to recognize Russian rule over Georgia and cede territory in the Caucasus. Shortly thereafter other concessions were obtained including the cessation of Armenian territory, the granting of commercial privileges in the Persian Empire, and the right to maintain a naval force in the Caspian Sea. Russia subsequently incorporated much of Central Asia into its empire in a series of military campaigns waged from 1865 to 1876. By the latter part of the nineteenth century, Great Britain had become apprehensive about continuing Russian drives toward Afghanistan, the stepping stone to India, and Persia. Nonetheless, these tensions abated without major incident when Great Britain and Imperial Russia entered into an agreement in 1907 that divided Persia into three spheres of influence—a northern Russian zone, a southwestern neutral zone, and a southeastern British zone—as well as acknowledging and limiting British influence in Afghan affairs solely to matters of foreign policy.

Until the October 1917 revolution, Russian interests in the Middle East were confined primarily to its southern frontiers, that is, toward the Ottoman Empire, Persia, and Afghanistan. Russian expansionism was motivated by a complex mix of factors including the desire to accumulate power, to delineate and expand its frontiers, fear of foreign encroachments, reaction to Western resolve to limit Russian westward expansion, and desires to exploit the region's resources, to gain access to strategic trade routes and waterways, and to find markets for finished products, which were uncompetitive in the West. In the Arab core of the Middle East, however, only a minor Russian presence existed, facilitated by gradually expanding commercial contacts and occasional concern for Orthodox populations living under Ottoman rule.

Following the founding of the Soviet state in 1917, it appeared that a new factor would determine the parameters of Soviet foreign policy: Marxist-Leninist ideology. In the immediate aftermath of the revolution, the Bolshevik leadership turned its attention westward in anticipation of revolutionary uprisings in the developed states of Europe. Its enthusiasm and patience withered, however, as revolutions failed to erupt except for two short-lived experiments in Hungary and Bavaria. Moreover, the Western powers were beginning to aid counterrevolutionary forces seeking to overthrow the Bolshevik government, and were to intervene themselves in Russia in 1918. Meanwhile, the sobering dictates of geography, economic privations, and security concerns goaded the Soviet leadership into more familiar patterns of Czarist foreign policy. In practice this translated into refocusing attention southeastward. The Soviets felt that the peoples of the Middle East and Asia shared a similar colonial experience with them and all held strong resentment toward the European powers. At the Congress of the Peoples of the East (1920), held under the auspices of the Communist International (Comintern), the Soviet delegates emphasized the unity of the Soviet workers' government with people oppressed by colonialism and pressed for the adoption of revolutionary slogans emphasizing liberation from imperialist domination. These efforts continued throughout the period between World Wars I and II as the Soviet Union adopted a position that favored Arab nationalism and sought to work through the small and ineffective Communist parties in Arab lands and in Palestine.[4] In effect, traditional Russian designs on the Middle East found expression even through the prism of Marxism-Leninism.

The Soviet Regime did not forsake conventional diplomacy in pursuit of its interests in the region. The first state with which it established diplomatic relations was Afghanistan (1919), followed by Iran and Turkey in 1920. The same year it endorsed the establishment in Gilan, Iran, of a Soviet Republic. In 1921, it signed treaties with Iran, Afghanistan and Turkey—the first in a series of "Treaties of Friendship" intended to break the diplomatic isolation of the Soviet Union. Subsequent agreements included the Soviet-Turkish Treaty on Friendship and Neutrality (1925), the Soviet-Iranian Treaty on Guarantees and Neutrality (1927), the Treaty of Friendship and Trade between the USSR and Yemen (1928), and the Treaty of Neutrality and Mutual Non-Aggression with Afghanistan (1931). In 1929, Iran and Turkey, among other states, signed the Soviet-sponsored Litvinov Protocol, which was intended as a regional followup to the Kellogg-Briand Pact outlawing war. The thrust of Soviet foreign policy was to secure legitimacy; that is, the acceptance by the international community of the USSR's sovereignty and independence. The civil war (1917–1922), with the intervention of European, U.S., and Japanese forces, taught the unseasoned Bolshevik leadership that a pariah state can never be assured of the inviolability of its borders and that legitimacy was the prerequisite to enhanced security. The Soviet Union perceived no immediate threat from the states of the Middle East in the interwar period,[5] but rather saw their role as central to the legitimation process. To a lesser extent it was also advantageous to seek good relations with the nationalist forces of the area, hoping to encourage their resistance against Britain—then the region's dominant power.

World War II facilitated a more active pursuit of traditional Soviet interests in the Middle East. In the Molotov-Ribbentrop negotiations (1940), the Kremlin made clear its intentions: "The focal points of the territorial aspirations of the Soviet Union would presumably be centered south of the territory of the Soviet Union . . ." and later elaborating that "the area south of Batum and Baku in the general direction of the Persian Gulf is recognized as the center of the aspirations of the Soviet Union."[6] Soviet interest in Turkey and the Straits was also reiterated. In 1941, through a treaty arrangement with Great Britan (which occupied the southern part of Iran), the USSR occupied a portion of northern Iran, primarily in response to concerns of increasing Iranian ties with Nazi Germany. It later encouraged a separatist movement in Iranian Azerbaijan in an effort to extend its influence. The end of hostilities provided conditions that facilitated further Soviet actions; Britain exhausted and devastated by the war, sought to narrow, and in some cases to terminate, its overseas commitments. In the Middle East this meant a gradual British withdrawal from the Arab core and the Persian Gulf regions, and the Soviet Union attempted to capitalize on the new strategic situation.

At first the Soviet Union's attention focused on Greece and Turkey, but in both cases its efforts were thwarted by U.S. military and economic aid provided under the aegis of the Truman Doctrine (1947). The Truman Doctrine was followed by the Baghdad Pact (1955), which was meant to be a permanent, collective security arrangement aimed at limiting Soviet encroachments in the area and included in its membership Great Britain, Iran, Iraq, Pakistan, and Turkey as well as the United States as a "fully cooperating though not signatory power."[7] In addition, Turkey joined NATO in 1952. Moscow viewed these developments as part of a global, U.S.-sponsored effort to threaten the Soviet Union militarily by penetrating a traditional sphere of Russian/Soviet interest and activity. The USSR reacted by shifting its focus within the region to the predominately Arab core of the Middle East and supported, albeit on a small scale, Arab independence movements and their demands for the withdrawal of Western influence from the area. It also supported Zionist aspirations for the termination of the British Mandate and the establishment of a Jewish state in Palestine. This marked an important watershed in that the Soviet state was projecting its influence and becoming active in an area traditionally considered beyond the scope of its vital interests.

In the Arab core, initial Soviet support for Israel was complemented by a hostile attitude toward the Arab League (founded in 1945), which was described as a "reactionary bloc" and a British instrument aimed at undermining the national liberation movements in the Middle East. In 1949, Soviet policy began shifting in the belief that its objectives in the Middle East could not be achieved by supporting Israel. From 1949 to 1953, Moscow's position with regard to the Arab-Israeli conflict was formally neutral, though characterized by a continuous deterioration in Soviet-Israeli relations and a corresponding improvement in relations with the Arab states. During the next two years, Moscow shifted to a cautiously pro-Arab stance that in 1955 became a policy of full diplomatic support for the Arabs in their anti-Israel and anti-West positions. That year also witnessed an important arms agreement between Egypt and the Soviet Union with Czechoslovakia acting as intermediary. The deal broke the West's monopoly over arms exports to the Middle East and was a crucial show of support for those Arab states who had become alienated from the West by European and American support for Israel. In addition, other efforts were undertaken to woo the Arab states such as the extension of economic aid, highly publicized contacts between Arab and Soviet dignitaries, and the subsidized education of Arab students in Soviet bloc universities. By the outbreak of the Suez crisis in 1956, the basic pattern of Soviet involvement had been established: the exploitation of Arab anti-Western sentiments, support for the radical Arab states and, later, the Palestine Liberation Organization in their struggle against Israel, and the selective involvement in various inter-Arab rivalries. Interregional rivalry had provided Moscow with the first foothold in the area, and any significant alleviation in the intensity of that rivalry threatened to weaken the Soviet position, at least in the short run, and potentially open the way for increased U.S. influence.

Support for those states and actors aligning themselves against Israel has been a consistent theme of Soviet foreign policy toward the Arab-Israeli zone since 1955, the extent of that commitment having been dramatically augmented over the years. By the outbreak of the June 1967 Arab-Israeli war, the Soviet Union had expanded considerably its economic and military assistance to the major Arab protagonists, Egypt and Syria. The Arab's humiliating defeat at the hands of the Israelis in 1967 further strengthened the USSR's commitment to its clients. In addition to reequiping and upgrading the armed forces of the two Arab countries, the USSR introduced in Egypt during the War of Attrition (1969/70) SA-3 surface-to-air missiles manned by Soviet personnel and provided Egypt, just before the outbreak of the October 1973 war, with advanced "Scud" battlefield-support surface-to-surface missiles. During the course of the October 1973 war, the Soviet Union undertook the military resupply of Egypt and Syria, an action that the Politburo had avoided previously.[8] Egypt's growing estrangement from the Soviet Union in the early 1970s induced the USSR to expand its ties with Syria in the expectation of that country's becoming the focus of anti-Israel and anti-U.S. Arab radicalism. This entailed greater Soviet participation in Syria's military establishment as well as the expansion of diplomatic, political, and other contacts between the two states.

Soviet support for the PLO also increased considerably. Soviet-PLO contacts were initiated during PLO Chairman Yasser Arafat's visit to Moscow in 1968. They progressed to the Soviets directly supplying arms to the PLO (1972), to Soviet advocacy of a separate

Palestinian state (1974), to Arafat's reception by Soviet General Secretary Leonid Brezhnev and the opening of a PLO representative office in Moscow (1977), and reached an acme with the upgrading of that office to full diplomatic status (1981). To Moscow, the persistence of the Palestinian issue assures the USSR access to the Arab confrontation states as well as indirect contact with the moderate Arab states. The Soviet embrace of the PLO has not been wholehearted: the USSR has not accepted the official PLO position calling for the destruction of Israel nor has it been willing to lend full support to an organization so racked with internal dissension and internecine fighting, which came particularly to the fore in late 1983 when pro-Arafat forces clashed with Syrian-backed rebel PLO units in Lebanon. Moreover, Moscow has shown considerable anxiety over Arafat's association with Arab moderates such as King Hussein of Jordan and President Hosni Mubarak of Egypt. In general, the Soviet position toward the PLO has emphasized the need to retain unity among its ranks if it is to remain an effective anti-Israel force in the Middle East.

In the 1960s, Soviet attention in the Middle East began to focus on the southern tier—Turkey, Iran, and Afghanistan—as well as to turn increasingly in the direction of the Persian Gulf/Red Sea area and North Africa. Rising nationalist sentiments and growing domestic instability had undermined the unity of the Central Treaty Organization (CENTO) and the Soviet Union attempted to capitalize on this by shifting from a policy of open hostility to one of engagement, encouraging neutrality and emphasizing the nonbelligerency of the USSR.

In the 1960s and 1970s, as Turkey became increasingly alienated from the United States, especially following the Cyprus crises, the USSR attempted a rapprochement with its traditional adversary. Political and economic contacts were fostered and, in 1974, the Soviet Union came out in support of Turkey's invasion of Cyprus, initiating a period of expanding relations between the two countries.

In the case of Iran, Soviet approaches first came in the form of economic development aid and broadened to include trade and even minor military transfers. On the whole, the relationship remained low-key, however, given the Shah's close association with the United States, and was significantly curtailed following the revolution in 1979, although the USSR has attempted to improve relations.

Soviet policy gained when, in 1978, a pro-Soviet, Marxist-Leninist faction assumed power in Afghanistan. Ties between the two countries were consolidated with the signing of a Treaty of

Friendship and Cooperation that same year followed by the extension of Soviet economic and military aid. By 1979, however, the Afghan government's attempts at fundamental reforms created such widespread popular resistance that it threatened to topple the regime. With the intention of ensuring continued influence in Afghanistan,[9] to preclude the precedent of a Soviet-backed, Marxist-Leninist regime being brought down by a popular revolt, and to guarantee the continuation of a friendly buffer on its southern border, Moscow decided to invade the country and bolster the existing regime.

Toward the Persian Gulf/Red Sea region, Soviet initiatives proved only partially successful as the majority of states tended to be suspicious of Moscow's intentions, given its association with various radical Arab states. Soviet amity with Marxist South Yemen was especially irksome since Aden was supporting insurgents against its neighbors and facilitating the USSR's access to the region through provision of naval bases and airfield facilities. The Soviet Union nonetheless developed an economic and limited military supply relationship with North Yemen and Kuwait while also promoting small-scale trade with states of the region.

Finally, as its naval presence gradually extended to the Mediterranean, the Soviet Union formed an interest in improved relations with the states of North Africa. By the mid 1970s, both Algeria and Libya had become significant customers for Soviet military equipment and openly supported radical Arab causes and movements favored by Moscow. Moreover, in the event of an outbreak of hostilities between the superpowers, a Soviet naval presence in the Mediterranean would assure the USSR an interdiction capability against European shipping, including tanker traffic, as well as provide a forward position for operations against NATO forces and bases in Southern Europe and Turkey.

Russian/Soviet history attests to the importance proximity can have to a state's foreign policies. Its location adjacent to the Middle East has sensitized the USSR to developments in the region that potentially affect its security. More recently, oil has played a prominent role in defining Soviet interests in the Middle East. The Soviet interest in the region's oil resources is often seen by Western observers in negative-strategic terms.[10] The assumption is that the Soviets want to control Persian Gulf oil because through its denial the USSR could significantly affect the economic and defense capabilities of Western Europe, Japan and, to a lesser degree, the United States. There is, however, little evidence in Soviet behavior to indicate that this is a central objective of Moscow.

The Soviet Union has never interfered in the shipment of oil through the Gulf or any other transit point and official discourse seldom raises the topic except in terms of the United States fabricating a "Soviet threat" as a pretext for U.S. intervention in the area.[11] The USSR is sensitive to the importance of Gulf oil to the West and Japan and recognizes that the United States has made a commitment in the Carter Doctrine to maintain the free flow of that resource. Moreover, the Soviet Union has an interest in maintaining stable trade relations with Western Europe, given the growing Soviet dependence on Western European markets to absorb its exports of energy products as well as to provide the USSR with capital equipment and technology. In sum, several factors militate against the USSR's seeking to gain control over Gulf oil, not the least of which is that such a move would most likely risk a confrontation with the United States.

There is, however, growing evidence to suggest that access to foreign oil supplies increasingly is becoming an important economic concern of Soviet policy. In 1977, the Central Intelligence Agency (CIA) projected a severe energy shortage for the USSR by the mid-1980s that would result from a growing demand for energy that outpaced domestic production.[12] The CIA went on to suggest that the Soviet Union would probably become a net importer of oil. Although these projections were revised to suggest that the USSR would become a net importer of oil at a later date,[13] the central point remains that whereas Soviet exports of oil continue to increase, domestic production is declining. In 1960 the USSR was producing 2.9 million barrels of oil a day (mbd). By 1970, output had more than doubled to 7.0 mbd, and it continued to increase, at a slower rate, to 11.7 mbd in 1980. Production peaked in 1983, started to decline in 1984, and dropped further in 1985. Despite the officially projected 2 percent increase in oil production for 1985, Soviet oil output for that year fell 2.6 percent.[14]

The USSR, nonetheless, has been steadily increasing its oil exports to Western markets in order to enhance its hard currency position. In 1970 exports of oil accounted for about 18 percent of the USSR's total hard currency exports, but by 1980 that figure had risen to over 50 percent and by the mid-1980s it was estimated to be about 60 percent.[15] This was made possible by rising production levels throughout th 1970s, by the steeply increasing prices paid for oil in Western markets and, to a lesser degree, by putting pressure on Moscow's East European clients to look to other sources to meet their growing energy requirements. More recently the Soviet Union has had to boost its oil exports in part because of the deleterious effects of cuts in the price of OPEC oil, which forced the USSR to reduce the price of its crude exports and hurt its foreign currency position.

In order to further increase its oil exports, the USSR also undertook measures to achieve domestic conservation, placed increased emphasis on the substitution of gas for oil, and reexported oil bought from countries such as Iran, Iraq, and Libya.[16] The Soviet Union also began to negotiate the purchase of oil from moderate Arab producers—including Saudi Arabia.[17]

The Soviet Union also sees the Middle East as an important source of hard currency, particularly through the sale of arms. The bulk of Soviet arms exports to the Third World are destined for the Middle East—almost 61 percent for the 1979–1983 period[18]—and states paying in hard currency or on a barter arrangement of oil-for-guns (Algeria, Iraq, and Libya) are prominent among Moscow's Middle Eastern customers. In 1970 arms sales comprised about 17 percent or $400 million of the Soviet Union's total hard currency exports. By 1980 the share had risen only one percent, but arms exports for hard currency now totalled $4.2 billion.[19] Current estimates put arms export earnings as a percentage of total Soviet trade earnings in the range of 25 percent or $7.9 billion in 1984.[20] The Middle East accounts for most of the Soviet Union's arms sales for hard currency. The Soviet trade relationship with the Middle East has been hampered, however, because, with the exception of military hardware, the USSR produces little of what the Middle Eastern states want. Moreover, the states of the region tend to prefer Western goods rather than Soviet products because their quality is generally deemed superior.

A final factor shaping Soviet interests in the Middle East is the region's relative instability, which the Soviet Union has sought to exploit by actively supporting those states and groups that adopt anti-United States and anti-imperialist orientations. This, in turn, has fostered a deepening reliance on the USSR for material and diplomatic/political support and helped to promote Soviet encroachment in the region.

THE MIDDLE EAST IN RECENT SOVIET PERSPECTIVE

Soviet policymakers and political commentators deal with the Middle East in terms of four sub-regions or sectors: the southern tier, the Persian Gulf/Red Sea sector, the Arab-Israeli sector, and North Africa.[21] The southern tier comprises those countries contiguous to the Soviet Union—Turkey, Iran, and Afghanistan—and

Soviet interests in the area derive largely from these states' proximity to the USSR and their potential to become a security concern. In general, since both Turkey and Iran developed ties with the United States to balance what they preceived to be an expansionist neighbor to the north, the thrust of Soviet efforts has been in the direction of preventing the establishment of military alliances, such as the Baghdad Pact (later the Central Treaty Organization), between these countries and the West. Soviet approaches to the two countries have emphasized basic state-to-state intercourse such as trade, development aid, and cultural and political exchanges in order to demonstrate that concerns about the belligerency of the USSR are unfounded, and remove the rationale for participation in any security arrangements. The Soviet Union has also tried to encourage neutralism and defiance of U.S. initiatives and exhortations. In the case of Turkey, expanding Turkish-Soviet cooperation in various fields, such as trade and scientific and cultural exchanges, is repeatedly highlighted in Soviet commentaries. An article in *International Affairs* by I. Leonidov noted the general improvement in Soviet-Turkish relations,

> . . . confirmed by the 1972 Political Declaration and the 1978 Political Document which contained the important thesis on the readiness of the sides to adhere to the principles of the non-use of force or threat of force in their relations and the refusal to allow acts of aggression and subversion against other states to be launched from their territories.[22]

Soviet approaches to Turkey have emphasized that while Turkey is a member of NATO, this "does not raise insurmountable obstacles to developing goodneighbourly relations between the two countries."[23] In particular, Moscow has been sensitive to what it views as NATO plans "to turn Turkey, and especially its areas bordering the Soviet territory, into launching pads for deploying medium-range nuclear missiles" as well as initiatives to involve the country in U.S. military and political "schemes."[24]

The Soviet Union fostered good relations with Iran prior to the overthrow of the Shah. Thereafter, Moscow gave cautious support, at first, for the regime of Ayatollah Khomeini. Soviet pronouncements stressed the necessity of preventing U.S. efforts to subvert the revolution and reestablish U.S. influence in the country. Toward this objective Andrei Gromyko and other foreign policy officials portrayed the Soviet Union as acting in the interest of its neighbor by tying the security of the Soviet state to that of Iran:

American imperialism, fearing to lose its military-political bridgehead in Iran, which it used to stifle the national liberation movement in that part of the world and to threaten the southern borders of the USSR, started to prepare plans for direct military intervention in the internal affairs of Iran threatening the country's sovereignty. Under these circumstances, Leonid Brezhnev gave a decisive warning to the USA and other Western countries regarding interference in the internal affairs of this country. "Let it be perfectly clear . . . that any, and in particular any military interference in the internal affairs of Iran—a country that borders directly on the Soviet Union—will be viewed by the USSR as affecting its own security."[25]

These efforts drew a mixed response from Teheran as the Khomeini regime was deeply suspicious of Soviet intentions. A more reserved Soviet attitude toward developments in Iran was adopted after the fundamentalist Moslem leadership branded the USSR, along with the United States, as imperialistic, following the invasion of Afghanistan in 1979. When Iran called for unity among all followers of Islam, Soviet leaders became concerned that the Khomeini regime would seek to export its revolution to the USSR's southern territories, which include sizable Muslim populations (numbering some fifty million).[26] Relations with Iran deteriorated still further in the fall of 1982 when Teheran cracked down on the Iranian Communist (Tudeh) party, dissolving it in May 1983 and expelling 18 Soviet diplomats. Soviet commentary thereafter became openly critical of Iran's internal policies as well as leaning increasingly toward Iraq in the Gulf war.

In regard to the conflict between Iran and Iraq, which was initiated in September 1980 by Iraq, the Soviet Union has emphasized that the war only benefits "U.S., Israeli, Zionist, and reactionary interests" in the region. The Gulf war, according to a Soviet commentary, prevents the two countries from participating

> . . . in the anti-imperialist struggle waged by Libya, Syria, the PDRY, Algeria, the Arab Palestinian people, and other progressive Muslims. The war has adversely affected Muslim unity against the imperialists and Zionists, because not all Muslim countries hold the same attitudes toward the Gulf war. Thus, this makes the stand and position of the Muslim countries against their common enemy—American imperialism and Zionism—weak. The Gulf war makes it easy for the imperialists to attain their designs in the area. The war provides them with a readymade excuse to transfer U.S. forces—the RDF—to southwest Asia for staging threatening military maneuvers in the region by forces armed with nuclear weapons. While the guns roar between Iran and Iraq, the United

States is busy making military preparations against Muslim countries like Libya.[27]

Soviet-Afghan relations had been developing on a steady path since the early 1950s, having been fostered by Afghan animosity toward Pakistan as well as a general Cold War climate that encouraged the taking of sides. Fundamentally, the Soviet invasion of Afghanistan in December 1979 was undertaken to prevent the country from moving away from a relationship that had been built up over the years and which, by 1978, included an openly pro-Soviet, Marxist-Leninist party in the seat of power. Officially, the Soviet Union explained its forces had been "invited" to come to the aid of a neighbor and ally beset by "direct threats from the outside." In considerable detail, Leonid Brezhnev explained the Soviet position shortly after the invasion:

> The unceasing armed intervention, the well advanced plot by external forces of reaction created a real threat that Afghanistan would lose its independence and be turned into an imperialist military bridgehead on our country's southern border. In other words, the time came when we could no longer fail to respond to the request of the government of friendly Afghanistan. To have acted otherwise would have meant leaving Afghanistan prey to imperialism ... To act otherwise would have meant to watch passively the origination on our southern border of a seat of serious danger to the security of the Soviet state. . . . The only task given to the Soviet contingents is to assist the Afghans in repulsing the aggression from outside. They will be fully withdrawn from Afghanistan once the causes that made the Afghan leadership request their introduction disappear.[28]

The Persian Gulf/Red Sea sector is of vital concern to Soviet policymakers and is generally treated as an extension of the southern tier. The USSR is sensitive to the global importance the region has assumed as access to Persian Gulf oil has become of vital strategic concern to the United States, Western Europe, and Japan, and as the United States has assumed a growing position in the Gulf, committing itself through the Carter Doctrine to maintaining the free flow of that oil by all necessary means. An article in *New Times* by Dmitri Volsky emphasized the dangerous thrust of U.S. policy toward the region as well as the security threat posed by the U.S. presence in the Gulf and the Indian Ocean: "the long-term aim is to establish U.S. military control over the 'oil tap'. . . , to grip the Moslem world in a vice, and, most important, to create an additional military springboard on the southern frontiers of the U.S.S.R."[29] Similarly, Gagik Drambyants, also writing in *New Times*, asserted that the Gulf war has provided U.S. policymakers with

... a pretext for the further expansion of their military presence in the Middle East and the Indian Ocean, for the setting up of new military bases there, and for stepping up their arms buildup with the object of establishing American military and political control over one of the richest oil-producing areas of the world. Washington's strategy is projected at arrogating to itself the right to be the sole arbiter of the destinies of the Persian Gulf countries and guarantor of stability in the area.[30]

In the Persian Gulf/Red Sea sector, the Soviet Union maintains close relations only with the People's Democratic Republic of Yemen (PDRY). A Soviet Foreign Ministry official, Valery Sukhin, described Soviet-PDRY relations as "not merely multifacted.... They are characterized by their completeness, by their 'totality'... They are all-embracing."[31] Strong ties with the PDRY has enabled the USSR to establish a sizeable presence in the country (some 2,325 economic and 1,100 military technicians from the USSR and Eastern Europe were stationed in the PDRY in 1984[32]) and has facilitated the acquisition of important support facilities for the expanding Soviet naval presence in the Indian Ocean and Persian Gulf.[33]

Other states of the region have been wary of Soviet approaches, particularly in light of the USSR's support for South Yemen, which has shown a propensity to stir up internal discontent and engage in military hostilities with its immediate neighbors—North Yemen and Oman. The Soviet Union, nevertheless, acknowledges a

...growing desire of Persian Gulf states to pursue a more balanced foreign policy. The Soviet Union's unchanging policy of supporting the Arab people of Palestine in their just struggle and the Arab nations in their fight against Israel's aggressive expansionist policy has earned it the respect of the monarchs in the region. The constructive Soviet stance with regard to issues bearing upon the situation in the Persian Gulf has also played a definite role.[34]

In approaching the states of this region the USSR has emphasized its peaceful intentions based on mutually beneficial trade relations and respect of state sovereignty. In connection with this the Kremlin has tried to portray itself as a "peace broker," supporting the plan to make the Indian Ocean a zone of peace, which was put forward by the nonaligned countries and adopted in similar form by the UN General Assembly in 1971. The USSR has also announced its own proposal for the demilitarization and neutrality of the Persian Gulf, which Leonid Brezhnev presented in 1980. The five point Brezhnev plan, advanced at the outbreak of the Gulf war, is more in the direction of dislocating rather than replacing U.S. influence in the area and entails the following proposals:

1. Not to establish foreign military bases in the Persian Gulf and on the littoral islands, and not to station nuclear or other weapons of mass destruction there;
2. Not to use, or threaten to use, force against the Persian Gulf states, and not to meddle in their internal affairs;
3. To respect the status of nonalignment chosen by the Persian Gulf states, and not to attempt to draw them into military alliances with nuclear powers;
4. To respect the sovereign right of the Persian Gulf states to their natural resources; and
5. Not to create obstacles or threats to normal trade and the use of sea communications linking these states with other countries.[35]

While not of the same strategic significance to the USSR as the southern tier or the Persian Gulf/Red Sea region, the Arab-Israeli sector has received considerable attention from policymakers and political commentators in the Soviet Union. The struggle against Israel is viewed as one of the most enduring factors promoting Arab unity and presents for the Soviet Union, through its support for the Arab cause, opportunities for the extension of its influence in the region. From the Soviet perspective, the United States collaborates with Israel's "ruling Zionist circles" in order to facilitate territorial, political, and economic expansion in the Middle East.[36] To effect this, they have pursued a strategy of *"divide et impera,"* creating and exacerbating divisions within the Arab camp by promoting "separate deals and partial solutions" such as the Camp David Accords. Evgeni Primakov, a prominent Soviet Middle East observer, argues that Camp David can never lead to a comprehensive settlement in the Middle East because it is "aimed at leading Egypt away from its posture of confrontation, thereby undermining the position of the Arabs and creating conditions which would make it easier for Israel to pursue its expansionist course against an Arab world weakened by Egypt's withdrawal."[37] The Israeli invasion of Lebanon in June 1982 is portrayed by Soviet commentators as the logical outcome of this policy of separate deals:

> Camp David in action—is in short the escalation of Israel's acts of aggression. . . .It was precisely after Egypt, the biggest and most industrialized country in the Arab world, was put out of the struggle in which Israel succeeded to annex East Jerusalem and then the Golan Heights, bomb the atomic research centre in Iraq and perpetuate other aggressive sallies against the Arab countries. . . .[T]he recent aggression in Lebanon . . .[is] the price that has been paid for Sadat's separate deal with Israel and the U.S.A.[38]

Soviet initiatives toward the Arab-Israeli sector have been two-pronged: diplomatic and strategic. On the one hand, the Soviets affirm the sovereignty of Israel as recently restated by General Secretary Mikhail Gorbachev: "We took part in the establishment of the State of Israel. We recognize the sovereignty of that state and its right to exist and to have security. But as for how security is understood by the ruling circles of Israel and by us, we have large differences here."[39] They emphasize, however, the need to reach a comprehensive settlement of the Arab-Israeli conflict, one that brings together all involved parties including the PLO, the Soviet Union, and the United States. Moscow has forwarded several proposals, the latest of which was on July 30, 1984.[40] Similar to the Arab position adopted at the Fez Summit Conference,[41] the Soviet position is based on a rejection of the forcible seizure of territories and calls for:

> ...the withdrawal of the Israeli forces from all the Arab territories occupied in 1967 and also from Lebanon; respect for the inalienable right of the Arab people of Palestine, the sole lawful representative of which is the Palestine Liberation Organization, to self-determination, including their own independent statehood; the return to the Arabs of the eastern part of Jerusalem; respect of the right of all states to a secure and independent existence; termination of the state of war; mutual respect of each other's sovereignty, independence and territorial integrity; international guarantees of a settlement which could be provided by the permanent members of the Security Council or the Security Council as a whole.[42]

Concomitant with efforts toward a comrehensive settlement the Soviet Union has attempted, according to Y. Glukhov writing in *International Affairs,* to promote its own strategic alliance in the aftermath of Camp David by calling for

> ... the broadest possible actions in the Arab world and in every country against the humiliating and shameful Treaty; closer cooperation between the progressive and patriotic forces and regimes in the Arab countries with a view to forming the widest possible militant front; stronger cooperation and alliance with the Soviet Union.[43]

The "Steadfastness and Confrontation Front," comprising Syria, South Yemen, Libya, Algeria, and the PLO, was seen as fulfilling such a mission by striving to be a regional grouping aligned against Israel and any Arab state concluding a separate peace with the Jewish state. Bickering among the participants, divided reaction to the Soviet invasion of Afghanistan, and disunity within the PLO hampered the effectiveness of the Front. Moreover, the role of Egypt as the major confrontation state was not replaced by any other state even though the Soviet Union had banked on Syria's becoming the region's bulwark against Israeli expansionism. An article in *International Affairs* by F. Nikiforov nevertheless stressed that the

> . . . fight for a just and all-encompassing Middle East settlement is the focus of Soviet-Syrian interaction. The core of this struggle is the demand (to offset the course of the USA and Israel for separate deals) for the convocation of an international conference on the Middle East in whose proceedings all interested sides could take part as equals. . . . [Moreover, the Soviet Union assesses] highly the consistent anti-imperialist line of Syria which is upholding the Arab's national interests and legitimate rights. With Syrian support the Lebanese national-patriotic forces inflicted palpable blows to US-Israeli plans in that country. The American-NATO forces were forced to leave Lebanon, and the Lebanese government later announced the annulment of the Lebanese-Israeli "peace" agreement of May 17, 1983, which infringed on the sovereignty of Lebanon and posed a threat to the security of other Arab states. Under such circumstances, the Israeli government had no other choice than to announce the withdrawal of the occupation forces from Lebanon.[44]

While the USSR has consistently stated, since the early 1970s, that the PLO is the sole and legitimate representative of the Palestinian people, divisions within the organization's ranks have been recognized by Moscow as a major weakness, detracting from its ability to wage the campaign against Israel. In particular the struggle for leadership within the PLO has placed Soviet decision makers in an uncomfortable position: when the USSR's ally, Syria, attempted to dominate the PLO by setting up its own rival Palestinian faction and bypassing Arafat, the Kremlin sought to avoid having to choose between the pro-Arafat forces and those of the Syrian surrogate. Echoing Politburo sentiments, then-Foreign Minister Andrei Gromyko expressed "deep concern over the unnatural fractricidal clashes among Palestinians, irrespective of the cause" and stressed that the PLO would be a more effective force in the Middle East if it were unified and worked closely with "the national patriotic forces of the Arab world, above all with Syria."[45]

From the Soviet perspective, the Palestinian issue is "a major political factor that serves to cement the Arab peoples' struggle against Israeli aggression and imperialist schemes in the region."[46] The short-lived Amman Agreement of February 11, 1985, between Yasser Arafat and King Hussein of Jordan,[47] which was a joint PLO-Jordanian approach to peace in the Middle East, was interpreted in the Soviet Union as a move that threatened to undermine the unity of the PLO. In particular, it

> ... threw overboard the problem of an independent Palestine state, weakened the independent status of the PLO as the exclusive legitimate representative of the Palestine people, and as an equal partner in the settlement process.[48]

Turning to North Africa, Soviet policymakers and political commentators do not give much attention to this sector and focus primarily on the mutually beneficial trade relations with states of the region, the advocacy and participation of Algeria and, especially, Libya in "progressive" Arab causes and movements, and the strategic significance of the Mediterranean. Libya is seen as an important radicalizing factor in North Africa, challenging the *status quo* regimes of the area, acting as a check on U.S. encroachments and supporting various terrorist groups. The official Soviet news agency, *TASS*, has described Soviet-Libyan relations as based on mutual interests and cooperation, particularly in North Africa, where the two countries have "asserted the need for the hotbeds of tension prevailing there to be eliminated and confirmed their readiness to make constructive efforts in the interests of strengthening peace, security, and cooperation for the good of the peoples of the region."[49] General Secretary Gorbachev, after meeting with Libyan leader Muammar Qaddafi in mid-October 1985, also reaffirmed "the broad coincidence of our positions on the more important and pressing international issues, those connected with the Middle East and Africa above all."[50]

There has been a heightened Soviet concern over U.S. involvement in the Mediterranean. A commentary in *Izvestia*, the official Soviet government newspaper, has argued that Washington's intentions in the Southern Mediterranean are directed at transforming the area into a "zone of U.S. imperial pretensions":

> There is the U.S. striving to lay its hands on the tremendous wealth, especially oil, ... attempts to intimidate the national liberation movement of the peoples of the Arab East and the African Continent, and the readiness to interfere in the internal affairs of those countries where changes displeasing to Washington are taking place. ... But the main matter is the U.S. military-strategic designs aimed at transforming the Mediterranean into a bridgehead for the implementation of its aggressive schemes against the Soviet Union and other socialist countries.[51]

The Soviet Union regards itself as a "Black Sea and, consequently, a Mediterranean power" and asserts that its naval buildup in the Mediterranean has been undertaken to check the U.S. presence, which directly threatens the USSR with its nuclear capability while also enabling it to "conduct local wars and perform police functions."[52] The USSR has also tried to muster support for the creation of a demilitarized Mediterranean zone. Similar to Brezhnev's Persian Gulf proposals, the thrust of this initiative is to alleviate the threat to the USSR of medium-range missiles based in Southern Europe and Turkey. Among the proposals are:

> ... that the naval activities in these regions should be limited, that the establishment of foreign military bases and the deployment of nuclear arms there should be banned, and that the threat of force and interference in the internal affairs of the countries in these regions should be prohibited.[53]

INSTRUMENTS OF POLICY

The Soviet Union has employed a range of policy instruments to secure its interests in the Middle East. In broadest terms, they fall into three categories: military support and aid, diplomatic-political initiatives, and trade and economic assistance. One of the most prominent tools of Soviet policy is military, which takes several forms including the transfer of military equipment, support for the military activity of others, the use of surrogates, and direct involvement in military conflict.

The Soviet Union has been willing to sell, often on concessionary terms, armaments to several Middle Eastern states. For the 1979–1983 period, 61 percent of all Soviet arms exports to the Third World went to states of the southern tier and to other Middle Eastern countries such as Algeria, Libya, and Syria (see Table 3.1). In addition, direct or indirect arms transfers to guerrilla and terrorist organizations like the PLO have become an increasingly major component of Soviet policy, as demonstrated by the substantial quantities of Soviet weapons captured and destroyed by Israeli forces in Lebanon in 1982.

Following the 1973 oil price increases and the consequent influx of petrodollars to the Middle East, the Soviet Union has been less willing to transfer arms on concessionary terms.[54] In effect, arms sales have assumed an important commercial value for the USSR as

TABLE 3.1: Soviet and Eastern European Arms Exports to the Middle East, 1979–1983 (millions of U.S. dollars)

Recipient	USSR	Eastern Europe	Total	USSR as Percent of Total
Afghanistan	1,800	20	1,830	98.4
Algeria	3,200	—	3,660	87.4
Egypt	40	50	5,645	0.7
Iran	975	45	5,365	18.2
Iraq	7,200	1,290	17,620	40.9
Jordan	230	—	3,430	6.7
Kuwait	30	—	450	6.7
Libya	5,800	1,115	12,095	48.0
PDRY	1,500	—	1,510	99.3
Syria	9,200	520	10,530	87.4
Yemen	1,200	260	2,355	51.0
Middle East	31,175	3,300	86,975	35.8
Third World	51,280	4,025	137,375	37.3

Source: U.S., Arms Control and Disarmament Agency, *World Military Expenditures and Arms Transfers, 1985*, Pub. 123 (August 1985), pp. 131–34.

payment has been increasingly demanded in advance in hard currency or in exchange for commodities that are then reexported to earn hard currency. In many instances, arms that are exported are state of the art. This is in sharp contrast to the 1950s and 1960s, when the Soviets sold arms that were primarily surplus, refurbished, or obsolete equipment. Beginning in the 1970s, the Soviet Union introduced into the Middle East some of its most advanced systems, including the MiG-25 interceptor, the T-72 main battle tank, and the SA-5 air defense and SS-21 surface-to-surface missiles. These systems are sometimes provided in export versions, without their most sophisticated components.

Finally, technical assistance has played a growing role as a follow-on to state-of-the-art arms transfers. Military personnel from the USSR and Eastern Europe perform advisory, maintenance, and training functions, and in 1984 there were almost 12,000 of these personnel stationed in the Middle East (see Table 3.2).

The persistence of regional instability has fuelled a demand for the import of military goods and services and facilitated the USSR's efforts at developing relationships with states throughout the

TABLE 3.2: Soviet and Eastern European Military Technicians in the Middle East[a] (number of persons, rounded to nearest five)

	1965	1970	1975	1979	1984
Middle East	2,105	8,840	5,905	7,615	11,900
World	3,635	10,125	8,220	15,865	21,335

Sources: U.S. Central Intelligence Agency (CIA), National Foreign Assessment Center, *Communist Aid Activities In Non-Communist Less Developed Countries, 1979 and 1954–79,* Publ. ER 80-10318U (October 1980), p. 6; CIA, Directorate of Intelligence, *Handbook of Economic Statistics, 1985: A Reference Aid,* Publ. CPAS 85-10001 (September 1985), pp. 122–23.

[a]Excludes Afghanistan.

Middle East. In turn, these relationships contribute to the expansion of Soviet influence as well as creating dependencies based on the provision of new and replacement equipment, spare parts, and ancillary military services. Finally, military assistance has provided a mechanism through which the Soviet Union is able to increase ties to the moderates of the region like Jordan and Kuwait, both of which, rebuffed by U.S. refusals to provide certain types of advanced weapons, have turned on occasion to the Soviet Union for the provision of arms.[55]

In general, the Soviet Union's military assistance program has not been without its drawbacks. While central to establishing and expanding relations with states of the region, the surge in arms exports has not necessarily led to a commensurate increase in the USSR's influence in those states. Egypt was heavily dependent on the supply of Soviet military equipment and ancillary services (in 1972 there were an estimated 15–20,000 Soviet military advisors and technicians in Egypt) but Egypt and the Soviet Union disagreed on the nature, delivery, and use of Soviet arms and there was friction between Egyptian officers and Soviet advisors. Egyptian leaders were also concerned about the Sovietization of the military and the satellitization of their country. Egypt severed its military association with the USSR in 1972. In the case of Iraq, concern over excessive dependence on the Soviet Union led that state to diversify its sources of supply, and Algeria has also recently moved in this direction, showing a renewed interest in purchasing arms from the United States and other suppliers. Libya, on the other hand, has adopted a policy from the outset of diversifying its sources of arms supply.

A more complex, though less frequently employed, Soviet policy instrument is support for the military activity of its Middle East clients. In 1970 during the War of Attrition between Egypt and Israel, Soviet pilots flew combat missions against Israel in response to a request from President Gamal Abdul Nasser for additional Soviet military aid to counter Israeli deep interdiction air strikes in Egyptian territory. On the whole, this move had a positive outcome for the Soviet Union: although pilots were lost in encounters with the Israeli air force, Soviet prestige in the Arab world was bolstered because of its willingness to come to the direct aid of Egypt. The Soviet Union has also supported Syria in opposition to Israel's military intervention in Lebanon. In addition to replacing military equipment lost during the fighting with Israel in 1982—including substantial numbers of aircraft—the Soviet Union supplied Syria for the first time with long-range SA-5 surface-to-air missiles and mobile battlefield-support SS-21 surface-to-surface missiles, the latter having a dual capability of delivering either nuclear or conventional weapons. The only other country to take delivery of the SA-5 has been Libya (1985), while Syria remains the exclusive recipient of the SS-21. Moreover, in the case of the SA-5 delivery was made to Syria even prior to deployment in Eastern Europe. An estimated 5,000 Soviet military personnel were also sent to Syria in late 1982 and early 1983 to operate, and to train the Syrians to use, the missile systems. By mid-1985, however, some 3,000 of those military technicians had been withdrawn, suggesting that the USSR had turned responsibility for the missiles over to the Syrians.

Another policy instrument is the sponsoring of surrogate states. In the past, South Yemen acted on behalf of Soviet interests, in part by serving as a center for Soviet weapons transshipment, aid disbursement, and training for terrorist and other radical groups such as the Popular Front for the Liberation of Palestine, the Japanese Red Army, and Spanish Basque separatists. It provided a base of operations for, and channeled Soviet aid to, rebels operating in the Dhofar province of Oman and played a key role in facilitating the massive Soviet airlifts of weapons to Ethiopia in 1977/78. Finally, it has made available to the Soviet Union airfield and port facilities on the island of Socotra and at Aden.

The USSR also has used its relationship with Libya to assist in the transshipment of Soviet weapons to other Soviet clients. In April 1983, for example, four Libyan transport planes, ostensibly loaded with medical supplies bound for Nicaragua, landed for refueling in Brazil. On inspection by Brazilian authorities, the planes were discovered to be transporting military equipment, including anti-aircraft emplacements, rocket launchers, rifles, machine guns and at least two disassembled trainer planes, all of which were of either Soviet or Czechoslovak manufacture.[56]

Finally, Soviet Middle East policy has relied on direct involvement in military conflict. The USSR invaded Afghanistan in 1979 to consolidate a pro-Soviet, Marxist-Leninist regime and to neutralize Afghan internal opposition and, by the end of 1985, retained an estimated 120,000 troops in the country. This represents the first instance since the 1940s in which the Soviet military has been involved overtly and directly in combat outside the Soviet bloc. Given U.S., European, and Japanese interests in and resolve to maintain the integrity of the Persian Gulf (in addition to the geographic illogic of using Afghanistan as a jumping off point), it is doubtful that the invasion was part of a broader Soviet military effort to secure control over the entire Gulf region or its oil resources. Moreover, since the British withdrawal from India, Afghanistan has not played a strategic role in the designs of any Western state. As such, the Soviet use of the military instrument should be considered *sui generis* and not a precedent for a more adventurous form of Soviet involvement in the Middle East.

Diplomatic-political measures are another policy instrument widely utilized in the Middle East. Major Soviet diplomatic-political initiatives have included the conclusion of treaties, the expansion of relations to moderate Arab states, the fashioning for itself of a permanent role in the Arab-Israeli peace process and, lastly, the maintenance of party-to-party contacts. More treaties of "Friendship and Cooperation" have been concluded between the USSR and various Middle Eastern states than with all other states combined, excluding the network of agreements binding the states of Eastern Europe and the Soviet Union into the Warsaw Pact framework. In the last decade and a half, the USSR has entered into treaty relationships with Egypt (1971, abrogated in 1976), Iraq (1972), Afghanistan (1978), South Yemen (1979), Syria (1980), and North Yemen (1984), and has tried, unsuccessfully to date, to obtain one with Libya. The 1978 Treaty of Friendship and Cooperation between the Soviet Union and Afghanistan provided the legal pretext for the invasion of that country under a clause that permitted the parties to "take appropriate measures to ensure the security, independence and territorial integrity of the two countries."[57] In general, these treaties commit the Soviet Union to facilitate its partners' independence and security. In practice this has meant the institutionalization of relationships based on the long-term supply of military hardware and economic aid, which creates and perpetuates dependence on the Soviet Union and serves as a vehicle for the wielding of Soviet influence. Success in creating this dependence has varied, however. Iraq, formerly heavily dependent on the Soviet bloc, especially for military aid, was able to reduce its dependence on the USSR by securing armaments from France and others as well as expanding trade ties with various Western states. In November 1984, Iraq also restored diplomatic relations with the United States, which had been suspended since the June 1967 Arab-Israeli war. Nor have commitments made in treaties been rigidly binding or faithfully implemented: The USSR took more than two years following the outbreak of the Gulf war to reinstate military deliveries to Iraq, in spite of being committed in the 1972 Treaty of Friendship and Cooperation to coordinate with Iraq "their positions to remove the threat that has arisen or to restore peace" as well as "to develop their cooperation in the matter of strengthening their defence capacity."[58] Changing circumstances in the conflict and the deterioration of its relations with Iran influenced the Soviet decision.

In recent years, the Soviet Union has expanded its relationship with states such as Saudi Arabia, the United Arab Emirates (UAE) and others in the Persian Gulf that are known for their moderate stance in Arab politics and their anti-Communist orientation. The USSR has or had at one time diplomatic relations with Saudi Arabia, Morocco, Kuwait, Jordan, and the UAE, although diplomatic missions were not established nor representatives accredited to all (see Table 3.3).

In 1985, Kuwait and the UAE were the only Gulf states with which the Soviet Union had diplomatic relations. Soviet efforts to expand its influence in Kuwait have met with little success because of Saudi Arabia's influential role in Kuwaiti and Gulf affairs as well as Kuwait's desire to maintain a posture of nonalignment. The occasional and limited sale of armaments has facilitated the more significant inroads. The USSR was successful in establishing full diplomatic relations with the UAE in late 1985. The UAE had expressed interest in the past in exchanging diplomatic missions with the USSR, but Saudi Arabia was instrumental in preventing the country from taking any steps beyond initial contacts made in the early 1970s. Finally, an agreement to open relations with Oman was reached in late 1985 and is a significant development. Not only is Oman one of the United States' closest allies in the Gulf, but the country in the past has also been extremely wary of Soviet approaches because the USSR had channeled aid via South Yemen to rebels operating in the Dhofar province of Oman. It appears that

TABLE 3.3: Chronology of the USSR's Establishment of Diplomatic Relations with the States of the Middle East

Date	Country (comment)
April 7 – May 27, 1919	Afghanistan
May 20, 1920	Iran
June 2 – Nov. 29, 1920	Turkey
August 6, 1924	Hejaz (February 16–19, 1926, with Kingdom of Hejas, Nejd and its dependencies. From 1932: Kingdom of Saudi Arabia. No diplomatic missions established or representatives accredited)
Nov. 1, 1928	Yemen (Diplomatic missions not actually established until 1955. Full diplomatic relations established Oct. 31, 1955)
May 16, 1941	Iraq (Interrupted Jan. 3–8, 1955; restored July 18–19, 1958.)
July 6–26, 1943	Egypt
July 21–29, 1944	Syria
July 31 – August 3, 1944	Lebanon
May 15–18, 1948	Israel (Interrupted June 9, 1967, following the June 1967 Arab-Israeli war)
August 31 – Sept. 4, 1955	Libya
June 11 – July 11, 1956	Tunisia
August 29 – Sept. 4, 1958	Morocco
March 19–23, 1962	Algeria
March 11, 1963	Kuwait
August 20, 1963	Jordan
December 1–3, 1967	South Yemen
December 8–23, 1971	United Arab Emirates (Full diplomatic relations established Nov. 13, 1985a)
September 26, 1985	Oman (Agreement on exchange of representativesb)

aPravda (November 16, 1985): *Abu Dhabi Domestic Service*, November 15, 1985.
bIzvestia (September 27, 1985).
Source: A. Akhtamzyan, "The Chronicle of the USSR's Establishment of Diplomatic Relations with Foreign Countries," *International Affairs* (Moscow) 5 (May 1984), pp. 138–41.

the 1985 agreement represents a Soviet guarantee that the territorial integrity of Oman will henceforth be respected.

The Soviet Union would like, at a minimum, to expand its representative presence to other states of the region. In the case of Saudi Arabia, the USSR plays on Saudi disquietude over developments in Iran and mutual concerns about the Camp David peace process while also attempting to build on contacts it had with the country prior to the establishment of the Kingdom of Saudi Arabia in 1932. The Soviet Union had opened diplomatic relations with Saudi Arabia in the 1920s, but no missions were established as Saudi leaders subsequently refused to recognize the Soviet Union or any other Communist state. Moscow continues to press for the exchange of diplomatic representatives, although little official Saudi interest has been forthcoming. In approaching Saudi Arabia and other Gulf states the USSR has also tried to underscore the positive aspects of the Soviet system as well as the freedom of religion granted to its Moslem populations, although it is not clear whether the latter point is credible in the Arab world.

Approaches have been made to other moderate states in different sectors of the Middle East. In the Arab-Israeli sector the Soviets have courted with varying degrees of success Jordan, Egypt, and Lebanon as well as Morocco in North Africa. On the whole, the Jordanians have been hesitant about developing close ties with the USSR, but this has not prevented them from expanding commercial relations or turning on occasion to the Soviet Union to purchase arms. An important diplomatic gain for the Kremlin came in the spring of 1984 when Jordan's King Hussein advocated including the Soviet Union in any peace negotiations and settlement in the region.[59] Notwithstanding, many factors work against the establishment of a strong Soviet presence in Jordan including the country's fundamentally moderate stance in Arab politics, its long association with the United States, its antagonism toward some of the USSR's friends in the region (Syria and Libya), and its continuing suspicion of Soviet intentions toward the Middle East.[60]

The Soviet Union has had some success in improving ties with Egypt. From the outset of Anwar Sadat's tenure in power, Soviet-Egyptian relations were characterized by increasing estrangement and mutual animosity. They reached a low with the withdrawal of the Egyptian ambassador to the USSR in 1978, a move taken in response to harsh Soviet criticism of President Sadat's peace initiative toward Israel. Egypt later expelled the Soviet ambassador and six embassy aides in 1981. Hosni Mubarak's assumption of leadership following Sadat's assassination in 1981 brought a thaw in Soviet-Egyptian relations as the new President sought to distance Egypt somewhat from the United States and to reintegrate the country into the Arab fold. In the case of Lebanon, the Soviet Union has attempted to foster better relations through the offer of economic and military aid, augmenting its efforts after the withdrawal of United States and West European forces from the country in 1984. Although the response of the Lebanese government has been non-committal, the fluidity of the political situation in Lebanon and strong Soviet ties with Syria add to the prospects for the realization of a Soviet role in the country. Finally, Soviet approaches toward Morocco have met with some success, being based for the most part on trade and aid programs. A major factor hampering Soviet initiatives has been Moscow's cordial relations with Morocco's traditional adversary, Algeria, as well as its advocacy and support for the Polisario rebels in the Western Sahara. In maintaining a neutral posture on the conflict in the Sahara, the Soviet Union's Eastern European allies have, in fact, made considerably more progress in establishing a presence in Morocco.

Perhaps the most extensive USSR diplomatic-political efforts have been expended to secure an increased role in the Arab-Israeli peace process. The principal objective of Moscow's approaches has been to achieve a return to the concept of a reconvened Geneva Middle East Peace Conference. That conference only met once, in December 1973, following the October War, and was attended by representatives from the USSR, the United States, Egypt, Jordan, and Israel (Syria refused to participate). The United States and the Soviet Union served as co-chairs of the conference.[61] In the Soviet view, the Geneva Conference created the framework for the institutionalization of a role for the Soviet Union in the Middle East peace process and provided the USSR with access to all the major parties to the conflict.[62] The Conference was not reconvened and Moscow accused the United States of substituting

> ... partial, separate steps on a bilateral basis for the cardinal solution of the principal questions of Middle East settlement ... [and of focusing] its main efforts on prying away Egypt from other Arab states and reorienting foreign policy from cooperation with the Soviet Union and other socialist countries to cooperation with the West.[63]

Soviet hopes for participation in the peace process were rekindled in 1977 when Secretary of State Cyrus Vance and Foreign Minister Andrei Gromyko issued a joint statement on the Middle East calling for, among other things, a comprehensive settlement of the

Arab-Israeli conflict "within the framework of the Geneva peace conference . . . with participation in its work of the representatives of all parties involved in the conflict."[64] The Carter administration believed that the Soviet Union could play a constructive role in the peace process and, under correct circumstances, would participate in the promotion of economic development and stability in the Middle East.

The communique was abandoned quickly by the United States because of domestic protest in the United States and opposition from both Israel and Egypt. The Soviets interpreted this as another move to exclude them from the peace process, signaling a resumption of a strategy of "bilaterial separate bargains." The Soviet Union currently seeks a return to the procedures envisaged by the joint statement, in part because it invited the USSR back into the Arab-Israeli peace process for the first time since the conclusion of the October War in 1973. At present, there is little prospect for that to happen as long as the Reagan administration holds the view that the Soviet Union is the major impediment to peace and stability in the Middle East. Moreover, the major parties to the conflict such as Egypt and Israel are reluctant to have Soviet participation, while others, notably Syria, would like to see Soviet participation, but have shown little commitment themselves to participate. In the final analysis, the fundamental dilemma facing the Soviet Union is that of seeking, but not being able, to establish for itself a constructive and permanent role in the Middle East peace process.

A discussion of diplomatic-political means is not complete without considering Soviet relations with the Communist parties of the Middle East. In general, the performance of the various Middle Eastern Communist parties has been dismal and it is doubtful that the USSR considers these organizations significant in their respective countries' political dynamics. In some states, no party organization of consequence exists (Bahrain, Libya, Saudi Arabia); in others the party is proscribed (Egypt, Iran, Jordan, Turkey) or strictly controlled by the regime in power (Iraq, Syria). The two instances of ruling Communist parties are in South Yemen and Afghanistan, while Lebanon and Israel have been the only democracies in which the Communist parties have had a moderate degree of success in terms of membership and participation in politics.

Soviet policy toward the Middle East has emphasized the role of state-to-state relations while assigning a position of secondary importance to party-to-party contacts. The establishment of diplomatic relations with various Middle Eastern states was central to the Soviet Union's strategy to break out of the diplomatic isolation imposed on it by the West following the October 1917 revolution. Moreover, the Middle East is an area of long-standing Russian/Soviet interests, which has prompted Moscow to establish relations with as many states as possible in order to gain influence over regional developments. The Soviet leadership maintained sound relations with Egypt in the 1950s and 1960s even though Egypt's communists were being brutally persecuted by Nasser. The same is true in Syria and Iraq.[65] The USSR rationalizes its support for regimes that persecute local Communist parties by noting that socioeconomic conditions in these countries are not ripe for the development of genuine worker/peasant movements; nonetheless, they are capable of making a positive contribution in the broader struggle between imperialism and socialism through their adoption of anti-imperialist and nationalist policies as well as espousal of certain socialist tenets. The USSR's objective then becomes, at a minimum, to reinforce those currents that are interpreted as "progressive" (e.g., anti-imperialism), while discouraging those which are detrimental to Soviet interests.

The final category of policy instruments encompasses trade and economic assistance. In general, Soviet trade with the states of the Middle East is not significant and has declined as a percentage of total trade (see Tables 3.4 and 3.5). In descending order of magnitude, the top five Middle Eastern countries importing Soviet goods for the decade 1975–1984 were Iran, Afghanistan, Egypt, Turkey, and Iraq; those Middle Eastern countries exporting to the USSR over the same period were Afghanistan, Egypt, Syria, Turkey, and Algeria.[66] Exports from the Middle East to the USSR tend to be comprised of fuels, industrial consumer goods, and textiles and clothing while the Soviet Union exports machinery and equipment, and arms (this last component is not reported in Soviet trade statistics but is assumed to make up most of the unspecified commodities category).[67]

Economic considerations play a role in determining Soviet trade relations with states in the Middle East. In particular the Soviet Union has benefited from increased hard currency earnings through trade with states like Algeria, Iraq, and Libya. Political motivations also contribute to the direction and terms of trade. The fundamentally anti-Communist orientation of the Gulf states has hampered the USSR's efforts to develop trade relations of consequence with these countries.[68] In the southern tier, trade has been instrumental in serving as a basis upon which other relations, including political, are built. It has also functioned as a vehicle through which the Soviet Union seeks to demonstrate its peaceful intentions toward

TABLE 3.4: Soviet Imports[a] from the Middle East (millions of U.S. dollars)

Country[b]	1960	1965	1970	1975	1980	1984
Afghanistan	17	19	33	86	397	358
Algeria	—	4	49	97	94	15
Egypt	121	143	293	606	128	136
Iran	19	19	—	54	—	—
Iraq	3	3	5	—	—	—
Israel	—	1	—	—	—	—
Jordan	—	—	—	—	—	—
Kuwait	—	—	—	—	—	—
Lebanon	4	2	3	10	23	21
Libya	—	—	—	—	—	—
Morocco	4	12	14	46	123	43
Oman	—	—	—	—	—	—
PDRY	—	—	—	—	—	—
Qatar	—	—	—	—	—	—
Saudi Arabia	—	—	—	—	—	—
Syria	8	19	17	55	117	203
Tunisia	2	1	3	9	5	2
Turkey	5	20	29	74	169	108
UAE	—	—	—	—	—	—
Yemen	1	—	1	—	—	—
Mideast	184	243	447	1,037	1,056	886
World	1,851	2,467	4,523	19,321	35,263	34,897
Mideast / World	9.9%	9.9%	9.9%	5.4%	3.0%	2.5%

[a]Imports are FOB.

[b]For all countries, data for one or more years derived; see yearbooks for methods.

Sources: International Bank for Reconstruction and Development (IBRD) and International Monetary Fund (IMF), *Direction of Trade: A Supplement to International Financial Statistics, 1960–64,* 1964, pp. 382–83; IBRD and IMF, *Direction of Trade Statistics Yearbook, 1964–68,* 1968, pp. 385–86; IMF, *Direction of Trade Statistics Yearbook, 1970–76,* 1976, pp. 259, 292; IMF, *Direction of Trade Statistics Yearbook, 1982,* 1982, pp. 387–88; IMF, *Direction of Trade Statistics Yearbook, 1985,* 1985, pp. 392–93.

these states. Prior to its intervention in Afghanistan in 1979, the USSR had become one of that country's major trading partners in addition to disbursing substantial sums of development aid. Iran and Turkey, despite strong ties with the West, became trading partners of the Soviet state. In the aftermath of the Iranian revolution, Soviet efforts were directed at maintaining normal relations, facilitated by trade between the two countries, in the face of an increasingly anti-Soviet Iranian attitude. In the case of Turkey, through

TABLE 3.5: Soviet Exports to the Middle East (millions of U.S. dollars)

Country[a]	1960	1965	1970	1975	1980	1984
Afghanistan	32	55	34	76	455	410
Algeria	2	10	41	65	48	44
Egypt	70	76	88	212	70	160
Iran	18	11	53	210	647	577
Iraq	20	30	49	94	123	109
Israel	—	—	1	—	—	—
Jordan	—	3	6	4	17	29
Kuwait	—	5	7	5	14	9
Lebanon	4	5	12	18	25	22
Libya	—	3	9	20	62	26
Morocco	6	9	30	67	138	95
Oman	—	—	—	1	—	—
PDRY	—	2	1	5	8	7
Qatar	—	—	—	—	2	—
Saudi Arabia	—	—	6	3	50	17
Syria	11	6	25	48	41	127
Tunisia	3	5	3	5	26	39
Turkey	8	15	35	67	164	219
UAE	—	—	4	6	3	5
Yemen	4	—	3	8	13	5
Mideast	178	235	407	914	1,906	1,900
World	1,517	2,291	3,913	13,080	32,426	32,816
Mideast/World	11.7%	10.3%	10.4%	7.0%	5.9%	5.8%

[a]For all countries, data for one or more years derived; see yearbooks for methods.

Sources: International Bank for Reconstruction and Development (IBRD) and International Monetary Fund (IMF), *Direction of Trade: A Supplement to International Financial Statistics, 1960–64,* 1964, pp. 382–83; IBRD and IMF, *Direction of Trade Statistics Yearbook, 1964–68,* 1968, pp. 385–86; IMF, *Direction of Trade Statistics Yearbook, 1970–76,* 1976, pp. 259, 292; IMF, *Direction of Trade Statistics Yearbook, 1982,* 1982, pp. 387–88; IMF, *Direction of Trade Statistics Yearbook, 1984,* 1985, pp. 392–93.

the development of a substantial trade relationship and the extension of development aid, the USSR was able to lay the foundation for a broader accommodation with its NATO neighbor. In fact, Soviet-Turkish relations have assumed a remarkably businesslike character, exhibiting a lessening of traditional Turkish mistrust of Russian/Soviet designs vis-à-vis the Straits and other strategic territories.

In other sectors of the Middle East, trade has served as a basis for reinforcing ties with the USSR's more staunch allies, particularly

Syria and Libya, and was a factor in recent improvements in relations with Egypt and Morocco. Trade has also facilitated the maintenance of ties with Iraq despite deteriorating relations between the two countries over the last decade and, although on a small scale, continues to be an important component of North Yemeni-Soviet relations. The ability of the Soviet Union to translate trade relations into influence should not be overstated: the Soviet share of most Middle Eastern countries' trade is not sufficiently large to provide significant market power, thus rendering ineffective such measures as boycott or restriction of trade. At best, Soviet influence gained through trade relations can be described as an ability to gain political favor rather than as the capability to discourage or to punish.

Another important economic instrument is development aid. Soviet aid takes several forms: the extension of economic credits and grants, the delivery of turnkey enterprises, the acceptance of repayment in local currency or the product of Soviet-aided plants, participation of Soviet technicians in a country's development projects, and the subsidized training of foreign students in the USSR. From the outset, economic aid has had more of a distinctively political character than trade and was utilized as a means of securing access to and expanding influence in particular countries, especially those of strategic significance to the USSR. Economic benefits have also accrued to Moscow in terms of significantly expanded trade relations with the major recipients of Soviet aid.

On the whole, the cost of Moscow's foreign economic assistance program has been minimal running at the equivalent of less than one-tenth of one percent of the Soviet GNP.[69] The Middle East has been the single largest recipient of Soviet development aid (see Table 3.6), but the recipients of that aid have varied, reflecting changing political alignments and opportunities for the expansion of Soviet influence. For the 1954–1966 period, the three states receiving the highest disbursements were Egypt, Afghanistan, and Iran. In the five-year period 1967–1972, the top three recipients were Iraq, Turkey, and Egypt, followed by Morocco, Turkey, and Afghanistan for the 1973–1978 period; and finally by Turkey, Iraq, and Afghanistan for the five-year period 1979–1984. The number of Middle Eastern states receiving Soviet aid has declined over the entire 1954–1984 period. Moreover, strategic concerns appear to dominate Soviet decisions on the direction and magnitude of development aid as reflected by the disproportionate amount going to the states of the southern tier. The Soviet aid program to the Middle East also

TABLE 3.6: Soviet Economic Credits and Grants Extended to the Middle East, 1954–1983 (millions of U.S. dollars)

Country	1954–66	1967–72	1973–78	1979–84	1954–84
Afghanistan	565	261	425	1,231	2,482
Algeria	236	189	290	565	1,280
Egypt	1,001	299	—	360	1,660
Iran	330	232	188	—	750
Iraq	184	365	150	1,453	2,152
Jordan	—	—	25	—	25
Morocco	44	44	2,000	—	2,088
PDRY	—	14	115	—	129
Syria	233	84	150	—	467
Tunisia	34	—	55	27	116
Turkey	6	524	1,850	1,600	3,980
Yemen	92	—	44	—	136
Middle East	2,725	2,012	5,292	5,236	15,265
World	5,453	2,937	7,585	10,614	26,589
Mid. East/World	50.0%	68.5%	69.8%	49.3%	57.4%

Sources: U.S., Department of State, Bureau of Public Affairs, Office of Media Services, *Communist States and Developing Countries: Aid and Trade in 1974,* Special Report no. 23 (February 1976), table 2; U.S. Central Intelligence Agency (CIA), *Communist Aid to Less Developed Countries of the Free World, 1975,* Publ. ER 76-10372U (July 1976), pp. 32–33; CIA, *Communist Aid to the Less Developed Countries of the Free World, 1976,* Publ. ER 77-10296 (August 1977), pp. 11–13; CIA, National Foreign Assessment Center (NFAC), *Communist Aid to Less Developed Countries of the Free World, 1977: A Research Paper,* Publ. ER 78-10478U (November 1978), pp. 5–6; CIA, NFAC, *Communist Aid Activities in Non-Communist Less Developed Countries, 1978: A Research Paper,* Publ. ER 79-10412U (September 1979), pp. 7–10; CIA, NFAC, *Communist Aid Activities in Non-Communist Less Developed Countries, 1979 and 1954–79: A Research Paper,* Publ. ER 80-10318U (October 1980), pp. 18–20; Department of State, Bureau of Intelligence and Research, *Soviet and East European Aid to the Third World, 1981,* Publ. 9345 (February 1983), pp. 17–18; CIA, Directorate of Intelligence, *Handbook of Economic Statistics, 1984: A Reference Aid,* Publ. CPAS 84-10002 (September 1984), p. 110; CIA, Directorate of Intelligence, *Handbook of Economics Statistics, 1985: A Reference Aid,* Publ. CPAS 85-10001 (September 1985), p. 110–11.

as growing Soviet involvement in North Africa.

Soviet development assistance has been channeled primarily to large, public sector, showcase projects such as the Aswan Dam in Egypt, the Nasiriyah power plant in Iraq, the Euphrates Dam in Syria, Iran's first steel mill near Isfahan, the Karabuk steel mill in Turkey, and the Jalalabad Power and Irrigation Project in Afghanistan. In so doing, Moscow has gained a recognition for development aid that is far in excess of actual program outlays.

Moreover, aid commitments almost always tie the recipient to the purchase of Soviet goods and services. The Soviet Union has also encouraged states to enter into broad, long-term cooperation agreements such as the 1978 $2 billion framework agreement with Morocco for the exploitation of Moroccan phosphates. Such agreements are intended to synchronize a state's planning cycle with that of Moscow, thus establishing a more solid basis for joint economic planning and assuring the USSR of continued access to sources of vital raw materials.

The provision of technical services is another aspect of Soviet aid that has gained in importance and size in recent years. In 1984, there were 100,400 Soviet and Eastern European economic technicians in various Middle Eastern countries, compared with 24,450 in 1975 and 7,145 in 1965.[70] Among the states of the Middle East, the greatest concentration of technicians is in states holding large hard currency reserves; Algeria, Iraq, and Libya alone retained 82 percent of all Soviet and Eastern European technicians posted to the Middle East in 1984.[71]

The Soviet Union also provides subsidized academic and technical training programs in the Soviet Union and Eastern Europe for its aid recipients. Students from the Middle East make up a significant portion of the Third World students being educated in the USSR and Eastern Europe. While the actual benefits accruing to the Soviet Union from this program are difficult to gauge, the Kremlin may have concluded that its influence would be enhanced should a generation educated in the USSR and Eastern Europe assume positions of leadership and responsibility in the developing world.

PROSPECTS

Of the external powers involved in the Middle East, the Soviet Union (and before that, Russia) has demonstrated one of the longest records of continuous interest and involvement. In the distant past, the Middle East was seen as a potential threat to Russia's security, an opportunity for territorial expansion, and an outlet for Russian goods. Later, as Russian power and prestige grew appreciably, the Middle East became the focal point of competition between Russia and other imperialist powers for territory and influence. With the ascension to power of the Bolshevik government in 1917, the Soviet Union assumed a new role: through the initiation of diplomatic relations and the fostering of cordial ties with the states of the region, the USSR sought to break the diplomatic-political isolation imposed on it by the Western powers. This proved a successful first step in the state's efforts to establish its legitimacy in the international community. Following World War II and the gradual retirement of the European powers from the Middle East, the Soviet Union sought to extend its influence to new sectors of the region. These efforts, however, did not go unchallenged as a new element was introduced into the Soviet Union's foreign policy calculations—the superpower competition.

This latter factor has been pivotal in transforming Soviet approaches to the region. Superpower competition globalized issues such as the Arab-Israeli conflict, Western oil dependence, and various inter-Arab rivalries. The extent and nature of Soviet involvement consequently was linked to estimates concerning the possibility of U.S. involvement and the overriding, but implicit, priority of avoiding direct armed confrontation with the United States.

On the whole, Soviet policy in the Middle East has had a mixed record of success. Significant inroads were achieved in the 1950s and 1960s, facilitated especially by the extension of military and economic aid, but the momentum of those early efforts subsided as there developed a growing sense of disillusionment with the Soviet Union among a number of Middle Eastern states. Egypt and other close allies became disgruntled with Soviet assistance and involvement, and the invasion of Afghanistan demonstrated that the USSR was less of a disinterested party helping the countries of the Middle East resist imperialism and more of a superpower seeking to promote its own, narrow interests. Nevertheless there persists a general recognition among states and actors of the region that the Soviet Union has been and will continue to be an important factor in the Middle East. It has long-standing interests in the area, some related directly to its own security, and the USSR retains a capacity to influence the decisions and actions of the region's key states.

Prospects for peace and stability in the Middle East remain conditioned on, at a minimum, Soviet acquiescence. This is not to imply, however, that the USSR is the most significant external actor in the Middle East. The Soviet Union has not displaced the United States nor even matched its accomplishments in the region. The United States' close involvement in regional issues, especially the Arab-Israeli conflict and ancillary issues, is a significant factor affecting Soviet policy. Despite Washington's setbacks in the Middle East, especially after Lebanon, Soviet positions in the region have not been appreciably strengthened. The USSR remains outside the mainstream of efforts to promote peace in the region and its closest friends—notably Syria and Libya—are those most adamantly opposed to any peace settlement that would recognize the State of Israel. Moreover, the dispute within the PLO has complicated Moscow's relations with that organization as well as with other central participants in the Arab-Israeli dispute. As such, Soviet policy toward the Middle East will continue to emphasize entrenchment—a consolidation of existing positions—and consequently, we are likely to witness the Soviet Union continuing to hold as one of its central objectives in the Middle East the circumvention of U.S. peace initiatives. The USSR has little incentive to see their successful outcome and, at the same time, lacks the influence to move the major participants in an alternative direction. At present, such a policy is in the Soviet interest and the USSR possesses the capability to see it effectively implemented.

NOTES

1. Two excellent surveys of Russian history are Nicholas V. Riasanovsky, *A History of Russia*, 4th ed. (New York and Oxford: Oxford Univ. Press, 1984); and George Vernadsky, *A History of Russia* (New Haven, CT: Yale Univ. Press, 1929).

2. Riasanovsky, *A History*, p. 265.

3. Russia was not to achieve territorial gains as significant on its southern frontiers as it had after the First and Second Turkish wars. Russian drives toward the Middle East and the Indian subcontinent were subsequently challenged by European imperialism, which was determined to contain Russian expansionism. In particular, the *status quo* powers of Europe agreed that the preservation of Turkey's independence, at least nominally, was intrinsic to the balance of power in Europe. Initially Russia accepted this premise as its campaigns against Turkey were never fought with the objective of destroying the opponent and, on occasion, it even aided Turkey when internal divisions threatened the fabric of Ottoman suzerainty. The limits of Europe's tolerance of Russian designs on Turkey were eventually exceeded, however, and resulted in the Crimean War (1854–1855) in which the combined forces of France, Great Britain, and Sardinia supported the Turks in their struggle against Russia. The conclusion of hostilities witnessed a defeated Russia accepting the humiliating provisions contained in the Treaty of Paris (1856) which, among other things, stipulated the cession of territory to Turkey and the neutralization of the Black Sea.

4. George Lenczowski, *The Middle East in World Affairs*, 4th ed. (Ithaca and London: Cornell Univ. Press, 1980), pp. 777–78.

5. Immediately after World War I, Turkey, Iran, and Afghanistan found common ground with the Soviet Union in resisting Western encroachments, and all held a commitment to revolutionary change, though differing in degree and substance. Shortly thereafter relations deteriorated between the USSR and its neighbors, prompting Turkey, Iran, Iraq, and Afghanistan to enter into the Saadabad Pact in 1937, which was widely interpreted as being directed against the Soviet Union.

6. U.S., Department of State, *Documents on German Foreign Policy, 1918–1945*, vol. 7, 1960, pp. 565, 715.

7. George Lenczowski, *Soviet Advances in the Middle East* (Washington, D.C.: American Enterprise Institute, 1971), p.47.

8. Jon D. Glassman, *Arms for the Arabs: The Soviet Union and the War in the Middle East* (Baltimore and London: Johns Hopkins Univ. Press, 1975), p. 131.

9. Prior to the 1979 invasion, the USSR had become Afghanistan's largest source of economic and military assistance and the country's most significant trading partner. For the 1975–1979 period, the Soviet Union had a total of $450 million in economic aid agreements with Afghanistan, which represented an increase of $150 million over the previous ten-year period. There were 3,700 Soviet and Eastern European economic technicians in Afghanistan prior to the invasion, and some 5,000 Afghan students had been trained in Soviet economic institutions and 1,600 in technical institutes. The Afghan economy was also highly dependent on Soviet markets to absorb its exports of natural gas. Central Intelligence Agency (CIA), National Foreign Assessment Center (NFAC), *Communist Aid Activities in Non-Communist Less Developed Countries, 1979 and 1954–1979: A Research Paper*, Publ. ER 80-10318U (October 1980), p. 64.

10. For a discussion of this and related questions see Jonathan B. Stein, *The Soviet Bloc, Energy, and Western Security* (Lexington, MA and Toronto: Lexington Books, 1983).

11. Soviet military sources are the exception: see, for example, V.D. Sokolovskiy, *Soviet Military Strategy*, trans. Harriet Fast Scott, 3rd ed. (New York: Crane, Russak & Co., 1975), p. 28.

12. See CIA, NFAC, *Prospects for Soviet Oil Production*, Publ. ER 77-10270 (April 1977); CIA, *The International Energy Situation: Outlook to 1985*, Publ. ER 77-10240U (April 1977); and CIA, NFAC, *Prospects for Soviet Oil Production: A Supplemental Analysis*, Publ. ER 77-10425 (July 1977).

13. See CIA, NFAC, *The World Oil Market in the Years Ahead: A Research Paper*, Publ. ER 79-10327U (August 1979).

14. "Oil troubles for Russians," New York *Times* (June 5, 1985); "Output lags for Soviet oil," New York *Times* (January 13, 1986); and "Where the good oil news is bad," *Economist* (January 25, 1986), p. 64. See also Thane Gustafson, "The origins of the Soviet oil crisis, 1970–1985," *Soviet Economy* 1 (April–June 1985), pp. 103–35.

15. Calculated from data in CIA, Directorate of Intelligence, *Handbook of Economic Statistics, 1985: A Reference Aid*, Publ. CPAS 85-10001 (September 1985), p. 70; and "Oil trouble for Russians," New York *Times* (June 5, 1985).

16. "Trade winds blow East again," *Economist* (April 7, 1984), p. 67; and "Russia drills less oil, Opec keeps it cheap," *Economist* (June 8, 1985), p. 65.

17. In particular, substantial quantities of Saudi crude were bought in the first quarter of 1984. See "War or no, oil market stable," New York *Times* (July 7, 1984). The Soviet Union may actually have reduced its exports of oil to the non communist countries by as much as 25 percent in 1985. See "Where the good oil news is bad," *Economist* (January 25, 1986), p. 64.

18. Based on data in U.S., Arms Control and Disarmament Agency (ACDA), *World Military Expenditures and Arms Transfers, 1985*, Publ. 123 (August 1985), pp. 131–34. Syria is also a significant importer of Soviet arms, financing its military imports from subsidies provided by Saudi Arabia, Kuwait, Libya, and other Middle Eastern states.

19. Based on data in Joan Parpart Zoeter, "U.S.S.R.: Hard currency trade and payments," in U.S., Congress, Joint Economic Committee, *Soviet Economy in the 1980's: Problems and Prospects*, vol. 2, 97th Cong., 2nd sess., 1982, pp. 502–04.

20. William H. Lewis, "Emerging choices for the Soviets in Third World arms transfer policy," in ACDA, *World Military Expenditures, 1985*, p. 31; and based on data in CIA, *Economic Statistics, 1985*, p. 71.

21. The responsible departments in the Soviet Ministry of Foreign Affairs are the

Middle Eastern Countries Department (the southern tier); the Near Eastern Countries Department (the Persian Gulf/Red Sea and Arab-Israeli sectors); and the First African Department (North Africa).

22. I. Leonidov, "Turkey: A web of unsolved problems," *International Affairs* (Moscow), 8 (May 1984), p. 57.

23. V. Stepanov, "Prospects for Soviet-Turkish cooperation," *International Affairs* (Moscow), 3 (March 1985), p. 78.

24. Leonidov, "Web of unsolved problems," p. 56.

25. A.A. Gromyko and B.N. Ponomarev (eds.) *Soviet Foreign Policy, 1945–1980*, 2nd vol., 4th ed., revised and enlarged, trans. David Skvirsky (Moscow: Progress Publishers, 1981), p. 618.

26. For a discussion of this and related issues see Alexandre Bennigsen, "Mullahs, Mujahidin and Soviet Muslims," *Problems of Communism* 33 (November/December 1984): 28–44; and Yaacov Ro'i (ed.), *The USSR and the Muslim World* (London: George Allen & Unwin, 1984).

27. Unattributed commentary, Moscow, in Persian to Iran, January 15, 1986; in *Foreign Broadcast Information Service: Soviet Union* (January 17, 1986), pp. H5-6.

28. "Leonid Brezhnev's answers to questions by a Pravda correspondent, 12 January," *News and Views from the USSR* (Washington, D.C.: Soviet Embassy Information Department, 1980), p. 3. See also M. Arunova, "Democratic Afghanistan: The path of struggle and construction," *International Affairs* (Moscow), 5 (May 1985), pp. 46–52.

29. Dmitry Volsky, "Observer's view: Guided reaction," *New Times* 23 (June 1984), p. 11.

30. Gagik Drambyants, "Middle East: Thunderheads over the Persian Gulf," *New Times* 10 (March 1984), pp. 14–15.

31. Quoted in "Massacre with tea: Southern Yemen at war," New York *Times* (February 9, 1986).

32. CIA, *Economic Statistics, 1985*, p. 123.

33. The civil war that brought down the government of President Ali Nasser Mohammed al-Hassani in January 1986 appears to have caught Soviet policymakers by surprise. The Soviet Union avoided taking sides in the struggle, evacuated more than 3,000 personnel stationed in South Yemen, and came out in support of the new leader, Haidar Abu Bakr al-Attas only after the outcome of the struggle had become clear. In effect, the USSR's close association with South Yemen over the past two decades provided it with only minimal influence on the course of events that took place at the beginning of 1986.

34. D. Zgersky, "U.S.S.R.–Oman: Establishing relations," *New Times* 41 (October 1985), p. 9.

35. A. Usvatov, "Comment: The Gulf Crisis," *New Times* 25 (June 1984); p. 9. See also V. Ustinov, "Zones of peace and international security," *International Affairs* (Moscow), 12 (December 1984), pp. 119–25.

36. O. Kasyanov, "Crimes of imperialism and Zionism in Lebanon," *International Affairs* (Moscow), 9 (September 1984), p. 53.

37. Evgeni M. Primakov, "The USSR and the developing countries," *Journal of International Affairs* 34 (Fall/Winter 1980/81), p. 280.

38. V. Volgin, "A conspiracy of Zionism, imperialism and reaction," *International Affairs* (Moscow), 10 (October 1982), p. 85.

39. Mikhail S. Gorbachev, "Joint press conference with Francois Mitterrand in Paris, October 4, 1985," in *A Time For Peace* (New York: Richardson & Steirman, 1985), p. 293.

40. For the text see "The Soviet Union's proposals on a Middle East settlement,"

New Times 32 (August 1984), pp. 4-5.

41. See "Text of Final Declaration at Arab League Meeting," New York *Times* (September 10, 1982).

42. Leonid Medvedko, "Middle East: There is a way out," *New Times* 37 (September 1984), p. 8. See also A. Ustyugov, "A way to a just peace in the Middle East," *International Affairs* (Moscow), 10 (October 1984), p. 72.

43. Y. Glukhov, "Arab interests betrayed," *International Affairs* (Moscow), 6 (June 1979), p. 86.

44. F. Nikiforov, "Who builds up tension in the Middle East," *International Affairs* (Moscow), 9 (September 1985), p. 128.

45. "Gromyko calls for P.L.O. unity," New York *Times* (November 24, 1983).

46. V. Gurev, "The Middle East and the cobweb of Camp David," *International Affairs* (Moscow), 11 (November 1985), p. 69.

47. For the text of the agreement see "P.L.O. Pact with Jordan," New York *Times* (February 24, 1985). On February 19, 1986, King Hussein announced the termination of Jordan's efforts to effect a joint peace strategy with Yasser Arafat, citing the PLO's lack of genuine cooperation. See "Hussein drops a yearlong effort to join in peace bid with Arafat," New York *Times* (February 20, 1986).

48. V. Konstantinov, "A Middle East settlement and its opponents," *International Affairs* (Moscow), 1 (January 1986), p. 106.

49. "Soviet-Libyan Communique," TASS (March 19, 1983).

50. Quoted in D. Zverev, "U.S.S.R.-Libya: Common views," *New Times* 43 (October 1985), p. 8.

51. "The Mediterranean: Area of cooperation or seat of tension?" *Izvestia* (March 28, 1983).

52. See *The Soviet Navy in War and Peace* (Moscow: Progress Publishers, 1980), especially chp. 4.

53. A. Osipov, "NATO's militaristic strategy in the Middle East," *International Affairs* (Moscow), 4 (April 1985), p. 65.

54. Concessionary terms have entailed, typically, discounts from list prices averaging 40 percent, but running as high as 75 percent, rates of interest of 2 percent, and repayment accepted over eight-to-ten-year periods and in local currency. Orah Cooper and Carol Fogarty, "Soviet economic and military aid to less developed countries, 1954–78," in U.S., Congress, Joint Economic Committee, *Soviet Economy in a Time of Change*, vol. 2, 96th Cong., 1st sess., 1979, p. 650.

55. In 1975, King Hussein threatened to turn to the Soviet Union for arms after having gone through exhaustive efforts to obtain an air defense package from the United States. Further dissatisfaction with U.S. treatment of Jordan prompted him to make good on that threat in 1981 and again in 1985. Although not the first order for Soviet arms, Kuwait in 1984 concluded an arms agreement with the USSR after a request for "Stinger" surface-to-air missiles was turned down by the United States. For elaboration see Alexander J. Bennett, "Arms transfer as an instrument of Soviet policy in the Middle East," *The Middle East Journal* 39 (Autumn 1985), pp. 745–74.

56. See "Brazilians hopeful of accord on Libyan planes," New York *Times* (May 1, 1983).

57. "Soviet-Afghan treaty of friendship, good-neighbourliness and cooperation, 5 December 1984," *Survival* 21 (March/April 1979), pp. 92–93.

58. "Treaty of Friendship and Co-operation Between the Union of Soviet Socialist Republics and the Republic of Iraq," in *The Policy of the Soviet Union in the Arab World* (Moscow: Progress Publishers, 1975), pp. 178–83.

59. See "Excerpts from interview with the King of Jordan," New York *Times* (March 15, 1984); and "King Hussein calls for Soviet role in Mideast," TASS (April 8, 1984).

60. In the summer of 1985 there were also reports that the USSR was seeking a restoration of diplomatic relations with Israel, which had been broken in 1967, but apparently nothing materialized. See "Israeli Radio reports a Soviet offer on new ties," New York *Times* (July 20, 1985); and "Hints of Soviet shift on Israel doubted," New York *Times* (November 12, 1985).

61. At the Conference, Soviet Foreign Minister Andrei Gromyko put forward his government's position on a just political settlement of the conflict that held many of the same points as UN Security Council resolutions 242 and 338 and was to serve as a basis for all future Soviet pronouncements. It called for "the withdrawal of Israeli troops from all Arab lands occupied in 1967, respect for the sovereignty, territorial integrity, and political independence of all Middle East nations, including Israel, and the safeguarding of the legitimate rights of the Arab people of Palestine." Gromyko, *Soviet Foreign Policy*, p. 503.

62. Diplomatic relations had been broken with Israel following the June 1967 Arab-Israeli war, while relations were maintained with Syria in spite of its decision to boycott the conference. The USSR had had contacts with the PLO since 1968 although the organization was not invited to participate.

63. Gromyko, *Soviet Foreign Policy*, p. 503.

64. "Soviet-American Joint Statement on the Middle East," *Pravda* (October 2, 1977).

65. Since its founding in 1921, the Egyptian Communist party has operated almost continuously illegally and has been the object of occasional persecution. At present it does not claim significant popular support nor is it the focus of opposition to the government, which is comprised of a broad spectrum of groups and parties ranging from the extreme left to the religious right. Between 1973 and 1979 the Iraqi Communist party was allowed to participate, though not actively, in Iraq's National Progressive Front. This was terminated *de jure* in 1979 after party members were given the choice of either submitting to the ruling Ba'ath party's directives or giving up their political posts. Their representatives were subsequently ousted from the Cabinet and participation ended *de facto* in 1978 when the party fell victim to a series of bloody purges, decimating its leadership. In Syria, the Communist party has been more successful in working with the ruling Ba'athists. Syrian Communists have held several cabinet posts since 1972 and the party officially participates in the National Progressive Front, which is led by the Ba'ath party and includes various nationalist currents. Participation by the Communists has been tolerated because the party lacks widespread popular support and thus is not perceived as a threat by the regime. See the annual *Yearbook on International Communist Affairs*, produced by the Hoover Institution, Stanford University.

66. Calculated from data in International Monetary Fund, *Direction of Trade Statistics Yearbook*, various years.

67. Alan H. Smith, "The influence of trade on Soviet relations with the Middle East," in Adeed Dawisha and Karen Dawisha (eds.), *The Soviet Union in the Middle East: Policies and Perspectives*, (New York: Holmes & Meier Publishers, 1982), pp. 120–21.

68. Some of Moscow's Eastern European allies—notably Poland, Czechoslovakia, East Germany, and Romania—have had more success than the USSR in establishing a presence through trade in the Gulf as well as in other states where Soviet efforts have made little or no headway.

69. CIA, *Communist Aid Activities, 1954–79*, p. 8.

70. Excludes Afghanistan. CIA, *Communist Aid Activities, 1954-79*, p. 10; and CIA, *Economic Statistics, 1985*, pp. 122–23.

71. CIA, *Economic Statistics, 1985*, pp. 122–23.

III
EUROPE

4

Europe

Bernard Reich and Patrick Coquillon

In the latter part of the twentieth century the two global superpowers—the United States and the USSR—have become the primary external actors in the Middle East; historically, however, the major outside powers were European. The expansion of the spheres of interest of several European powers in the nineteenth century and the dismemberment of the Ottoman Empire at the beginning of the twentieth century brought the Middle East into direct contact with Europe. The European presence in the Middle East had military, economic, and political components as well as a lasting cultural influence, but the sum of its multinational dimension was, and remains, clearly less salient than the national policies of the several major European states. It was not a *European* presence that developed in the Middle East in the twilight of the Ottoman Empire, but rather the presence of individual European powers, locked in an uneven match marked by intense rivalries in their quest for control of portions of the region. Britain and France were major actors, while Italy and Spain played minor roles, and other European states, such as Germany, played virtually none at all. The powers were not linked in a common effort to influence regional developments, as has begun to occur today with the European Community (EC), but rather they concentrated on pursuing individual interests in competition with each other. While the intramural competition continues, there is now also a common dimension in the positions adopted by the EC.

The European powers view the Middle East in terms different from those of the superpowers, and while some of their interests overlap, especially with those of the United States, others do not. They are influenced by a host of factors, such as their colonial presence and history in the region, which do not affect the superpowers and which have found expression in different interests, sometimes compatible with those of the superpowers, sometimes clearly in conflict.

In a general sense there is a compatibility between the policies of the West European states and those of the United States. The fundamental security interest of the West in the Middle East is to prevent the region from falling under hostile, usually defined as Soviet, influence. Also shared is the concern that no regional conflict should escalate to involve external powers in a major war or threaten to affect other Western interests. Interest in the region's oil resourses—for both strategic and commercial/economic (profits from production and marketing of oil and from provision of goods and services paid for with petrodollars) reasons—remains high. Access to oil is closely related to transit rights, including the unimpeded passage of ships through waterways such as the Suez Canal, the Straits of Hormuz, and the Bab el-Mandeb. Landing and overflight rights for aircraft are mutual concerns of the European powers and the superpowers. European interests derive from geographic proximity, often common (though usually colonial) history, and the political and military implications for Western Europe of Middle East regional developments.

West European security and prosperity are dependent on the Middle East, especially its oil resources, although some European states are less vulnerable than others. The United Kingdom and Norway, because of the North Sea production and reserves, are less dependent than Italy, Germany, and France, which continue to rely on Middle East oil. (See Table 4.1.) The traditional trade in oil has been supplemented—especially as Arab petrodollar accounts have grown—by major Middle Eastern purchases of European exports such as machinery and advanced technology; Europe and the Arab world have become major trading partners. Nevertheless Europe has also maintained long-standing political, cultural, and economic ties with Israel. (See Tables 4.2 and 4.3.)

The ability of the various Western States to achieve their goals has varied over time. The shift of regional primacy from the European powers to the superpowers began at the end of World War II, but the pace varied in different portions of the region at different times. It became evident that the old mechanisms of preserving influence, at least politically, were no longer effective. The French had to leave Syria and Lebanon and the British gave up the Palestine mandate. Later, Morocco, Tunisia, and Algeria became independent. The attempt undertaken by Great Britian and France to regain their

TABLE 4.1: Sources of EC Crude Oil Imports, 1973–1983 (in percent)

Year	Total	OPEC	Near and Middle East	Africa	Eastern Europe	Norway
1973	100	94.6	69.2	26.2	2.3	0.2
1978	100	89.2	71.0	21.2	4.4	1.8
1979	100	88.8	68.0	22.9	4.5	2.0
1980	100	86.0	65.5	23.3	5.2	2.3
1981	100	81.7	63.7	22.2	5.8	2.4
1982	100	76.9	52.5	27.5	8.4	3.5
1983	100	70.8	40.7	33.3	11.0	5.0

Source: *EUROSTAT: Energy Statistics Yearbook (1978–1983)*, Statistical Office of the European Community.

once dominant political positions during the Suez crisis of 1956 failed and marked the termination of the classic pattern of Western intervention in the affairs of the Middle East. The receding of the European colonial presence has taken considerable time, and the nature of the withdrawal and the remaining linkages has varied. Italy's defeat in World War II led to the end of its role in Libya soon thereafter, but Spain remained in parts of Morocco until the middle of the 1950s and in the Spanish Sahara until the 1970s. It still retains a presence in Ceuta and Melilla (enclaves in Moroccan territory). France's control of Syria and Lebanon was terminated during World War II, in Morocco and Tunisia in the mid 1950s, and in Algeria in 1962. The termination of the British role often went through two stages: granting of nominal independence, followed by the actual end of British dominance. Thus Egypt and Iraq achieved nominal independence long before the vestiges of British influence were removed from those states in the 1950s. South Yemen became independent in the late 1960s and most of the Gulf states not until the 1970s. The process of withdrawal was often complex, and sometimes (such as in the case of Algeria) bloody, while in some instances (such as in the Gulf) it proceeded with few complications. The withdrawal process, like the colonial period that preceded it, colored the perceptions of the regional states (as well as of the retreating powers) and of future relations between the external and the regional powers.

With the post-World War II alterations came the beginning of a longer-term and more significant alteration in the Western presence in the Middle East, as the United States assumed, albeit gradually, the role of the leading Western power and the formerly-dominant European powers became secondary actors.

TABLE 4.2: EC Imports from the Middle East, 1977–1984 (millions of European Currency Units, ECU)

Country	1977	1978	1979	1980	1981	1982	1983	1984[a]
USA[b]	2604	2852	3420	4460.	4959	5383	5348	6063
Index	100	109.5	131.3	171.2	190.4	206.7	205.3	232.8
Rank	1	1	1	1	1	1	1	—
Saudi Arabia[c]	1310	1026	1470	2509	3683	2603	1364	976
Index	100	78.3	112.1	191.4	281.1	198.6	104.0	74.5
Rank	2	2	2	2	2	2	7	—
Libya	3910	3291	4972	6564	7092	9142	9339	9542
Index	100	84.1	127.1	167.8	181.3	233.7	238.8	244
Rank	13	15	14	12	11	9	10	—
Algeria	2099	2006	2762	4028	6063	8642	7732	8854
Index	100	95.5	131.5	191.8	288.8	411.7	368.3	421.8
Rank	20	23	21	19	13	10	12	—
Iran	7602	6928	4433	2798	2554	7127	6932	7867
Index	100	91.1	58.2	36.7	33.5	93.7	91.1	103.4
Rank	6	6	16	21	25	13	13	—
UAE	3067	2567	3117	4375	4643	3920	3337	2141
Index	100	83.6	101.6	142.6	151.3	127.7	108.8	69.8
Rank	17	19	19	16	17	19	21	—
Iraq	4117	4591	6137	7948	2996	2866	3682	2827
Index	100	111.5	149	192.9	72.7	69.5	89.4	68.6
Rank	12	12	11	9	21	21	19	—
Egypt	738	1051	1442	2253	3343	2739	2976	3682
Index	100	142.4	195.3	305.2	452.9	371.1	403.2	498.9
Rank	44	37	32	24	19	23	27	—
Israel	1025	1235	1372	1627	1707	1793	2048	2561
Index	100	120.4	133.7	158.8	166.4	135.8	199.8	249.8
Rank	35	32	30	36	37	33	34	—
Turkey	—	830	941	986	1341	1611	2047	2760
Index	—	100	113.3	118.7	161.5	194	246.6	332.5
Rank	—	44	47	50	42	39	35	—

[a]Calculation for one year on the basis of the first five months.

[b]EC exports to the United States are noted for comparison. Values of U.S. exports are in 10 million ECU.

[c]Value of Saudi exports are in 10 million ECU.

Sources: EUROSTAT, *Monthly External Trade Bulletin (1952–1983)* Special Number; *Ibid.*(March 1985)–(Luxembourg: Office des Publications des Communautes Europeenes, 1985).

TABLE 4.3: EC Exports to the Middle East, 1977–1984 (in millions of European Currency Units, ECU)

Country	1977	1978	1979	1980	1981	1982	1983	1984[a]
USA[b]	2061	2326	2521	2678	3717	4291	5028	6433
Index	100	112.8	120.9	128.5	178.4	205.9	243.9	312.1
Rank	1	1	1	1	1	1	1	1
Saudi Arabia	4774	5818	6548	7487	10442	12880	13953	15046
Index	100	124.4	139.4	159.4	222.4	274.3	298.5	321.9
Rank	10	6	5	7	5	4	5	—
Iraq	1793	1940	2694	3865	7083	8904	4643	3528
Index	100	108.1	150	215.2	394.5	495.9	258.9	196.7
Rank	24	21	17	15	10	8	16	—
Algeria	3689	3670	3854	4754	5583	5334	6147	6814
Index	100	99.4	104.4	128.8	151.2	144.5	166.6	184.7
Rank	11	10	11	11	14	13	—	—
Egypt	17749	1891	2391	3207	4265	4436	5264	5806
Index	100	108.1	136.5	183.1	243.5	253.2	300.9	331.9
Rank	26	23	20	19	17	17	14	—
Iran	5404	5924	2277	3284	4199	3652	6884	7296
Index	100	109.6	42.1	60.7	77.8	67.5	127.3	135
Rank	6	5	22	18	18	22	9	—
UAE	1557	1616	1802	2088	2684	3270	2994	3120
Index	100	103.7	115.6	134	172.3	209.9	192.2	200.3
Rank	26	28	27	28	24	23	25	—
Israel	1489	1641	1789	1691	2194	2544	3424	3382
Index	100	110.2	120	113.4	147.2	170.7	229.9	227.1
Rank	28	27	28	33	29	28	23	—
Turkey	2168	1569	1611	1836	2185	2476	2977	3809
Index	100	72.3	74.2	84.6	100.7	114.1	137.3	175.6
Rank	20	30	32	29	30	31	26	—

[a]Calculations for one year on the basis of the first five months.

[b]EC exports to the United States are noted for comparison. Values of U.S. exports are in 10 million ECU.

Sources: EUROSTAT, *Monthly External Trade Bulletin (1952–1983)* Special Number; *Ibid.* (March 1985)—(Luxembourg: Office des Publications des Communautes Europeenes, 1985).

THE EUROPEAN COMMUNITY

Traditionally the European relationship with the Middle East has taken a primarily bilateral form, although the European Community (EC) has become a major new element, introducing a multilateral dimension to the political and economic links between these areas.

The Economic Dimension

The European Economic Community (EEC) was created by the Treaty of Rome of 1957 and included, as original members, West Germany, France, the Netherlands, Italy, Belgium, and Luxembourg. They were joined by Great Britain, Denmark, and Ireland in 1973; by Greece in 1981; and by Spain and Portugal in 1986. With the progressive implementation of the Treaty of Rome, the EEC has come to have far-reaching effects on the exports of a number of countries, the effects on the exports from the Middle East having been especially significant.

Since its inception the EEC has devoted particular attention to its economic relations with the Mediterranean region, beginning to develop this approach soon after the EEC became a functioning entity in January 1958. The Rome Treaty recognized the special status of North Africa, previously colonized by France and Italy. While still a French territory in 1958, Algeria also came fully under the provisions of the EEC Treaty although it did not become a member. The EEC states developed closer relations with the northern Mediterranean littoral states through Association Agreements with Greece (effective November 1, 1962) and with Turkey (effective December 1, 1964). These envisaged a gradual removal of tariffs, eventually leading to full membership in the EEC, as well as financial support by the Community. Although these arrangements were principally economic in character, their political/military overtones were obvious and the United States pressed for the completion of negotiations to tie the two NATO partners more closely to Europe. During the 1960s and early 1970s, a number of other agreements were concluded containing economic or politico-economic elements, but the Turkish and Greek models were not repeated and the treaties with Israel, Lebanon, Morocco, Tunisia, Malta, Cyprus, and Egypt, and the initial agreements with Spain and Portugal, were largely restricted to the establishment of preferential trade relations.

The EEC took a pragmatic approach to strengthening Mediterranean states and, at the same time, contributing to the political stabilization of the region. No general conception of the form that relations should take with third parties in general, or with the Mediterranean states in particular, had been developed, however, and the multiplicity of treaties often became confusing and unmanageable—quite apart from the fact that individual agreements with different Mediterranean states began to produce contradictions in Community policy and led to demands for equal treatment. In early

1972 the European Council directed the European Commission to make proposals for a "global Mediterranean policy," which it did in July 1972. At a summit in Paris in October 1972 the Community decided to negotiate a series of cooperation and association agreements with almost all the non-member states of the Mediterranean littoral region—a policy known as "the global policy for the Mediterranean." These treaties would include full access to the Community market for industrial goods, preferential access for agricultural produce, economic cooperation, and financial and technical assistance by the Community. The nature of each treaty would be determined by the circumstances peculiar to each country.

The "global policy" did not achieve extensive agreement between the EEC and the Mediterranean states, which was hardly surprising in view of the multiplicity of competing interests among the Europeans themselves, among the Mediterranean states, and in their bilateral relationships. In June 1973 four association agreements (with Greece, Turkey, Malta, and Cyprus) became operative in the same month that the EEC decided to begin negotiations with the states of the Middle East and North Africa aimed at concluding a series of trade and cooperation agreements. The rationale behind the negotiations was the existence of historical relationships, the responsibility to extend a helping hand to these countries, and the need to develop a spirit of cooperation in the region. Trade with the states in the Mediterranean area, including extensive oil shipments (which had almost trebled between 1960 and 1970), has continued to grow and represents a significant share of total EEC trade with non-European countries.

Of the Arab countries in the Eastern Mediterranean, Lebanon was the first to sign a trade accord (in 1965). The agreement was modified and extended into a preferential agreement in 1972. Egypt signed a similar accord that same year. Since 1977, these countries and Syria have become parties to a broad cooperation agreement, emphasizing economic, technical, financial, and commercial collaboration through a suitable institutional mechanism.

In April 1976 the EC signed cooperation agreements with the three countries of the Maghreb, Algeria, Morocco and Tunisia. They were the outcome of a long process the origin of which dates back to the Treaty of Rome. It was not until after the independence of Algeria that Morocco and Tunisia officially requested, in October 1963, the opening of negotiations on an association agreement of unlimited duration that would deal with financial and technical cooperation and labor questions as well as trade arrangements. Exploratory talks began in late 1963, and after lengthy negotiations agreements were finally signed in March 1969. Although they established an association, the agreements were restricted to trade issues and failed to provide for the more extensive cooperation that was to come later. Over the long term the 1969 agreements were geared to establishing a free trade area; they gave Morocco and Tunisia unhindered access to the Community market for nearly all their industrial products and preferential arrangements for certain agricultural products. The agreements were officially sanctioned at the Paris Summit in October 1972, which paved the way for parallel negotiations with all three Maghreb countries concerning full cooperation agreements. The negotiations began in July 1973 and were completed in the first half of January 1976; the new agreements were then signed in April 1976 and entered into force on November 1, 1978. Their aim was to establish wide-ranging cooperation between the partners with the purpose of promoting the economic and social development of the Maghreb countries through trade and cooperation in the economic, technical, financial, and social arenas. The agreements established free access to EEC markets for raw materials and industrial products not generally covered by the common agricultural policy. Agricultural exports to the Community had to be examined carefully in order to avoid conflicts between the interests of agricultural producers on both sides. The Community used precautionary measures such as quotas and import calendars to control agricultural imports from the Maghreb countries. Financial protocols were annexed to each agreement and some guarantees were provided for Maghreb guest workers in the EEC states but these proved unworkable.

In 1977 the EC signed cooperation agreements, similar to those with the Maghreb states, with Egypt, Jordan, Lebanon, and Syria; these came into force in 1977 and 1978. Industrial products were exempted from EEC tariffs by 1979 and agricultural products were granted a wide range of tariff concessions. Substantial financial assistance in the form of aid and loans was granted by the EEC.

Israel became the third country to establish a diplomatic mission to the EC in January 1959. Israel's action reflected various factors, especially concern about the effect of the EEC on Israeli exports. Israel has traditionally benefited from the export of large quantities of its products to EEC countries. Economic considerations were supplemented by political factors including Israel's fundamental ties with Europe based on historical, cultural, and social linkages. But, despite these considerations, Israel's earliest overtures were repulsed and only later negotiations resulted in an arrangement between Israel and the EEC. In June 1964 Israel established contractual links with the EEC in the form of a three year trade agreement. The agreement provided for the temporary and partial suspension of the common external tariff duties on some twenty industrial and commercial products and the removal, in whole or in part, of the quantitative restrictions still applied by member states in their trade with Israel. In return, Israel made a declaration of intent to facilitate the importation of Community products. A joint committee was set up to promote the implementation of the agreement and the development of trade.

Both parties regarded the 1964 agreement as a modest beginning, laying the foundation for the further growth of trade between the Community and Israel. Nine months before that agreement expired, Israel proposed the conclusion of an association agreement. The ensuing negotiations were long and difficult. Although exploratory talks between Community and Israeli representatives began in January 1967, it was not until October 1969 that the Council of the Community authorized the opening of official negotiations. The new preferential agreement was signed in Luxembourg on June 29, 1970 and came into force on October 1 of that year.

To avoid a break in contractual relations, the 1964 agreement was renewed on a number of occasions until the preferential agreement came into force. The 1970 agreement was a significant step forward in strengthening the contractual links between the Community and Israel. The advantages granted to Israel were considerably greater than in the past and, for its part, Israel undertook to offer some reciprocity on imports from the Community.

After the official accession of Britain, Ireland, and Denmark to the Community in January 1973, the Commission drew up proposals seeking to define the content of the EEC's overall Mediterranean approach in the fields of trade, economic, technical, labor, and financial cooperation. This preparatory work led to the adoption of negotiating directives by the Council at its meeting of June 24/25, 1973. Negotiations with Israel began on July 18, 1973. In the meantime, the two parties had signed a supplementary protocol postponing the application of provisions of the 1970 agreement on trade between Israel and the new member states. This was extended twice, first in 1973 and then until the conclusion of negotiations, which lasted for two years. The new agreement between Israel and the Community of Nine was officially signed in Brussels on May 11, 1975, coming into force on July 1 of the same year. The purpose of the 1975 agreement, which was the first concrete result of the Community's overall Mediterranean policy, was to consolidate and extend commercial and economic relations established in 1964 and 1970. In February 1977 additional protocols, including a financial protocol laying the framework and providing the means for closer economic cooperation with the Community, were signed.

The objective of the 1975 agreement was to gradually establish an industrial free trade zone between the Community and Israel and also to grant Israel considerable concessions in agriculture. Tariff reductions were in effect for more than 80 percent of Israel's exports to the Community. These preferential agreements were all the more important because agricultural exports were a major portion of Israel's foreign trade and because the European Community was the primary market. A cooperation council supervises the implementation of the cooperation objectives and replaces the joint committee that was set up by the 1975 agreements. Its role is to draw up resolutions and recommendations necessary for the attainment of the objectives of the cooperation agreement.

Despite the extensive existing agreements, there is some question about the future prospects of economic cooperation between the EC and its Mediterranean partners, because of the admission of Spain and Portugal. The Iberian Peninsula is an agricultural giant that is geographically attached to Europe and possesses considerable productive capacity. The goods that the Peninsula might sell to its European partners are precisely the ones that the Community buys from its Mediterranean neighbors. Israel, Tunisia, Algeria, and Morocco fear losing vital outlets as a result of Spain's and Portugal's accession to the Community. Because of its geographical proximity, low costs of transportation, and preferential tariffs, Spain could severely affect Israel, which already in 1983 suffered from European protectionist measures. The European market is indispensable to Israel for both imports and exports, especially since it is isolated politically and economically in the Middle East and cannot penetrate Eastern markets. But the Arab-Israeli conflict and Europe's dependence on oil imports seem to have constrained the Community in its relations with Israel.

The enlargement of the Community to include Spain and Portugal led to considerable divergences among the European members concerning appropriate polices, although there appeared to be agreement that the EC must maintain the traditional patterns for imports from the Mediterranean countries and from Morocco in particular. In March 1985 the European Commission adopted guidelines consisting of a number of guarantees for the Maghreb countries and Israel: maintenance of effective access to the Community markets for present flows of sensitive agricultural products such as citrus fruit, tomatoes, olive oil,and wine; free access to the Community markets for industrial products, including the reintroduction of free trade arrangements for textiles as quickly as possible; and continuation of financial and technical cooperation, which provides support for economic and social development efforts.

Overall, the Mediterranean countries have been disappointed with the Community and its efforts to facilitate a link between them and the EEC. The general trend toward self-sufficiency in Europe at the expense of Morocco, Tunisia, and Israel, which have vital interests in trading with the Community, has affected this viewpoint. Israel in particular affirms that maintaining trade relations is, for Europe, as much or more a political decision as an economic imperative. Algeria is less concerned economically by the Community import restrictions but supports the other Maghreb states. Turkey feels excluded from the Mediterranean policy after the admission of Greece in January 1981. Jordan and Eygpt hope that European financial assistance will be strong enough to be helpful. Lebanon and Syria pay much more attention to the Lebanese civil war than to their economic relations with the Community. This demonstrates the divergence of interests not only among Arabs but also among all Mediterranean countries and bears out the economic, political, religious, and social differences between the North, the South, the East and the West of the Mediterranean region. These differences represent considerable obstacles to a global and coherent Mediterranean policy, which the Community has been trying to formulate since 1972.

It is unlikely that Europe will achieve its ambitious goals in the Mediterranean region, the ultimate task being to respect its obligations toward those Mediterranean countries seriously threatened economically—and maybe politically—after the Community enlargement.

Efforts to extend the EC connection to the Persian Gulf have not made substantial progress. Since the EC is the Gulf states' main trading partner, in January 1980 the Europeans, at the initiative of German Minister for Economic Affairs Otto Graf Lambsdorff and German Foreign Minister Hans-Dietrich Genscher, proposed the negotiation of bilateral agreements with the Gulf states. The initiation of an EC-Gulf states dialogue was designed to avoid the political issues that had brought the Euro-Arab dialogue to a halt after the Camp David accords and the Egypt-Israel Peace Treaty. Six years after the decision to develop trade relations between the EC and the Gulf states, Arab and European parties continued to reaffirm their willingness to sign an overall cooperation agreement. In March 1985 both sides agreed that "it was in their mutual interest to aim to conclude a comprehensive, mutually beneficial, all embracing agreement to foster the broadest possible commercial and economic cooperation between the Gulf Cooperation Council (GCC) and the European Community."[1] Despite these perspectives concrete action to implement them has been lacking.

The Political Dimension

Growing political cooperation has been a feature of the European Community in recent years, and although the members are far from a common policy on most issues, there is increasing coordination. These trends have been especially noteworthy concerning the Middle East, despite the members' varying interests in the region. Most European countries have emotional sympathies favorable to Israel and economic interests that tend to favor the Arab states. This has helped to foster a general desire to achieve peace and stability in the area as a goal in itself and as a means of furthering other interests, especially economic, in the region.

The six members of the EC began an effort to reach a coordinated foreign policy position as a means of strengthening European political unity as early as November 1970 in Munich. At that time the Middle East was discussed by the ministers among themselves and then "for information" with representatives of the four states which then were candidates for Community membership.

On May 13/14, 1971 in Paris, the foreign ministers of the six member states considered a position paper on the Middle East prepared by a group of experts from their foreign ministries that raised the essential questions of the Arab-Israeli conflict and gave the impression that the EC wanted to pressure Israel concerning the territories it had occupied in the 1967 war. The working paper was never officially made public, although there were press reports suggesting that it was based on UNSC Resolution 242 and contained comprehensive and detailed views on the solution of the Arab-Israeli conflict that focused on free movement in the Suez Canal, concern for the Palestinian refugees, the question of Jerusalem, and the creation of a demilitarized zone. It favored the Arab perspective in its interpretation of Resolution 242, reflecting France's pro-Arab stance and West Germany and Italy remained reserved toward the report. The Europeans recognized the complexities of the issues and the difficulties of translating general principles into specific actions. Although the experts were asked to revise their report, the 1971 document could be considered the first effort at a coordinated

European policy on the Middle East as opposed to the policies of individual European states. The United States did not greet it with enthusiasm, Israel rejected it, and it was generally criticized in Europe. Among the criticisms of the document was its obvious pro-Arab orientation, the feeling that it resulted from European reliance on Arab oil, and the belief that Europe lacked the ability to implement its suggestions. The members of the EC not only had different historic ties with the Middle East, but their political approaches were different. Although an official common policy on the Arab-Israeli conflict was not agreed upon at that time, the attempt did provide a basis for future European approaches, especially after the 1973 war.

The October 1973 Arab-Israeli war and the embargo by Arab oil producing states had a shock effect on Western Europe, although the Arab effort was in fact directed against only one European state, the Netherlands. The result was a heightened European concern and interest in the Arab-Israeli conflict and a growing commitment to play a role in the peace process that emphasized differences between the views of the United States and those of its European allies. On October 13, 1973 the nine members of the EC issued an appeal for the termination of hostilities that "will help...to open the way to a proper negotiation" toward a solution based on Resolution 242.[2]

The EC's formal reaction to the developing situation came on November 6, 1973 in Brussels, when the nine Foreign Ministers issued a statement in which they urged the combatants to return to the positions they had occupied when the initial October 22 ceasefire went into effect.[3] They called for negotiations for a just and lasting peace in accordance with UNSC Resolution 242 in all of its parts.

> They consider that a peace agreement should be based particularly on the following points:
> I. the inadmissibility of the acquisition of territory by force;
> II. the need for Israel to end the territorial occupation which it has maintained since the conflict of 1967;
> III. respect for the sovereignty, territorial integrity and independence of every State in the area and their right to live in peace within secure and recognized boundaries;
> IV. recognition that in the establishment of a just and lasting peace account must be taken of the legitimate rights of the Palestinians.[4]

They declared "themselves ready to do all in their power to contribute to that peace." The declaration reflected the need for the

Europeans to adopt a coordinated policy and represented a compromise between the positions of the various states.

Despite the notable achievement of securing agreement to issue a joint statement, there were important discordant voices within the Community, U.S.-European relations were adversely affected, and Israel denounced what it viewed as the pro-Arab perspective as a "policy of expendiency" to help ensure European supplies of oil. The Arab world was receptive to it and, as a consequence, Europe decreased the risks of another oil embargo. When the Organization of Arab Petroleum Exporting Countries (OAPEC) met on November 18, 1973, the EC states were exempted from the 5 percent cutback in production scheduled for December of that year. The Arab Summit, which met in Algiers on November 26–28, 1973, responded to the earlier EC statements by noting the affinities between Europe and the Arab world and by stressing the importance of cooperation between the two areas.

The events connected with the war also affected the United States-Europe dialogue on the Middle East and related alliance issues. The Europeans felt slighted for a number of reasons, including non-consultation by U.S. Secretary of State Henry Kissinger and by their exclusion from the December 1973 Geneva Conference on the Middle East chaired by the United States and the Soviet Union.

The European summit in Copenhagen reaffirmed the November position in a communique issued on December 15, 1973. It also affirmed the need for "negotiations with oil-producing countries on comprehensive arrangements comprising cooperation on a wide scale for the economic and industrial development of these countries, industrial investments, and stable energy supplies to the Member Countries at reasonable prices."[5] On the whole, little was achieved, however.

The October War of 1973 marked the beginning of sustained European efforts to ensure its oil supplies. While the earlier concepts of greater economic cooperation reflected in the Mediterranean policy of the EC helped to form the basis of this effort, the oil crisis provided the stimulus to concrete efforts to deal with both concerns. For the Arab side the war marked the beginning of an initiative to secure support from the West, and particularly from the Western European allies of the United States, for the Palestinian cause in opposition to Israel. Diplomatic support and economic cooperation became the twin objectives of the Arab effort. The war had suggested a connection between economic and political issues and provided the basis for establishment of a Euro-Arab dialogue between the EC and the Arab League to explore the possibilities of cooperation between Europe and the Arab world. Underlying the effort was the interdependence of the two regions. Substantial trade results from the fact that Europe is dependent on Arab sources for much of its petroleum and that the Arab world seeks European products and technical aid for its economic development.

THE EURO-ARAB DIALOGUE

The Euro-Arab dialogue was launched in the winter of 1973 and established in 1974. On March 4, 1974 the nine members of the EC called for a meeting between the Community and designated Arab representatives to set up the machinery for a formal dialogue, beginning with working groups of experts to define areas of potential cooperation. The dialogue was formally instituted at the Ministerial level in Paris on July 31, 1974, but the first plenary session was not convened until June 1975 in Cairo. There were issues in dispute between the parties from the outset. The Europeans were primarily interested in ensuring the reliability of oil supplies at reasonable prices and in guaranteeing access to Middle Eastern markets to sell goods and services to help pay for the oil. The Arabs were interested in a broad range of subjects, including technology transfer and investments, but the primary interest was in securing European support on Arab-Israeli issues and European efforts to influence U.S. policy in that regard.

Before the dialogue could start, the delicate political problem of recognizing the PLO as the "sole legitimate representative" of the Palestinians had to be faced. The Arabs decided that the PLO, as a member of the Arab League, would take part in the first discussions scheduled for November 1974. The Europeans opposed the decision and the meeting was cancelled. The Arabs and Europeans finally arrived at the "Dublin formula" on February 15, 1975, which provided that there would be two delegations—one European and one Arab—and each participating group was free to select its own delegates, who would not necessarily be political representatives of their respective states.

At the first plenary meeting that took place in Cairo from June 10 to 14, 1975, the "Euro-Arab experts" adopted a joint memorandum in which they stressed the desire to revitalize their historical ties and reduce the technological gap. To achieve these goals working committees would focus on a range of questions. In November 1975, the experts adopted a common report on the basis of the results of the preceding meetings. In May 1976 the general committee representing the central authority of the Euro-Arab dialogue met in Luxembourg. The second meeting of the general committee took place in Tunis in February 1977. Following the third and fourth sessions of the general committee in Brussels in October 1977 and in Damascus in December 1978, the experts proposed a first project, but inter-Arab rivalries, especially resulting from Egypt's exclusion from the Arab League following the Camp David accords and the Egypt-Israel Peace Treaty, brought the activities of the dialogue to a halt.

The European Community sought to revive the dialogue but after a series of meetings between the Secretary General of the Arab League and representatives of the European Commission, the Arabs agreed to revive the dialogue only if the EC would lend more significance to the political aspect of Euro-Arab relations. In June 1980 the nine heads of states and governments in the EC and their foreign ministers met in Venice where their deliberations focused on developing a political dimension to the dialogue. The Venice Declaration (discussed below) provided a basis for trying to restart the dialogue.

In Luxembourg in November 1980, European and Arab representatives agreed on the modalities to relaunch the dialogue: a meeting of ministers should be held before the summer of 1981 to discuss political and economic questions and an ad hoc group, composed of representatives of the European Commission and of the Arab League, was entrusted with preparing for the Euro-Arab foreign ministers meeting. The meeting was postponed primarily because of inter-Arab disagreements. Although active preparations were made in 1981 and 1982 to renew the dialogue, Sadat's assassination in October 1981 and the Israeli invasion of Lebanon in June 1982 precipitated a new impasse in the Euro-Arab dialogue that lasted until 1983.

The dialogue remained in a "semi-somnolent state" until 1983 when a new European initiative was launched to influence the development of the Middle East peace process. EC heads of government who met in Brussels in March declared that "the Palestinian people and the PLO should take the opportunity by declaring themselves in favor of peace negotiations." The Europeans attempted to influence the talks in Amman between Arafat and the King Hussein concerning a settlement based on the September 1982 Reagan peace initiative. The Community initiative had no tangible results but put the Europeans in a favorable position to renew Euro-Arab cooperation. The Hamburg Symposium in April 1983 brought about the resumption of contacts between Arab and European representatives, primarily in the cultural field. Although some substantial progress for cooperation at the socio-cultural level was made by the participants, little else followed.

In June 1983 the EC ministers decided to go ahead with the EC-Israel financial protocol, the signing of which had been delayed after the Israeli invasion of Lebanon. Arab reaction to the agreement was negative and the Secretary General of the Arab League asked the EC to revise its position on peace in the Middle East and demanded that the EC members take a clearer stand regarding Israel's actions. He argued that the Arab peace plan adopted at the Fez Summit provided an adequate base for the resolution of the conflict.

The Arab reaction did not limit itself to these verbal pronouncements. In December Jordan's King Hussein encouraged Europe to make it understood that the Soviet Union must play a role in the peace process and noted that he expected Europe to play a "fully positive" role. Soon after King Hussein's visit, the fifth session of the general commission of the Euro-Arab dialogue was convened. While no statement was issued at the end of the meeting, it was significant that high level political discussions were resumed for the first time in five years. Although some members of the Arab League described the meeting as a total fiasco, most Arab and European representatives remained optimistic and reaffirmed their joint desire to pursue the dialogue. The meeting of the cultural committee in Tunis in January 1984 confirmed the common desire to cooperate, and emphasis was put on the cultural aspects of Euro-Arab relations, such as vocational training in Tripoli, Libya, and the possibility of meetings between young Europeans and Arabs. Euro-Arab relations seemed positive on the eve of the sixth meeting between Arab ambassadors and the members of the European Parliament at the Arab League office in Brussels on April 23, 1984. The Arabs were definitely willing to continue the dialogue and created a mission to visit the various European governments to explain the Arab position concerning the Iran-Iraq conflict and to convince the European parties not to supply arms to Iran.

The Euro-Arab dialogue serves a basic purpose for the Europeans—to create relationships and mechanisms to enhance the security of oil and gas supplies. The dialogue deals with industrialization, infrastructure, agriculture, trade, finance, science, technology, and related areas of cooperation including cultural and social exchanges. There have been relatively few results owing to a number of factors including the exclusion from discussion of energy questions such as oil prices and reliability of supply. At the same time, the Arab states have sought support for the development of their own refineries and petrochemical industries as well as other industrial projects, which threaten to compete with European capacities. The Europeans have insisted that the Arab-Israeli conflict not be included on the agenda, although they have expressed their position on that conflict in final communiques issued after each of the general sessions. Other elements have intruded as well, particularly attempts by the Arab states to influence the European relationship with Israel. Nevertheless, there has been an advantage to the dialogue—contacts and interpersonal relations of significant political value have been established. The objective of the Euro-Arab dialogue had little to do with reconciliation between Europe and the Arab world; it limited itself to creating structural cooperation between two complementary and neighboring regions. This cooperation, which was motivated by the economic interdependence of the two regions, could only be realized in conjuction with a solid political basis. It did not automatically mean that Arabs and Europeans should have identical political views; the community sought to create, rather, a climate of reciprocal confidence and of mutual entente.

Many EC officials are skeptical of the future of the Euro-Arab dialogue. The stalemate after 1979 highlights the fact that the dialogue has been strongly affected by political developments. Because of the link between economic and political issues, it has been difficult to pursue cooperation at the technical or economic levels without resolution of political problems.

The Euro-Arab dialogue has consistently been faced with a major problem; the large number of participants and their inability, especially within the Arab League, to agree with each other. Often bilateral interests have outweighed multilateral arrangements. A more political factor affecting the dialogue has been a tension between the Arab desire to focus on political issues and the European determination to separate politics from economics. The Euro-Arab dialogue is nevertheless likely to remain a feature of relations between the two regions for some time to come. The common interests identified in the 1970s have changed, but in some ways they have become more salient. The Europeans are less dependent on Arab petroleum in a period of excess supply and falling prices, although they have become increasingly involved in Arab markets. The Arabs still look to Europe for a Western political perspective different from that of the United States concerning the Middle East. They also foresee Europe becoming increasingly important as a market for Middle East products such as petrochemicals. The multinational character of the discussion reveals the perceived common West European interest in building bridges to the Arab World.

THE VENICE DECLARATION

In the latter part of the 1970s the EC ventured cautiously into the Middle East political arena. Official statements by the EC became more supportive of the Palestinian perspective and began to consider not only refugee matters but broader political concerns, including the concept of the legitimate rights of peoples. When the United States, during the Carter administration, expanded its perspective to include the political dimension of the Palestinian issue the EC moved in a similar direction. In London in June 1977 the EC spoke of Palestinian national identity and of a Palestinian homeland, and offered to participate in the peace process. In its declaration of June 29, 1977 the European Council noted:

> The Nine have affirmed their belief that a solution to the conflict in the Middle East will be possible only if the legitimate right of the Palestinian people to give effective expression to its national identity is translated into fact, which would take into account the need for a homeland for the Palestinian people.[6]

At the same time the European leaders emphasized the need for negotiations among all the parties involved leading to a lasting, comprehensive peace:

> In the context of an overall settlement, Israel must be ready to recognize the legitimate rights of the Palestinian people; equally, the Arab side must be ready to recognize the right of Israel to live in peace within secure and recognized boundaries.[7]

The Sadat initiative created a dilemma for the EC and eventually elicited a cautious reaction of support and a reiteration of the European perspective that a comprehensive peace was appropriate. In the initial period following Sadat's visit to Jerusalem, the EC reduced its role to that of support for the extant diplomatic process. As the negotiations seemed to be getting nowhere, various European leaders became involved in efforts to prod the parties, especially through pressure on Israel, but to little avail.

The success of the Camp David Summit elicited a positive response in Europe although there was some dismay as a consequence of the strongly negative Arab reaction. This helped to condition a muted European reaction to the Egypt-Israel Peace Treaty of March 1979 and a stress on the need to continue the process and not to allow it to become a separate peace. The EC declaration of March 1979 emphasized the Palestinian right to a homeland and condemned Israeli settlements in occupied territories. Although the Europeans occasionally worked with the United States in relatively minor efforts to promote peace and stability in the Middle East, on the major issues there was a policy divergence. By early 1980 European leaders seemed prepared to take unilateral action because of their concern about the failure of the Camp David process to make adequate progress and their perspective that U.S. policy could no longer be conducted by the Carter administration in a coherent manner. The Venice Declaration was both a reaction to the Camp David process and the product of a decade of cooperative European efforts to reach a Middle East policy.

The statement on the Middle East issued in Venice (the Venice Declaration)[8] on June 13, 1980, noted that the heads of state and ministers of foreign affairs "agreed that growing tensions affecting this region constitute a serious danger and render a comprehensive solution to the Israeli-Arab conflict more necessary and pressing than ever." They believed "that the traditional ties and common interests which link Europe to the Middle East oblige them to play a special role and now require them to work in a more concrete way towards peace. . . ." The envisioned terms of a settlement were outlined, the crucial elements of which included: "All of the countries in the area are entitled to live in peace within secure, recognized and guaranteed borders. . . . A just solution must finally be found to the Palestinian problem, which is not simply one of the refugees. . . ." They noted further "that they will not accept any unilateral initiative designed to change the status of Jerusalem" and that there is "the need for Israel to put an end to the territorial occupation which it has maintained since the conflict of 1967." They noted that "they are deeply concerned that the Israeli settlements constitute a serious obstacle to the peace process. . . ." In order to proceed with their proposals they "decided to make the necessary contacts with all the parties concerned. . . ." Their approach was to be based on UNSC resolutions 242 and 338 and would seek to promote two principles: "The right to existence and to security of all the states in the region, including Israel, and justice for all the peoples, which implies the recognition of the legitimate rights of the Palestinian people." The Europeans argued that the Palestinian people and the PLO "will have to be associated with the negotiations."

For the first time the Community expressed a common political view on the Middle East and called for sustained diplomatic action. The declaration's operational component included a directive to the President of the EC Council of Ministers to make contacts among the parties and an agreement to follow up on the results of those meetings. The then-president of the European Community's Council of Ministers, Luxembourg's Foreign Minister Gaston Thorn, headed a fact-finding mission to the Middle East in August 1980 designed to assess the possibility of replacing Camp David with the European initiative. The U.S. preference for its own approach and Egyptian and Israeli opposition dimmed the prospects for a substantial European initiative. Sadat seemed prepared to allow President Jimmy Carter to continue his efforts. Israeli opposition was much stronger and focused on the European effort to include the PLO despite the PLO's professed aim of eliminating Israel. Israel was concerned because the European states had not taken part in the Camp David peace process and by their declaration endangered what Israel considered to be a successful peace process while also encouraging holders of extremist views. The Israelis also were disturbed because the declaration contained preordained views ignoring Israel's interests and the situation in the Middle East; they saw it as a one-sided statement in that it accepted the Arab views in their entirety and disregarded Israel's position. In a statement issued on June 15, 1980 the Israeli Cabinet said:

> Nothing will remain of the Venice decision but a bitter memory. The decision calls on us and other nations to bring into the peace process that Arab SS which calls itself 'the Palestine Liberation Organization' .... all men of goodwill in Europe, all men who revere liberty, will see in this document another Munich-like capitulation to totalitarian blackmail and a spur to all those seeking to undermine the Camp David accords and derail the peace process in the Middle East. . . .[9]

The PLO argued that the declaration ignored fundamental factors for the establishment of a just peace in the area and the essence of the Arab-Israeli conflict. It noted that the statement was vague and contained contradictions, while it failed to recognize the PLO as the sole legitimate representative of the Palestinian people. The PLO nonetheless welcomed the move but called on the European states to take more independent stances and to free themselves from U.S. policy. A number of Arab states provided circumscribed approval.

The negative reactions of the parties to the Venice Declaration convinced many of the Europeans directly involved that the approach was appropriate—any statement criticized by both sides must be of some ultimate utility in resolving the problem.

The Venice Declaration provided evidence that the Europeans could formulate a common initiative toward the Arab-Israeli conflict and it became a starting point for further political cooperation despite some criticism from various quarters in Europe. It also reflected a compromise in the individual positions of the various European states. It articulated a European perspective that there should be a European-U.S. division of labor and that the Europeans should adopt a more active and assertive role with regard to the problems of the Middle East, most notably the Arab-Israeli conflict. To a significant degree this was based on the view that U.S. influence in the region had declined and that the United States could not adequately protect all Western interests in the region, especially those that were primarily European. An additional factor was a European view that the Arab perception of the role Europe might play in the Middle East had changed substantially, especially in the wake of Camp David, and that the Arabs would welcome such an initiative. This was seen as a result of the perceived failure of U.S. policy and closer Euro-Arab connections in part stimulated by their mutual dialogue. Political developments in the region after the adoption of the declaration soon demonstrated the limits of the EC's influence and role, however.

The primary question was whether the EC not only would, but could, act in support of its statements. After June 1980 the European Community did not take any significant steps to implement the declaration. On the contrary the attitude of the Community was reserved. Despite the Thorn fact-finding trip, the European Ministers who met in Brussels in September 1980 seemed to back away from their declaration. The outbreak of the Iran-Iraq war provoked a division in the Arab world and diverted attention from the Arab-Israeli conflict.

The United States also greeted a European initiative negatively. The general political climate between Europe and the United States was already tense because of the debate on disarmament, and Washington believed that the EC might be tempted to emphasize its independent role in the conflict to offer the Third World an alternative to the choice of the superpowers. On the other hand any European initiative had limited chances of success because of political incompatibilities between Israel and Europe.

In Luxemburg on December 2, 1980 the heads of state and government of the EC were reported to have approved in secret an internal working document that was, in fact, a European peace initiative, to serve as a "viable alternative" in the event of the failure of the Camp David process. Nevertheless the initiative seemed not to be as viable as it first appeared.

EC efforts to implement the Venice Declaration did not make substantial progress owing to a number of factors. The U.S. presidential elections in November 1980, which brought Ronald Reagan to power, led several European countries, especially Britain, to take a wait-and-see attitude to determine if the new president would continue the Camp David process. Also, the Europeans wished to do nothing that might harm the chances of the Labor opposition in the Israeli national election scheduled for June 1981. When Menachem Begin again became prime minister it made European efforts more difficult. The French presidential election in May 1981 brought to power Francois Mitterrand, who seemed favorable to Camp David and hostile to the Venice process. He attempted to reduce the French pro-Arab influence in the EC in the hope that Europe could at least become an honest broker. He argued that a Kissinger-style step-by-step approach was the appropriate policy to solve the Arab-Israeli conflict. In addition, a number of new elements were introduced into the equation: the assassination of Sadat and the uncertainties surrounding the policies of his successor; the publication of the Fahd Plan; the waiting period before Israel completed its evacuation from the Sinai; and the Falklands war, which monopolized European attention and provisionally eliminated Great Britain as the moving force behind an initiative on the Middle East.

Each of these events reduced the possibility of success of the initiative. But, beyond the unfavorable constellation of events, the European failure can be attributed to more fundamental causes. The Europeans have engaged in declaratory diplomacy—they issue declarations or working papers that offer solutions rather than engaging in any intense diplomatic efforts. They also suffer from the fact that rather than being the effort of a single government, the policies are the result of a compromise among six or more governments; the policy thus reaches a high level of complexity that makes it difficult to pursue. Europe also has lacked the massive economic and military commitment associated with superpower, especially U.S., efforts.

It is even more noteworthy that the declarations received no significant follow up, and generated no real commitment, in the area. The most highly developed activity of the Europeans since the Venice Declaration has proved to be the ritual visits to the Middle East of the presidents of the Council of Ministers. The economic aid of the Common Market to the parties to the dispute has been very limited. In the military realm there is even less of a role: the MFO and the Multinational Force in Beirut are not European interventions although troops of European states are involved, arms sales have remained bilateral, and there is no European force capable by itself of regional intervention.

Finally, the lack of European success is intimately related to the internal crises of the EC. Europe suffered from an accumulation of disabilities in its efforts to implement the Venice Declaration. It had little credibility and influence in the region, especially with Israel, and it was suspect to the United States. It sought to secure an Arab response that might facilitate the process but was unsuccessful. It could not broker a deal because of a lack of influence with both sides in the conflict as well as an inability to secure any real acceptance of the European approach and role.

By the time of the announcement of the Reagan initiative in September 1982 the European effort had effectively come to a halt and the European Community was prepared to defer to the efforts of the President of the United States, although continuing to criticize the U.S. effort. It could link itself to the President's proposal without abandoning Venice and without admitting that it had failed to secure any significant achievement for the declaration.

In sum, the Europeans had little choice but to support the Reagan initiative/Camp David negotiations process, and the alternative role that the EC hoped to play was transformed into little more than a supportive one. Whatever its influence in the Arab or the Palestinian camp, Europe did not possess sufficient leverage in the Middle East to play a major independent role.

After the Israeli invasion of Lebanon in June 1982 the Europeans condemned Israel's actions but also condemned terrorist action against Israel. The EC's position toward the Palestinian question remained similar to that expressed in the Venice Declaration. At the end of June the foreign ministers declared that Israel would only find the security it needs "by satisfying the legitimate aspirations of the Palestinian people." The EC remained convinced that the PLO should be associated with negotiations and after the massacres of Palestinians at Sabra and Shatila, the President of the European Council of Ministers met for the first time with PLO representative Farouk Kadoumi. This contributed to a worsening of the Community's relations with Israel.

The United States had requested European participation in the multinational force in the Sinai after Israel's April 1982 withdrawal and sought the EC's assistance in helping to solve the Lebanese problem. After the invasion of Lebanon another Multinational Force including French, Italian, and British contingents joined the U.S. Marines to supervise the evacuation of the PLO from Beirut, but these were bilateral efforts and did not engage the EC. By September 1982 the Middle East had become an area of entente between the EC and the United States. Reagan's September 1, 1982 "fresh start" initiative corresponded to a view that the Europeans had held for some years. Reagan's concerns about Israel's extention of its law and jurisdiction to the Golan Heights in December 1981 and the war in Lebanon in June 1982 contributed to closer relations between the United States and Europe. Europe deferred to Reagan and his initiative, although there were signs of agitation and complaint from Britian and other Europeans by 1984/85 that the United States was not doing enough to promote the effort.

European differences with the United States have been most pronounced in regard to the issues resulting from the Iranian Revolution and the Soviet invasion of Afghanistan. European governments were reluctant to follow President Carter's lead in imposing economic and symbolic reprisals against the USSR after the invasion of Afghanistan and in initiating long-term countermeasures to guarantee the security of the Persian Gulf. Openly criticizing the inconsistency, unpredictability, and absence of consultations that had characterized recent U.S. foreign policy, they were apprehensive of a return to the kind of cold war confrontation with the Soviet Union that had preceded detente. At the same time, they were concerned that economic sanctions against Iran would be ineffectual or counterproductive, further endangering Western energy supplies while accomplishing nothing to secure the release of the U.S. hostages taken in Teheran in November 1979. The reluctant decision of some European governments to support the Olympic boycott, the trade embargo against Iran, and similar measures, was born less of their own conviction than of a recognition of the need to retain close working relations with the United States.

The EC attitude toward the Iran-Iraq war has been reserved. At the beginning of the war, the EC Council of Ministers met to exchange views on the conflict. The Community published a neutral statement in May 1982 and offered to take a mediation role to put an end to the hostilities. After the Iranian counterattack in July 1982, economic exchanges between Europe and Iraq diminished. In March 1983 the foreign ministers of the Community expressed their concern that the continuation of the conflict increasingly threatened the stability and the security of the whole region. With none of the previous initiatives having succeeded in bringing peace to the area, the European Community continued to call for a ceasefire, the cessation of all military operations, and the withdrawal of forces to internationally recognized frontiers, and a just and honorable settlement negotiated in accordance with the resolutions of the UN Security Council and acceptable to both parties.

From the viewpoint of economic exchanges, Iran was the first to reduce considerably its oil exports to the Community in 1980, followed by Iraq in 1981 and 1982. Because of Teheran's poor relations with the West after the revolution in 1979, Iranian imports from the Community consistently decreased until 1982, while Iraqi imports increased from 1977 to 1982.

In December 1983, at the Euro-Arab meeting in Greece, the Europeans reaffirmed their neutrality and called on Iran and Iraq not to commit any act of war or take any measure that would endanger free navigation in the Gulf and lead to an escalation of hostilities.

CONCLUSION

The EC's approach to the Middle East was primarily trade-oriented until the end of the 1960s. The European ambition was to create a huge interregional market based around the Mediterranean. This project was confronted with the difficulty of establishing a common agricultural policy in Europe and of contributing to the development of basic, solid economic structures in the Mediterranean states. The Arab-Israeli dispute, which was already the central issue of the Middle Eastern conflict, gained momentum in 1967 and in 1973. At the same time Europe became increasingly dependent on Middle Eastern oil, and with that the necessity to support politically the Palestinian cause in exchange for an Arab promise not to use the oil weapon became the central preoccupation of European decision makers from 1970 onwards.

The Euro-Arab dialogue was seen as a means of promoting structured cooperation between the two regions but it has yet to achieve substantial, tangible results. Similarly Europe's ability to propose its own peace initiative to solve the Palestinian question is limited in both accomplishment and prospect. There is no doubt that the Europeans are aware that their contribution to an Arab-Israeli settlement will remain limited. This is due not only to the fact that every European statement or initiative is a result of compromise among the various European states, but also because the Europeans realize that in reality they have little leverage to implement their policy if the parties concerned are unwilling to accept them or if they clash with those of the United States. The EC thus faces a series of difficulties: to reach a compromise position that retains some merit, to define its role in a precise and clear manner, to become credible and acceptable to the parties to the conflict, and to coordinate its activities with those of the United States. Realistically, it can do little more than to try to foster a dialogue on the issues in contention.

Despite the greater activism of Europe policy in the Middle East since the beginning of the 1970s, Europe has not become a power that exerts any discernible influence on the course of regional events or developments. The European Community generally has been impotent and frustrated as EC policies have failed to achieve positive results. Although the Europeans are sceptical about the U.S. chances of getting much further with the Camp David process, they have yet to suggest a better approach. There is also a reluctance to do anything that might undercut the U.S. approach.

The United States and Europe have similar but not identical interests in the Middle East. Both have political, cultural, and economic links with both Israel and the major Arab states and share a concern for the security of the region and the stability of its individual states. But European dependence on Middle Eastern oil is not shared by the United States. For Europe the economic link, enhanced by historical connections, has been an important factor. Europeans also believe that the absence in Europe of significant Jewish communities or Zionist lobbies has permitted them to pursue policies more balanced than those of the United States on the Arab-Israeli issue. Nevertheless, despite some sharp criticism of Israel, the European states remain committed to Israel's survival.

The playing of a political role, begun in the decade of the 1970s, remains a central component in the European approach to the Middle East, although its tangible successes remain, as yet, limited in scope and accomplishment.

NOTES

1. *Bulletin of the European Communities* 6 (June 1983), pp. 41–43.
2. Federal Republic of Germany, Press and Information Office of the Federal Government, *European Political Co-operation*, 3rd Ed. (Bonn, 1978), p. 66.
3. *Ibid.*, p. 67.
4. U.N. Document S/RES/242.
5. *European Political Co-operation*, p. 82.
6. *Ibid.*, p. 159.
7. *Ibid.*

8. "Venice, from the European Council to the Western Summit," *Bulletin of the European Communities Commission* 6 (1980) p. 7.

9. Israeli cabinet statement of June 15, 1980 in *Survival* (September/October 1980), pp. 227–30.

5
Great Britain

Rosemary Hollis

The role of the United Kingdom in the international relations of the Middle East was of greater significance in the past than it is today. More than any other external power, Britain played a predominant role in shaping the modern Middle East during the first half of the twentieth century.

THE HISTORICAL RELATIONSHIP

The Early Years

The appeal made by Pope Urban II to European Christians, in 1095, to mount a crusade to rescue the Christian Holy Lands from the domination of Moslems marked the beginning of direct and persistent contact between England and the Middle East. After the Crusades and until the nineteenth century the main form of British presence in the region was the merchant adventurers, and the trading companies that they set up. By the seventeenth century British trade relations with the Middle and Far East were administered by two companies, granted monopolies in these regions by the English crown. The Levant Company, otherwise known as the Turkey Merchants, was founded in 1581, having negotiated with the Ottoman Sultan both access to trade in his dominions and protection for the British traders themselves. The protection was granted in the form of "Capitulations," also enjoyed by the French, which afforded the foreigners various exemptions from local laws and taxes, and were to become a bone of contention with the local population over time. The East India Company, trading with India, was granted its charter in 1600.

Having started out as a trading nation, Britain evolved into an imperial power. The protection of its trading activities and its colonial possessions, and the access to communication routes essential to both, became central components of British foreign policy. The British Raj in India became the "Jewel in the Imperial Crown," the most prized colonial possession for the British. By 1800 British interests in the Middle East revolved around two fundamental concerns: first, protection of the routes to India, both the northern route through the Persian Gulf and the southern route across Egypt to Suez and the Red Sea; and second, prevention of domination of the region by rival powers, notably France or Russia. Napoleon's invasion of Egypt in 1798 and the revelation of his plans to negotiate a treaty with Persia in 1807 served to galvanize Britain's resolve to protect those interests and curtail incursions by France.

From this time, British involvement in the Middle East evolved in two distinct spheres, partly reflecting the existence of the two routes to India and partly the division of administrative responsibility for the region between London and Bombay, stemming from the historical division of trading activities between the Levant and the East India Companies. In the sphere centered on the Persian Gulf and administered from Bombay, the main British objectives in Persia were to develop trade relations, prevent incursions into the northern reaches of the imperial possessions in India, and guard against Russian expansion toward the Persian Gulf and the Indian Ocean. The primary concern in the Gulf was to prevent local Arab tribes from raiding or disrupting British shipping.

The formalization of British relations with the Arab sheikhs of the Gulf littoral began in 1798 with a treaty with the Sultan of Muscat. By the General Treaty of Peace of 1820 and the Maritime Truce of 1835 the erstwhile pirate leaders of the Lower Gulf coast were bound to cease armed conflict at sea. The Treaty of Peace in Perpetuity, signed in 1853 by the Trucial Sheikhs, as they became known, added a clause for enforcement by the British navy. The treaties served to protect British merchant traffic and other commercial activities in the Gulf from interference by piracy or local disputes. Between 1880 and 1916 more extensive protective agreements were negotiated with the Trucial Sheikhdoms, entitling Britain to conduct their foreign relations, handle their security problems, and maintain order in the region. These arrangements were to remain in place essentially until the end of the 1960s.

A policy of support for Ottoman authority in the interior of the Arabian Peninsula, as a way of protecting British interests, proved unrealistic in these outer reaches of the Ottoman Empire, and in

1839 the British annexed Aden, which developed into a flourishing port and coaling station for steamships coming to and from Suez. The government of India was responsible for running the colony and port facilities in Aden, as well as for supervising relations with the Arab principalities along the Gulf and dealings with the Ottoman province of lower Mesopotamia. From 1860, the diplomatic posts in south and east Persia were staffed from India, and London assumed responsibility for Teheran, Tabriz, Isfahan, and Shiraz.

British relations with the states along the Suez route gradually developed into a more active presence than was the case in the Gulf. Whenever the prospect loomed of either the French or the Russians acquiring territory in Europe or Asia at the expense of the Ottomans, the posture adopted by the United Kingdom (U.K.) was one of support for Ottoman authority, or, on occasion, direct involvement itself, as in the acquisition of the island of Cyprus, in the eastern Mediterranean, by the Treaty of Berlin of 1878. Britain's efforts to arrange favorable terms for its agents and traders was to lead to growing involvement in Egypt where Ottoman control was ineffectual. In 1875 the British prime minister bought the Egyptian khedive's shares in the Suez Canal when financial difficulties forced him to offer them for sale. This move gave Britain and France ownership of the Canal. It was in the interest of protecting this commercial concern that in 1876 they took joint control of Egypt's ailing finances and, in 1882, the British occupied Egypt.

Direct British intervention in Egypt proved difficult to reverse: there seemed no immediate prospect of finding a suitable surrogate to govern Egypt with appropriate deference to British interests. The importance of Egypt to British interests was growing because of a decline in British influence with the Ottoman Sultan, the increasing value attached to the Canal, and a new drive to rationalize the British presence in Africa, exemplified by the reconquest of the Sudan in 1898, which resulted in the establishment of an Anglo-Egyptian condominium there.

In the early twentieth century British policy in the Middle East shifted. The accelerating decline of Ottoman authority, the formation of an alliance between Russia and France in 1894, and the demonstration of British military deficiencies when put to the test in the Boer War, together obliged the U.K. to accept sharing a few of the spoils in the Middle East with rivals. In 1903 Germany won the concession for a Baghdad railway; in 1904 the British conceded a free hand to France in Morocco in return for the same for themselves in Egypt, and in 1907 they came to an agreement with Russia to divide Persia into separate spheres of influence.

World War 1 and Conflicting Arrangements

World War 1 brought British political and military involvement in the Middle East to a new level, and by the close of the postwar peace negotiations the U.K. had become the predominant power in the region.

A number of factors influenced British policy and strategy in the Middle East during World War 1. First, India was considered as vital an interest as ever, having become the primary military base for British forces outside the U.K. The British-officered Indian army numbered a quarter of a million men and was used for "policing" the empire far beyond India's shores. India was also Britain's single most valuable commercial asset, accounting for almost 10 percent of total U.K. trade. There was thus no question of the need to protect the routes to India. A second factor was that the Ottoman Empire sided with Germany, which made it an opponent of British ambitions in the region as well as an obstacle to Britain's communications with its ally Russia. Meanwhile, given the anticipated demise of the Ottoman Empire, the British wanted as much influence as possible over the division of the spoils. An additional concern was that Arab nationalism was taking effect as a new force in the region, one that it would be better to placate than to confront. Lastly, overt intervention having already become the policy in Egypt, direct military action elsewhere was facilitated both logistically and psychologically.

Britain's decision to launch the Gallipoli Peninsula campaign was designed to open a second front to relieve the pressure in Europe, but it had added attraction as a way to position the British at the helm in Constantinople, ready for the postwar dissection of the Ottoman Empire. This possibility also occurred to Britain's allies, and Britain had to balance a policy of protecting its assets and lines of communication in the region, as well as recruiting Arab nationalism to its cause, with the need to reassure its allies. This led it into a tangle of promises and undertakings to the different parties concerned with the region.

In 1914 Britain declared Egypt a Protectorate and sent an expedition to secure the British position at the head of the Gulf in Mesopotamia. The following year Britain was obliged to clarify its position with its allies, and the Constantinople Agreement, the first of a number of secret agreements on the future of the Middle East, was reached in March 1915 with France and Russia. Russia's claim to Constantinople and the Turkish Straits was accepted, while France made known its interest in Syria. Concurrently, the British administration in Cairo was exploring the possibility of sponsoring an Arab revolt against the Ottomans, under the leadership of Sherif Hussein of Mecca, the go-between in this endeavour being T.E. Lawrence (Lawrence of Arabia).

A correspondence between Sir Henry McMahon, British High Commissioner in Egypt, and Sherif Hussein was conducted between July 1915 and January 1916, the purpose of which was to encourage the Sherif to revolt, in return for British recognition and support, subject to various modifications, for independence of the Arabs in the regions demanded by the Sherif. The key letter in respect to the British position on both Syria and Palestine was written by McMahon dated October 24, 1915. The Sykes-Picot Agreement, negotiated by Mark Sykes for Britain and Georges Picot for France in May 1916, embodied different provisions.

The Sykes-Picot Agreement and the McMahon letter of October 24, 1915 coincided on some points, including the expectation that the British would control Southern Mesopotamia and that the French would control the coastal zone of what is now Lebanon and Syria. They both provided for the independence of the "Arab peoples"—subject to differing but unspecified conditions. That Arabia would belong to the Arabs was also taken for granted by both. The documents differed, however, on three main points: (a) By the Sykes-Picot Agreement alone, Britain was to have complete control of a small enclave containing the ports of Haifa and Acre; (b) In regard to Syria, Hussein was given the impression that this would be independent, while France was assured that France would be the sole source of "advisers and foreign functionaries"—implying French supervision there; (c) On Palestine, the Sykes-Picot Agreement was specific—Palestine was to have an international administration, "the form of which is to be decided upon after consultation with the other allies, and the representatives of the Shareef of Mecca."[1] The McMahon letter, however, was unclear on Palestine. Britain, it said, "was prepared to recognize and support the independence of the Arabs," subject to three exceptions: in the coastal areas "lying to the West of the districts of Damascus, Homs, Hama and Aleppo;" in the regions affected by "our existing treaties with Arab chiefs" (the Gulf littoral); and in regions in which "the interests of our ally, France" limited Britain's freedom to act alone. The word translated as "district" in the first of these exceptions was *vilayet*, which could also be translated as "province," with somewhat different connotations. The discrepancies between the McMahon correspondence and the British agreement with the French were revealed in November 1917, when the Bolsheviks made public all secret agreements in the Tsar's records. At that point the

Sherif was effectively soothed, but controversy based on these documents was to surface again later.

The Arab revolt against the Ottoman Empire was launched with British help in June 1916. In March 1917, the British forces in Mesopotamia took Baghdad, and the following December, Jerusalem was captured. In the meantime, on November 2, 1917, Foreign Secretary Lord Balfour wrote a letter to Lord Rothschild stating the position of the U.K. government on Jewish/Zionist aspirations, which has become known as the Balfour Declaration:

> His Majesty's Government views with favour the establishment in Palestine of a national home for the Jewish people, and will use their best endeavours to facilitate the achievement of this object, it being clearly understood that nothing shall be done which may prejudice the civil and religious rights of existing non-Jewish communities in Palestine, or the rights and political status enjoyed by Jews in any other country.[2]

After the triumphal entry into Palestine and Damascus of both the regular forces under General Sir Edmund Allenby and the Sherif's nationalists under the tutelage of Lawrence, the French and British issued a statement on November 8, 1918, declaring their objective in the war to have been the complete emancipation of the peoples oppressed by the Turks and the establishment of national governments and administrations deriving their authority from the initiative and free choice of the indigenous populations. For immediate practical purposes, however, Allenby turned to the Sykes-Picot agreement as the most comprehensive guide for allocating pressing administrative tasks.

Drawing Up the Map of the Middle East, 1918–1922

Drawing up agreements to apportion all the spoils at the end of World War I was bound to be a lengthy and complicated task, and the designation of boundaries in Europe took first priority. Consequently, decisions on the various claims to control in the Middle East were not reached until the San Remo Conference in 1920. Even then the British left the final decisions on how they intended to conduct themselves in the territories under their control until a conference in Cairo in 1922. This allowed considerable time for ad hoc arrangements to affect British and Arab perceptions.

At the end of the war, British influence was paramount in Egypt, Sudan, Palestine, Mesopotamia, the sheikhdoms along the Arabian coast of the Gulf, and the Arabian Peninsula itself. The type of arrangements devised for dealing with each of these areas varied.

After long deliberations, it was announced in February 1922 that the Protectorate of Egypt would be abolished, and on March 1, 1922, Egypt theoretically became an independent state. In practice, however, the British retained considerable control by reserving the right to maintain troops there to defend Egypt and the Canal, to protect foreign minorities, and to control the Sudan "until such time as it may be possible by discussion and friendly accommodation on both sides to conclude agreements in regard thereto between His Majesty's Government and the Government of Egypt."[3]

The Ottoman territory of Mesopotamia, thereafter Iraq, was granted to Britain at San Remo as a League of Nations Mandate. Rioting immediately ensued and British troops from India were used to quell the outbreak. In 1921 control was transferred from the India Office to the Colonial Office in London, and on August 23, 1921, Feisal, the son of Sherif Hussein whom the French had just ousted from Damascus, was crowned King of Iraq as a British gesture of recompence. On October 10, 1921, Britain signed a treaty with Feisal in which it undertook to provide the "State of Iraq with such advice and assistance as may be required during the period of the present Treaty, without prejudice to her national sovereignty." Iraq was to have diplomatic representation in London and to apply for membership in the League of Nations. Provision was made for constitutional development and there were no religious or financial safeguards attached to the treaty. In December 1925 the province of Mosul was incorporated in Iraq.

In Persia the British sphere of influence agreement with Russia had lapsed with the Bolshevik revolution in 1917 and subsequent attempts by the British to negotiate a favorable treaty directly with the Persians collapsed. Commencing with a coup d'etat in 1921 Reza Shah gradually consolidated personal power and effected the exclusion of Britain from Iranian affairs, except as the foreign power principally responsible for the production of Iranian oil.

On the Arabian shores of the Gulf the nineteenth century British "exclusive treaty" arrangements with the sheikhdoms remained undisturbed by the war. In the Arabian Peninsula, meanwhile, the U.K. had gained a new ally in Abdul Aziz ibn Saud, who in 1925 captured Mecca from Sherif Hussein and added the Hejaz to the newly created Kingdom of Saudi Arabia. In May 1927, Saud signed the Treaty of Jiddah with the British, which stressed "the complete and absolute independence of the dominions of his Majesty the King of the Hejaz and Nejd and its Dependencies." In return, Britain gave him its protection.

The British retained their settlement at Aden, which was transmuted in 1937 into a Crown Colony administered from London instead of India. The British-Yemeni Treaty of Sana had been signed in 1934 in an effort to prevent Yemeni interference in the area under British protection, but ambiguities persisted and produced disputes at a later date.

The British Mandate in Palestine proved to be the thorniest issue. By agreement at the San Remo Conference, Britain took official charge as Mandatory authority in Palestine and Transjordan on July 24, 1922. The terms of the Mandate included provision for a Jewish national home in Palestine, incorporating the Balfour Declaration into the text. As the Mandatory authority, Britain had full control over foreign, defense, administrative, and legislative policy, at the same time being bound "so far as circumstances permit (to) encourage local autonomy" and preserve freedom of conscience. According to Article 4, "an appropriate Jewish Agency for the purpose of advising and cooperating with the administrator of Palestine in such economic, social and other matters as may affect the establishment of the Jewish National Home and the interests of the Jewish population in Palestine"[4] was to be set up. The same provision was not considered necessary to represent the concerns of the Arab population at this point, and subsequently they were to resist the notion of representation parallel to that of the Jews. Consequently, the British dealt with the Jews through a single interlocutor, but not so the Arabs.

To coincide with the publication of the Mandate the government issued a policy document in July 1922, later referred to as the Churchill White Paper, clarifying the meaning of the Balfour Declaration. It reaffirmed that Palestine as a whole was not to be converted into a Jewish National Home, only that such a home should be founded in Palestine. It also stressed that the British government would not contemplate "the disappearance or subordination of the Arab population, language or culture in Palestine." Far from easing the situation this document served to obstruct Zionist aspirations without securing Arab goodwill. Subsequently, every time Britain produced a plan for the future of Palestine it was greeted with disapproval from one or both sides and Britain recoiled from implementing it by force. The result was vacillation.

The Churchill White Paper also offered clarification of exactly what Sir Henry McMahon had proposed to Sherif Hussein in his letter dated October 24, 1915. The undertaking, it said, excluded from its scope the portions of Syria lying to the west of the district of Damascus and the whole of Palestine west of the Jordan River.

According to the Mandate, Britain was entitled to make such provision as it considered suitable for the administration of the territories lying between the Jordan and the eastern boundary of Palestine, as ultimately determined, and to postpone or withhold application there of such provisions of the Mandate as it deemed inapplicable. Sherif Hussein's son Abdullah was already installed as ruler of Transjordan (spanning both banks of the Jordan), and in 1923 he was promised independence in the future. The arrangement was formalized in a treaty with Abdullah in 1928, whereby he was given his own machinery of government, with British tutelage over financial and foreign policy concerns.

The Assumption of British Predominance, 1922–1945

From 1922 to the outbreak of World War II the arrangements by which Britain enjoyed predominance in the Middle East remained essentially unchanged. Except in Palestine, Britain's position, which was founded on a combination of self-confidence and, ultimately, the strength of the Indian Army, was not seriously challenged. At the same time, Britain did little to assuage the forces of nationalism that would eventually challenge British predominance when recourse to the Indian Army was no longer an option.

Disturbances in Palestine became endemic by the end of the 1920s, as the number of Jewish immigrants rose steeply. Troops were brought in from Transjordan, Egypt, and Malta to restore order, but successive government statements concerning immigration policy and quotas, which attempted to reassure both the Jewish and Arab communities, succeeded only in fuelling anxiety in both.

On the eve of World War II, a U.K. Royal Commission recommended partition of Palestine. Since the proposal was not acceptable to the communities on the spot, it would have had to be enforced by the British. Given the growing global tension at this time, Britain decided to shelve the problem of Palestine's political future. The Palestine White Paper of May 17, 1939 was designed to shore up the situation in the short term. It placed limitations on Jewish purchases of land, fixed an annual total for Jewish immigration for five years, after which further increase was to be dependent upon Arab acquiescence, and there were to be no arrangements made for independence without consulting the Jewish community.

The Palestine White Paper was the first of a number of emergency measures designed to meet British needs in World War II. British policy in the Middle East in World War II was dictated by the traditional concerns of protecting the empire and its communications and preventing rival powers from encroaching on British spheres of influence, as well as protecting new ventures in oil exploration.

After Germany invaded the Soviet Union in 1941, the U.K. and the Soviet Union jointly occupied Iran, to prevent the Iranian government from obstructing supplies on their way across Iran from the Allies to the USSR. They partitioned the country between them for the duration of the war. Britain also put all its Middle East administrations on a war footing for the duration of the war, regardless of the fact that the region was only involved directly in the fighting until the Allied victory at Alamein in 1942.

The British Decline, 1945–1955

In the aftermath of World War II Britain was faced with an array of impatient claims for new arrangements in the Middle East. This placed it in a difficult situation, since it was evident to the British government by now that new dangers, such as the ambitions of the Soviet Union and the growing importance of oil, were beginning to threaten its interests there.

The British presence in the Gulf had been dictated originally by the imperatives of imperial communications. By coincidence, it was in territories under British influence at Kirkuk, Basra, Kuwait, Qatar, and Abu Dhabi, as well as in neighboring Iran, that oil became a potential for economic gain. In 1948, the year after India had gained its independence, demand for Middle Eastern oil began to grow and thereby came into being a new incentive to safeguard sea and land routes from the area.

As both consumer and exploiter of oil, Britain's interests dictated maintaining as much influence in the Middle East as possible, but the postwar exhaustion of British resources left it without any major bargaining chips with which to do so. Between March 1946 and January 1948 the British attempted to renegotiate treaty arrangements throughout the region, and everywhere—except Transjordan and the Trucial sheikhdoms—they failed. Arrangements along the Gulf littoral remained unaltered. In the case of Transjordan they were able to negotiate reentry rights for 25 years, for which the Jordanian king was heavily criticized by his neighbors.

In Iran the British forces of occupation withdrew from the southern provinces, as promised after their entry in 1941. When the Soviet troops in the north failed to follow suit Britain was not able to help Iran drive them out, although it had no wish to see them remain.

In Greece and Turkey, meanwhile, the U.K. had been the power primarily responsible for bolstering national defenses. In March 1947 the announcement of the Truman Doctrine by the government of the United States signalled that it was to take responsibility for Western strategic interests in the vicinity of Greece and Turkey. Theoretically American and British interests were sufficiently similar that this should have been a source of relief for Britain. In fact, having to bow to superior American strength required some adaptation in Britain, especially when this was accompanied by pressure from Washington on behalf of both Arab self-determination and Jewish interests in Palestine.

In August 1945 President Truman appealed directly to British Prime Minister Clement Attlee to allow the immediate admission of 100,000 Jewish refugees to Palestine. In response Attlee proposed the creation of an Anglo-American Committee of Inquiry to study the Palestine problem. A committee of nonofficial citizens was duly appointed and eventually unanimously endorsed a report recommending immediate entry for 100,000 Jews, continuation of the Mandate, pending execution of a trusteeship by the United Nations, and removal of land transfer limitations. Both governments reserved judgment and appointed an official committee to recommend approaches to implementation. The result was the Grady-Morrison plan, which revived a British prewar project for a federalized Jewish-Arab Palestine and made further Jewish immigration dependent upon joint Jewish-Arab consent.

The Zionists were bitterly disappointed. Civil strife in Palestine intensified, and in February 1947 Britain, under pressure from the Jews, the Arabs, and the Americans, declared itself unable to deal with the situation and referred it to the UN. The British refused to cooperate with implementation of the UN partition plan and in May 1948 withdrew from Palestine. As soon as this was accomplished the Jewish National Council proclaimed the independence of the state of Israel and the first Arab-Israeli war broke out.

In the wake of this conflict and the onset of the Cold War, Britain joined France and the United States in the Tripartite Declaration in 1950, undertaking to monitor the supply of arms to the region. In Egypt Britain seemed for a while to be able to come to terms with the new regime, which had seized power by coup d'etat in 1952, and which turned out to be relatively efficient. In 1953, an agreement was reached between the British and the Sudanese that gave the Sudan independence after a transitional period. In 1954, an accommodation was reached with the Egyptians on the status of the Suez Canal, such that British troops were to be "completely withdrawn from Egyptian territory...within a period of twenty months from the date of signature of the present Agreement." A proviso was made, however, that in the event of an armed attack by an outside power on Egypt or any country that was a party to the treaty of joint defense (between Arab League States, signed in Cairo on 13th April 1950), or on Turkey, Egypt still offered to the U.K. such facilities as might be necessary in order to place the base on a war footing and to operate it effectively.[5]

British relations with Iran underwent a serious crisis at the beginning of the 1950s. In 1951, the Iranian government nationalized the oil industry, thereby dispossessing the Anglo-Iranian Oil Company (AIOC). Efforts to negotiate compensation for this move failed and Iranian politics were overtaken by anti-Western extremism, which the young Shah was unable to contain. In 1953, a period of mounting economic and political chaos in Iran was brought to a close with a military coup d'etat, aided by both U.S. and British intelligence, and the Shah's authority was restored. Following this, arrangements were made for an international consortium of oil companies to operate Iranian oil fields and share the profits with the government, and the AIOC received some compensation.

Demonstrating a continuing desire to preserve the Middle East from Soviet machinations but unable to confront such a challenge alone, from 1955 Britain participated in the Baghdad Pact. This had value for Britain as a way to further its interests without bearing all the burden of costs, but it also presented problems, since the inclusion of Britain was labelled imperialistic by Arab nationalists, and the other signatories therefore became targets of popular criticism. In 1956 Britain came into direct confrontation with the leader of Arab nationalism, Egypt's President Gamal Abdul Nasser.

Debacle: 1956

In September 1955 Egypt announced that it had concluded an arms deal with Czechoslovakia. This represented an opening for the Soviet Union in the heart of the Middle East, which could render irrelevant such instruments of containment as the Baghdad Pact. The cause of radical Arab nationalism that Egypt championed, meanwhile, presented a mounting threat to the British position of influence in Jordan and Iraq. In July 1956 the British government followed the lead of the United States in withdrawing its offer of a loan to Egypt's President Nasser to finance the building of the Aswan Dam. Then,on July 26, 1956, Nasser nationalized the Suez Canal.

On the surface, the next few months constituted a period of continuous negotiation between the British and French shareholders and the Egyptian government to come to some form of mutually acceptable settlement for the future running and protection of the waterway. In fact, this time was spent by Britain and France, in collusion with Israel, making arrangements to seize the Canal by force. The Israelis took the opportunity to make a preemptive strike at Egypt's military forces, since they expected them to be used against Israel.

On October 29, 1956, Israel launched its attack on Egypt. The following day, in London, the British and French governments officially protested to the ambassadors of Israel and Egypt and issued an ultimatum stating that they were both to withdraw to lines ten miles back from each side of the Canal, so that British and French forces could occupy the Canal zone. Neither side responded and the British and French launched their attack on Egyptian airfields on October 31. On November 5, Allied paratroopers began landing at Port Said. The international condemnation of this demonstration of force by the U.K. and France was overwhelming, and the United States demanded Allied and Israeli withdrawal without compromise. On November 6, Britain called for a ceasefire and the war was over. The evacuation of British troops was completed by December 22.

The Suez invasion was specifically the work of Prime Minister Anthony Eden and his Cabinet rather than the British Foreign Office. Eden had become convinced that Nasser was a threat to the stability of the Middle East in general and British interests in particular and the invasion had been intended, from his point of view, not merely to retrieve control of the Canal but to replace Nasser with either direct Anglo-French control or a government more suited to the tastes of both the British and French governments. However questionable the actual objectives, in the post-imperial era, the plan was also hopelessly ill-conceived. Insufficient attempt was made to ascertain the likely response of the United States, or to plan for U.S. opposition; the delay of the Anglo-French invasion to maintain the pretense of a unilateral Israeli attack was poor military strategy, allowing Egypt time to rally its defenses; and the hypocrisy of colluding with Israel eliminated whatever gains Britain had accrued with the Arabs since World War II by dissociating itself from Zionism.

For the U.K., the Suez adventure of 1956 had achieved the complete obverse of what had been intended. The Allies were obliged to pay for the material damage, while Nasser gained in both power and prestige. The reputation of Britain in the Middle East reached an all time low, and criticism was voiced throughout the Commonwealth. The episode also had an adverse effect on Anglo-American relations. The U.S. reputation in the region was boosted by its demonstration of firmness and impartiality. The announcement of the so-called Eisenhower Doctrine on December 31, 1956 signalled the shift of responsibility for Western interests in the Middle East to the United States coincident with the nadir of British influence.

The Last Phase of Direct Involvement, 1956-1971

On July 14, 1958, a coup d'etat overthrew the monarchy in Iraq and with it the last vestiges of British influence there. Responding to a request from Jordan for a demonstration of support for the regime, British paratroopers made a visit to Amman, at the same time as U.S. marines landed in Lebanon. The Iraqui revolution did not, however, spill over, and the troops were shortly withdrawn.

This episode marked the dwindling of the British presence in the Middle East to its last outposts on the Gulf littoral and in Aden Colony. For a time the government proposed to incorporate these into plans for policing the Indian Ocean as part of the strategy of the Western Alliance for containing communism and protecting oil supplies.[6] In 1959 an Arabian Peninsula command was built and a unified command created at Aden. As it turned out the new policy did not endure. A combination of pressure for independence in the protected areas and a new political mood in Britain, which favored divesting the country of foreign responsibilities that it could ill afford, brought almost complete withdrawal "East of Suez" within a decade.

Since creating a Legislative Council for Aden in 1947, the colonial authorities had been obliged by nationalist pressure to yield more and more autonomy to the inhabitants. At the same time, their attempts to bring order to the surrounding region (which was to become South Yemen), through the creation of an Eastern and a Western Protectorate, had failed to prevent chronic warfare among tribal groups. In 1959 the Western States of the Protectorate were induced to sign a Treaty of Federation under British protection. In 1962, Britain linked Aden to the Federation, in an effort to create a more viable economic and administrative unit.

This move was taken on the eve of a republican coup in neighboring Yemen, following which Britain gave backing to the royalist opposition there, while Nasser's Egyptian armed forces came to the support of the nascent republican regime. The violence extended into Aden itself and the Federation rapidly lost what little authority it had. In 1966 the British announced that the Aden base was no longer tenable and that they intended to leave by 1968. The planned withdrawal turned into a shambling retreat, completed by November 1967.

Britain had no direct involvement in the hostilities during the 1967 Arab-Israeli war. As soon as the conflict began, Britain's initial response was to impose an arms embargo on all the combatants, its duration conditional on similar actions by the other powers. When these were not forthcoming, Britain lifted its embargo after only twenty-four hours. The Arab states, for their part, subjected Britain to an oil embargo, imposed simultaneously on the United States and West Germany. This did not last long but served as a warning. The U.K. was instrumental in bringing the UN Security Council to concur on appropriate peace terms. Lord Caradon, head of the British delegation to the UN, drew up Resolution 242, which was passed unanimously and has become a milestone in the history of the Arab-Israeli conflict.

Arrangements to maintain the British presence in the Gulf, despite the abandonment of Aden, were devised in 1966 partly to accommodate British military contingents that could no longer be based in South Arabia. The British Empire in the Far East had been almost completely dismantled, but it took a while for military planning and deployment to adjust to new political realities. By 1967 the British military presence in the Gulf amounted to 6–7 thousand servicemen in Bahrain and Sharja and 3,400 more on Masira Island, off the Omani coast. Both Kuwait and Oman had by this time attained independence coupled with special treaty relations with Britain. The Sultan of Oman had exchanged letters with the British government in 1958, by virtue of which Britain extended military assistance. In 1961 the ruler of Kuwait exchanged letters with Britain that established Kuwait as a fully independent state, bound to Britain only by a treaty guaranteeing British assistance to Kuwait if requested. That request came within a month of independence in response to a threat from Iraq, but a brief show of force by Britain ended the crisis without a shot being fired. The other Gulf sheikhdoms under British protection since the nineteenth century, Bahrain, Qatar, and the seven Trucial States that eventually became the United Arab Emirates (UAE), were still linked to Britain on foreign policy and defense matters.

In January 1968 the Labor Government of Harold Wilson announced its intention to withdraw British forces "East of Suez," including those in the Persian Gulf, by the end of 1971. The Labor Party was ideologically uncomfortable with retaining imperial possessions or dictating the politics of others, but the decision was actually precipitated by a sterling crisis in 1967, resulting in the devaluation of the pound by 14 percent and the need to cut national expenditure considerably and quickly. The Tory Government that took over at Westminster in June 1970 toyed briefly with the idea of reversing the Labor decision, but consultations with the Gulf sheikhdoms revealed their preference for independence and the difficulties of reversing policy. In August 1971 Bahrain declared its independence, followed by Qatar in September. Shortly thereafter, the formation of the United Arab Emirates was announced, encompassing Abu Dhabi, Dubai, Sharjah, Ajman, Umm al-Quwain, Ras al-Khaimah, and Fujairah.

New treaties between Britain and each of the newly independent states were concluded by the end of 1971. The earlier protective agreements were repudiated, and provision was made for consultations "in time of need," encouragement of cooperation in the educational, scientific, and cultural fields, and maintenance of existing relations between Britain and these states in respect to trade and commerce.

Britain's departure from the last outposts of its predominance in the Middle East was accomplished relatively smoothly, and the U.K. has fostered amicable relations with the governments of the newly independent states ever since. Elsewhere in the region, hostility to Britain had apparently reached its climax with the Suez debacle in 1956, and subsequently, relations between Britain and governments in the Middle East began improving gradually. The period since 1971 has witnessed a readjustment by Britain to its contemporary needs and objectives in the Middle East, characterized by expressions of mutual respect and understanding by the British government and many of the Arab heads of state.

BRITISH INTERESTS IN THE MIDDLE EAST

British interests in the Middle East are a complex mixture of political, military, economic, and cultural imperatives. The U.K. is primarily a trading nation, for which access to overseas markets and raw materials is essential. British interest is maintained in the Middle East as a lucrative export market for British products and services; source of sizable foreign investment and sterling deposits; source of oil supplies essential to the Western alliance; center of oil exporting countries with crucial influence on the international oil market; location of a large number of British overseas business operations and expatriate personnel warranting both assistance and protection; strategic communications link between Europe and the East; location of recurrent conflict with potentially destructive effect on other interests and world peace; territorial boundary of the Soviet Union, separating it from access to a warm sea; object of expansionary ambitions of the Soviet Union; potential ground for superpower confrontation; potential source of tension between Britain and its European and Atlantic allies; traditionally an area of British influence and expertise.

Closer examination reveals that all these interests are interconnected, the pursuit of one potentially enhancing vulnerability to another, so that all of them must be balanced and managed attentively and concurrently. The following discussion of British interests, therefore, should not be taken to imply that they can be neatly isolated or ranked, and sometimes the means to attaining one interest constitutes another interest in itself, such as the location of British personnel and equipment in the area.

The unilateral interest of Britain in access to Middle East oil supplies has undergone a major change since 1973. In that year, 75 percent of total British oil consumption came from the Gulf; a decade later, this figure had dropped to 14 percent. While the share of oil in the domestic fuel market dropped over the period, the change is primarily due to the discovery and drilling of North Sea oil. In 1983 Britain was, for the first time, a net exporter of energy and ranked fifth among world oil producers. According to industry estimates the U.K. supplies are expected to have reached their peak in 1985. This suggests that while Britain has enjoyed a respite from dependence on Middle East oil, in contrast to Japan and to a lesser extent France and West Germany, its interest in the security of oil supplies will not diminish in the long term. Even in the short term, as a member of the Western alliance, Britain shares a NATO requirement for uninterrupted oil supplies to the Western industrial economies. Threats to the flow of oil are depicted as emanating both externally, as from a Soviet expansionary move, and internally, as from disruptions in supplies caused by conflagrations like the Iranian revolution or the Iran-Iraq war.

The fact that Britain has become an oil producing and exporting nation has added a new and crucial dimension to its interests in the Middle East. Sudden or dramatic shifts in both the level of supply and the price of oil on the world markets have an immediate impact on the market for Britain's North Sea oil, on the government tax revenues from North Sea oil sales and, by extension, on the health of the pound sterling. Very steep rises in the price of oil accompanied by shortages, such as occurred in 1973 and 1979/80, result in debt crises for developing countries and contractions in consumer markets in the developed economies, which Britain can only partially offset with its own oil revenues. Equally perilous is a dramatic fall in oil prices and a supply glut, which makes it unprofitable to exploit North Sea oil at the same pace as hitherto, especially as the most accessible fields have already been tapped and additional supplies are relatively more expensive to drill. Third World producers outside the Middle East are then obliged to increase oil supplies further to maintain the same level of income, since they have no reserve funds upon which to draw. The Arab members of OPEC, meanwhile, are forced to draw on their reserves and reduce both their investments on the international money markets and their capital expenditures, with adverse effects on the British economy.

This last consideration raises the question of British interest in the Middle East because of the wealth accrued by Middle Eastern oil producing countries since the early 1970s. Oil wealth attracts British interest for three reasons: it constitutes a source of investment in British property, stocks, and reserves; it fuels development and construction projects in the Middle East, which constitute a growth market for British exports and services; and it is channeled into aid projects in less wealthy developing nations, which creates an additional source of business for British contractors.

In specific terms, investment by Arab governments in the U.K. has reached the level where substantial withdrawals could have damaging repercussions for the British economy. The largest investors have been Kuwait and Saudi Arabia, although all the Arab oil producing countries have acquired some holdings. When interest rates are favorable the London banks have attracted short term deposits, while longer term ventures have included considerable Arab acquisitions of real estate. The preference of Arab investors in Britain has been for portfolio rather than direct stock holdings. Private investors from the Middle East also hold substantial amounts in deposits and property and have shown interest in investing in those industries with which they have had direct dealings. It is estimated that Middle East wealth accounts for approximately one third of overseas deposits, documentary credits, and trade financing of the British banking system,[7] not to mention the considerable business for British banks and insurance brokers in the region itself. Not surprisingly, therefore, a primary consideration for Britain in its relations with the Middle East is to prevent the withdrawal of Arab investments from Britain, to attract additional deposits, and to stimulate interest in business ventures in the United Kingdom.

Since the nationalization of the major oil interests in the producing countries in the Middle East during the 1970s, direct British investments in the region have not been a major consideration, although the operations of British companies and finance houses are obviously assets to be nurtured and protected. As the size of British holdings in the oil industry was being reduced, however, the potential for both visible and invisible exports was expanding dramatically. In the early 1980s the growth in Middle East markets and development projects leveled off somewhat, but for Britain they still account for around 10 percent of visible, and up to 15 percent of invisible, exports. This constitutes Britain's third largest market, after Europe and North America. Apart from a dip between 1979 and 1980, British trade with the Middle East has been in surplus since 1977. In terms of the British defense industries, the region has absorbed around 50 percent of British defense sales since 1975. It has also been the largest overseas market for British consultants and building and civil engineering contractors. Even with the end of the boom period in Middle East development, it is a key area for the export of British goods and services, to be both cherished and further exploited.

The interests discussed thus far arise from qualities intrinsic to the Middle East. British strategic and military concerns in the area are the product of external factors that impinge on the Middle East, such as the East-West confrontation and its effects on local conflicts and tensions. To be more specific, Britain has strategic military interests in the Middle East in four respects, all interrelated: containing expansionist ambitions of the Soviet Union, preserving access to the oil supplies of the Middle East to service its own needs and those of the NATO alliance generally, preventing violent upheavals in the region, and using the area for communications and military intelligence on a routine basis.

If the Soviet Union succeeded in expanding into the Middle East, its gain would almost certainly be a direct loss for Britain and its allies. Acquisition of a direct outlet to the sea, or of any significant proportion of the oil reserves of the Persian Gulf region, by the Soviet Union would vastly increase the maneuverability and economic strength of the USSR, as well as its potential for a stranglehold on the Western economies.

An actual invasion or annexation of part of the Middle East by the Soviet Union represents the most serious danger to be averted in the Middle East, though it is not considered by the British as an imminent threat. At a less critical level, there is an interest in retaining friendly relations with the governments of the Middle East to facilitate the operation of British and allied security arrangements and communications in the Mediterranean and in the Indian Ocean.

Even though Britain's global defense posture has been reduced dramatically from the level and extent of military deployment maintained during its imperial days, Britain retains military bases, naval detachments, and radar and telecommunications installations in enclaves all over the world. The communication lines between the British military base on Cyprus, in the Eastern Mediterranean, and a small Royal Naval detachment in the Indian Ocean lie across the Middle East. These two installations are used to monitor movements and communications in the Soviet Union and other portents of instability or hostility in the region generally. Freedom to operate these security arrangements and to come and go between them is a British interest dependent on political and military developments in the Middle East.

The preservation of free access to its own security installations, and the prevention of developments likely to make a Soviet invasion of the Middle East a more imminent possibility depend as much on factors in the region itself as on external considerations. Even though Britain is alert to the danger posed to its security and prosperity by an incursion into the Middle East by the Soviet Union, it does not consider this danger either so imminent or so overwhelming as to warrant an urgent military response in the region. The assessment in Britain is that the Soviet Union is not strong or adventurist enough to undertake an invasion of the Middle East without more conducive circumstances developing in the region itself. Consequently, the priority for Britain is to seek to avert developments in the region that could make communist subversion or an expansion of Soviet involvement more likely.

Britain is interested in bolstering the security and stability of friendly regimes in the region to perpetuate access to oil and export markets, but it recognizes, especially in the wake of the fall of the Shah in Iran, that overt "Westernization" may fuel nationalist and fundamentalist opposition to friendly regimes. If Britain or any of the other Western trading nations fail to exercise the necessary restraint, long-term security interests are jeopardized for short-term trading advantages. Perceiving this dilemma, Britain sees one of its interests in the Middle East as being the management of local developments so that they do not produce destabilizing influences that threaten the collapse of friendly regimes.

In the same connection, the persistence of the Arab-Israeli conflict is seen by Britain as threatening the stability of the region on two counts: on the one hand, the disaffection of Palestinians dispersed throughout the region makes them a focus for unrest and radicalism, and on the other, the conflict could flare up into war again if it is not resolved. Such a war, as demonstrated in the past, commits the superpowers to backing clients on opposing sides and could lead to a superpower confrontation.

The connection between local conflict in the Middle East and the superpower confrontation is not simple or direct. In its reading of what is at stake here, Britain differs from the United States, viewing the latter as somewhat of a liability in this regard. The British do not see Soviet ambitions as the most imminent danger to stability in the Middle East but rather the persistence of indigenous sources of tension which, if not resolved, could draw in the superpowers. Paradoxically, the United States is regarded by Britain as potentially the most destabilizing or inflammatory influence in the Middle East because of the precedence given to its friendship with Israel and the priority it periodically accords to the perceived Soviet threat in the Middle East. Too much concentration on building strategic alliances, with U.S. military basing rights, it is argued, will have the counterproductive effect of alienating the local people against such "imperialist" behavior, and thereby fuelling radical opposition movements. At the same time, concentration on dealing with the external threat posed by the Soviets deflects attention from the immediate problems, above all the Arab-Israeli conflict. Britain's perception is that the United States fails to see the centrality of the conflict to the protection of Western interests in the Middle East and fuels the tension by its unwavering support of Israel.

These concerns devolve into two specific preoccupations for Britain in the Middle East. First is the effort to handle the effects of statements and actions of the United States. Second is the desire to prevent provocative behavior by local governments or groups arising from tensions in the region, which could have repercussions for the stability of Britain's relations with its allies. Britain's interest is to balance its commitment to its NATO allies with its reading of the forces at work in the Middle East. In the quest for profit in the expanding markets of the Middle East a need has been identified to prevent local pressures from causing serious rifts and disagreements between Britain and its European allies in the competition for contracts. Again, Britain's interest lies in finding a balance between short-term gains and the danger of fuelling an anti-Western backlash; this will only be effective if it is done in concert with other advanced trading nations.

Less prominent, but none the less important, are British interests in promoting personal and cultural ties with the Middle East. The encouragement of young people from the region to pursue higher education or training in Britain serves two purposes. It provides useful income for British colleges, and it instills in the visitors a familiarity with British practices, language, and culture, which has long-term benefits for Britain after they return to their own countries. The promotion of the use of English as a second language is also a British objective, to reinforce a traditional use of British legal jargon, business practices, and contract law in many parts of the Middle East, which facilitates continued access for British companies.

Greater understanding and familiarity with Britain and its language is also an objective for Britain in its quest to promote stable development in the region and aid the containment of crises and radicalism. Britain wants its advice to be heeded on matters of human rights concerns or misunderstandings between Washington and Arab governments. Consequently, it is a British interest to have a continuing dialogue with as many factions and leaders in the region as feasible.

POLICY POSITIONS AND OBJECTIVES

In keeping with the identification of a range of strategic, political, and economic interests in the Middle East, the British government develops and promotes its own policy positions on the main issues or problems of the region.

Arab-Israeli Conflict

Since the Suez debacle in 1956 Britain has not been in a position to exercise direct influence in the Arab-Israeli sector of the Middle East. Since the 1967 war it has, however, stated its position on the conflict and the various schemes put forward to resolve it. As a permanent member of the UN Security Council it has voiced its opinion in that forum and supported active use of the United Nations in resolving the conflict. More recently, as a member of the European Community (EC), it has been committed to finding a common European position to bring pressure for a resolution.

In the aftermath of the Arab-Israeli war of 1967, the UN Security Council adopted landmark Resolution 242 on November 22, 1967. The wording of the Resolution in respect to territories occupied by

Israel during the war is intentionally imprecise, a piece of diplomacy devised by Lord Caradon, the British representative. The official British position since 1967 has made specific reference to Resolution 242 as the basis for a settlement between Israel and its neighbors, and has been exemplified in British support for Resolution 338 after the October War in 1973. The U.K. has stressed the requirement for Israeli withdrawal, periodically criticizing Israeli settlement policy in this connection. On the question of the Palestinians, the British position has shifted from concern for a refugee problem mentioned in Resolution 242 to support of Palestinian rights to self-determination.

The subject of the Palestinians was raised by Foreign Secretary Sir Alec Douglas-Home in a speech he made at Harrogate in October 1970. While reaffirming support for the existence of Israel, he spoke of the "legitimate aspirations" of the Palestinians and their desire for "a means of self-expression." Having joined the European Community in 1973, the British government was a party to the statement issued by the Community after the 1973 war, which provided that "in the establishment of a just and lasting peace, account must be taken of the legitimate rights of the Palestinians." In an address to the United Nations in 1976 Foreign Secretary Richard Crosland referred to a "land for the Palestinians." The joint EC position was made more explicit in a statement made on behalf of the Nine at the United Nations in December 1976 affirming: "We have...made clear that the exercise of the right of the Palestinian people to the effective expression of its national identity could involve a territorial basis in the framework of a negotiated settlement." An EC statement issued on June 29, 1977 called for a "homeland for the Palestinian people."

The gradual evolution of the British position on the Palestinian question since the passage of Resolution 242 was confirmed on June 13, 1980 with the release of the Venice Declaration by the European Community. British Foreign Secretary Lord Carrington took an active role in drafting the Venice Declaration, and he later countered criticism of it from the United States with the explanation: "What we have done is to occupy ground which had to be occupied, ground in which Europe is seen and should be seen to be proposing something which is demonstrably fair to both sides and anybody who says it isn't, really hasn't read the Venice Declaration."[8] Carrington claimed that, given the loss of momentum in the Camp David process after the Egypt-Israel Treaty was signed in 1979, it was important to reassure the moderate Arab governments that the West was not neglecting the peace process.

It was with this in mind that Lord Carrington visited Saudi Arabia in 1981 on behalf of the EC to "explore the thinking which lay behind the principles set out by Crown Prince Fahd in August," in the belief that "there may be ways in which it [the Fahd approach] can be built on to bring peace nearer."[9] The visit also provided Carrington with an opportunity to discuss with the Saudis proposed British participation in the Multinational Force and Observers (MFO) in Sinai, being set up by the United States to facilitate Israeli withdrawal in accordance with the Egypt-Israel Treaty. The MFO, to which Britain contributed a headquarters unit (37 men), was obviously linked to the Camp David process, so Carrington reiterated that while Britain endorsed the objectives of the Camp David approach, it did not regard its provisions for the Palestinians as sufficient and would be active in exploring alternatives.

Clarifying the implications of the Venice Declaration, as his government saw them, Foreign Secretary Francis Pym (who succeeded Carrington in 1982) explained to the Conference of Jewish Leaders from the Commonwealth, on November 30, 1982:

> On the Palestinian side, the term we and our European partners have used to summarize their rights is self-determination. This has been much misunderstood....What we mean by it is that circumstances must be created in which the Palestinian people through a choice of their own can express their political aspirations and sustain their political identity. Clearly this expression of identity could take various constitutional forms. President Reagan's proposal for self-government in association with Jordan is one. A state is obviously another, and it would be illogical for the 10 countries of the European Community to seek to rule this option out, having supported the Palestinians' right to choose.
>
> The key point is that the Palestinian act of political choice will need to be made in the light of political realities. The final outcome must of course be accepted by all the parties involved, including Israel.[10]

The Venice Declaration had been designed to trigger new progress in the search for a settlement of the Arab-Israeli conflict. It was superseded, however, by President Reagan's initiative of September 1, 1982, alluded to by Mr. Pym. This was considered sufficiently promising in Britain to obviate the need to pursue a separate approach in Europe. The British Foreign Secretary welcomed it with much enthusiasm, indicating that by its embodiment of the dual principles of security for Israel and the rights of the Palestinians, the U.S. initiative was "very close to the ideas and opinions being expressed by Britain and the other European countries for a year or two now."[11] Even so, it was acknowledged that the U.S. position still differed from that of the British in that it did not explicitly endorse the Palestinian right to self-determination or envisage a role for the Palestine Liberation Organization (PLO) in the negotiations. In concert with its European partners, Britain also welcomed Fez "two", the plan based on the Fahd approach, which emerged from the Arab League summit shortly after Reagan's announcement of his initiative. This was seen as a demonstration that "the Arabs are now agreed that it is time to devote their energies to a political solution to the Palestinian question."[12] Greater clarity on the subject of recognition of Israel was regarded as essential by Britain if negotiations were to progress.

Between the issuance of the Venice Declaration in 1980 and early 1986, the British government has spoken of a need to associate the PLO with negotiations for a settlement, arguing that it enjoys considerable support among Palestinians in the occupied territories and elsewhere, and that it is difficult to imagine a viable settlement without its participation. Britain has not, however, recognized the PLO as the sole representative of the Palestinians and has avoided the issue of formal recognition on the grounds that the U.K. only affords such status to sovereign states. It has been British policy to maintain contacts with the PLO at an official, but not Cabinet, level and periodically British ministers have offered to talk to the PLO should this prove useful in the pursuit of peace.

When the Arab League proposed to send a delegation, headed by King Hassan of Morocco, to discuss Fez II with European governments in the Fall of 1982, Mrs. Thatcher refused to meet them because of the inclusion of a PLO representative. The Prime Minister challenged the organization to recognize Israel and confirm its renunciation of terrorism. She met with a reconstituted delegation—minus the PLO representative—the following year. In September 1985, while on a five day visit to Egypt and Jordan, Mrs. Thatcher signalled a shift in British policy by inviting two members of the PLO executive committee to London as part of a joint Jordanian-Palestinian delegation. The invitation did not amount to formal recognition of the PLO, but the talks between the delegation and the Foreign Secretary would have constituted the first Cabinet level contact with the PLO.[13] The move was part of an effort to support King Hussein's 1985 peace initiative, but, as will be discussed below, the talks did not take place and the British position on contacts with the PLO became even more circumspect while King Hussein himself announced the breakdown of his discussions with PLO leader Yasser Arafat in February 1986.

The British position on the status of the occupied territories is that any changes made unilaterally by Israel to alter its physical or demographic character are illegal, including actions to alter the status of Jerusalem. The Israeli settlement policy is regarded as a violation of the Fourth Geneva Convention, while Israel's extension of civil law to the Golan Heights is seen as tantamount to annexation and thus contrary to international law, apart from being unconducive to a settlement.

The established position of the British on the Arab-Israeli conflict was summarized anew by Foreign Secretary Sir Geoffrey Howe in a speech at the Middle East Association in London on February 14, 1984, in which he said "a bargain will have to be struck in which Israel recognizes the Palestinians' right to self-determination, and the Palestinians accept Israel's right to exist within secure and recognized borders. Both sides of this bargain are important."[14] In terms of the peace process British policy embodies the dual objectives of applying pressure on moderate Arabs, including elements in the PLO, to take the step of recognizing Israel, at the same time as applying pressure in Washington for the United States to lean more heavily on Israel to persuade it to concede territory in the West Bank in return for peace. This dual approach is epitomized in the British response to the initiative taken by King Hussein of Jordan in 1985.

In a speech to the House of Commons on April 25, 1985, Foreign Secretary Sir Geoffrey Howe reported that he and the Prime Minister had been encouraging Washington to explore the potential of King Hussein's efforts to secure a joint approach with the PLO.[15] The strongest signal of British support for the initiative came when Mrs. Thatcher visited Egypt and Jordan in the Fall of 1985, the first such visit to these countries by a British Prime Minister. At the end of her visit to Jordan Mrs. Thatcher announced her invitation to a joint Jordanian-Palestinian delegation to visit London for talks, calling it a "fresh and constructive step" in support of King Hussein's peace initiative.[16] In the event the Foreign Secretary did not meet with the Palestinian members of the delegation, owing to a disagreement between them and the British over the wording of a statement designed to preface the discussions. The statement contained explicit references both to the right of Israel to exist within secure and recognized borders and to the right of the Palestinians to self-determination. The failure of the London talks constituted a serious setback to the personal efforts of the Prime Minister in support of King Hussein's initiative.

The following May Mrs. Thatcher, during a visit to Israel, urged Israel to allow the Palestinians in the West Bank and Gaza to elect their own representatives, depicting this as "the best way" to "encourage the emergence of responsible political leaders ready for peace."[17] Talking to reporters later, she said she could not see a role for the PLO in peace negotiations "unless the PLO renounces terrorism, accepts Resolution 242, the United Nations Resolution, which of course implies Israel's right to exist, and they would recognize that explicitly." Asked to explain her understanding of self-determination for the Palestinians, she responded that she did not envisage an independent Palestinian state, as "that would cause endless problems and would never be acceptable," suggesting instead that "the most popular and most acceptable—widely acceptable—idea is for the West Bank to be part of a federation with Jordan."[18]

The U.K. government's position on an international conference, as supported by the Soviet Union, as well as a component of the Jordanian and Egyptian initiatives in 1985, is that "the prerequisite of any progress is that the parties should agree among themselves that there is a basis for discussion. That is the most important first stage."[19] The involvement of other powers, including the Soviet Union, is to be expected in the long run. By contrast, the vital necessity for the United States to take an active role in the process and to encourage the moderate Arab interlocutors for their pains has received repeated emphasis, and government statements indicate a persistent effort to press this point in Washington.

Lebanon

When Israel invaded Lebanon in June 1982, the British government joined the other members of the EC in condemning the Israeli invasion and calling for the complete and prompt withdrawal of Israel's forces. They also urged the withdrawal of "all foreign forces except those which may be authorized by a legitimate and broadly representative Government of Lebanon whose authority would be fully re-established over all its national territory."[20]

In early 1983 a small British contingent of nearly one hundred troops joined the Multi-National Force of Americans, French, and Italians stationed in Beirut as part of an international effort to aid the quest for peace in the region. The tiny British presence was a token gesture, compared with the 4,200-strong force contributed by the other powers. Benefiting from the army's experience of tours of duty in Northern Ireland, the contingent was able to guard the Ceasefire Commission and run a mobile patrol unit, surviving virtually unscathed until withdrawal in Spring 1984. The troops were recalled in the wake of the unilateral decision by the Americans to withdraw their Marines following heavy casualties and accusations of partisanship, at which point it was decided that the British contingent could no longer carry out its former role.

Aside from this, the British concentrated on promoting more extensive use of UNIFIL and other UN agencies to bring order to Lebanon. Speaking in February 1984, Foreign Secretary Sir Geoffrey Howe explained his government's position:

> A weak and divided Lebanon would be a powder keg which could blow up at any moment into a major crisis, sucking in its neighbors and bringing the Superpowers to a dangerous confrontation. It is therefore in our interests, as well as those of the Lebanese people themselves, that Lebanon should enjoy peace and independence.[21]

Howe went on to explain that the thrust of British diplomacy at that time was to put together multinational support for wider UN deployment in Lebanon, in conjunction with the Lebanese army. Contacts were made with the Soviet Union and Syria, as well as Western allies. The British position urged the full withdrawal of Israeli troops, with security arrangements in South Lebanon put in the hands of UNIFIL and the Lebanese. The withdrawal of Syrian troops was also considered necessary, to be worked out in accordance with the wishes of the Lebanese government. Lastly, the need for the Lebanese to produce a representative government that could be trusted by all the various communities was acknowledged.

As the cycle of violence in Lebanon persisted and Israel pulled out the majority of its own armed forces, Britain continued to lament the damage to Lebanon. In a statement to the House of Commons on June 26, 1985, Minister of State for Foreign and Commonwealth Affairs Richard Luce said: "We deplore recent appalling acts of violence and lawlessness in Lebanon. We continue to believe that an improvement in security can only be achieved by agreement between the Lebanese themselves. Our primary concern is for the suffering of the civilian population. This month we donated a further 500,000 pounds to the International Committee of the Red Cross Lebanon Appeal."[22]

The Iran-Iraq War

The British attitude regarding the Iran-Iraq War reflects fear of an extension of the conflict to the surrounding region and possible superpower confrontation, not unlike the government's "powder keg" description of the situation in Lebanon. British policy was summarized by Foreign Secretary Sir Geoffrey Howe in a speech to the House of Commons on March 22, 1984:

> The Government's policy on the Gulf war remains one of strict neutrality. Beyond that, we want the war ended. A negotiated peace is desperately needed, but the belligerents will need to cooperate with the UN and with the other countries and organizations that have offered their good offices. We do not, at the moment, see an independent role for the United Kingdom in the process of mediation, but we support the efforts of the Secretary General....Finally, although the House will not expect me to go into details about contingency planning, I should say that we are very much aware of the dangers and possible consequences of escalation, and that we shall be ready if need arises, to work with others to protect our interests and those of our friends....all diplomatic channels should be exhausted before considering any question of military or other action to clear the straits. If events did move in that direction, it would be important to ensure that the Soviet Union had no misunderstanding of our intentions."[23]

An embargo on arms supplies to both combatants was agreed to by some of the Western powers, including Britain, when the war first broke out in September 1980. This has not prevented supplies from arriving to both sides. France came under considerable criticism from Britain for supplying Super Etendards and Exocet missiles to Iraq, which London maintains have facilitated Iraqi attacks on tanker traffic in the Gulf. The British have not been above the reproach of their allies themselves, however. In 1984, for example, the government approved export licences for logistic support ships and marine engines for Iran. Responding to questions about the possible violation of the embargo a Foreign Office spokesman told Parliament: "There is no absolute definition (of what is military). We must decide to what extent it might exacerbate the conflict."[24] The United States and Arab governments in the Gulf expressed dismay. The British government has stated repeatedly, however, that the U.K. has supplied no lethal items to either side since the fighting began.

When the number of civilian casualties escalated in 1985 Britain backed the call by the UN Secretary General to end attacks on civilian targets and participated in diplomatic representations made by the EC to Teheran and Baghdad, urging Iran and Iraq to respond to UN appeals.

The International Context

British policy is not just a reaction to developments in the Middle East itself but also a response to the imperatives of international alliances, organizations, and confrontations. The decision taken by the British government in 1968 to withdraw British forces "East of Suez" signified recognition that Britain is not and cannot act as a global power of the first rank. The country has lost its overseas capital assets and must survive on visible earnings from trade without the cushion traditionally provided by invisible earnings. While it may wish to exercise influence on world events it can have an impact only in conjunction with other powers.

The imperatives of these realities were made clear during the 1973 Arab-Israeli war and its aftermath. From the outset of hostilities Britain was studious in its policy of non-intervention. It imposed an arms embargo on both sides, which was maintained until the disengagement agreements that were concluded in 1974. In effect, this had more of an effect on Israel than on the Arab belligerents. Britain resisted giving assistance to the United States in its emergency measures to airlift arms to Israel, although access to British bases on Cyprus, for example, would have considerably facilitated U.S. operations. Prime Minister Edward Heath complied with the Arab oil producers' requirement not to divert British oil supplies to embargoed countries (including close allies in Europe, such as the Netherlands), thereby avoiding an embargo on Britain. In sum, British policy in 1973 was to put sensitivity to the Arab cause marginally ahead of other considerations, such as the inconveniences suffered by its allies.

British attentiveness to the concerns of moderate Arab leaders has been consistent since the early 1970s, and for a number of reasons in addition to material self-interest. The perception of Israel as the "underdog" deserving of British sympathy has been replaced by that of a militarily strong and politically self-righteous regional power that is indulged in its transgressions by its benefactor, the United States. Now rid of the responsibilities and baggage of global power, the U.K. is better placed to understand how U.S. and Soviet activities in the region must appear to local governments. It has also discovered that its advice and support can now be received with less suspicion than was previously the case.

As Britain learns the companionship of secondary power status, the United States is experiencing the loneliness and distrust attendant on superpower status. This is amply reflected in the positions of the two in the United Nations. In the early years of the United Nations,

Britain and the United States, as among the victors of World War II and founding members of the organization, shared a common status, at least in appearance. Now the United States is often singled out for criticism in a forum that has become preoccupied with Third World concerns, the North-South divide, and the hegemony of the superpowers. That Britain is not thus singled out, nor automatically sides with its Atlantic ally when the votes are counted, is an indication that Britain is both sensitive to the reality of such changes and aware of the need to balance loyalty to its ally with other considerations.

If the cumulative effect of regional and global developments has militated against Britain adopting a stance in the Middle East that is identical with that of its U.S. ally, the evolution of the EC has conveniently presented an alternative way to proceed. The European Community was established with primarily economic and some internal political objectives in mind. It was not envisaged that it would become a new actor in international diplomacy to the extent that it has. Drawing together the approaches of its European allies to produce an EC policy on the Middle East is an appealing role for the British Foreign Office. It offers the opportunity to demonstrate cooperation with the EC, to ameliorate accusations of obstreporousness by Britain on other EC concerns, as well as adding weight to British policy perspectives.

British policy in the Middle East is to bring pressure to bear on both the United States, because of its relations with Israel, and on moderate Arab leaders, to encourage both to work toward a settlement of the most pressing political question in the area, the Arab-Israeli conflict. Membership in the EC, and to a much lesser extent in the UN, is used by Britain to enhance the pressure, since alone it has ceased to exercise much power.

ACTIVITIES AND POLICY INSTRUMENTS

Two general points require attention before describing how British policy is put into effect. First, the process by which foreign policy is formulated in Britain must be distinguished from practices prevailing in the United States or France, for example. Second, this has implications for the priority accorded different instruments of policy.

When discussing British foreign policy the assumption can usually be made that of all the government departments the Foreign and Commonwealth Office (FCO) is the primary influence in the formulation of policy. Members of the Cabinet are obviously the arbiters in the decision-making process, and individual Foreign Secretaries and Prime Ministers will favor certain priorities. The Foreign Secretaryship of Lord Carrington was expected to produce more vigorous activity than usual by Britain in pursuit of a settlement of the Arab-Israeli dispute. After he resigned in 1982 (in connection with the Falklands war) the initiative was taken by Mrs. Thatcher, who had emphasized boosting British exports to the Middle East, especially in armaments, and in 1985–86 she took a personal interest in the peace process as well. Aside from this, the role of Parliament and Parliamentary committees is relatively insignificant, except as a vehicle for giving public voice to government policy. There is not a tradition of deferring to general public opinion on foreign policy questions and although lobby organizations do exist, the system is not geared to afford them an important role.

The nature of the process and the leadership enjoyed by the FCO in that process makes the traditions and opinions of the diplomatic corps of considerable importance in orienting national policy. With respect to the Middle East this is especially the case, since it has been the practice to train relatively large numbers of diplomats in the language and politics of the Middle East, given the large number of postings there. The Arabists at the FCO are prevalent in the upper echelons of the department. They are perhaps the most cohesive group internally, and they have built up close personal connections in the Arab states and with their representatives in London, which are at least as important as institutional liaisons. These factors together account for close expert attention to British policy in the Middle East, which can be expected to continue for another two or three decades.

This raises the second point concerning the priority afforded different instruments of policy. Traditionally, the Foreign Office dealt primarily with political questions in the Middle East, to which trade, especially military sales, was subordinate. Since the withdrawal "East of Suez" by 1971, trade and commercial concerns have assumed much greater importance, especially in the Persian Gulf. While this shift of emphasis has been acknowledged in the FCO, the type of expertise developed in the diplomatic service and the mechanisms for coordinating policy with the Treasury and Department of Trade, or the business community, have not changed dramatically. It should not be assumed, therefore, that the British government manipulates the pieces in exact accordance with carefully planned policy objectives. British policymakers and implementers are primarily absorbed with reacting to developments rather than shaping them, coping with problems rather than solving them.

The traditional mode of conduct in the Middle East was overt political control or informal supervision through exclusive treaty arrangements, all underpinned by British military strength. Now the only states with which Britain retains treaties of friendship are Bahrain (1971), Qatar (1971), and the UAE (1971), in addition to a formal arrangement with Oman (1958) on military matters. Gunboat diplomacy is certainly not an option now, and Britain's policy is implemented in diverse and far less dramatic ways.

Diplomatic Activity

By the end of 1971 the U.K. had withdrawn the last of its official bases from the Middle East. Since that time the British government has sought to promote its objectives and conduct relations with groups or governments in the region through both the UN and the EC, as well as exerting influence in Washington. This activity has taken place concurrently with bilateral diplomatic contacts with Middle Eastern countries.

One type of diplomatic contact is the state visit by representatives of the government. This can take place at various levels: departmental, junior ministerial, ministerial, the Prime Minister in person, members of the royal family, and the Queen. British withdrawal from the Gulf was accomplished on amicable terms and relations with the Arab Gulf states have been generally very friendly ever since. In 1979 Queen Elizabeth made a tour of the Gulf states, including Kuwait and Saudi Arabia. This was the first visit by a British monarch to the area. In 1981 Prime Minister Margaret Thatcher went to Qatar, the UAE, Oman, and later Bahrain, and in 1985 she visited Egypt and Jordan. King Hussein of Jordan has visited London often for high level consultations. Oman's ruler, Sultan Qaboos, made his first state visit to the U.K. in 1982; other rulers from the Emirates have been more frequent visitors, and many members of the ruling families from the Arab Gulf states spend time in Britain in pursuit of a range of personal interests, from banking, to breeding race horses, to studying for doctorates. This allows for continuous informal dialogue in Britain itself.

The chief purpose of Margaret Thatcher's visit to the Gulf was to boost British exports. Other top level visits have been designed to show support for specific developments in the peace process. In March 1984 the Queen made her first official visit to Jordan, responding to an invitation issued in 1968. The trip was initially designed to bolster President Reagan's designation of King Hussein as key to the peace process, but when it took place U.S.-Jordanian relations were less warm and controversy surrounded some passing remarks made by Her Majesty about the situation in the West Bank. Challenging the British to demonstrate impartiality, the Israeli President issued an invitation to the Queen to visit Israel, while he was in London in April 1974, but a response from the palace was not expected to be issued speedily. Mrs. Thatcher's visit to Jordan and Egypt in 1985 signalled both support for the efforts of King Hussein and President Mubarak to further the peace process, and the Prime Minister's involvement in promoting arms deals with both countries.

British-Israeli relations went through a very cool period following the Israeli invasion of Lebanon, which prompted condemnation in London and the imposition of an arms embargo pending Israeli withdrawal. Contacts improved somewhat in the wake of Shimon Peres' accession to the premiership in September 1984, and Mrs. Thatcher's visit to Israel in 1986, the first of a serving Prime Minister, signalled the end of a period of tension. In 1984 Foreign Secretary Sir Geoffrey Howe visited Israel, Saudi Arabia, Syria, and Egypt, and Defence Minister Michael Heseltine went to Jordan and Egypt. During Howe's visit to Syria the government in Damascus demonstrated the distinction drawn there between U.S. and European perspectives on the Arab-Israeli conflict. A Syrian official urged Britain to instigate greater EC involvement, asserting "Europe understands the Middle East better than the United States does. The European view may not correspond with ours, but it is more negotiable."[25]

Britain does not maintain the same level of contact with all groups and governments in the region. As already mentioned, contact with the PLO has been circumscribed. Contact with the various factions in Lebanon has been limited since terrorist attacks forced the closure of the British Embassy in East Beirut, as well as the evacuation of British civilian personnel from Lebanon at the same time as the British contingent of the MNF was pulled out in early 1984. A handful of diplomats have remained in West Beirut to operate a minimal service. Terror was also the reason behind a break in diplomatic relations with Libya. A London policewoman died when a gunman inside the Libyan embassy shot at demonstrators outside in April 1984.

In April 1986 Prime Minister Thatcher responded positively to a request by the United States to allow the use of U.S. aircraft based in Britain for a raid on Libya, in retaliation for Libya's support of international terrorism. After the raid, she made a statement to the House of Commons detailing evidence of Libyan support for the outlawed Provisional Irish Republican Army, which dated back to 1973, indicating that Britain had its own reasons for wishing to see Libyan activities curtailed.

The British Embassy in Tehran was closed in 1980 following the Iranian revolution. Since then a small team of British diplomats have operated out of the British interests section of the Swedish Embassy. The Iranian Embassy in London, meanwhile, was left deserted after it was stormed by the SAS (special forces) to release it from takeover by an anti-Khomeini group. The official British stance on the Iran-Iraq war is impartiality and when France led an effort in the UN Security Council to condemn Iranian activities, Britain obstructed it. In keeping with its relatively low-key stance, when British tanker traffic has been damaged by either Iran or Iraq, the policy in London has been to lodge a formal complaint with the government concerned. FCO and Ministry of Defence officials have indicated that Britain hopes to be well placed to pick up business from both belligerents, as soon as hostilities end.

Military Sales and Projects

According to government records (see Table 5.1) the Middle East has absorbed some 50 percent of Britain's defense sales in the late 1970s and early 1980s. The exact value of each deal that is struck is not always made public. Following World War II British arms sales were designed more to meet the security requirements of newly independent colonies than as a commercial endeavor. By the 1970s, however, the emphasis had shifted. From the mid 1970s to the mid 1980s its main customers have been in the Gulf. Deals have included 12 Hawk training aircraft for Kuwait ($105m), 24 Hawk Mk-61 aircraft for the UAE ($156m), some 30 Chieftain tanks, Jaguar fighter aircraft, and various missiles for Oman, as well as nearly 300 Chieftain tanks for Jordan ($430m).[26] And the following year, 1985, was a record year for British arms sales. Constituting Britain's biggest single deal to date, Saudi Arabia signed a memorandum of understanding for the sale of 72 Tornado fighter-bomber aircraft and 60 jet and turboprop trainer aircraft. With spares, support, and training the deal could be worth 4 billion pounds. Britain agreed to receive part cash and part crude oil in payment. Oman contracted to buy Tornados worth some 250 million pounds, and Jordan and Egypt signed defense packages worth 270 million and nearly 100 million pounds, respectively, both of which incorporated credit arrangements offered by the U.K.

TABLE 5.1: Destinations of U.K. Exports of Defense Equipment (millions of pounds sterling)

	1975	1976	1977	1978	1979	1980	1981	1982	1983	1984
Total identified Sales	198	218	356	392	393	537	613	904	919	825
NATO Countries and Other Western Europe	52	43	48	77	82	111	172	185	206	175
Middle East and North Africa	91	128	162	202	127	158	239	405	506	311
Percent of Total	46	59	46	52	32	29	39	45	55	38
Asia and Far East	20	12	19	46	63	134	124	192	137	108
Sub-Saharan Africa	5	12	10	18	36	121	67	97	55	201
Latin America and Carribean	30	23	117	49	85	13	11	25	16	30

Source: U.K. Ministry of Defence, *Statement of the Defence Estimates 1981* (vol. 2), p.21 and *1985* (vol.2), p. 12.

Prior to the Iranian revolution, Britain had profited from the Shah's appetite for arms, in the British case notably tanks and hovercraft. Officially, Britain is embargoing all shipments of arms to either Iraq or Iran for the duration of their war. There has also been a British ban on arms to Israel since the invasion of Lebanon.

Partly as a legacy of the period of British ascendancy in the Middle East, British military training and expertise has a high reputation in a number of Middle East capitals. King Hussein of Jordan and Sultan Qaboos of Oman are themselves products of the Sandhurst Military Academy. During the campaign against a rebel movement in the Dhofar region of Oman between 1965 and 1975, Britain, along with Jordan and Iran, seconded forces to the Sultan's army. British military advisors have remained in Oman on the understanding they are there to tide over a transition period while local officers are undergoing modern training, though this does not apply to expatriate British officers serving there on contract, of which there are several hundred. In 1985 there were nearly 200 British loan service personnel in Oman, the largest arrangement of its kind. They were totally integrated with the Omani forces, with Britain providing the commander and key operational appointments. The extent of British military involvement in Oman constitutes an exceptional case in British Middle East policy. Around 100 British service personnel have also been on loan to Kuwait. The cost of the loan service is borne mostly by the host government.

The loan of personnel forms part of a scheme for supplying advisors in support of defense sales. In 1985, for example, a small team was in Qatar helping to introduce Rapier missiles to the armed forces, and another was in the UAE instructing in the use of Hawk aircraft. Since 1980 the International Military Services Division of the U.K. government's Defence Export Services Organisation has won two contracts from the Iraqi armed forces: one to repair tanks, the other to educate Iraqi air force cadets. A private concern in England, run by ex-RAF officers, trained some 80 Iraqi military pilots in 1984. In 1981 the same contractor trained 20 pilots from the UAE.

Operations conducted by the British armed forces in the Middle East since the Dhofar rebellion in Oman include participation in the MFO in Sinai in 1982, in the MNF in Lebanon in 1983/4, and in 1984 five British mine-hunters worked with American and French vessels to sweep the Gulf of Suez and the Red Sea, at Egypt's request, following eighteen mysterious explosions. The Royal Navy discovered one Soviet-made mine before the area was declared clear. A Royal Naval flotilla of two warships and an auxilliary vessel has been in the Indian Ocean for some years and has patrolled the Gulf periodically during the course of the Iran-Iraq war. In 1984, two company level excercises were conducted from Oman, involving RAF Nimrod maritime patrols in anti-submarine warfare training and Tornados in low-level navigation and weapons training.

Other Trading Activities

British trade with the Middle East has undergone a major transformation over the last decade. Britain is not currently dependent on Middle East oil and, while it will eventually become a net importer again, this will not become a significant factor in relations with the region for the foreseeable future. A drop in Britain's energy surplus, from 6 billion pounds in 1983 to 5 billion pounds in 1984 was largely the result of a long and damaging strike by coal miners, which necessitated importing more heavy crude to make good the drop in coal supplies. This caused the amount spent on oil imports to rise by 69 percent, to 4.1 billion pounds, which should be interpreted as an exception, not a trend.[27]

Of course, because oil is now a major factor in the U.K. economy, movements in international oil prices immediately rebound on it. This affects most notably the government's tax income and sterling's exchange rate, as well as affecting the profitability of hydrocarbon fields and the pace of future exploration and development. The U.K. has not cooperated directly with OPEC on oil prices, though consultations are continuous on a bilateral level. It is official British policy to regard some lowering in oil prices, as has happened recently, as healthy, yet too great a drop is considered likely to trigger an international banking collapse. The possibility of drilling in Iran and Iraq reaching pre-war levels if the war ends could help to produce this scenario. All of which suggests reason for ambivalence about a speedy end to the war.

In the meantime, in contrast to ten years ago, Britain has become a net exporter to the Middle East. The Middle East represents Britain's third largest market, after Western Europe and North America. The favorable trend in the balance hides a drop in Britain's share of the Middle East market over the past ten years, to under 10 percent, however, which is evidence of the heightened competition for business in the region.

U.K. exports to the region increased from 4,104 million pounds in 1979 to 6,545 million pounds in 1984 (see Table 5.2). Exports to

TABLE 5.2: U.K. Exports to the Middle East, 1979–1984 (millions of pounds sterling)

	1979	1980	1981	1982	1983	1984
Arab Countries						
Total	3,320	3,645	4,615	5,423	5,289	4,896
$m equivalent	7,044	8,479	9,358	9,492	8,023	6,542
% of world	7.8	7.7	9.1	9.8	8.7	6.9
Israel						
Total	271	231	212	224	355	393
$m equivalent	574	537	430	393	538	525
% of world	0.6	0.5	0.4	0.4	0.6	0.6
Other Non-Arab Countries						
Total	513	676	705	701	1,046	1,257
$m equivalent	1,098	1,573	1,430	1,226	1,587	1,679
% of world	1.2	1.4	1.4	1.3	1.7	1.8
Middle East						
Total	4,104	4,551	5,532	6,348	6,690	6,545
$m equivalent	8,707	10,588	11,218	11,112	10,149	8,747
World Total	42,804	47,364	50,998	55,538	60,534	70,511
$bn equivalent	90.8	110.2	103.4	97.2	91.8	94.2
Middle East as						
% of world	9.6	9.6	10.9	11.4	11.1	9.3

Source: U.K. Department of Trade & Industry, *U.K. Overseas Trade Statistics,* and *Middle East Economic Digest* (MEED).

Arab countries in the region were worth 3,645 million pounds in 1980, rose to 5,289 million pounds in 1983, and levelled off to 4,896 million pounds by 1984. Saudi Arabia was the biggest individual market, with sales rising by 20 percent from 1982 to 1.5 billion pounds in 1983, nearly one fourth of total U.K. sales, before dropping some 6 percent the following year. Exports to Iraq rose by 40 percent from 1981 to 875 million pounds in 1982, before tailing off to 343 million pounds in 1984. Other major importers were the UAE, Egypt, and Kuwait. Exports from the UK to the non-Arab countries of the region have also risen in value since 1980, but not consistently. U.K. exports to Iran, the major non-Arab importer in the region, dipped to 334 million pounds in 1982, from 403 million pounds the previous year, rising to 703 million pounds in 1984.

The UK share of the Saudi market, about 6 percent, is accounted for largely by machinery and transport equipment and manufactured goods, though this is set to change with the 1985 arms deal. U.K. contractors have lagged well behind their competitors, with only 1 percent of Saudi construction contracts, though consultancy operations are thriving, with some 35,000 U.K. nationals supplying skilled labor in 1984. After a healthy record up to 1982, British exports to Iraq dropped by half the following year, due largely to the continuing disruptions of the Gulf war. Sales to Iran have improved somewhat, however, since plummeting after the revolution.

Imports from the Middle East to the UK (see Table 5.3) amounted to 3,784 million pounds in 1979, nearly 8 percent of total imports, and declined to 2,905 million pounds, nearly 4 percent of the total, in 1984. Commensurate with the overall trend, there has been a continuous decline since 1980 in imports from Arab countries, amounting to 1,811 million pounds in 1984, as compared with 4,239 million pounds in 1980. However, imports from the non-Arab countries have gradually risen since 1980. Having dropped dramatically at the end of the 1970s, imports from Iran have gradually increased. In 1984 their value stood at 368.5 million pounds, over two and a half times greater than the value for the previous year.

Developments in British trading and contracting practices in the UAE illustrate the trend in a number of Arab oil-producing states. Local firms are increasingly acquiring the necessary skills to bid for new contracts in competition with foreign companies. British contractors are succeeding to the extent that they are ready to adapt, that is, take on cooperative ventures with local companies, supplying the most specialized expertise themselves, or diversifying into new areas.

TABLE 5.3: U.K. Imports from the Middle East, 1979–1984 (millions of pounds sterling)

	1979	1980	1981	1982	1983	1984
Arab Countries						
Total	3,097	4,239	3,689	3,131	2,096	1,811
$m equivalent	6,571	9,862	7,482	5,481	3,180	2,420
% of world	6.39	8.52	7.21	5.5	3.2	2.3
Israel						
Total	228	233	256	275	314	393
$m equivalent	483	541	519	482	476.5	525
% of world	0.47	0.47	0.5	0.48	0.5	0.5
Other Non-Arab Countries						
Total	459.5	285	394	555	405	701.5
$m equivalent	975	662	799	972	614	937.5
% of world	0.95	0.57	0.77	0.97	0.6	0.9
Middle East						
Total	3,784	4,757	4,340	3,962	2,815	2,906
$m equivalent	8,028	11,066	8,800	6,935	4,271	3,883
World Total	48,467	49,773	51,168	56,940	65,993	78,705
$bn equivalent	102.8	115.8	103.8	99.7	100.1	105.2
Middle East as						
% of world	7.8	9.6	8.5	7.0	4.3	3.7

Source: U.K. Department of Trade & Industry, *U.K. Overseas Trade Statistics,* and *Middle East Economic Digest* (MEED).

A habitual lament of some British businessmen has been that the British government is less committed to assisting and promoting British contractors than is the case with their foreign competitors. To supplement market intelligence provided by the British Overseas Trade Board, a variety of trade associations and advisory bodies came into being before the boom in Middle East markets began in the early 1970s, notable among which are the Arab-British Chamber of Commerce, the Middle East Association, and the government's official advisory body, The Committee for Middle East Trade (COMET), which has mixed public and private sector membership. The Conservative government that took office in 1979 worked to redress some of the grievances of businessmen, as is demonstrated by the Prime Minister's visit to the region to promote trade, especially in armaments, and new attention to "soft" credit packages since 1985. It is also the case that, whatever Britain's privileged position in the Gulf market prior to 1971, after the oil price boom began it was inconceivable that Britain alone could meet the needs of the oil rich states, while the states themselves prefer to spread business among a number of foreign nationals. If they are to compete, British companies need more than Embassy support and the occasional state visit, they have to have their own local bases and contacts, which may not, in turn, be cost-effective for the amount of work available.

There also has been criticism of the refusal of the U.K. government to intervene in trading practices on a rather different count. For decades Arab nations have sought to boycott merchandise from companies that do business with Israel. Certificates of origin are required for each transaction. In Britain these are mostly handled by the Arab-British Chamber of Commerce, but the Board of Trade processes some. Other countries, including the United States and France, have established penalties for companies complying with this practice. Periodically voices have been raised in the British Parliament in favor of ending the boycott but to no avail. Partly as a result, U.K. trade with Israel in the mid 1980s dropped to 6 percent of the Israeli market, whereas thirty years earlier it was 85 percent.

Finance, Aid, and Investment

The Middle East has not been a priority area for British overseas development aid. Since 1971, the annual allocations for the region have been about two percent of total bilateral aid. The bulk of bilateral aid is made available to British dependencies and Commonwealth countries, which does not include any Middle East countries (except Cyprus). The proportion of public expenditure on aid spent bilaterally has been decreasing overall, and that distributed through multilateral organizations, notably the EC, the World Bank Group, and UN agencies, has been rising. Total British public expenditure on aid in 1984 was 1.3 billion pounds, of which 40 percent was assigned to multilateral organizations. This compares with a total of 1 billion pounds in 1980 and 0.3 billion pounds in 1971, of which 27 percent and 11 percent respectively were spent through multilateral agencies.

As the figures in Table 5.4 reveal, the largest recipients of British bilateral aid to the region, which includes technical cooperation and project loans, are the Sudan and Egypt. In the former case this is accounted for by the extremity of need and the historical association between the two countries. Egypt, meanwhile, has benefited from a specific effort by the British government to channel aid to areas where this will result in opportunities for British business. Britain provided 64 million pounds for public sector

TABLE 5.4: U.K. Overseas Aid—Gross Bilateral Aid, including Technical Cooperation, Middle East (thousands of pounds sterling)

	1980	1981	1982	1983	1984
Bahrain	3	—	—	—	—
Iran	10	20	—	—	—
Iraq	—	—	—	—	—
Israel	—	—	—	—	—
Jordan	4,682	7,086	3,308	2,747	6,105
Kuwait	—	—	—	—	—
Lebanon	56	142	1,624	20	34
Oman	384	452	663	641	570
Qatar	—	—	—	—	—
Saudi Arabia	1	—	—	—	—
Syria	308	456	443	1,748	568
U.A.E.	—	—	—	—	
Yemen, North (YAR)	2,725	2,540	2,842	3,756	3,103
Yemen, South (PDRY)*	1,335	1,835	855	798	969
Total Middle East, excluding North Africa	9,502	12,391	9,052	9,327	11,109
Egypt	12,246	8,124	7,478	10,573	15,404
Sudan	22,576	32,738	39,417	32,194	27,427

*Largely accounted for in pensions for former employees of British Aden Colony.
Source: U.K. overseas Development Administration (ODA), *British Aid Statistics 1978–92;* ODA, *British Overseas Aid 1983;* ODA, *Summary of Statistics of British Overseas Aid 1984.*

development projects in Egypt in 1983, 16 million pounds as a grant and the remainder as mixed credits from the Export Credits Guarantee Department (ECGD). Also in 1983, the ECGD agreed to guarantee 3 million pounds of credit provided by Chase Trade Finance for Egyptian importers and agents of British exporters. The U.K. has also provided 50 million pounds in aid and 100 million pounds in ECGD-backed credits for Cairo's waste-water project, thereby ensuring work for U.K. contractors and suppliers.

As Britian's share of the export market to the Middle East declined in the face of fierce competition, businessmen periodically complained about having to compete with foreign contractors who could link their bids to "soft" credit arrangements provided by their governments. Such complaints reached a crescendo when British companies competing for the Bosphorus Bridge contract in Turkey lost to a Japanese consortium able to offer better aid terms. In the wake of this, in August 1985 Trade and Industry Secretary Norman Tebbit indicated that, while he did not want to announce suddenly to the world that the U.K. is in the soft-loan game, the government "would be more flexible in offering aid in the form people like it rather than in the form it should be pre-ordained that they should have it."[28] Arrangements for payment on deals signed with Saudi Arabia, Egypt, and Jordan subsequently indicate early results for this policy shift.

In the case of contractors who suffered as a result of the Iranian revolution, the ECGD has paid out about 180 million pounds in compensation, and actually ceased providing guarantees for a period, excepting some provision for the Talbot car-assembly operation. Following a visit by an Iraqi delegation to the Prime Minister in 1983, meanwhile, the government agreed to provide 250 million pounds in medium-term credit, another indication of long-term optimism about British prospects in Iraq.

Neither the Iranian revolution nor the Iran-Iraq war has interfered much with the business of Iranian banks in London, which happens to host the largest concentration of Iranian banks abroad and the only overseas branch of Bank Markazi, Iran's central bank. As previously discussed, the importance of the City of London to Middle East banking and investment generally has remained a major consideration in British relations with the region, which has weathered the recession in Britain's economy.

Initially the trend was for the U.K. clearing banks and credit houses to establish operations in the Middle East, while large quantities of petrodollars were invested either on the London stock exchange or in London real estate. More recently, the growth of local banks in the Middle East has forced British giants such as Grindlays and British Bank of the Middle East to share the market. Brian Ashby, Middle East director of Lloyds Bank International, explained in 1983:

> The differentiation between local and international banks has narrowed in the past five years but the region still needs banks like us. We feel British banks' customer base and balance sheets are large enough for us to maintain our position and continue to work with the Arab banks.[29]

In parallel with trends in the industrial sector, British finance houses are thriving to the extent that they can offer specialized services or professional advice to local operations and governments. Arab banks, meanwhile, have expanded their bases in London. The prospects for British finance houses from the mid 1980s are for fiercer competition with Arab banks for a decreasing pool of surplus cash.

Educational and Cultural Exchanges

The two institutions officially responsible for promoting the British perspective in the Middle East (in broad terms, as opposed to the government stance) are the External Services of the BBC and the British Council. The BBC's Arabic Service is on the air 63 hours a week, and the Persian Service about 10 hours. According to a survey conducted in 1977 the BBC Arabic Service had the highest number of listeners of all Britain's foreign language services, and obtained regular audiences of 34 percent (200,000 adults) in urban Jordan, 13.5 percent (175,000) in urban Sudan, and 3.2 percent (325,000) in urban Egypt. In Jordan and the Sudan this made it more popular than the Voice of America, and it was able to match local services often.[30] In 1983 the BBC stated that, "mindful of the growing number of commercial and national stations round the Arab World," the Arabic Service has "laid particular emphasis on the strengthening of news and current affairs within the daily nine-hour schedule."[31] For its magazine, *Huna London,* the BBC claimed a readership of 70,000 in the Middle East. The publication also serves as a vehicle for British advertisers.

The British Council, fifty years old in 1984, is designed to promote British interests through cultural and educational exchanges. Fiscal discipline since the 1970s has forced the Council to trim its operations yet, in conjunction with BBC Eaternal Services, it remains a protected item on the Foreign Office budget, also receiving funds from the aid budget. Out of a total budget of 181.8 million pounds in 1984/5, it was estimated that 42 million pounds would be spent in the Middle East.[32] The Council has offices in Bahrain, Egypt, Iraq, Israel, Kuwait, Oman, Qatar, Saudi Arabia, Sudan, Syria, the UAE, and North Yemen, all of which run English classes, stage exhibitions, and administer exchanges.

The number of visitors to the U.K. from countries in the Middle East has been rising in recent years. In the first nine months of 1982 the number reached 600,000, an increase of 24 percent over the same period of 1981. In 1983 the rate rose by another 20 percent. The British Tourist Authority has estimated that Arabs constituted 6 percent of all visitors to the U.K. in 1982 and that they spent an average of 768 pounds each. This figure is likely to have risen further with the drop in the rate of exchange of the pound sterling.

Figures for British visitors to the Middle East are not so readily accessible, but a more significant measure of the relationship is the proportion of U.K. applicants for jobs abroad choosing the Middle East. The region has been the first choice for over 50 percent of the applicants for some years now. The primary motive has been higher salaries, and for male applicants the first choice has been Saudi Arabia. For some of the British expatriates, meanwhile, the Middle East still holds an attractive aura of mystery and romance that may be considered lacking in domestic British culture.

As the experience of foreign nationals in Iran in the late 1970s demonstrated, interchange purely on the basis of material incentives does not promote lasting understanding. Yet British human and cultural exchanges with the Middle East have penetrated to a deeper level. Courses in Arabic, especially for businessmen, were better subscribed to in Britain in the 1980s than they were when the political ties were ostensibly stronger. The establishment of the Centre for Arab Gulf Studies at Exeter University, partly with the stimulus of donations from the region, bears witness to a lively interest in greater understanding.

Training and educational institutions in Britain remain attractive for Middle Easterners, despite memories of the imperial connection. Partly because of it and Britain's proximity to Continental Europe, there is a perception of greater empathy with British, as opposed to American or Soviet culture, ties with which may offer more material rewards. In 1981/82 there were some 58,000 overseas students studying in Britain. Students from Iran, Iraq, and Cyprus ranked among the eight largest national groupings included in this figure. The more intensive British system of university instruction, with its favorable tutor-student ratios and shorter periods necessary for completion of courses than in most other Western countries, also offers an incentive for overseas students to qualify in Britain rather than other countries.

CONCLUSION

British expertise on Middle East history and politics has been acknowledged in the European Community and in the United States. The Foreign Office may be expected to try to capitalize on this in coming years, as the most appropriate way to enhance British influence over the politics of the region now that Britain lacks the military and economic power that it once enjoyed. Insofar as it possesses influence in Washington and Europe, this will be used to urge a settlement of the Arab-Israeli conflict along the lines of the Venice Declaration, and to maintain the present limits to the Iran-Iraq War.

In the wake of King Hussein's initiative to arrange talks between the United States and a Palestinian-Jordanian grouping in 1985 as a prelude to negotiations with Israel, Britain, under the personal leadership of Prime Minister Margaret Thatcher, showed a pronounced interest in supporting and furthering that initiative. This is partly a reflection of Britain's perception that the Arab-Israeli dispute is central to the future stability and prosperity of the region, as Arab leaders have long maintained.

The need to find a solution to the Palestinian question has become the unifying element in the various strands of British policy in the Middle East. Certainly Britain is very interested in preserving and extending its trade relations and commercial ties with the area. This cannot be achieved, however, without paying attention to the disruptive potential of the Arab-Israeli conflict. Equally, the area cannot be protected from religious fundamentalist or Soviet subversion without reference to this issue. The manner in which King Hussein has sought to deal with the question is deemed both courageous and appropriate by Britain. The heads of state and businessmen of the Middle East who share this perspective are likely to maintain a dialogue with the British government, on the assumption that Britain does have a role to play in the future of the Middle East, first because it apparently understands their anxieties, and second, because it is a close ally of the United States and may be able to convey those anxieties to Washington more effectively than they have been able to do.

NOTES

1. Sir Edward Grey to Paul Cambon, May 16, 1916. See the text of the Sykes-Picot Agreement and the Hussein-McMahon correspondence in U.S. Congress, Senate Committee on Foreign Relations, *A Select Chronology and Background Documents Relating to the Middle East*, 94th Congess, 1st Session, 1975 (Washington: U.S. Government Printing Office).

2. The Balfour Declaration, in *A Select Chronology*, p. 136.

3. Quoted in Ann Williams, *Britain and France in the Middle East and North Africa, 1914–1967* (New York and London: Macmillan, 1968), p. 42.

4. The British Mandate (1922), in *A Select Chronolocy*, p. 144.

5. Quoted in Williams, p. 117.

6. *Ibid.*, p. 137.

7. Committee for Middle East Trade (COMET), *Britain and the Middle East* (London: COMET, 1983), p.8.

8. Geoffrey Edwards, "National approaches to the Arab-Israeli conflict: Britain", in David Allen and Alfred Pijpers (eds.), *European Foreign Policy-Making and the Arab-Israeli Conflict* (The Hague: Martinus Nijhoff, 1984), p.55.

9. Lord Carrington, Secretary of State for Foreign and Commonwealth Affairs, to The Conservative Friends of Isreal, in London, November 2, 1981. Reproduced in British Information Services, Policy Statement, *The Middle East: European Peace Initiatives* (November 4, 1981), p.6.

10. Mr. Francis Pym, Secretary of State for Foreign and Commonwealth Affairs, at a Conference of Jewish Leaders from the Commonwealth in London on November 30, 1982. Reproduced in British Information Services, Policy Statement, *The Middle East: President Reagan's Proposals* (December 1, 1982), p.3.

11. Foreign and Commonwealth Office, *Background Brief, Britan and the Arab-Israeli Dispute since 1967* (January 1983), p.3.

12. Francis Pym, *The Middle East: President Reagan's Proposals*, p.6.

13. Roger Matthews, "Thatcher gives invitation to PLO," *Financial Times* (September 21, 1985).

14. Sir Geoffrey Howe, Secretary of State for Foreign and Commonwealth Affairs, at the Middle East Association on February 14, 1984. (Because Sir Geoffrey was in Moscow, the speech was read for him by Sir John Leahy.) Reproduced in British Information Services, Policy Statement, *Lebanon and the Middle East: British Proposals* (February 15, 1984), pp. 4–5.

15. Sir Geoffrey Howe to House of Commons, April 25, 1985. Reproduced in Central Office of Information (C.O.I), *Verbatim Service*, VSO38/85, p.9.

16. Roger Matthews, "Thatcher gives invitation to PLO."

17. Margaret Thatcher, speaking at a banquet in Israel on May 25, 1986. Reproduced in British Information Services, Policy Statement, *Israel and the Palestinian People* (May 27, 1986), p.4.

18. Margaret Thatcher, speaking in television interviews in Israel on May 27, 1986. Reproduced in British Information Services, Policy Statement, *Israel and the Palestinian People* (May 28, 1986), pp.2 and 4.

19. Richard Luce to House of Commons, April 25, 1984. *Official Reports*, House of Commons, Oral Answers, April 25, 1984, col.715.

20. Conclusions of the European Council, June 1982, in *Bulletin of the European Community 6-1982*, p. 16.

21. Sir Geoffrey Howe, *Lebanon and the Middle East: British Proposals*, p.1.

22. Richard Luce to the House of Commons, June 26, 1985. Reproduced in C.O.I., Press Service, Priority Information Press Release (June 26, 1985).

23. Sir Geoffrey Howe to House of Commons, March 22, 1984. Reproduced in News Department, Foreign and Commonwealth Office, *Promoting Britain's Interests Abroad: Some Key Foreign Policy Statements, June 1983–August 1984*, p.27.

24. David Black and Mark Hosenball, "Britain arms Iran's new attack force," *London Times* (October 14, 1984).

25. Henry Stanhope, "Syria urges Britain to take diplomatic lead," *London Times* (February 10, 1984).

26. International Institute for Strategic Studies, *Military Balance, 1979–80, 1980–81, 1981–82, 1982–83, and 1983–84*.

27. Dominic Lawson, "Energy surplus drops by 1 billion pounds" *Financial Times* (August 1, 1985). In this, Lawson reviews the latest edition of H.M.S.O.'s *Digest of the U.K. Energy Statistics 1985*.

28. Norman Tebbit, Secretary for Trade and Industry, interviewed in *Financial Times* (August 1, 1985).

29. Stephen Timewell, "Change of tack for U.K. banks", *Middle East Economic Digest*, Special Report on The United Kingdom and the Middle East (November 1983).

30. BBC, *Annual Report 1980*, p.59.

31. BBC, *Annual Report 1983*, p.54

32. The British Council, *Annual Report 1983-4*. p.44.

6
France

Timothy J. Piro

France has been an active power in the Middle East for centuries. Although the instruments and extent of its policies have undergone change over time, the primary goal, the promotion of French political, economic and military power, has not. The interests at stake have ranged from the protection of Christian values in the Holy Land to France's need for Persian Gulf crude oil. Its methods have included military invasion, colonial domination, and participation in the protective shield of the United Nations peacekeeping forces. Changes in the global context meanwhile have imposed various constraints on the range of options available to France in the pursuit of its objectives.

HISTORICAL LEGACY

French interest in the Near East, as it was termed in France, was of a religious nature initially. The first major French venture into the Near East was part of a European drive to push back the expanding Arab-Islamic Empire and to spread the Christian faith. In 732, the Saracens, the followers of Mohammed, crossed the Pyrenees to fight the Frankish army of Charles Martel near the town of Tours in the Loire Valley. Charles Martel triumphed and sent the message to other European leaders that Christendom would not fall to the invaders from the East. Believing itself to be the protector of the Christian faith, France sent forces to the Near East as part of its *mission civilisatrice*. This mission obligated France to preserve and defend the origins and holy places of Christianity. The First Crusade set out from France in the spring of 1096, and on July 14, 1099, the conquest of the Holy City of Jerusalem was complete. The Crusaders were not able to sustain their hold in Palestine, however, and in 1171 the Kurdish leader Saladin expelled them. Tamerlane's invasion of the Near East in 1400/01 marked France's return to Palestine.[1] In time, the economic and geographic advantages to be gained in the Near East supplanted French religious interest in the holy places.

The French presence in the Near East was formalized by the Treaty of Friendship and Commerce of 1535, signed by Sulayman I of the Ottoman Empire and Francis I of France. This treaty gave France important commercial rights in the Levant (what is now Syria and Lebanon). These privileges, or capitulations, provided the French with freedom of navigation and trade in Ottoman ports, and removed French traders from the jurisdiction of local courts. It also enabled France to extend its protection over Roman Catholics within the Empire, and gave French clergy the right to build new churches in the Holy Land. More importantly, the treaty initiated a rivalry among the larger powers of Europe (Britain, Spain, Austria, and Holland) for influence within the Ottoman Empire.

By the eighteenth century the French foothold in the Ottoman Empire and the declining influence of other European powers in the Far East, principally Portugal and Holland, made eastward expansion possible. A strong and friendly Ottoman Empire was considered the best guarantee of French interests in the Near East since it could serve as the geographic and commercial link with the Far East. Louis XV (1723–1748) established cordial relations with the Ottoman rulers in the Levant, and secured a place for France in Europe's expansion eastward. Land trade from the East passed mostly through Persia and what is now Iraq on its way to Syrian ports. From there, products were shipped to European cities along the Mediterranean littoral, notably the French cities of Marseille, Montpellier and Narbonne. Of additional concern to the French was the water route from the Indian Ocean to the Red Sea. Products were transported across Egypt on their way to Europe, thereby making the area around the Gulf of Suez strategically important. The Near East thus served the French, like the British, as an essential commercial link in their lucrative trade with the Orient.

The French Revolution of 1789 had two consequences for French activity in the Near East. First, the change in governments brought France into a bloody confrontation with the Ottoman Empire. Second, the French revolutionary motto of "Liberté, Egalité, Fraternité" left a lasting impression on the various peoples of the Ottoman Empire and was, perhaps, the most significant force that awakened their nationalist aspirations. France would encounter the resultant nationalist fervor later in revolts in the Maghreb and the Levant.

Napoleon's invasion of Egypt in 1798 was the First Republic's first major foreign venture. The initial reasoning behind the attack was to sever British communications with India. Napoleon eventually occupied Egypt and advanced into Palestine and Syria and as far north as Sidon in Lebanon. The expedition established a base for extensive commercial contacts between France and Egypt. However, the French occupation was too taxing in political and military terms, and it damaged relations with the Ottoman Empire and the British. In 1801, the French surrendered to the British, who then returned Egypt to the nominal control of the Ottoman sultan the following year. The rivalry with Britain for overseas expansion prompted France to search out other areas of interest to satisfy its colonial ambitions. While France retained and sought to protect its economic and religious interests in the Levant and in some parts of Egypt, it focused its imperial leanings elsewhere, particularly toward the Maghreb.

The French conquest of Algeria in 1830 had its origins in an unsettled debt problem between the Bey of Algiers and the French Consul in Algiers, although France offered the depredations of the Barbary pirates as justification for its intervention in Algeria. Presumably because of the threat the Barbary pirates posed to French shipping, France blockaded the Port of Algiers. However, France's decision to undertake military action was rooted in both domestic and international political concerns.

The restored French monarchy believed the Algerian campaign would bolster the increasingly unpopular rule of Charles X and enhance French prestige abroad. It saw the undertaking in Algeria as a way of demonstrating to the other European nations that France still had the will and capability of an imperial power.

The military expedition quickly forced the Bey's surrender, but the forces of Charles X suffered a defeat in the French elections and he abdicated on August 2, 1830. The new French government of Louis Philippe declared that it would remain in Algiers until the Barbary pirates were defeated. In fact, France remained in Algeria for 130 years.[2] So, through the beginning of the 18th century, the French rivalry with Britain for imperial dominance, the growing commercial contacts with Egypt and the Levant because of France's Far East trade, and France's domestic politics shaped French external policy toward the Near East and North Africa. Through a combination of trade and military expedition, France established itself as a major external power in the region.

THE MAGHREB AND THE LEVANT IN THE 19TH CENTURY

Economic and political considerations guided French policy in the Near East and North Africa during the nineteenth century. Economically, the Levant and Egypt provided the critical link with France's Far East trade, and supplied Europe with raw materials such as silk and cotton. Politically, North Africa served as a showcase for French imperial power.

France subdued Algeria, as well as Morocco and Tunisia, by military occupation. Humiliated in Europe by defeats in the Napoleonic wars and later the Franco-Prussian War in 1870, France sought new areas to assert its military and political power, and Algeria was an ideal choice for this activity given its proximity to France (500 miles). While France did not depend on Algeria for any essential resource, it did develop Algerian markets (wheat and grapes) and exported the produce to France and Europe, helping the French economy and assuring the incorporation of Algeria into the French Empire. Thousands of colonists were encouraged to go to Algeria and by 1848 the European population in Algeria reached 110,000.

As France consolidated its hold on Algeria, it extended its colonial ambitions to Morocco and Tunisia, despite protests from Britain. In order to prevent an Ottoman challenge to French rule in North Africa, France encouraged the Bey of Tunisia to borrow French capital at high rates of interest to build railways and ports and when Tunisia was unable to repay its loans, it was forced to accept French protection. France and Tunisia signed the Treaty of Kassar Said on May 12, 1881, giving France effective authority over the Bey and his territory.

The French expended more time and energy in Morocco than in Algeria and Tunisia because of the involvement of other European powers (notably Germany and Spain). Spain and France had been at odds with each other over Morocco since the late 1850s. France wanted to expand economic ties with Morocco (principally in the wool and mineral markets), while Spain envisioned diverting all of Morocco's trade to the Rif, the northern most region of Morocco, where Spain would have a significant commercial advantage. France and Spain signed separate agreements with Morocco establishing their respective zones of influence in the area. At the same time, Germany increased its trade with Morocco in a bid for influence in the Maghreb. The final settlement in April 1906 designated authority to the French and Spanish Protectorates, and Germany acknowledged French authority when France agreed to compensate Germany with the Cameroons.

The period from 1860 to 1914 was an active one for French commercial, military, and cultural activities in the Levant and Egypt.

Aware of France's increasing influence in the region, Louis Napoleon demanded the expansion of French clerical privileges in the Holy Land. In addition to this, France established cordial relations with key groups in the area in order to secure its holdings. Close ties were developed with the Maronites and other Christian groups in what is now Lebanon, between 1840 and 1860, based on shared religious values and Maronite control of important sectors of the economy in Mount Lebanon. French ties to the Christian groups of Mount Lebanon were so close that when violence broke out between the Christian and Druze communities in 1860/61, the French intervened on behalf of the Christians.

The traditional French interest in the holy places of Jerusalem led to a bloody confrontation with Tsar Nicholas I of Russia in the 1850s. The Russian defeat in the three-year-long Crimean War (1854–1856) resulted in French, British, and Austrian agreement to protect the Ottoman Empire from further Russian expansion and to preserve its territorial integrity. Moreover, the victory allowed France to expand its control over North Africa with minimal opposition from the Ottoman Empire.

Despite France's difficulties with Imperial Russia, French trade with the Levant and Egypt flourished. The French controlled the tobacco industry, several utilities, and more importantly, the railways in Syria and Lebanon. By the 1850s the sight of French steamers docking at the ports of Tripoli and Beirut carrying goods from the Orient became a common sight. The Levant also became a principal supplier of silk to France and Europe. The French also had concessions for port construction in Haifa and Jaffa. The establishment of lycées in Lebanon and Egypt for the children of French citizens brought French culture and language to the area. French missionaries established St. Joseph's University in Beirut in 1875. During this period of increased economic, political, and cultural activity in the Near East, France expanded its colonial holdings in the Far East with Indochina becoming the principal area of commercial interest. Egypt served as the critical juncture on a voyage to the Far East. This link was so important that the French explorer and engineer, Ferdinand de Lesseps, obtained a contract from the Egyptian viceroy, Ismail Pasha, in 1856 for the construction of a canal over the Isthmus of Suez. Opened in 1869, the Suez Canal guaranteed a faster and less expensive voyage for French and British ships on their way to the Orient. In addition to that, Egypt's textile industry provided Europe and France with a cheap source of cotton. So, in the last years of the Concert of Europe, France was able to link the distant parts of its empire through trade because of the unique geographic features of the Near East. At the close of the 19th century, French interest in the Near East and the Maghreb began taking on a more complex character. French interest in navigable waterways increased with the building of the Suez Canal. Likewise, the development of key industries in the Levant and North Africa further differentiated French economic interest in the area. While this occurred, successive French leaders safeguarded these interests through military domination, close collaboration with key groups in the area favorably disposed toward French influence, and the extention of French culture. Despite these changes, the desire to promote French colonial ambitions and political power continued to guide French policy. By the beginning of the twentieth century, France had established an extensive economic, military, and political presence in North Africa and the Near East rivalled only by Britain.

WORLD WAR I AND THE MANDATE

The outbreak of World War I had a profound effect on the Middle East. Of primary significance to the French was the correspondence between the British High Commissioner in Egypt (Sir Henry McMahon) and the Sherif Hussein of Mecca in 1915–1916, and the Sykes-Picot Agreement of 1916. In McMahon's letter of October 24, 1915, it was declared that Britain would support the independence of the Arabs in certain parts of the Middle East, excluding some areas in what is today Lebanon, such as the Maronite Christian enclaves.

The Sykes-Picot Agreement, signed between Britain and France on May 16, 1916, noted "that France and Great Britain are prepared to recognize and protect an independent Arab state or a Confederation of Arab states"[3] and laid the groundwork for the French Mandate in the Levant. Sir Mark Sykes of Britain and Francois Georges Picot of France exchanged notes that envisaged French control of the Levant coast in what is now Syria and Lebanon. The French delineated a "Greater Lebanon," which included Mount Lebanon, Beirut, Sidon, Tyre, southern Lebanon, the Bekaa Valley, and the Akkar Plain in the north. France believed that this larger region would make the Levant more economically viable and accommodating to its interests, by protecting the dominant position of Christian groups in the area.

Between World War I and World War II France ruled what later became Syria and Lebanon under a League of Nations Mandate that authorized France to advise and assist the native population and offer "services" that would "expedite" the development of these areas as independent states. Yet France's experience in Syria and Lebanon was marred by invasion and indigenous rebellion. France invaded Syria in 1920 and 1926 and employed a policy of *divide et impera* in the mandated areas in order to deal with the growth of Arab nationalism and the Syrian quest for a "Greater Syria"—the belief among many Arab leaders that Lebanon was part of historic Syria.

Realizing that its control over the mandated areas was waning, France began to transfer power gradually to the Syrians. The new Syrian parliament ratified a Franco-Syrian treaty in September 1936 in the hope that an eventual reunification with Lebanon would occur, but the French government refused to ratify the treaty. The Popular Front government of Leon Blum, reacting to the resurgence of German and Italian militarism, decided not to divest itself of its base in the eastern Mediterranean.

Another issue that complicated French policy in the Levant concerned the Sanjak (district) of Alexandretta, an area on the Syrian-Turkish border inhabited by Turks, Arabs, and Kurds. The Franklin-Bouillon agreement of 1921 entrusted France with the care of the Turks in Alexandretta. In May 1937 the Council of the League of Nations decided to grant the Sanjak full autonomy in its internal affairs, while Syria was entrusted with the administration of its foreign affairs. France and Turkey concluded a treaty in 1938 that guaranteed the security of the Sanjak and declared that it had a predominantly Turkish character. The following year France ceded the Sanjak to Turkey. This, along with French actions in Lebanon, set back Franco-Syrian relations and thwarted the Syrian dream of a "Greater Syria." Bearing out the persistence of that dream to this day, the Syrian Government has never established an embassy in Lebanon, regarding the country as an extension of Syria itself.

The Maghreb

Between the world wars, France expanded its economic, political, and military ties with the Maghreb, with penetration varying in both scope and method. For example the French military presence in Tunisia was never as large as that in Morocco or Algeria. The French in Tunisia never constituted more than seven percent of the entire population. Even its economic and political penetration into Tunisian society was limited. The Tunisians had control over some of the most fertile and prosperous land in the

Maghreb. The French also instituted bilingual training in French and Arabic, which had been discouraged in Algeria.

Unlike the situation in Tunisia, the process of incorporating Algeria into France was pushed forward during this period. Algeria became a source of cheap labor for French companies. Over 300,000 Algerians were working as laborers or soldiers in France by the end of World War I. In the quest for total domination of Algeria the French killed over three million Algerians, disbanded many tribes, and transformed the economy from its traditional production of cereals for domestic consumption to the production of wine for export.

The French never gained full control of Morocco. Incessant Moroccan resistance prevented France from dismantling the indigenous political and economic structure. Influential Moroccan families retained their priviledged positions and the Sultan continued to sign official decrees and legislation. Settlers from France and other countries built up European agriculture, banking, and industry in Morocco, and developed the Moroccan economy through the mining of phosphates. The construction of a rail and road network facilitated the transport and processing of these minerals for French companies.

Despite the differences in colonial penetration, all three countries experienced the beginning of indigenous rebellion that would later cause France severe foreign policy problems. Habib Borguiba's *Neo-Destour Party* in Tunisia, Abd al-Hamid Ben Badis' *Union Populaire Algerienne* in Algeria and Morocco's *Comité d'Action Marocaine* formed the political bases of the independence movements that would grip all three countries in the 1950s.

WORLD WAR II

The rise to power in France of Emile Petain's Vichy government did not alter the French policy in the Levant and the Maghreb. Most of the French civil and military administrators in the colonial and mandated areas refused to respond to pronouncements by Petain's opponent, Charles de Gaulle, and his Free French Committee. The principal aim of the Vichy government in the Levant was to prevent the infiltration of British forces from Palestine into Lebanon and Syria. The crisis that led to the British intervention in the Levant occurred in May 1941 when General Henri Dertz, the Vichy High Commissioner, permitted German aircraft to land and refuel at air bases in Syria to aid Rashid Ali's rebellion in Iraq. The avowed Vichy neutrality was broken, and Britain, assisted by Free French forces, invaded Syria and Lebanon in June 1941. General Dertz signed an armistice on July 14, 1941, and the British Middle East Command took control.

The removal of Vichy authority over the Levant hastened Syrian and Lebanese independence with formal proclamations of independence issued respectively on September 28, 1941, and on November 26, 1941. Despite formal emancipation, the leaders of Free France were unwilling to turn over the function and administration of government to the new republics until the war ended. France wanted to retain control and secure for the future all existing French rights, institutions, and privileges.[4] In March 1943 the Lebanese parliament adopted a resolution that expunged all references to France from the Constitution. In response to this, the new French Delegate General, Jean Helleu, arrested the President of the Lebanese Republic, Bishara al-Khuri, and a majority of his cabinet, and appointed Emile Edde the head of state and government. Anti-French riots broke out, and de Gaulle recalled Helleu and ordered Georges Catroux, Delegate General and Plenipotentiary of Free France in the Levant, to reinstate al-Khuri.

Syria experienced a similar crisis at the end of 1943 when it rewrote its constitution expressly omitting the French dependency clause. This prompted French forces to invade Beirut. These forces were withdrawn when British Prime Minister Winston Churchill threatened General de Gaulle with British intervention. Over the next two years, France staged a phased withdrawal from Syria and Lebanon. This caused an important cooling in Franco-British relations. The last French soldiers left Lebanon on December 31, 1946.

THE FOURTH REPUBLIC: (1946–1958)

The fall of Vichy France and the establishment of the Fourth Republic, with its weak executive and strong parliament, ushered in a new era in foreign policy. Three key events in the Middle East and North Africa were instrumental in changing the nature and direction of French policy in the region: (a) the rebellions in the Maghreb (particularly, in Algeria); (b) the establishment of close relations with Israel; and (c) the 1956 Suez Crisis.

The revolts in the Maghreb and Indochina were symptomatic of a decline in French political and military power on a worldwide scale. In Morocco and Tunisia the French strategy for dealing with these movements entailed controlling key sectors of the economy (the mining industry in Morocco and agriculture in Tunisia) in order to strengthen the Protectorates. While the independence movement was growing in Algeria, and taxing French military capabilities to a greater degree, France granted Morocco and Tunisia independence in 1956. It would now devote its full attention to Algeria, France's original conquest in the Maghreb and, for over 120 years, a showcase of French prestige and power.

France did not grant Algeria independence as quickly as it did to the other two nations in the Maghreb, arguing that Algeria was not a protectorate but rather a *departement*, an integral part of France itself. The French pursued somewhat conflicting policies in Algeria during the Fourth Republic. France wanted to improve the social and economic welfare of the Algerian population, while at the same time preserving a French Algeria and protecting the French and European minorities there. Unlike Tunisia and Morocco, Algeria's independence movement took the form of a bloody civil war that seriously taxed French military resources. The *Front de Liberation Nationale* (FLN) declared war on France on November 1, 1954. Violence erupted, continuing until Algeria's independence from France in 1962.

In order to quell the uprisings, the French sent Jacques Soustelle, who opposed the excessive use of force and was a supporter of de Gaulle, to Algeria to initiate new reform measures. The "Algerian Question," how France would untimately deal with the question of Algerian independence, occupied the center stage of French politics in 1956. The government of Prime Minister Guy Mollet pledged that it would achieve peace in Algeria. He believed that the rebels had little support, and that the French settler population would approve of indigenous autonomy for Muslims and Berbers in Algeria. Mollet sent over 400,000 soldiers to Algeria to quell the revolt and supported an *Algerie francaise*, the belief that "France without Algeria is not France."

The growing rebellion in Algeria and the withdrawal from Tunisia and Morocco left France with few allies in the Middle East and North Africa. Indeed, brutal attempts by France to end the Algerian rebellion made France the enemy of all Arab nationalists, especially Egypt's Nasser, whose influence in the Arab world was growing in the late 1950s. Nasser's overt support of the FLN greatly angered the French and helped promote French interest in establishing stronger ties with Israel. So, the French leadership promoted relations with Israel in part as a way of reasserting France's role in the Middle East.

Close cooperation between France and Israel in the political and economic realms characterized French Middle East policy during the Fourth Republic.[5] Israeli scientists were frequent visitors to the

Institut des Sciences Nucleaires et Techniques at Saclay near Paris. This cooperation eventually led to the French construction of the Dimona nuclear power plant in Israel's Negev desert. France also became the principal supplier of Israel's military. The French Mystere IV-A jet fighter and the AMX-13 main battle tank were the backbone of the Israeli Defense Forces. Other factors that nurtured the Franco-Israeli relationship were the political appeal of socialist Zionism, which made France's socialist leader Guy Mollet and Israel's Prime Minister David Ben Gurion ideological allies, and Israel's dislike of Gamal Abdel Nasser. Yet the growth of the relationship between France and Israel was not the only factor that contributed to the decline of French political and military prestige in the Arab world. Several international events helped to denigrate France's global role.

The disastrous defeat in Vietnam at Dien Bien Phu in 1954 and its accompanying humiliation was not an experience befitting a great power. In order to reassert themselves, French leaders believed a strong, hard-line policy in Algeria would command the respect of other nations, particularly the United States and the Soviet Union. The growing military, political, and economic rivalry between the United States and the Soviet Union contributed to France's inability to compete with the two superpowers on a global scale.

Apparently failing to grasp the significance of such limitations and eager to recapture its once dominant role in the Middle East, France, along with Britain and Israel, attacked Nasser's Egypt in November 1956 following Nasser's nationalization of the Suez Canal. Officially, Britain and France intervened in the conflict in order to separate the Egyptian and Israeli armies and keep the Suez Canal open for trade and passage. But Mollet and his Foreign Minister, Christian Pineau, held the view that Nasser was the key military supporter of the FLN in Algeria. They reasoned that a defeat of Nasser would reduce the military and political backing of the FLN, and justified the invasion on those grounds. Actually, however, Egyptian military support for the FLN was minimal.

Unable to withstand the combined pressure of the Soviet Union, the United States, and the United Nations, France, Britain, and Israel withdrew from the Canal Zone in 1957. The withdrawal left France in a highly uncomfortable diplomatic position in the Middle East. It had collaborated militarily, politically, and economically with Israel, and the Arab states, along with other emerging nations in the Third World, detested its aggressive designs on Algeria and Egypt. The domestic backlash from the Suez Crisis caused the government of Guy Mollet to fall in May 1957.

Believing that French leaders were not prosecuting the Algerian campaign aggressively enough, French generals staged a coup in Algiers in 1958 to express their frustration with the French war strategy. The event heralded the downfall of the Fourth Republic after a short twelve year tenure, characterized by splits within the governing socialist coalition over how to deal with French decolonization, and France's declining position in world affairs.[6] The Parliament dissolved itself and with the return of Charles de Gaulle, the hero of the French Resistance during World War II, as its President, the Fifth Republic was born on January 1, 1959.

THE FIFTH REPUBLIC

The establishment of the Fifth Republic signalled not only a change in French domestic policy but also a change in French foreign policy. De Gaulle's desire to restructure the government so that more power would rest with the executive instead of the parliament was reminiscent of Napoleonic authoritarianism. The decolonization that occurred in both the French and British spheres of influence after World War II had increased the number of states in the world, and de Gaulle believed that the nation-state was the key to global stability. He wanted to reassert French power on a world stage in which the French role would be neither pro-American nor pro-Soviet. Instead he advocated a policy of a "Third Force," which France would lead. The key word in this respect is *mondialisme*, or French presence worldwide. The methods envisaged for sustaining nonalignment in the face of the East-West rivalry were conflict resolution through diplomacy, an expanded role for the United Nations, with particular emphasis on the Security Council, and increased trade with the Third World.[7] De Gaulle believed that pursuing this policy of independence would reassert French power in the international arena and once again establish the "grandeur" of France as a world power. The Middle East and North Africa provided an ideal environment for this new policy, given the French experience in the Maghreb and the Levant. France could demonstrate that despite its colonial legacy, it could change for the better. In addition to this, de Gaulle saw the superpower conflict as a debilitating element in the political and economic development of the Third World. He believed that the developing countries would view a new France with no colonial ties as an alternative to superpower dependence. To accomplish this, however, France has to extricate itself from Algeria.

On September 28, 1958, de Gaulle placed a referendum before the French people concerning the Fifth Republic's Constitution, the composition of de Gaulle's government, and the French role in Algeria. The French people voted overwhelmingly to negotiate with the rebels and rejected a continuation of Algerian integration into France. The Evian Conference opened in May 1961 and negotiations lasted almost a year. De Gaulle hoped that the Algerians would still opt for some sort of association with France to protect France's growing oil interest there, but negotiations became deadlocked over the status of the European minority population in Algeria, and the future of the Sahara and its oil and minerals. In March 1962, France granted Algeria its independence with the understanding that economic cooperation would continue with France.

The granting of independence to Algeria was also key to de Gaulle's domestic program of preserving the strength of the Fifth Republic's new power-sharing arrangements. The Algerian war led to the downfall of at least four ministries in the Fourth Republic—Guy Mollet, Maurice Bourges-Maunoury, Felix Gaillard, and Pierre Pflimlin—and de Gaulle believed that granting independence to Algeria would be a measure of the Fifth republic's new vigor and stability.[8]

After the granting of independence to Algeria, de Gaulle began rebuilding France's image not only in the Middle East but also in the Third World. He believed that the unequivocal French support of Israel during the Fourth Republic was an obstacle to his policy of "grandeur." The election of de Gaulle to the presidency and the resolution of the Algerian question had the effect of eliminating the ideological and political alliance between Ben Gurion and the socialist leaders in the Fourth Republic, and diminished France's distrust of Nasser. France continued to supply Israel with military hardware and economic aid into the late 1960s, but the ties between the two states gradually weakened as de Gaulle pressed on with his new policy.

De Gaulle believed that nonalignment in the superpower rivalry and a closer working relationship with Algeria would establish France's anti-colonial credentials and thus entice other Third World countries to turn to France for economic, political, and military leadership. By the spring of 1963 all the Arab nations who had severed diplomatic relations with France following the Suez Crisis had reopened their embassies in Paris.

Algeria was the cornerstone of France's new Middle East policy for two reasons: First, it was a link to three regions: the Middle East, North Africa, and sub-Saharan Africa. Its Arab-Islamic culture and its relations with black Africa made it the "gateway to the Third World."[9] So, firm relations with Algeria would not only promote France's anti-colonial image in the Middle East, but in the Third World also. Second, the French economy during the Fourth and Fifth Republics was being transformed from one based on coal to one based on cheap Middle East petroleum.[10] So, good relations between France and the Arab suppliers of inexpensive oil would guarantee France a steady supply of petroleum. France and Algeria jointly governed the *Organisme de Cooperation Industrielle*, which was responsible for distributing French money to develop the Algerian oil industry. Algeria accounted for approximately 30 percent of French imported oil needs by 1969. Economic aid was also key to the new Franco-Algerian alliance—France provided in excess of $160 million in 1963 and over $150 million in 1964 in grant aid. These grants and industrial ventures provided France with a place in the Algerian economy and, thus, were a way of securing access to France's growing oil interest.

The 1967 Arab-Israeli war marked the beginning of a new period in French Middle East policy in terms of new issues and policy instruments, with the goal of a rejuvenated France in world affairs as always the guiding principle. The whole question of occupied lands and Palestinian refugees captured the diplomatic and political interest of French leaders, in common with the governments of other external powers. France, with its avowed desire to fight colonialism and promote its relations with the Arab world, saw the results of the war as an opportunity to come to the aid of the Arab states in their time of defeat. De Gaulle took advantage of that opportunity and played down French relations with Israel as a way of promoting a new and independent role for France.

De Gaulle believed that a solution to the tensions between Israel and the Arab states lay with the regional states as well as the "Big Four Powers" (the United States, the USSR, France, and Britain). On June 2, 1967, de Gaulle informed his Council of Ministers that whichever state resorted to armed conflict first would meet with French disapproval. De Gaulle imposed a general embargo on arms to the states in the crisis area on June 3. The embargo was aimed primarily at Israel, since the amount of French arms being sold to the Arab states was inconsequential. The rationale behind the embargo was to demonstrate to the Arabs that a new French policy was imminent. Following the war, the French supported UN Security Council Resolution 242 and official French policy deemed Israeli withdrawal from the occupied territories a prerequisite to any lasting peace in the area.

French concern to develop a more balanced policy in the Middle East did not stop with support for UN resolutions. De Gaulle pursued his four power peace initiative as a framework for settlement of the Arab-Israeli conflict during 1968/69. His "global solution" specified three conditions to end hostilities: (a) evacuation of the territories seized by force; (b) an end to the state of war; and (c) mutual recognition of each of the states involved.[11] The four power talks began in New York City in March 1969, but by June 1970 these talks had become deadlocked. Israel questioned the whole framework for negotiations since it believed two of the participants in the negotiations, France and the Soviet Union, were openly hostile to it; and, in any event, Israel believed the key to a resolution lay with the regional actors themselves and not with the outside powers. Also, the Rogers Plan put forward by U.S. Secretary of State William Rogers in December 1969, while not attaining general acceptance, served to deflect attention from the Four Power Talks and the French initiative fell by the wayside.

Franco-Israeli relations deteriorated further after the 1967 war. The Israelis had contracted with the French for 50 Mirage jets to be delivered in late 1968. Because the Israelis had used French planes in an attack on the Beirut airport in December 1968, the French tightened the ban on the sale of weapons to Israel in January 1969. De Gaulle noted that the embargo would apply to all the "confrontation states," namely Israel, Egypt, Jordan, Lebanon, and Syria. However this did not prevent France from selling Libya 110 Mirage jet fighters in 1970. That same year, Israel clandestinely seized five gunboats that it had previously contracted to have built from the port of Cherbourg. While over 50 percent of French arms sold abroad went to Israel between 1955 and 1964, that figure fell to just under 13 percent between the years 1965 and 1969.[12] The 1970s were destined to be an era of reconciliation between France and the Arab world.

The resignation of de Gaulle and the election to the presidency of Georges Pompidou did not alter the Gaullist doctrine of grandeur or the French tilt toward the Arab world.[13] The early 1970s witnessed requests from Saudi Arabia for the sale of armored personnel carriers and Alouette helicopters. By the 1973 Arab-Israeli war, France was establishing itself as an economic actor in an area of traditional British interest—the Persian Gulf. The war had set in motion a series of actions by the Gulf states that changed the nature and scope of French activity in the Middle East. The Arab oil embargo prompted France to choose a policy of close involvement with the Arab oil exporting states, for it underscored French vulnerability to the oil weapon. Oil accounted for approximately 70 percent of French energy consumption.[14] At the time of the 1973/74 embargo, France was receiving 73 percent of its imported oil from the Persian Gulf.[15] This stimulated the expansion of bilateral trade agreements between France and the Gulf states, principally Saudi Arabia and Iraq. French leaders believed state-to-state trade accords, and not a multilateral, European initiative on energy, would assure France of the most secure access to Gulf oil. The French also urged the Gulf states to arrange new terms of profit sharing with British and American oil companies to maneuver these companies from their traditional position of dominance in the international oil trade.[16] Much of the trade that France initiated with the Gulf states was military in nature, but contracts also were secured for the construction of airports in Iraq and hospitals in Saudi Arabia.

The election of Valery Giscard d'Estaing in 1974 perpetuated the pro-Arab policy in the Persian Gulf and Arab-Israeli sectors. The new President, more so than his predecessors, regarded the Palestinian question as the key to a stable peace. France agreed in 1975 to open a Palestine Liberation Organization (PLO) liason and information office in Paris, but it did not regard the PLO as the sole representative of the Palestinian people. The ban on the sale of weapons to the confrontation states was also lifted.

In concrete policy terms, France under Giscard became the first European Community (EC) member to link the Palestinian question to the overall peace process. France, on several occasions during Giscard's presidency, voted in the United Nations to criticize Israeli settlement policies in the West Bank. Nonetheless, Giscard did not go so far as to call for the establishment of a Palestinian state, but rather affirmed after a visit to Tunisia in November 1975 that the Palestinians had a right to a *patrie independente*, or independent homeland. Giscard did not actively endorse the Camp David peace process that began in 1977, or any other initiative that excluded the French. Giscard was an active member of the EC and a supporter of the "Euro-Arab Dialogue," which advocated political and technical cooperation, and cultural exchanges between Europe and Middle Eastern states.[17] His own policy emphasized France's role as a European and Mediterranean power, and Giscard generally worked within the framework of the EC to address the political difficulties of the Arab-Israeli conflict. During a trip to the Gulf in the spring of 1980 he went further than any of his predecessors in promoting the Palestinian cause by calling for Palestinian self-determination. In his final communique from this diplomatic venture Giscard noted that the plight of the Palestinians was not a refugee problem but was one of self-determination. This statement brought back memories of the

French colonial struggle with Algeria where "self-determination" meant the right to a state. In Amman, Jordan, Giscard stated that representatives of the Palestinian people must take part in any negotiations that would lead to a settlement of the Arab-Israeli conflict. A few months later, in June 1980, the French government joined in the Venice Declaration. Giscard also urged that members of the PLO be included in any future negotiations.

MITTERRAND AND FRENCH INTERESTS IN THE MIDDLE EAST

By the time of the May 1981 election of Francois Mitterrand as president, French policy in the Middle East and North Africa had established strong political, economic, and cultural ties with the Maghreb states, promoted a vast market for French goods in the Persian Gulf, and provided Egypt, Syria, and Jordan with a reliable trading partner. In regard to the Arab-Israeli conflict, France regarded itself and the Palestinians as key players to the resolution of the conflict. Mitterrand assumed office in 1981 with an avowed socialist compassion for the working class in France, an awareness of the economic and political underdevelopment of Third World countries, and a belief in the political and economic interdependence of states in world affairs. In the Middle East he sought to pursue a new approach to attain traditional French interests.

Mitterrand's interest in the Arab-Israeli conflict is a reflection of the Gaullist desire to play a more active diplomatic role in the peace process. Like de Gaulle, Mitterrand has sought to portray France to the states of the Middle East as a legitimate economic, political, and military "Third Force." The Middle East thus offers France an environment to reassert itself in world affairs. While endorsing the Camp David Accords as a first step toward a comprehensive settlement in the Middle East and contributing French forces and materiel to peace-keeping duties in the Sinai, Lebanon, and minesweeping operations in the Red Sea, Mitterrand criticized the Reagan initiative of September 1982 for not directly addressing the plight of the Palestinian people or, more importantly, providing France with a direct role in any negotiations. Mitterrand was critical of de Gaulle, Pompidou, and Giscard for being too "pro-Arab" in their view of the Arab-Israeli conflict. He wanted to redress this imbalance, since the overwhelming majority of France's 700,000 Jews supported his candidacy, and Mitterrand's

Parti Socialiste had been the primary supporter of Israel during the heydey of the Fourth Republic. A new posture on the Arab-Israeli conflict based on a more conciliatory approach toward Israel could guarantee France a role in future negotiations.

French cultural ties, the use of French as a second language in its former spheres of influence, particularly Lebanon and the Maghreb, play a key role in this continuing effort to promote French power. The Sorbonne, the University of Toulouse, and the *Ecole Pratique des Hautes Etudes* have become the leading choices of many young Arabs studying abroad. France's proximity to the Middle East and the business opportunities available there make it an ideal environment in which Arabs can study and learn about the West, and France in particular. Positive experiences with French education and society have helped to erase the French image as a colonial power. In 1980 there were approximately fifty thousand students from the Middle East and North Africa studying in France, comprising about half of the foreign student population of the country.[18] As de Gaulle made Algeria "the gateway to the Third World," Mitterrand has chosen to portray France as "the gateway to the West." The Maghreb states of Algeria, Morocco, and Tunisia play a special role in this policy, given their historical association with France. The large North African population in France, almost 1.4 million, makes it the largest minority in the country and establishes Islam as the second largest religion in France. In addition, the French population in the Maghreb exceeds 100,000. Mitterrand and other high government officials make frequent trips to all three states, and young French citizens (*coopérants*) are still offered the opportunity to do volunteer work in the Maghreb in place of military service.

France's economic interests in the Middle East are tied directly to its need for oil (see Table 6.1). Into the 1990's, oil will provide approximately one half of the energy that France consumes.[19] This need for petroleum has made the Persian Gulf and Algeria of vital economic interest to France. Mitterrand has continued to promote the large volume of trade, particularly in arms, with the Middle East and North Africa as a way of cementing links and offsetting the cost of oil. The Middle East and North Africa have consistently accounted for over ten percent of France's imports and exports (see Tables 6.2–4). Even though both imports and exports have declined as a percentage of total French trade during the Mitterrand presidency, the Middle East and North Africa have provided certain sectors of the French economy, especially the arms industry, with a lucrative market.

TABLE 6.1: French Oil Imports; the Middle East and North Africa, 1980–1984 (percentage of total oil imported*)

	1980	1981	1982	1983	1984
Iraq	21.6	2.9	2.0	2.8	4.4
Iran	1.4	1.6	4.5	6.1	5.0
Saudi Arabia	35.4	51.9	36.3	21.2	12.6
Kuwait	2.9	1.5	na	na	0.2
Qatar	2.3	3.0	2.6	1.2	3.0
UAE	6.7	7.8	7.7	7.7	6.0
Oman	0.1	0.4	0.7	1.2	na
(subtotal)	(53.4)	(69.0)	(54.0)	(40.2)	(31.2)
Algeria	4.1	4.5	7.7	8.0	7.1
Tunisia	0.1	0.6	0.4	0.4	1.0
Libya	1.8	1.6	2.8	4.9	4.8
Egypt	0.1	0.2	1.0	2.5	3.3
Syria	0.2	1.0	1.3	1.1	0.7
(subtotal)	(6.3)	(7.9)	(13.2)	(16.9)	(17.0)
Total	59.7	76.9	67.2	57.1	48.2

*Numbers rounded to the nearest decimal.

Source: Centre Francais du Commerce Exterieur, "Importations de Petrole Brut," *Commerce Exterieur de la France, Resultats Annuels—Annee 1984.*

Most of the imports from the Middle East include oil and combustible minerals, while France's chief exports to the area have included engine parts used in weapons systems, steel and metal used in industry, and electrical parts used in aircraft and radar systems. In 1984, France exported $11.42 billion worth of goods to the Middle East and North Africa and imports from the area reached $11.41 billion.

Although companies involved in the production of arms (Dassault, Panhard, Aerospatiale) have generated a great deal of this revenue, other firms have been instrumental also. The French construction company Bouygues, the engineering company Compenon Bernard, and the public works company SPIE-Batignolles have played key roles in securing contracts with the countries of the Persian Gulf. Bouygues obtained a $71 million contract for the construction of roads in Iraq, while SPIE-Batignolles secured a $744 million contract for the construction of the Baghdad International Airport.

TABLE 6.2: French Trade with the Middle East and North Africa, 1980–1984 (percentage of total French trade)

Country	1980 IMP/EXP	1981 IMP/EXP	1982 IMP/EXP	1983 IMP/EXP	1984 IMP/EXP
Israel	.23/.23	.26/.33	.24/.36	.28/.41	.26/.32
Turkey	.16/.46	.23/.39	.21/.28	.22/.23	.27/.28
Lebanon	.01/.31	.00/.34	.00/.36	.00/.40	.00/.26
Jordan	.00/.18	.01/.21	.00/.18	.01/.17	.00/.17
Syria	.09/.29	.31/.30	.21/.22	.18/.22	.22/.23
Egypt	.09/1.17	.14/1.13	.30/1.08	.5/1.2	.57/1.0
Libya	.49/.60	.42/.90	.56/.45	.81/.37	.80/.23
Sudan	.04/.08	.04/.10	.03/.14	.03/.11	.00/.10
Djibouti	-/-	.00/.00	.00/.00	.00/.00	.00/.00
Cyprus	.01/.05	.01/.06	.02/.07	.01/.07	.01/.20
Ethiopia	-/-	.00/.00	.00/.00	.00/.00	.00/.00
Somalia	-/-	.00/.00	.00/.00	.00/.00	.00/.00
Iraq	4.12/.97	.60/1.44	.35/1.55	.48/.89	.76/.74
Iran	.51/.65	.40/.66	.79/.35	.92/.40	.75/.19
Saudi Arabia	6.46/1.31	10.01/1.84	6.34/2.12	3.33/2.0	2.1/2.5
Kuwait	.61/.27	.35/.21	.10/.34	.19/.50	.18/.77
Qatar	.50/.08	.67/.09	.51/.20	.20/.21	.49/.12
UAE	1.42/.42	1.75/.50	1.41/.59	1.21/.43	.9/.3
Bahrain	.00/.04	.04/.03	.01/.06	.02/.06	.00/.00
Oman	.02/.04	.08/.03	.12/.08	.19/.06	.00/.00
N Yemen	.00/.14	.00/.14	.00/.13	.00/.13	.00/.12
S Yemen	.00/.02	.02/.03	.17/.04	.04/.03	.00/.00
Morocco	.57/1.07	.53/1.18	.53/1.21	.56/.90	.58/.86
Algeria	1.27/2.36	1.99/2.34	3.42/2.31	2.93/2.6	2.7/2.9
Tunisia	.29/.84	.36/.95	.34/1.00	.37/.93	.41/.81
Total*	16.8/11.5	18.2/14.6	15.7/13.2	12.5/12.4	11.0/12.2

*Rounded to the nearest decimal.
Source: Centre Francais du Commerce Exterieur, *Commerce Exterieur de la France, Resultats Annuels—Annee 1984.*

As a consequence of France's interest in oil and trade in the Middle East, Mitterrand views a stable military, political, and economic environment for French investment with acute regard. The French believe that Khomeni's penchant to export his fundamentalist Islam, Colonel Qadaffi's meddling in Egypt and the Maghreb, and any large-scale military conflagration such as the Iran-Iraq war pose threats to the long-term French interests in the

TABLE 6.3: French Exports to the Middle East, 1980–1984 (Millions of U.S. dollars*)

Country	1980	1981	1982	1983	1984
Israel	262	332	331	337	297
Turkey	516	396	255	209	253
Lebanon	349	345	333	363	243
Jordan	198	211	168	159	153
Syria	329	307	199	205	217
Egypt	1298	1152	993	1110	943
Libya	676	916	417	336	209
Sudan	92	106	133	101	94
Djibouti	—	1	38	70	71
Cyprus	—	63	64	66	181
Ethiopia	—	23	41	42	39
Somalia	—	11	7	9	18
Iraq	1082	1464	1424	810	680
Iran	721	669	326	369	180
Saudi Arabia	1468	1879	1954	1810	2266
Kuwait	298	35	311	453	711
Qatar	95	96	187	107	100
UAE	423	517	537	391	280
Bahrain	—	45	7	25	38
Oman	40	32	73	54	72
N. Yemen	—	144	118	117	110
S. Yemen	—	33	44	27	37
Morocco	1193	1204	1117	824	794
Algeria	2638	2384	2125	2446	2686
Tunisia	935	973	922	862	752
Total	12,613	13,338	11,212	11,342	11,424

*Numbers are rounded to the nearest decimal.

Exchange Rates: 1980, \$1 = FF4.2; 1981, \$1 = FF5.4; 1982, \$1 = FF6.6; 1983, \$1 = FF7.6; 1984, \$1 = FF8.8.

Source: "Statistics," *France & the Middle East, MEED: Special Report* (April 1985), p. 30.

region, and ultimately the supply and safe transit of oil to France. Mitterrand's relations with Qadaffi have been difficult, given the opposing 1983 French and Libyan interventions in Chad. The deployment of 3,000 French troops in Chad, from August 1983 to November 1984, to bolster the government of Hissen Habre strained relations with Libya because of Qadaffi's support of Chadian rebels.

TABLE 6.4: **French Imports from the Middle East, 1980–1984 (millions of U.S. dollars*)**

Country	1980	1981	1982	1983	1984
Israel	311	316	275	291	272
Turkey	214	274	239	236	276
Lebanon	20	6	4	3	4
Jordan	1	7	5	15	11
Syria	121	371	239	185	222
Egypt	130	170	340	525	582
Libya	685	505	638	850	811
Sudan	52	48	40	34	31
Djibouti	—	1	0.3	1	0.3
Cyprus	—	10	18	14	10
Ethiopia	—	27	26	36	32
Somalia	—	1	0.6	0.4	1
Iraq	5693	726	404	503	782
Iran	683	482	905	966	773
Saudi Arabia	8822	12140	7289	3500	2126
Kuwait	849	424	115	204	183
Qatar	700	811	591	211	504
UAE	1925	2111	1614	1271	924
Bahrain	—	45	7	25	6
Oman	26	99	135	208	28
N. Yemen	—	—	—	4	0.1
S. Yemen	—	21	195	37	7
Morocco	774	640	604	589	592
Algeria	1769	2412	3926	3085	2819
Tunisia	399	436	386	389	418
Total	23,174	22,083	17,996	13,182	11,414

*Numbers are rounded to the nearest decimal.

Exchange Rates: 1980, $1 = FF4.2; 1981, $1 = FF5.4; 1982, $1 = FF6.6; 1983, $1 = FF7.6; 1984, $1 = FF8.8.

Source: "Statistics," *France & the Middle East, MEED: Special Report* (April 1985), p. 30.

Despite that, Libya has supplied France with a larger percentage of its imported oil since Mitterrand's election. In 1981 France received less than two percent of its imported oil from Libya. By 1984 that figure had reached close to five percent. Even though Qadaffi's rhetoric had not been commensurate with his deeds, Mitterrand regards Qadaffi's anti-Israeli and anti-Western leanings as undermining his desire to pursue a rapprochement with Israel, and to keep open vital lines of communication and transit. Regardless of the Libyan leader's views on the Middle East, there has been negotiation between the two nations over Chad regarding French and Libyan military deployments, albeit through Moroccan mediation.

Geographically and strategically, Mitterrand continues to view the Middle East and its key waterways as a vital link in France's military supply lines. The French Foreign Legion base in Djibouti (the largest overseas French base, with 3,900 Legionnaires), French naval strategy in the Indian Ocean, and the French port at Reunion off the coast of Madagascar—all depend on the free passage of French ships through the Suez Canal and the Bab al-Mandeb to execute France's military policies in sub-Saharan Africa.[20] Any attempt to close those waterways is of significant concern to Mitterrand. Because of that, France keeps a number of naval frigates near the Persian Gulf in case of such an emergency. Those waterways would take on an added significance if there were a military crisis in Europe. France's armed forces depend on oil from the Persian Gulf to execute their continental missions. Thus any attempt to blockade the Straits of Hormuz, or the other key waterways in the Middle East, would be regarded as a threat to France's national security.

The Middle East is both a market and a gateway to the Third World, which make it an ideal environment for the projection of French power. In that regard French interest in the Middle East since the Crusades has not changed. Mitterrand's interest in a renewed and active France is in evidence in his desire both to play a more significant role in the Arab-Israeli conflict and to establish more extensive commercial relations with the countries of the Persian Gulf. In fact, Mitterrand's general interest in open sea lanes, stable economic and political environments, and French cultural exposure antedates his administration. His Middle East objectives and policy instruments, however, differentiate him from his predecessors.

MITTERRAND AND FRENCH POLICY TOWARD THE MIDDLE EAST

Mitterrand has outlined his foreign policy as centered around three basic principles: (a) that all countries should be guaranteed basic human rights; (b) French independence in global affairs must be maintained; and (c) a commitment to achieve a new international economic order must be made.[21]

The Arab-Israeli Conflict

In August 1982 Mitterrand set forth his principal goals in the Middle East. He described French policy in the Middle East as one of presence, balance, and peace. The hallmark of this policy was protection for Israel's territorial security within safe and recognized borders, a homeland for the Palestinians, and the assertion of Lebanese sovereignty within its borders, which Israel violated in June 1982.[22]

The Mitterrand presidency has been characterized by a change concerning the Arab-Israeli conflict, but he has found that regional conflict and the policies of the states in the area have thwarted his new initiatives. In reality his record in office has been one of reaction to events rather than a new foreign policy.

There have been key differences between Mitterrand and his predecessors in the emphasis this new foreign policy has followed. Unique to this policy was a rapprochement with Israel. Mitterrand supported the Camp David Accords, unlike his predecessor's criticism of the agreement. In August 1981 he sent Pierre Marion, head of French intelligence, to Israel for extensive talks with his Mossad (Israeli intelligence) counterpart, whereas Giscard had avoided all contact with the Mossad. Former Prime Minister Claude Cheysson, in a visit to Israel at the end of 1981, also reiterated that France opposed a European initiative along the lines of the Venice Declaration. Mitterrand was also the first French head of state since de Gaulle to visit Israel. Yet, his initiative ran into difficulty from the beginning. One month after the socialist victory in France in May 1981, Israel bombed a French-built nuclear reactor in Iraq and France condemned the bombing as an act of aggression. The Israeli bombing of Beirut in July 1981 and its annexation of the Golan Heights in December of that year worsened relations between the Begin and Mitterrand governments. In this period of deteriorating relations, Mitterrand postponed his scheduled trip to Israel from January to March 1982. Traditionally French ties with Israel were with the Israeli Labor Party, and not the conservative parties of the Likud coalition that governed Israel at the time. However the fact that Mitterrand finally did visit Israel in March of 1982 reflected his determination to change the direction of French Middle East policy. The Israeli invasion of Lebanon in June 1982 saw a further erosion of Franco-Israeli relations and quelled Mitterrand's desire to improve relations.

Israeli actions were not the only factors that led to a deterioration in relations between France and Israel. French policy on the

Arab-Israeli conflict caused Israel to repudiate French initiatives. Although France embraced UNSC Resolutions 242 and 338, which only referred to the Palestinian "refugee" component of the Arab-Israeli conflict, France subsequently took the position that the Palestinians were the key to any overall settlement of the Arab-Israeli conflict. When Mitterrand took office, former Prime Minister Pierre Mauroy issued a communique stating that all interested parties (including the Palestinians) should take part in any negotiations. Unlike the Venice Declaration of December 1980, Mauroy failed to mention the PLO. However, Mitterrand proposed that a Palestinian "homeland" was key to any overall settlement, noting that Israel's right to live within secure and recognized borders is concomitant with the Palestinians' right to choose their own political destiny, "within the limits of the territories on which it lives."[23] In January 1982 Mitterand proposed that a Palestinian state was a necessity to eventual resolution of the conflict. Mitterrand thus carried the French posture beyond the policy of Giscard. France now perceived the Arab-Israeli conflict as an Israeli-Palestinian struggle over legitimacy and territory.[24] That demarche in foreign policy was in stark contrast to that which France in general and Giscard in particular had pursued in the past. While Giscard regarded a European framework, in the form of the Venice Declaration, as the best negotiating posture for France, Mitterrand believed that breaking ranks with his European compatriots might guarantee a place for France in the peace process.

Mitterrand's trip to Israel in 1982 was meant to show concern not only about Israel but also for the plight of the Palestinians. It was significant that in Mitterrand's speech to the Israeli Knesset, there was no mention of the EC. While Mitterrand embraced the principles of the Venice Declaration, he believed that a European initiative could succeed only if the regional actors in the conflict demanded it. The goal was now to conclude a series of smaller agreements with regional states that might lead to the global peace that France and the rest of Europe had traditionally desired. These smaller agreements included Mitterand's friendship with members of Israel's Labor Party, his support of moderate Arab states such as Jordan and Egypt, and France's convergence of economic interests with the states in the Persian Gulf, and aimed at providing a reasonable role for France in peace negotiations. What these understandings did was create the appropriate conditions for a French initiative in the Arab-Israeli sector. So, acting alone, France proposed the Franco-Egyptian Draft Resolution to the UN Security Council in July 1982, calling for all of the states in the region to live within secure and recognized borders in accordance with UNSC Resolution 242, mutual and simultaneous recognition between all of the interested parties, and representation of the Palestinian people, including the PLO, at peace negotiations.[25] It entailed a renewed interest in the Palestinians, allowed France limited penetration into the Arab-Israeli conflict, and promoted French prestige among the moderate Arab states. Mitterrand still insists that the Franco-Egyptian Draft Resolution offers the best possible chance of securing a workable negotiating framework for the participants in the conflict. However the Reagan initiative of September 1982, the French withdrawal from Lebanon, and the February 1985 Jordanian-PLO agreement on negotiations have overtaken what little momentum the French initiative had.

The Persian Gulf

French policy toward the Persian Gulf, through arms sales and various trade accords, has been designed to establish France as an economic, military, and political power worthy of Arab confidence. This policy is directly related to France's interest in the unhindered passage of oil to France. In pursuit of that objective, Mitterrand has sought to convince Arab leaders of the Gulf that France was still a reliable and profitable market despite the country's new socialist label. Mitterrand has also sought to diversify sources of imported oil so France can reduce its reliance on the Persian Gulf, and he has tried to offset the threat to that supply of oil posed by the Iran-Iraq war by openly supporting Iraq economically and militarily.

Arab leaders were wary of the socialist victory in France, because of Mitterrand's previous public support of Israel and of Mitterrand's pledge to put moral considerations back into French arms sales policy (which they interpretted as cutting back on such sales). Within a week of Mitterrand's election, Arab financiers withdrew about $8 billion from Parisian banks, followed by another $15 billion over the next two to three months.[26] In order to regenerate the Gulf states' confidence in France, French officials travelled to the Persian Gulf stressing the reliability of France as a trading partner. Former Foreign Minister Claude Cheysson affirmed that "France's state interests were paramount and took precedence over party options,"[27] and that the new socialist government would honor all previous contracts that France had signed with the Gulf states. Mitterrand also sought to dispel fears that his prior record of support of Israel would change the direction of French policy in the Arab-Israeli conflict. Mitterrand indicated that he held in high esteem the views of moderate Gulf leaders on the Arab-Israeli conflict. He embraced King Fahd's August 1981 Peace Plan, which called for the creation of a Palestinian state on the West Bank with Jerusalem as its capital. Mitterrand has also praised Fez II, the plan based on Kind Fahd's approach, which the Arab League agreed to shortly after the promulgation of Reagan's September 1982 initiative, for providing a framework for the peace process.[28] The Arab-Israeli conflict was used, thus, as a means to bridge the political and economic gaps between France and the moderate Gulf states at the beginning of the Mitterrand presidency.

The second French goal in the Persian Gulf was to assure access to oil supplies. The Iran-Iraq war posed a direct threat to this objective. At the beginning of the war, France received 21.6 percent of its imported oil from Iraq. In 1981, one year after the war began, Iraq provided less than three percent of France's imported oil. The cutoff of Iraqi oil prompted the French to turn to other Arab suppliers, including Algeria and Libya, as well as to non-Arab suppliers such as Nigeria and Britain to meet its energy needs. The Gulf war thus forced France to diversify its oil supplies and to develop its nuclear power industry.

France's official attitude toward the Gulf war has centered on support for Iraq's sovereignty and independence, and the need for a negotiated solution between Iran and Iraq. However support for Iraq by Mitterrand's government has gone far beyond bulletins from the Quai d'Orsay. Its commitment to Iraq has been manifested in economic and military terms, embodying French resolve to challenge a real threat (Islamic fundamentalism) or potential threat (a Soviet incursion into the area) to French military and economic interests. France's naval capabilities in the Indian Ocean would facilitate the speedy access to vital sea lanes in the Persian Gulf if a crisis were to threaten the passage of oil. In that regard, Mitterrand's policy is not at all different from that of Giscard. In fact, his continuity in policy objectives has allowed France to compete in the Gulf for its share of the market, and has been instrumental in establishing France as an important military and economic power in the region.

POLICY INSTRUMENTS

France has used selected policy instruments both intensively and extensively in the Middle East. Traditionally, those initiatives have been multilateral in nature. However each president of the

Fifth Republic has interpreted the relation of France to other external powers and to the local actors differently. De Gaulle sought a global solution with the participation of the United States, the USSR, Britain, France, and the regional actors. Giscard, on the other hand, preferred a more European-based strategy emphasizing France's role as a Mediterranean power. Finally, Mitterrand has not regarded European participation or the involvement of every regional power in the area as a sine qua non for meaningful negotiations. The key difference between Mitterrand's approach and his predecessors is that he leaves room for France to pursue its own initiatives if warranted. Since Mitterrand does not feel it incumbent upon himself to establish a uniform European policy, his method of embracing the United Nations and select multinational approaches has provided France with the opportunity to reestablish itself as an important actor in the Arab-Israeli conflict. When the issue concerns the vitality of the French economy, Mitterrand, like his predecessors, has used arms sales, military cooperation, and bilateral trade accords to promote French power. He has employed this policy instrument most effectively in the Persian Gulf. Mitterrand has continued to use foreign aid as a policy instrument but its effectiveness varies throughout the Middle East and North Africa. Finally, he has used the Presidential visit to demonstrate symbolic changes in French policy.

Multilateral Initiatives

France's participation in UN forces and other multinational efforts has spearheaded French efforts to implement its policy of "grandeur" with regard to the Arab-Israeli conflict. De Gaulle's acceptance of UNSC Resolution 242 in November 1967, his quest for a "global" solution, and Giscard's embrace of the Venice Declaration in 1980 are examples of the multilateral approaches France has employed. It was the 1978 Israeli invasion of Lebanon, however, which provided France with the opportunity to go beyond mere words and to establish a military presence in the Middle East. When Israel withdrew its forces from southern Lebanon, the United Nations Interim Forces in Lebanon (UNIFIL) was created, and France committed 700 soldiers to peacekeeping duties in southern Lebanon. Justifying its presence on the basis of the UNIFIL mandate allowed France to avoid some of the criticisms when a large, industrialized nation intervenes in another nation's domestic affairs. Mitterrand has continued to pursue such multilateral initiatives with an even more multinational emphasis. France increased its troop commitment to UNIFIL to 1,200 in May 1982, was one of the 10 countries to participate in the multinational observer force in the Sinai when Israel withdrew, and joined in minesweeping duties in the Red Sea in 1985 when Libya was suspected of seeding the area with mines.

The most striking example of Mitterrand's new multilateral approach was France's participation in the multinational peacekeeping force (MNF) in Lebanon, along with the United States, Italy, and Britain, from September 1982 to March 1984. Participating in this force projected direct military and political influence into an area of traditional French interest. France's contingent also served several larger objectives. First, France wanted to present the MNF as a legitimate option in lieu of the United States or the Soviet Union to which Arab and underdeveloped countries could turn. The Israeli invasion gave Mitterrand the chance to promote French policy independence in the Middle East by voicing criticism of the Israelis, of the more radical elements of the PLO, and of the United States for its perceived support of the Israeli invasion.

Second, the presence of French troops was intended to bring the Palestinian issue to the forefront of any proposed settlement between the Arabs and the Israelis. The stationing of the French contingent in the Sabra and Shatila refugee camps identified the French with the Palestinians. In so doing, the French hoped to ride the fine line between endorsement of a "terrorist" group and support for the hopes and legitimate aspirations of a beleaguered people in exile.

Third, the French believed that the deployment of troops in West Beirut would have an indirectly beneficial effect on Franco-Israeli relations. The French, while condemning Israel's "offensive military attitude" reiterated that there would be no solution to the Arab-Israeli conflict without Arab recognition of Israel's right to exist.[29] At the height of the Israeli siege of West Beirut, France insisted that it would be unproductive to isolate Israel in a UN vote. French policy sought to reconcile support for both the rights of Palestinians and legitimate Israeli security concerns. This balancing act, however, has neither exempted French nationals from a series of kidnappings in West Beirut by pro-Iranian militia groups because of French support for Iraq, nor saved France from a terrorist attack that claimed the lives of 58 French soldiers in Lebanon in October 1983. While France did retaliate for the attack on its military compound, it did not do so in conjuction with the other members of the MNF. This independence of action is evidence of the French struggle for autonomy in foreign policy. Since the MNF was not a European initiative, France had room to promote its own peace plan, along with Egypt, at the UN. Although the essence of the plan embraced the principles of the Venice Declaration, it was the closest France had come to pursuing its own Middle East peace initiative.

Arms Sales and Military Cooperation

Arms sales are the second significant method that France has used to expand its role in the area. Many countries in the Middle East, particularly Egypt, Saudi Arabia, and Iraq, have regarded French arms sales as a way of diversifying their military hardware and offsetting U.S. influence in the area. The French, on the other hand, have viewed the sales as a way of paying for large purchases of oil from the Gulf. Over 76 percent of French arms sales (totalling almost $4.7 billion) were with the countries of the Middle East and North Africa in 1984. Over 70 percent of that hardware was ground equipment such as radar and tanks, 25.7 percent was aircraft, and 3.7 percent was naval.[30] It should be noted, however, that Mitterrand's exploitation of this policy instrument was inevitable, despite the fact that many Arab countries, particularly in the Gulf, had believed he would reduce the sale of military hardware.

The increase in French military manpower since the 1960s enlarged the number of units available for foreign intervention, and so required the French economy to sustain the costs of developing logistical capabilities to ensure the projection of military power abroad. The enhanced capabilities of the French military together with French dependence on Middle Eastern oil set the stage for the creation of a large arms export industry during the Giscard presidency as a way of offsetting oil costs and meeting the needs of France's military establishment. The sale of arms supported a larger industrial base than would have been possible otherwise. Arms sales abroad benefited French military technology, and thus improved the country's defense posture.[31] A result of that policy has been the development of an economic infrastructure in France that makes the cost of maintaining a domestic arms industry tolerable.[32] Former French defense minister Charles Hernu highlighted the importance of the arms industry to the French economy when he indicated that of the 720,000 people employed by the Defense Ministry, over 143,000 are civilians. He also mentioned that over 300,000 workers and engineers were employed in such industries as the National Asrospace Industry Company, Thomson-CSF, Dassault, Renault Industrial Vehicles, Panhard, and Saint Etienne. Subcontracts from these companies underwrite almost one million jobs in related activities.[33] Such statements from a member of a socialist government are evidence of the concern the socialists have for the structure of the defense industry and its relation to the smooth functioning of the French economy. In addition to this, the large number of workers in France whose jobs are connected to the sale of arms provides a unique bloc of voters in favor of increased arms sales abroad, regardless of the ideological disposition of a foreign leader.

Most of the arms contracts signed under Giscard were with the Arab states, principally Saudi Arabia and Iraq. The delivery of French arms to the Middle East more than doubled between 1974 and 1977 from $1.4 billion to $3 billion. A review of selected countries in this area will highlight the extent to which the French have penetrated this zone of traditional British influence. The French relationship with the Persian Gulf has been a highly satisfactory one for all of the parties due to the practicality of the relationship. As a result of this, France has succeeded in promoting its image as a major economic, political, and military power in the area.

Saudi Arabia

In late 1973 and early 1974 France agreed to sell the Saudis 38 Mirage III jet fighters, 150 AMX-30 tanks, and a number of naval frigates and minesweepers. Previously France had sold some equipment to Saudi Arabia but nothing on the scale of these sales.[34] In December 1974 an arms deal totalling $825 million was signed that included the provision of 250 AMX-30 main battle tanks, 259 armored cars, Alouette III helicopters, and the "Crotale" surface-to-air missile system. That arms sale constituted the first large-scale French arms commitment to the Saudis. The Crotale missile system and its accompanying artillery pieces took 4 years to deliver during which time a successor had already been planned. The decision to sell the "Shahine," or Falcon's Eye, was made in December 1978, and its parts will be delivered after 1985.[35]

Since 1978 the Franco-Saudi arms relationship has blossomed. The principal deals involved the "Sawari" (named after the naval battle of Dat al-Sawari in 655 A.D., where the Arabs defeated the Byzantines) arms contracts, which were part of a general accord in naval cooperation concluded in May 1980.[36] The deal totaled $3.45 billion and included the sale of four guided missile frigates armed with ship-to-ship missiles, 24 Dauphin helicopters armed with air-to-surface missiles and carried on board the frigates, and two 10,800 ton military oil tankers.[37] In January 1984 France delivered the

Shahine air defense missile system. This entire arms agreement cost the Saudi government between $4.1 and $4.7 billion. Saudi Arabia has accounted for approximately $7 billion in arms revenues for France since the beginning of 1980, which makes it France's number one arms customer. The arms agreements with the Saudis reflect the French desire to establish itself as a military and political power in the Persian Gulf, and France's regard for the stability of of Saudi Arabia. Table 6.5 catalogues some of the major arms agreements that France and Saudi Arabia have signed.

TABLE 6.5: France: Selected Weapons Agreements—Saudi Arabia

Year	No. Ordered	Weapon	Year of Delivery	No. Delivered
1980	96	Otomat Surface-to-air miss.	—	—
1980	4	F-200 class frigate	1984–87	—
1980	2	Durance class oil tanker	—	
1980	24	SA-365 Dauphin helicop.	1982 1983	4 10
1980	200	AS-15TT air-to-surface missile	1982 1983	50 50
1980	104	Crotale surface-to-air missile	1980	
1983	—	Shahine landmobile air defense missile system	For Deliv. From 1985	

Total cost: $3.45 billion

Sources: SIPRI, *World Armaments and Disarmament, SIPRI Yearbook: 1984.* (London: Taylor & Francis, 1984), p. 255; and IISS, *The Military Balance: 1981–1982* (London: International Institute for Strategic Studies, 1981), p. 115.

The Saudi-French arms relationship has been economically profitable for France and militarily beneficial for the Saudis. Although Saudi Arabia ranked third in 1984 behind Britain and Nigeria as a source for French petroleum, it still provided a large portion of France's total energy requirements. Mitterrand has been intent on promoting Saudi Arabia as a staunch ally and has continually emphasized cooperation between the two countries. Whether it be siding with Iraq in the Gulf war or embracing the Fahd Plan as a means of resolving the Arab-Israeli conflict, the French regard their relationship with Saudi Arabia as economically and politically significant.

Iraq

The Soviet Union had been the principal military and political supporter of Iraq since the coup in 1958, which overthrew the monarchy and installed an anti-Western regime. However, Iraq began to pursue a closer military relationship with France in the mid 1970s to diversify its sources of military supplies, and to give it access to Western credits without compromising its anti-American posture.[38] In 1974 France signed a contract with Iraq that provided for the transfer of 40 Alouette III helicopters. This was followed in 1976 with the sale of ten Super Frelon helicopters and in 1977 with the sale of 36 F-1C Mirage fighters and 100 Puma and Gazelle helicopters.[39] France's interest in establishing a close military assistance relationship with Iraq was largely to guarantee the supply of Iraqi oil to France; by 1980, Iraq accounted for 21.2 percent of the oil imported by France.

The socialist orientation of Francois Mitterrand has not prevented France from selling arms to Iraq despite Sadam Hussein's dictatorial rule. In fact, relations between the two countries have been amicable during his presidency. The frequent visits to France of Deputy Premier Tariq 'Aziz to secure both arms and economic credits demonstrate the cordiality of relations. Table 6.6 catalogues some of the major arms agreements between France and Iraq.

After the Israelis bombed the Iraq's French-built nuclear reactor in June 1981, Mitterrand personally agreed two months later to rebuild it as long as the Iraqis promised not to use it for military purposes. France also delivered four Mirage jet fighters to Iraq after that Israeli attack. These were the first of sixty to be delivered. Iraq purchased over $680 million worth of weapons from France in 1982, including 30 Mirage F-1 fighters. Iraq had already bought the

TABLE 6.6: France: Select Weapons Agreements—Iraq

Year	No. Ordered	Weapon	Year of Delivery	No. Delivered	Cost
1981	150	AMX-30	1982	15	—
		Roland missile	1983	15	—
1982	3	Super Frelon helicop.	—	—	—
1982	85	155 GCT 155 mm self-prop. gun	—	—	$680 mil.
1982	29	Mirage F-1C fighter/ interceptor	1983	15	
			1984	14	
1983	5	Super Etendard fighter	1983	5	
	20	AM-39 Exocet air-to-surface missile	1983	20	

Sources: SIPRI, *World Armaments and Disarmament, SIPRI Yearbook: 1984* (London: Taylor & Francis, 1984), p. 242; and IISS, *The Military Balance: 1981–1982* (London: International Institute for Strategic Studies, 1981), p. 115.

Roland anti-aircraft system worth $1.7 billion from France, and the addition of the Mirage fighters contributed significantly to its military capability.[40] These deals contributed to Iraq's becoming—in addition to Saudi Arabia—one of the two largest recipients of French arms by the early 1980s.

As a sign of France's growing support for Iraq in its war with Iran, France decided to lend Iraq 5 Super Etendard fighters, one of France's most sophisticated weapons, in June 1983.[41] Iraq had previously employed Super Frelon heavy helicopters and Mirage F-1 interceptors for most of its offensive operations. The Super Etendard fighter bomber gave the Iraqis a longer bombing range and improved aerial capabilities against the Iranian air force's F-4 Phatom jet. It was not until March 1984, however, that Iraq first used these planes in a bombing run near Kharg Island.

Iraq has since used these planes quite often, especially against tankers loading oil near Iran, but it is doubtful that they will alter the present balance of forces in the Gulf. The loan is evidence that France is willing to train and equip the Iraqis with the most sophisticated military equipment. Nevertheless, the impact of this weapon is primarily psychological. It symbolizes France's commitment both to Iraq and the Gulf, which is based on France's interest in securing the safe passage of oil and providing French business with a safe environment for investment.

Egypt, Qatar, Kuwait, the UAE.

Egypt and the smaller Gulf states have also bought significant amounts of arms from France. Egypt, Qatar, Kuwait, and the UAE concluded contracts for the purchase of Mirage jet fighters in the 1970s and 1980s.[42] Egypt, in particular, has had close military relations with France. Deliveries have included Gazelle helicopters, AMX-30 main battle tanks, and Exocet missiles. The French agreement with Kuwait in 1984 for the sale of 13 Mirage jet fighters also provided training for Kuwaiti pilots. Other accords between France and the Gulf States have included the sale of six Super Puma helicopters with Exocet missiles to Kuwait and 36 Mirage 2000 jet fighters to the UAE in August 1983.

Foreign Aid, Bilateral Trade Accords and the State Visit

While arms sales provide the most dramatic evidence of French penetration into the Middle East, foreign aid, the conclusion of non-military trade accords, and Mitterrand's use of the presidential visit are also indispensable instruments of French policy.

Since 1980 France's official development aid has reached around four billion dollars annually, or 0.7 percent of the nation's gross national product. Most of this is in the form of bilateral development assistance, grants, and technical assistance to the recipient country. The Maghreb states and the Middle East have accounted consistently for approximately thirteen percent, or around $500 million, of France's official development assistance.[43] Some of this aid is channelled through international organizations such as the UN and the EEC. Egypt was the largest recipient of French foreign aid in 1983 in the Middle East and North Africa, receiving almost $136 million. In Egypt, however, France has been hurt by the weakness of the Franc compared with the strength of the dollar, which makes U.S. assistance much more desirable. Additionally,

France has given no official development aid to most of the Gulf states since the mid 1970s, thereby excluding this channel as a key instrument of French policy in the region. With that in mind, the ability of French companies to compete with other foreign companies in the Middle East offers a more effective instrument of penetration.

The involvement between the state and private industry in France has created a convergence of interests in the Middle East. Private industry's pursuit of profit and the government's desire for a larger role in Middle East affairs facilitates close cooperation between the two, and thus provides France with a greater opportunity to demonstrate its economic and technological power. French companies contracted for nearly $944.3 million with the Arab states of the Middle East from April 1984 to March 1985. In Egypt, French companies have been awarded contracts to build the Cairo subway, a new airport, and the country's first nuclear power plant. Other large contracts have included the construction of oil refinery equipment in Iraq and the building of military complexes in Saudi Arabia.

Mitterrand has also used the presidential visit to highlight his policies in the Middle East. In two countries, Israel and Syria, Mitterrand's visits were unique penetrations into the region. In November 1984 Mitterrand became the first French head of state to visit Damascus since Syrian independence. His visit highlighted France's desire to play a more active role in the area and also demonstrated France's recognition of the importance of Syria to any peace settlement between the Arabs and the Israelis.

The president's trip to Israel reflected his desire to improve relations with the Israelis. Likewise, Shimon Peres' December 1984 visit to Paris, the first by an Israeli prime minister in 20 years, reopened old channels of communication between the two countries. During the visit the French revealed that negotiations were under way for the sale of two nuclear reactors to Israel. Mitterrand has also visited several Maghreb states and was the first president of the Fifth Republic to receive an Algerian head of state (in November 1983). He has viewed continuing high level of contact with the Gulf states as indispensable to achieving France's Middle East objectives.

ACHIEVEMENTS, EVALUATIONS, PROSPECTS

Since its initial venture into the Middle East, France's primary goal has remained the promotion of French military, economic, and political power. In Algeria in the 1840s an aggressive colonial domination accomplished this objective. In the 1980s the sale of Mirage F-lC jet fighters and the French contingent of UNIFIL carry on that tradition. French activity in the area has undergone substantial change. Most recently, Mitterrand's own foreign policy has witnessed changes in some of the goals and, ultimately, the policy instruments used to attain French objectives. While Mitterrand has employed policy means different from his Fifth Republic predecessors to attain French objectives, he has generally been faithful to the Gaullist doctrine of autonomy in French foreign policy.

In regard to the Arab-Israeli conflict, France wanted to become more involved in the peace process. Mitterrand believed adopting less of a European approach and improving relations with Israel would accomplish this. His efforts, however, have not been successful. Relations between France and Begin's Israel were hampered by a number of Israeli actions: the bombing of Iraq's French-built nuclear reactor in June 1981; the invasion of Lebanon in June 1982; and the accelerated pace of the construction of West Bank settlements. The October 1985 Israeli bombing of a PLO base in Tunisia has further damaged bilateral ties. Mitterrand's attempt at a significant departure from the Israeli policy of his predecessors has not provided France with a more stable negotiating posture. Mitterrand's dealings with Israel have exhibited the same frustrations that characterized the policies of de Gaulle, Pompidou, and Giscard—Israeli positions conflict with French objectives and policy instruments. Any rapprochement now will ultimately depend on Israel's pursuing what France regards as more moderate policies toward its Arab neighbors.

As for the reassertion of French power in this diplomatic arena, the results are mixed. By undertaking a more active military, political, and economic role in the region, the Mitterrand presidency has been able to exploit opportunities and policy positions not available to the United States or the Soviets. By virtue of its mid-level size, France can solve such peripheral problems as PLO and Israeli prisoner exchanges, as well as Yasser Arafat's retreats from Lebanon. France nonetheless remains unable to solve the larger and more essential question of the Arab-Israeli conflict, primarily because many of the local actors and principal parties to the conflict, Israel, the United States, and Jordan, do not view France as an absolutely necessary element to permanent stability in the region. Adopting the Franco-Egyptian Peace initiative as preliminary to an international conference with Soviet participation would also run contrary to the U.S. and Israeli goal of preventing Soviet penetration into the Middle East. No matter what France has proposed, it has been unacceptable to one or the other superpower, or to the regional actors. Multilateral initiatives, like a UN peacekeeping force, may help France win favor with the more moderate Arab states and the PLO but are of little interest to Israel. It regards such methods as hostile and would rather deal with nations on a state to state basis. As long as France continues to assert itself in this conflict through the UN, it will have difficulty with Israel, and the overarching goal of reasserting the grandeur of France in this sector will remain elusive.

In the Persian Gulf, French policy has succeeded for the simple reason that it was presented with an easier task to accomplish. The French and Arabs in the Gulf have complementary interests—oil and trade. In the Arab-Israeli conflict, no such working relationship exists. The issues of occupied territories and a Palestinian state cannot be solved through the enticement of economic credits, a new missile system, or proclamations by the UN; whereas in the Gulf, French arms sales and bilateral trade agreements have been instrumental in establishing France as a power in the region. A measure of success for French policy in the region is that in 1984, for the first time since 1973—when OPEC quadrupled its oil prices—France moved into a trade surplus with the states in the Middle East and North Africa, wiping out a trend of trade deficits with the region. On balance, the French have achieved their goal of promoting France as an economic and military power in the Gulf. In the Persian Gulf, France is a major external power because of its convergence of interests with the regional states. Such a convergence of interests has eluded France with regard to the Arab-Israeli conflict, and, consequently, France has been unable to secure for itself one of the key roles to the conflict's resolution that it has traditionally desired.

So, a number of domestic and international factors will influence French foreign policy in the Middle East and North Africa in the future. Domestically, the election in 1986 of a rightwing majority in the National Assembly and the appointment of Jacques Chirac as the new Prime Minister presents Mitterrand with an opposition party at the cabinet and legislative levels. As long as the Gaullist dogma of Presidential preeminence in foreign policy is maintained, Chirac's opposition coalition should not interfere with Mitterrand's Middle East policy. While disagreement exists within the government regarding France's role within Europe and Mitterrand's renewed Atlanticist vigor, his goal of a rejuvenated France pursuing a role for itself in the Middle East peace process and of a strong French commercial presence in the Gulf is not faced with much opposition. The structure of the defense industry and its relation to the French economy make it in the interest of a great number of French laborers for arms sales to Iraq, Saudi Arabia, and Egypt to continue. Internationally, France's need for oil, its interest in protecting its former spheres of influence from both internal and external aggression, and its desire to promote French military, political, and economic power will continue to affect France's posture as an external power in the Middle East. It is this complex mix of pragmatic national considerations and idealism that guides French policy in the Middle East and North Africa.

NOTES

1. A comprehensive survey of French activity during the Crusades is found in Steven Runciman's three volume work, *A History of the Crusades* (Cambridge: Cambridge Univ. Press, 1954).

2. The French colonial experience in the Maghreb is treated extensively in Jamil M. Abun-Nasr's *A History of the Maghrib* (Cambridge: Cambridge Univ. Press, 1975).

3. Text: "Tripartite Agreement on the Partition of the Ottoman Empire: Britain, France, and Russia," in J. C. Hurwitz, *The Middle East and North Africa in World Politics, A Documentary Record*, Vol. 2: *British-French Supremacy, 1914–1945* (2nd ed.) (New Haven: Yale Univ. Press, 1979), pp. 62–64.

4. Stephen Hemsley Longrigg, *Syria and Lebanon Under French Mandate* (London: Oxford Univ. Press, 1958), p. 321.

5. An excellent survey of French relations with Israel during the Fourth and Fifth Republics is found in Sylvia K. Crosbie, *A Tacit Alliance: France and Israel from Suez to the Six-Day War* (Princeton: Princeton Univ. Press, 1974).

6. Miles Kahler treats this phenomenon at length in his book *Decolonization in Britain and France* (Princeton: Princeton Univ. Press, 1984).

7. Edward A. Kolodziej, *French International Policy Under de Gaulle and Pompidou: The Politics of Grandeur* (Ithica: Cornell Univ. Press, 1974), p. 42.

8. While de Gaulle was a strong proponent of an *Algerie francaise*, he reasoned toward the end of the Fourth Republic that the bloody civil war was an obstacle to French grandeur not only in the Third world but also in Europe. The benefits of retaining Algeria—asserting French military strength during an era of superpower dominance; French control over Algerian oil; and unwillingness to yield to the demands of a communist- and socialist-inspired movement—were not commensurate with the disadvantages—400,000 French soldiers bogged down in Algeria and French inability to devote the proper amount of time and material to its European responsibilities. See *Ibid.*, pp. 453–62, for further elaboration.

9. *Ibid.*, p. 464.

10. See Robert J. Lieber, "Energy policies of the Fifth Republic," in William G. Andrews and Stanley Hoffmann (ed.), *The Impact of the Fifth Republic on France* (Albany: State Univ. of New York Press, 1981), p. 181.

11. See "La politique de la France," *Revue Francaise de Science Politique* 19 No. 2 (1969), pp. 414–28.

12. See Stockholm International Peace Research Institute (SIPRI), *The Arms Trade with the Third World* (New York: Humanities Press, 1971), p. 251. For a detailed discussion of the difficulty involved in procuring reliable statistics on French arms sales, see Edward A. Kolodziej, "Measuring French Arms transfers: Problems with ACDA data," *J. Conflict Resol.* (June 1979), pp. 195–225.

13. See Daniel Collard, "La politique Mediterraneenne et Proche-Orient de G. Pompidou," *Politique Etrangere* 43 No. 3 (1978), pp. 283–306.

14. American Petroleum Institute, "World energy consumption and fuel shares: History, 1960, 1973, 1979," *Petroleum Data Book Petroleum Industry Statistics* III No. III (September 1983), Section 1, Table 1.

15. Centre Francais du Commerce Exterieur, "Importations Francaises de petrole brut," *Commerce Exterieure de la France, Resultats Annuels—Annee 1978.*

16. For a discussion of French foreign economic policy at the time of the 1973 embargo, see John Zysman, "The French State in the international economy," in Peter J. Katzenstein (ed.), *Between Power and Plenty* (Madison: Univ. Wisconsin Press, 1978), pp. 255–95.

17. For a fine discussion of the "Euro-Arab Dialogue," see David Allen, "Political Cooperation and the Euro-Arab Dialogue," in David Allen, Reinhardt Rummel, and Wolfgang Wessels (ed.), *European Political Cooperation: Towards a Foreign Policy for Western Europe* (London: Butterworth Scientific, 1982), pp. 69–82.

18. United Nations Educational, Cultural, and Scientific Organization (UNESCO), *Annual Statistics: 1984* (London: Index Printers, 1984), Table 3.16.

19. American Petroleum Institute, "Base scenario midprice projections, 1985, 1990, and 1995," *Petroleum Data Book: Petroleum Industry Statistics* IV, No. 3 (September 1984), Section 1, Table II.

20. For a discussion of France's military policy in Africa, see John Chipman's *French Military Policy and African Security* (London: International Institute for Strategic Studies [hereafter IISS], 1985), Adelphi Paper No. 201. For a discussion of French military policy in the Indian Ocean, see Pascal Chaigneau, "Ocean Indien: Les Velleites d'une zone de paix," *Defense Nationale* (April 1983), pp. 107–22.

21. "PS aide outlines Mitterrand foreign policy," *Espresso* (May 16, 1981), p. 8. Translated in the Foreign Broadcast Information Service (FBIS) *Daily Report: Western Europe* May 27, 1981, p. K2. (All FBIS translations will be from the *Daily Report: Western Europe.*)

22. These principles did not differ fundamentally from the ones Claude Cheysson had underlined in the year previous to the Israeli invasion. Those included: (a) The right of all states, Israel as well as a Palestinian state, to live within secure and recognized borders; (b) identical rights for all people including the right to a homeland and to self-determination; (c) negotiations among the forces in the region. See Dominique Moisi, "La France de Mitterrand et le conflit du Proche-Orient: Comment concilier emotion et politique?" *Politique Etrangere* 47, No. 2 (1982), pp. 395–402.

23. *Le Monde* (December 30, 1982), p. 3.

24. Claude Imperialia and Pierre Agate, "France," in David Allen and Alfred Pipers (eds.), *European Foreign Policy-Making and the Arab-Israeli Conflict* (The Hague: Martinus Nijhoff, 1984), p. 8.

25. *Le Monde* (July 30, 1982), p. 3.

26. Frank Spooner, "Sustaining a regional commitment on all fronts," *MEED Special Report: France and the Middle East* (April 1983), p. 2.

27. "Cheysson comments on foreign policy issues," *Agence France-Presse* (June 3, 1981); translated by FBIS (June 3, 1981), p. K1.

28. *Le Monde* (November 26, 1982), p. 8.

29. *Le Monde* (June 9, 1982), p. 4.

30. *Le Monde* (April 17, 1985), p. 1.

31. Frederick Seager, "New directions in French Middle East policy," *Middle East Review* (Spring/Summer 1982), p. 50.

32. See Andrew J. Pierre, *The Global Politics of Arms Sales* (Princeton: Princeton Univ. Press, 1982), p. 86.

33. *Le Figaro* (September 4–10, 1982), pp. 54–55.

34. In 1968 France agreed to sell Saudi Arabia light armored personnel carriers; see *Le Monde* (February 10, 1968), p. 5. In January 1969 Saudi Arabia asked France for the sale of 6 Alouette III helicopters; see *Le Monde* (January 23, 1969), p. 6, and Stockholm International Peace Research Institute, *World Armaments and Disarmament: SIPRI Yearbook 1972* (New York: Humanities Press, 1972), p. 128.

35. For a more detailed discussion, see "Livraison des 'Shahine' à l'Arabie Saoudite jusqu'en 1981", *Air et Cosmos* (June 28, 1980), p. 49.

36. Shahram Chubin, "La France et le Golfe: Opportunisme ou continuité?" *Politique Etrangère* 48 No. 4 (Winter 1983), p. 880.

37. See SIPRI, *World Armaments and Disarmament, SIPRI Yearbook: 1981* (London: Taylor & Francis, 1981), pp. 236–37; IISS, *The Military Balance: 1981–1982* (London: International Institute for Strategic Studies, 1982), p. 116; and "La France renforce la Marine d'Arabie Saoudite," *Air et Cosmos* (December 11, 1982), p. 39.

38. F. Roy Willis, *The French Paradox: Understanding Contemporary France* (Stanford: Hoover Institution Press, 1982), p. 75.

39. *Ibid.* This order was reduced in 1979 to 24 due to the desire on the part of the Iraqis to procure the Mirage 2000; see SIPRI, *World Armaments and Disarmament: SIPRI Yearbook 1980* (New York: Humanities Press, 1980), p. 146. This new order of Mirage F-1C fighters was delivered in the first few months of 1981; see *Le Monde* (February 3, 1981), p. 1.

40. For a more detailed discussion of the Roland anti-aircraft system, see "Irak, Nigeria, Argentine, et Venezuela, nouveaux, clients de Roland," *Air et Cosmos* (September 11, 1982), p. 42.

41. *Le Monde* (June 24, 1983), p. 1. These planes are on a three year lease to the Iraqis; see IISS, *The Military Balance: 1983–1984* (London: IISS, 1984), p. 129.

42. See SIPRI, *World Armaments and Disrarmament, SIPRI Yearbook: 1984* (London: Taylor & Francis, 1984), pp. 229–61; IISS, *The Military Balance: 1983–1984* (London: IISS, 1984), p. 130; and IISS, *The Military Balance: 1981–1982* (London: IISS, 1982), p. 115.

43. Organization of Economic Cooperation and Development: *Geographical Distribution of Financial Flows to Developing Countries: 1980–1983* (Paris: Organization of Economic Cooperation and Development, 1984).

IV
ASIA

Traditionally the focus of external interest in the Middle East has come from the European continent, while the Asian states have played only a marginal role. Recently, however, several Asian states—notably the People's Republic of China, Japan and Korea—have become noteworthy international actors and increasingly important factors in the Middle East strategic equation. China has been active for several decades and its role has elicited substantial interest while Japan and Korea are more recent participants, and have been less obvious in their activities. China has had limited trade with the area, but in other ways constitutes a potentially important participant in regional politics despite its limited efforts and achievements to date. Japan and Korea have loomed particularly large, primarily since the oil crisis of 1973, and the subsequent dramatic oil price increases that earned huge sums of petrodollars for the states of the region, creating markets for goods and services of unparalleled scope and importance for the Asian states seeking to expand their roles. They have become important powers in the region, notwithstanding restricting their activity to the economic sphere and avoiding a significant political role.

7

The People's Republic of China

Bernard Reich and Cheryl Cutler

In recent years the People's Republic of China (PRC) has emerged from relative isolation to a position of growing significance in the international community. It has become an important market for goods and services and a source of both raw materials and finished products. Its actions have influenced the policies of other powers in various regions and its views are considered of consequence beyond the Third World, in which it is a leading actor. It holds one of the permanent seats in the United Nations Security Council, where it can exercise a veto over Council action and utilize the forum to express concern over superpower activity in various parts of the world—including the Middle East, which has been a perennial Council issue. China's emergence has led to a mutual interest with the Middle East, two areas that historically, geographically, and traditionally have been distant.

Although there are records of ancient contacts and links as early as the eighth and ninth centuries, the Arab world was essentially on the periphery of the Chinese world, and the historical ties provided no firm basis for a twentieth century connection. Significant interactions date only from recent decades and even these generally are minor by regional standards.

Formal links between the PRC and the states of the Middle East were established slowly. Israel extended official recognition to the new PRC in January 1950, soon after the Revolution, but no diplomatic representation followed; full diplomatic relations were established between China and three Arab states (Egypt, Syria, and Yemen) in 1956. The PRC has since increased its regional and international diplomatic position considerably, especially compared with the Republic of China (Taiwan).[1]

China's view of Israel is ambivalent. Despite the fact that the two countries do not have diplomatic relations and that the accounts cannot be officially verified, there have been increasing reports of economic and commerical contacts between Israel and China in a number of spheres. China sees Israel as an anti-Soviet factor, but the instability associated with the Arab-Israeli conflict is identified as a vehicle for Soviet involvement in the region, providing opportunities to be exploited by Moscow. Since the end of the 1970s China has said that Israel has the right to exist as a state, but it continues to denounce Zionism and to call for the creation of a Palestinian homeland.

The PRC was the first state to recognize the PLO, which established an office, with ambassadorial status, in Beijing in 1965. PLO Chairman Arafat's visits to China have been at the level of a visiting head of state. China has been an important arms supplier of the PLO since the early 1970s. The PLO has been seen as one of China's few direct routes to Middle East involvement and China has remained supportive of the organization and of Arafat despite the 1982 war in Lebanon, which severely damaged the PLO's military and paramilitary base of operations and dissipated much of its power. And despite subsequent major internal PLO problems, China has continued to honor the PLO's requests for aid and to give rhetorical support to Yasser Arafat. Arafat visited the PRC again in May 1984 and was received with the ceremony accorded a visiting head of state.

Broader Chinese perspectives of the Middle East developed soon after the establishment of the PRC, and these came and continue to focus on foreign intervention as a root cause of the region's difficulties and on the fact that there is a potential for superpower confrontation in the Middle East. China's leaders have recognized the area as one of strategic significance to themselves as well as to the broader international community, but it has not been an arena of significant Chinese activity.

METHODS AND TECHNIQUES

The PRC has utilized a variety of methods in its efforts to increase its ties to, and expand its influence in, the Middle East.

A primary effort has been the championing of Third World causes, which has been an important Chinese lever for achieving influence among the members of that large bloc of states. The Chinese have provided strong rhetorical support for Third World positions as diverse as disarmament, nuclear free zones, technology transfer, the law of the sea, and the new international economic order and has utilized various forums, particularly the UN, to promulgate its views.

As a developing state, China has claimed a special connection with other Third World countries, including the Arab world. A major milestone was the Bandung Conference of African and Asian leaders in April 1955, at which Chou En-Lai emerged as a significant figure and where he met and established ties with Egyptian President Gamal Abdel Nasser, although Egypt's formal recognition of Beijing and an exchange of diplomatic missions did not take place until May 1956. The Egyptian decision should be seen not only in the context of the bilateral relationship but also in terms of Egypt's effort to convey a message to Washington, and particularly to Secretary of State John Foster Dulles, concerning the independent nature of Egyptian foreign policy. The relationship also helped to inaugurate Chinese ties to the Arab world.

China's leaders have sought to advance their ideas as to how Middle East problems should be solved. The main impetus of China's policymakers in the latter part of the 1970s and the early 1980s was their view that a possibility existed for a settlement of the Arab-Israeli conflict. They saw the Soviet Union as the primary supporter of the rejectionist Arab states who sought to ostracize Egypt and President Anwar Sadat and refused to participate in peace negotiations with Israel. Chinese leaders sought to promote Arab unity and to counter the Soviet Union's efforts to increase its influence.

In recent years China has sought to use an Islamic factor, claiming a "special relationship" with the Arabs because of a sizable Muslim population (estimated at 20 to 50 million) in China. Organizations such as the Chinese Islamic Association have been established to take advantage of this demographic factor. Muslim delegations have been dispatched as part of a broad diplomatic effort and Chinese Muslims have been allowed to make the pilgrimage (Hajj) to Mecca. Further, China has engaged in a propaganda campaign to undermine the Soviet position in the Arab-Islamic and, more generally, in the Third World, by characterizing the Soviet Union as the bane of the Third World and the enemy of Islam, as evidenced by its invasion of Afghanistan. Meanwhile, China has sought to portray itself as a defender of the faith.

An additional approach has been to establish party to party ties between the Communist party of China and both communist and noncommunist parties in the Middle East.

China has utilized trade with the Middle East as a diplomatic/political tool although it is extremely limited (especially when compared with that of the United States, Western European states, Japan, and the USSR) in both quantity and value. (See Tables 7.1 and 7.2.) Chinese trade consists mostly of light industrial products and some military equipment. Particularly problematic is the Chinese lack of sophisticated technology, especially in the area of arms supply, preferred by the states in the Middle East. Chinese trade nonetheless has performed an important political function. Trade relations with countries who had not yet recognized the PRC were exploited as quasi-diplomatic ties to bypass the question of recognition and, at the same time, to create a favorable atmosphere for it. China's Middle East trade also has been utilized to enlist Arab goodwill and support.

If China's trade with the Middle East has greater political than economic significance, this is even more the case with its aid policy. Chinese aid programs began in the mid 1950s but were generally small in value. Until 1963 Chinese aid offers to Arab countries amounted to the very modest sum of $18 million and was extended only to Egypt (in 1956) and Yemen (in 1958/9). In an unprecedented offer, in 1963/4 China agreed to give Arab countries $125 million in loans—undoubtedly to win Arab goodwill for the forthcoming Afro-Asian conference. As an integral component of its foreign aid in the Middle East, China has taken advantage of its enormous manpower surplus and sent large numbers of technical advisers (some 20,000 in 1983) to assist in implementing its programs.

Chinese arms exports to the Middle East have increased in recent years primarily as a function of its role as a supplier, directly and indirectly, to both sides in the Iran-Iraq War. This is partly a consequence of the demand of both sides for low cost, easily maintained weaponry, items not readily available from the superpowers in this instance.

ASSESSING THE CHINESE ROLE

China is not a major factor in the Middle East, either in economic or military terms, and its political influence is more nebulous and less effective than that of the other powers. At the same time, because of its growing significance in the global strategic configuration and its importance as an adversary to the Soviet Union, its role is likely to grow in consequence. It appeals to the Arab states because of its emphasis on sovereignty, independence, and cooperation against external intervention.

China's interest and effort has not resulted in substantial achievements and Chinese leaders have been aware of their inability to affect significantly developments in the area. Such influence as China does possess derives more from its prestige and general global standing than from any particular ability to make its power felt in the Middle East. Technically, its military equipment is regarded as some 15 years behind that of the superpowers, and other major (especially European) suppliers, and China is not regarded as a major source of arms supplies for the region's states, which possess mostly highly advanced military equipment. Similarly, China's resources and economic position preclude it from becoming a major trading partner with any of the primary regional states or a major aid donor to the more needy states.

China's dilemma in the Middle East arises not only from a relative lack of power to promote its views but also as a consequence of its approach to world politics. Realistically it seeks no regional position for itself, nor a sphere of influence, but supports independence for regional states as a means of thwarting the imperialist designs of other powers, particularly the Soviet Union. The Chinese have long considered the Middle East a key battlefield for the superpowers in their struggle for global supremacy. Thus, for example, since the 1970s the Chinese have feared that Soviet control of the strategic crossroads and oil resources of the Middle East would lead to Soviet predominance in Europe and subsequently to a possible assault on the PRC. The Soviet invasion of, and continued presence in, Afghanistan seems to confirm that view; China sees in this a potential direct threat to itself as a consequence of further encirclement by hostile (i.e., Soviet) forces. The Middle East is thus an arena of Sino-Soviet rivalry because of the extensive Soviet interests and involvement in the region.

The means employed by China to realize its interests have varied over time. They have supported national liberation movements and revolutionary organizations but they have also sought to gain the support of legitimate governments. In all instances their level of direct involvement has been limited. Their military, economic, and political capabilities have been minimal and they have been unable to apply significant pressure on the Arabs to push them to adopt Chinese perspectives. The lack of effective leverage has left them with little more than political rhetoric in their drive for a Middle Eastern role.

Different cultural backgrounds and political belief systems have been an impediment to Chinese success. There is little to connect the communist ideological perspectives of the Chinese and

TABLE 7.1: China, Exports to the Middle East (millions of U.S. dollars)

Country	1973	1974	1975	1976	1977	1978	1979	1980	1981	1982	1983	1984
Bahrain	17[a]	26[a]	33[a]	35[a]	57[a]	—	—	—	21	14	11	8
Egypt	24[a]	17[a]	34[a]	41[a]	47[a]	54[a]	69	215	173	256	205	167
Iran	19[a]	101[a]	48[a]	85[a]	122[b]	65	37	121	163	41	267	155
Iraq	33[a]	46[a]	62[a]	52[a]	79[a]	69	135	124	190	122	35	55
Israel	—	1[a]	1[a]	1[a]	2[a]	1[a]	1[a]	—	—	—	—	—
Jordan	—	12[a]	8[a]	13	20[a]	—	—	—	435	1,263	1,516	1,235
Kuwait	33[a]	42[a]	45[a]	68[a]	118[a]	93	136	157	122	111	99	85
Lebanon	14[a]	18[b]	21[b]	25[b]	28[b]	—	—	—	96	30	29	23
Libya	32[a]	52[a]	10[a]	62[a]	50[a]	22	37	50	126	168	47	59
Oman	3	4[a]	7[a]	6[a]	7[a]	—	—	—	15	11	10	11
Qatar	4	5[a]	6[a]	8[a]	13[a]	—	—	—	9	8	6	6
Saudi Arabia	—	3[a]	4[a]	16[a]	30[a]	37	68	136	220	183	149	133
Syria	22[a]	46[a]	41[a]	33[a]	46[a]	—	—	—	89	72	166	343
United Arab Emirates	19[a]	41[a]	52[a]	45[a]	75[a]	—	—	—	47	79	68	63
Yemen	4[a]	12[a]	30[a]	23[a]	33[a]	—	—	—	381	328	81	57
Yemen (P.D.R.)	3[b]	2[b]	1[b]	1[b]	—	—	—	—	34	40	53	36
Middle East (not specified)	—	—	—	—	—	—	—	—	2	—	—	—
Total	237	428	403	514	727	322	483	803	2,120	2,725	2,742	2,435

[a]Data derived from partner country for the entire year.

[b]Data extrapolated for the entire year.

Source: International Monetary Fund, *Direction of Trade Yearbook 1980* and *Direction of Trade Statistics Yearbook, 1985.*

276

TABLE 7.2: China, Imports from the Middle East (millions of U.S. dollars)

Country	1973	1974	1975	1976	1977	1978	1979	1980	1981	1982	1983	1984
Bahrain	—	8[a]	17[a]	20[a]	17[a]	—	—	—	—	—	23	18
Egypt	21[a]	38[a]	58[a]	57[a]	38[a]	63	57	97	126	61	68	50
Iran	—	—	—	—	—	54	31	59	2	89	—	—
Iraq	3[b]	3[b]	3[b]	3[b]	3[b]	57	49	128	4	8	11	8
Israel	—	—	—	—	—	—	—	—	—	—	—	—
Jordan	—	—	—	—	—	—	—	—	7	5	27	29
Kuwait	17[a]	22[a]	3[a]	11[a]	44[a]	33	39	42	10	23	50	26
Lebanon	2[a]	3[b]	5[b]	7[b]	8[b]	—	—	—	—	—	—	—
Libya	—	—	—	—	—	—	—	2	—	21	34	34
Oman	—	—	—	—	—	—	—	—	—	—	—	2
Qatar	—	—	—	8[a]	—	—	—	—	20	50	43	63
Saudi Arabia	—	—	—	—	—	—	—	16	12	10	19	28
Syria	32[a]	47[a]	25[a]	41[a]	61[a]	—	—	—	35	4	20	10
United Arab Emirates	—	—	—	—	—	—	—	—	—	—	—	13
Yemen	1[a]	3[a]	6[a]	3[a]	6[a]	—	—	—	3	2	—	—
Yemen (P.D.R.)	4[b]	6[b]	7[b]	8[b]	10[b]	—	—	—	4	—	—	—
Middle East (not specified)	—	—	—	—	—	—	—	—	—	—	—	—
Total	80	130	124	158	187	206	184	343	222	272	294	280

[a]Data derived from partner country for the entire year.

[b]Data extrapolated for the entire year.

Source: International Monetary Fund, *Direction of Trade Yearbook 1980* and *Direction of Trade Statistics Yearbook, 1985.*

most of the Arabs, except a very vague ideological opposition to imperialism. There is the fundamental Arab ideological, and to some extent practical, hostility to communism and Communists although there is something of an ideological appeal in China's strongly anti-colonial perspective and its anti-superpower, especially anti-Soviet Union, approach. Despite the logic of such an appeal, in practice neither China's anti-imperialist militancy nor domestic revolutionary example has developed much of a following in the Arab world.

China's attitudes were different not only from those of the Western powers but also, at a very early stage, from those of the Soviet Union. Whereas the Soviets were reluctant to use or advocate the use of force in the Middle East, the Chinese regarded the Middle East as an important strategic position—as the main battlefield against the West—and urged the Arabs to resist the West precisely to avoid another world war. The Chinese predated the Soviets in their belief in the potential long-term strength of Arab nationalism as a partner in the anti-imperialist front. Unlike the Soviets, they revealed little interest in the socio-political nature of the Middle Eastern regimes.

The influence and presence of the superpowers in the Middle East has further restricted China's ability to be an important regional force. Unlike some parts of Africa, where the Chinese were able to move into a political vacuum created by the reluctance of the great powers to become involved, the Chinese found no room in the Middle East for such penetration. Parts of the Middle East that had been under Western influence were, and to some extent still are, basically hostile to the PRC. In other sectors, where the Soviet Union had become predominant, the Chinese managed to establish diplomatic, economic, and cultural relations. However, as the Sino-Soviet conflict unfolded, it tended to damage the Chinese rather than the Soviet position in the region.

In addition to these objective circumstances there were also some very important subjective considerations affecting China's performance in the Middle East. Fundamentally, the Chinese have needed Arab support not so much to enhance China's position in the Middle East, but more negatively, to use against the two superpowers. Unlike these powers, China has never had much of an interest in territorial expansion or in building overseas bases. Consequently, the means for such ventures—such as a large navy, a strategic air force, or extensive aid programs—were not developed.

In principle, the Chinese have tried to avoid military or even political involvement in matters that have no direct bearing on

China's national security. China's foreign policy as well as its revolutionary strategy stresses self-reliance, meaning that Third World countries and national liberation movements should count primarily on their own resources in resisting foreign domination and intervention. China's support, whenever and wherever required by the Arabs, was generally restricted to rhetoric and symbolic aid. Peking also has tried to avoid any identification with the superpowers and refused to take part in international or UN initiatives involving the United States and the Soviet Union in the Middle East.

China's peculiar methods and aims in the Middle East and its primary concern with the superpowers were not always fully understood in the region and sometimes were deliberately distorted. For a long time the Chinese were portrayed by the Arabs as a disruptive, subversive, dangerous, and irresponsible element in the Middle East, seeking to promote a socialist revolution although there is not much evidence to substantiate these allegations. The Chinese usually defended Arab communism, condemned the Arab leaders, or supported local national liberation movements only in the context of opposition to foreign intervention and only at times when they perceived imminent "aggression" in the Middle East or elsewhere, occasions that required firm resistance. Considering the distance between China and the Middle East, China's limited economic, military, and transportation capabilities, and the lack of common background and traditional relations between Chinese and Arab communism, Chinese subversion in the Middle East has never been a serious threat.

NOTE

1. The People's Republic of China, diplomatic relations:

Country	Date of Establishment
Democratic Republic of Afghanistan	January 20, 1955
Arab Republic of Egypt	May 30, 1956
Syrian Arab Republic	August 1, 1956
Yemen Arab Republic	September 24, 1956
Republic of Iraq	August 20, 1958
Kingdom of Morocco	November 1, 1958
Democratic People's Republic of Algeria	December 20, 1958
Democratic Republic of the Sudan	February 4, 1959
Somali Democratic Republic	December 14, 1960
Republic of Tunisia	January 10, 1964

Country	Date of Establishment
Islamic Republic of Mauritania	July 19, 1965
People's Democratic Republic of Yemen	January 31, 1968
Socialist Ethiopia	November 24, 1970
State of Kuwait	March 22, 1971
Republic of Turkey	August 4, 1971
Islamic Republic of Iran	August 16, 1971
Republic of Lebanon	November 9, 1971
Republic of Cyprus	December 14, 1971
Hashemite Kingdom of Jordan	April 7, 1977
Sultanate of Oman	May 25, 1978
Socialist People's Libyan Arab Jamahiriya	August 9, 1978

(Note: A mission of the PLO was set up in Beijing on March 22, 1965.)

Source: *China Handbook* Editorial Committee, Compilers, *China Handbook Series: Politics* (Beijing: Foreign Languages Press, 1985), p. 175–90.

The Republic of China (Taiwan) maintains diplomatic relations with Saudi Arabia. These relations have included reciprocal visits of senior government officials, Taiwanese assistance in the medical field, and educational and cultural exchanges. The lack of formal diplomatic relations with other states of the region has not precluded contacts and reciprocal visits of officials and others and the establishment of commercial offices as well as trade.

8
Japan

Bernard Reich and Cheryl Cutler

Japan is a relative newcomer to the Middle East, and its adoption of political positions toward the region is an even more recent phenomenon, dating primarily from the October War of 1973 and the associated oil crisis. Prior to that, Japan maintained cordial diplomatic relations with both Israel and the Arab states but studiously avoided deeper involvement in the controversial political affairs of the Middle East for fear of jeopardizing its increasingly significant economic interests—its dependence on oil supplies and its search for new export markets. Ironically, those same economic concerns recently have motivated Japan to discard gradually its cautious approach and to address some of the Middle East's most controversial political issues. Although Japan has yet to assume a major, or even significant, political role in the region, it has made attempts to become more active in both the Arab-Israeli and the Persian Gulf sectors of the Middle East since 1973.

HISTORICAL TIES

Geographic distance and historical and cultural remoteness were among the factors contributing to Japan's lack of foundation for the development of relations with the Middle East. After the initiation of the "closed door" policy in 1639, Japan lost all contact with the Western world, through which it had first learned about the Middle East. Despite the restoration of foreign relations during the Meijing dynasty in the nineteenth century, Japan's contact with the Middle East remained almost nonexistent until the beginning of the twentieth century. Participation in the San Remo Conference at the end of World War I was the single example of Tokyo's political involvement. In the period between the World Wars, Japan's links to the region were economic, consisting mainly of the importation of Egyptian cotton and certain other raw materials and the establishment of a relatively small market for the export of some consumer goods.

Given the devastating effect that World War II had on Japan, little attention was given to the Middle East in the years immediately following the conflict. In 1952 Japanese policymakers undertook to achieve a number of related economic objectives and to avoid ideological and political entanglements that might have affected its ability to pursue commercial or financial interests. In addition to restoring Japan's international position and establishing its image as a peaceful democracy, Japan sought the rapid development of the country's war-ravaged economy and pursued the cultivation of foreign trade. Japanese plans for economic growth were impeded by its lack of natural resources, making it almost wholly dependent on foreign sources for raw materials, especially petroleum products. Compounding this was the fact that Japan had lost its major pre-war markets. The resultant quest for new export markets and the need to import vital energy resources directed Japan to the Middle East and dictated its policy in the region. Despite these limitations and the debilitating effects of World War II, the Japanese economy experienced tremendous growth in the first two decades after the war: the average annual growth of the Gross National Product reached nine percent in the 1950s, rising to eleven percent by the end of the 1960s. This rapid expansion, with its strong emphasis on industrial development, resulted in a sharp rise in the import of petroleum. Before World War II, Japan secured the majority of its oil from the United States, the USSR, and the West Indies, while very small quantities were supplied by Kuwait, Saudi Arabia, Iraq, and Iran. By the early 1970s the Arab oil-producing states had become the primary suppliers of Japan's growing fuel requirements as a result of the diminished availability from such sources as the USSR and Indonesia, the relatively low prices and high quality of Middle Eastern oil, and agreements with the American companies that had developed the oil fields of the Middle East.

Between 1952 and 1955, Japan either resumed or established diplomatic relations with Israel, Turkey, Egypt, Iran, Lebanon, Saudi Arabia, Jordan, and Iraq. Japan's fundamental approach was to disassociate itself from the internal political affairs and regional conflicts of the Middle East, thereby avoiding complications that might have negative economic ramifications. Since Japan purchased its oil from the major oil companies rather than from the producer-states in the period prior to the 1973 oil crisis, it was able to minimize direct contacts with the governments of the region. This arrangement tended to lessen the importance of close Japan-Arab relations and made it unnecessary for Japan to confront the internal political problems of the region or to be wholly responsive to Arab pressures to limit its relations with Israel. Tokyo's limited contact with the Arab states, and its wariness of being seen as pro-Arab, also was affected by Japan's awareness of the special relationship between the United States and Israel and the implications of this for its own relationship with the United States. Japan consequently sought cordial, though limited, relations with Israel as well. In December 1952 Israel opened a legation in Tokyo and in 1955 Japan established a diplomatic mission in Israel. In 1963 both countries raised the level of their legations to embassies. Economic relations did not develop apace. While there was trade between Japan and Israel, the Japanese government followed a policy of passivity with regard to the Arab boycott of Israel, declaring that compliance with Arab boycott demands was solely the decision of the firms concerned. Japan proved able to manage its relationship with Israel such that it avoided antagonizing the Arabs.

Japan's extensive dependence on petroleum imports was reflected in its trade balance with the oil-producing Arab states and Iran. The 1970 trade balance with Iran and Saudi Arabia showed a deficit of $817 million and $577 million, respectively. (See Tables 8.1 and 8.2.) Despite the importance of the Middle East oil-exporting states to Japan, and the fact that Tokyo was besieged with numerous Arab requests for development loans, few were offered and those that were, generally were characterized by high interest rates and numerous stipulations concerning the purchase of Japanese goods, thereby reducing the likelihood of their being accepted. As an alternative, Tokyo seemed to prefer to provide credit to local businessmen, many of whom were agents of Japanese firms, and to encourage private Japanese investment.

Japan was already heavily dependent on Arab oil prior to 1973 and a reliable supply seemed secure. However Japanese investment in and exports to the region were not as significant prior to 1973 as they were to become by the 1980s. Tokyo's receptivity to Arab requests for assistance and its amenability to the Arab position in the Arab-Israeli conflict increased dramatically after the Arab-Israeli war of October 1973.

THE OIL CRISIS AND JAPAN'S APPROACH TO THE MIDDLE EAST

Japan saw its interests and objectives in the Middle East, primarily

TABLE 8.1: Japan's Exports to the Middle East, 1960–1970 (millions of U.S. dollars)

Country	1960	1962	1964	1966	1968	1970
Total Trade	4,054.7	4,917.5	6,677.4	9,779.0	12,999.2	19,317.9
Total Middle East	156.6	165.8	245.2	361.6	463.6	557.1
Aden	15.6	18.3	29.0	—	—	—
Bahrain	4.5	5.6	6.7	7.4	12.0	14.7
Cyprus	0.4	1.2	2.3	4.3	4.9	11.3
Egypt	20.4	16.5	17.8	11.8	32.5	36.9
Iran	34.7	25.3	46.7	72.0	136.7	178.7
Iraq	18.8	14.5	17.4	28.2	41.3	15.9
Israel	2.5	6.1	13.9	20.6	13.6	20.0
Jordan	3.9	6.2	5.9	7.4	8.1	11.0
Kuwait	22.4	27.0	34.3	48.1	71.3	94.4
Lebanon	5.9	9.9	16.3	19.5	20.8	29.5
Trucial Muscat/Oman	4.7	4.0	7.5	1.4	2.3	2.4
Saudi Arabia	15.6	22.5	38.2	74.1	78.9	89.6
Syria	6.9	8.6	8.8	30.5	24.2	20.5
Trucial States	—	—	—	10.5	10.3	16.1
Yemen	—	—	0.1	25.7	4.8	12.4
Yemen (P.D.R.)	—	—	—	0.1	1.9	3.7

Source: International Monetary Fund, International Bank for Reconstruction and Development, *DIRECTION OF TRADE*, 1960–1964, 1966–1970.

the assurance of a steady supply of oil, severely threatened by the oil crisis associated with the October War of 1973. Since then Japan has made clear its concern about ensuring a secure and stable flow of oil. The 1973 war, the Iranian revolution, and the Iran-Iraq war have reinforced Japanese concern over the dependability of supply and price.

In response to the 1973 crisis, Japan launched a concerted effort to alleviate the problem. This involved a multifaceted approach—to reduce its dependence on oil, to encourage non-oil alternative energy sources, to ensure supplies by stockpiling, and to help ensure its sources of supply by expansion of its Middle East economic activity through closer cooperation with the Middle East oil-producing states.

Japan's initial actions focused on immediate responses to the crisis created by conflict and the decision of the Organization of Arab Petroleum Exporting Countries (OAPEC) to reduce oil production

TABLE 8.2: Japan's Imports from the Middle East, 1960–1970 (millions of U.S. dollars)

Country	1960	1962	1964	1966	1968	1970
Total Trade	4,491.7	5,634.9	7,947.4	9,522.5	12,984.5	18,881.1
Total Middle East	439.8	592.0	937.6	1,232.8	1,787.2	2,292.5
Aden	1.4	1.9	11.5	—	—	—
Bahrain	8.2	13.6	14.0	9.9	10.6	25.3
Cyprus	2.6	0.1	0.6	2.0	5.0	0.2
Egypt	18.6	10.6	21.8	20.6	63.8	117.5
Iran	25.0	88.7	202.3	362.5	632.5	995.3
Iraq	66.1	33.8	48.6	67.4	26.0	0.2
Israel	1.7	5.2	15.0	12.1	17.7	27.8
Jordan	—	0.2	0.6	0.2	0.5	0.1
Kuwait	205.3	262.5	282.0	290.4	307.7	308.3
Lebanon	0.6	0.5	0.2	2.1	1.4	1.7
Trucial Muscat/Oman	1.2	7.0	8.8	—	50.9	65.0
Saudi Arabia	105.6	165.2	329.7	462.5	612.6	666.6
Syria	2.7	0.8	1.6	6.4	11.5	18.7
Trucial States	—	—	—	7.8	18.5	16.8
Yemen	0.9	1.9	0.9	17.7	27.1	47.3
Yemen (P.D.R.)	—	—	—	1.2	1.4	1.8

Source: International Monetary Fund, International Bank for Reconstruction and Development, *DIRECTION OF TRADE*, 1960–1964, 1966–1970.

progressively by five percent each month from September 1973 production levels. Although friendly countries were assured they would continue to receive the same amounts as before, Japan was included among those states viewed as not supportive of the Arab position, and thus was to receive less oil in the months to follow.

Japan panicked, although, in retrospect, it is clear that the effect was more psychological than real. Japan was convinced that its economic growth would suffer significantly. On December 25, 1973, the initiators of the oil embargo reclassified Japan as a "friendly" country and, therefore, entitled to special privileges. The scheduled five percent cutback in oil production planned for January 1974 was cancelled and instead Japan became entitled to share in an increase in production of ten percent. In the announcement it was made clear that the oil Ministers had "noted the changes in the Japanese policy vis-à-vis the Arab cause which was conveyed through various ways and means. . . ."[1] They referred to the dramatic and rapid changes in Japan's policy between October and December 1973. At that time the Japanese government reevaluated its carefully cultivated policy of noninvolvement in the Arab-Israeli conflict and Japanese policy underwent a profound change—from relative lack of interest to calculated neutrality to a more vocal position in support of the Arab states in their conflict with Israel.

On October 26, 1973, Saudi Arabia's ambassador to Japan (acting as the representative of ten Arab states represented in Tokyo) received a *note verbale* from the Japanese Foreign Ministry's Administrative Vice-Minister that outlined Japan's attitude: "We sufficiently understand the various Arab nations' hope for restoration of their territory."[2] On November 6, this *note verbale* was presented in the form of an official statement issued by the chief cabinet secretary, making clear that the government supported the Arab interpretation of UNSC Resolution 242 of 1967 "that the Israeli Forces withdraw completely to the border line before the Six Day War." Japan declared its support for a just settlement of the Arab-Israeli conflict and made known that it "supports the UN Resolution, which recognizes the equality and the right of self-determination of the Palestinian people."[3] On November 22, 1973, the chief cabinet secretary issued another policy statement on the Arab-Israeli conflict illustrating Japan's new approach.

> The Government of Japan is of the view that the following principles should be adhered to in achieving a peace settlement. 1) The inadmissibility of acquisition and occupation of any territories by use of force; 2) The withdrawal of Israeli forces from all the territories occupied in the 1967 war; 3) The respect for the integrity and security of the territories of all countries in the area and the need of guarantees to that end; and 4) The recognition of and respect for the legitimate rights of the Palestinian people in accordance with the Charter of the United Nations in bringing about a just and lasting peace in the Middle East. The Government of Japan, deploring Israel's continued occupation of Arab territories, urges Israel to comply with these principles. The Government of Japan will continue to observe the situation in the Middle East with grave concern and, depending on future developments, may have to reconsider its policy towards Israel.[4]

The Japanese apparently believed that this would absolve them from the need for more substantive actions and that it would be a way to retain relations with Israel while simultaneously improving their links to the Arab states. The statement represented a significant departure from Japan's former policy of noninvolvement to one more readily acceptable to the Arab oil-producing states.

In extension of the new approach, Vice-Premier Takeo Miki visited the Arab oil-producing countries from December 10 to December 28, 1973. Miki met with Arab leaders in Saudi Arabia, Egypt, Abu Dhabi, Kuwait, Qatar, Syria, Iraq, and Iran. Yasuhiro Nakasone, then Minister of International Trade and Industry, visited Iraq and Iran, and other senior Japanese officials and former officials also travelled in the Arab world. The visits of high-ranking Japanese officials and the offers of economic and technical assistance they brought with them were designed to convey Japanese goodwill toward their host countries. For example, Vice-Premier Miki offered Egypt over a quarter of a billion dollars for the repair of the Suez Canal.[5] Some have referred to this frantic period in Japanese foreign policy as "oil begging" or "resource" diplomacy.

The Japanese statements and subsequent tours of the Arab world attained the desired results—the upgrading of Japan's status to a country deemed "friendly" to the Arab cause, just two months after the initial OAPEC decision to reduce oil allocations to non-friendly states.

The pro-Arab position of Japan's foreign policy in subsequent government statements made clear Japan's belief that the Palestine question is at the heart of the Middle East conflict and that peace and stability in the region depend on solving it. The pro-Palestinian posture of Japanese foreign policy was given added weight when Takeo Miki, a strong supporter of the Palestinian cause, became Prime Minister in late 1974. On February 5, 1975, Tokyo declared its willingness "to entertain a request from that organization (the PLO) for an office in Tokyo."[6] On December 19, 1976, a PLO office was opened in Tokyo and there were other Japanese efforts to develop closer ties between Japan and the Palestinians. In a January 1976 address to the UN Security Council, Ambassador Shizuo Saito declared, "The Palestinian question is the central issue of the Middle East problem. Without a solution of this question therefore, there can be no solution of the Middle East problem."[7] In 1977, then-Prime Minister Masayoshi Ohira said he "understood the rights of the Palestinian people included the right to establish an independent state of their own."[8] In 1980 Japan supported the European Community's Venice Declaration on peace in the Middle East, and in 1981 Japan endorsed a proposal by Saudi Arabian Prince Fahd that called, *inter alia*, for the creation of an independent Palestinian state with Jerusalem as its capital. Japanese friendship associations, sympathetic to the Arab cause and designed to promote better relations between the two peoples, were formed. The government of Japan endorsed the PLO as an important political body and in 1981 it unofficially supported, through a government-approved invitation extended by the Parliamentary League for Japan-Palestine Friendship, a visit by PLO Chairman Yasser Arafat.

The Japanese had planned to defuse the inevitable controversy surrounding Arafat's scheduled October 1981 visit with a visit the following month by Egyptian President Anwar Sadat. Following Sadat's assassination on October 6, 1981, however, the Japanese were hesitant about allowing Arafat to visit Tokyo since he had made no attempt to hide his jubilation at the murder of Sadat. Nevertheless, after Arafat agreed to Japanese demands regarding his conduct while in Japan, the visit proceeded as planned. During his meetings with the Prime Minister and the Foreign Minister, Arafat urged the West, especially the United States, to formally recognize the PLO, recognition being a necessary step, according to the PLO leader, toward the achievement of a comprehensive Middle East peace. While the outcome of the meetings had little effect on the course of events, Arafat's visit to Tokyo reflected Japan's belief that any peace initiative must have Palestinian participation.

ECONOMIC ASSISTANCE

Since 1973 Japan, in support of its effort to broaden its relations with the Arab oil-producing states, has actively pursued greater economic cooperation with them. In contrast to its previous reluctance to grant such credit, Japan entered into a number of foreign assistance arrangements, among which was a $1 billion loan to Iraq for the construction of an oil refinery and a $140 million loan to Egypt to be used for dredging the Suez Canal.[9] Japan's overall net disbursements (official loans and grants minus payments on outstanding loans) grew at an annual growth rate of 11.3 percent during the period from 1978 to 1983, from an average of $711 million during 1971 to 1973, to $3.76 billion by 1983.[10] Despite this growth and the fact that U.S. assistance during the same period grew at an annual rate of only 1.6 percent, total net disbursements from the United States in 1983 amounted to over $4 billion more than that provided by Japan. In their allocations to the Middle East, the discrepancy between U.S. and Japanese aid is even more significant. More than 65 percent of Japanese aid has consistently been provided to Asian recipients and since 1980 Japan's allocation of funds to the Middle East has shown a decrease in percentage and in real terms; from 10.4 percent or $204 million in 1980, to $201 million in 1983, just 8.3 percent of total Japanese aid allocations for that year.[11] In Egypt, for example, U.S. assistance exceeded $1 billion in 1984, compared with Japan's aid of $50.4 million in 1983, although the aid allocation for Egypt was Japan's largest single disbursement in the region.

Much of the money received in grants and loans by the states in the Middle East have been utilized for the purchase of military equipment and foreign arms sales have been a major tool for external powers seeking to gain influence in the region. Given Japan's refusal to supply military equipment as part of its general prohibition against arms sales, foreign aid has often been utilized as a surrogate in an attempt to strengthen relations between Tokyo and various regional states. But while Japanese allocations to the Middle East have increased in nominal terms, in a comparative sense those funds remain rather insignificant. In a region where security concerns predominate, the lack of arms sales, compounded by the relative paucity of foreign aid, reduce Japan's ability to increase its influence. It is unlikely that Tokyo will be able to utilize economic assistance as a key instrument of political policy in the Middle East.

Economic and Technical Cooperation

Since 1973 Japan has become involved in a number of joint economic projects in the Middle East. Japan's seeming lack of interest in other countries' domestic political affairs has made it attractive for developing cooperative ventures in the Islamic world. The period of greater economic cooperation between Japan and the Arab states began in March 1975, when Tokyo and Riyadh signed an economic and technical cooperation agreement that called for the dispatch of Japanese technicians to Saudi Arabia, the formation of a joint economic committee, and increased Japanese investment in Saudi Arabia.

The Japanese government works in close cooperation with such major Japanese companies as Mitsubishi, Marubeni, Nissho Iawai, and Mitsui. In addition to direct exports these companies, in conjunction with the government, have undertaken substantial joint venture projects in such countries as Saudi Arabia, Kuwait, and Iran, the latter being the recipient of the largest volume of Japanese overseas investment since World War II. Those funds were invested in a petrochemical project at Bandar Khomeini in southern Iran that was begun in 1973, at an estimated total cost of $1.3 billion, and that by 1979 had risen to about $3.5 billion.[12] It was the largest industrial project in Iran and was under construction by the Iran-Japan Petrochemical Company (IJPC), with Mitsui being the major member of the Japanese consortium that controlled a 50 percent interest in the project. The completion of Bandar Khomeini has been interrupted repeatedly by the Iranian Revolution and later by the Iran-Iraq war, and Mitsui has suffered heavy financial losses due to project delays.[13] Work on the project was suspended in February 1984 and eight months later the remaining Japanese personnel were evacuated from the site.[14] Despite this misfortune befalling the most ambitious Japanese project in Iran, Tokyo's continued commitment to Bandar Khomeini suggests an optimistic outlook for the area's economic potential.

Japanese businesses also have expanded their investments. In fiscal year 1979, direct overseas investment totalled $4.99 billion, of which 2.6 percent, or about $130 million, was invested in the Middle East.[15] At that time, direct Japanese investment in Saudi Arabia amounted to $19 million, a mere 0.4 percent of the total amount distributed. By 1983, direct Japanese overseas investment had grown to over $8.1 billion worldwide and while Japanese investment in the Middle East experienced a slight decrease in percentage terms, down to 2.1 percent, it grew in actual terms to $175 million.

JAPANESE EXPORTS

In the decade after 1973 the states of the Middle East rapidly expanded their imports of advanced nonmilitary equipment and technology, and Japan has been among the major suppliers to this market. In 1970 Japanese exports worldwide amounted to $19.3 billion, of which $557 million went to the Middle East (see Table 8.1). By 1980 Japanese exports to the region were valued at $13.2 billion. In the following year sales increased by more than $3 billion and although export revenue was lower in 1983, it was still more than $15.5 billion. As Table 8.3 indicates, Japanese exports to the Middle East increased dramatically in the period 1973–1981. In the past few years, however, sales to the region have fallen significantly. In 1984 Japanese exports to the area were valued at $12.95 billion and in the period between January and June 1985, sales amounted to $5.4 billion, a dramatic decrease from the levels of the early 1980s.[16] In 1984, the four largest customers in the Middle East for Japanese goods and services, Saudi Arabia, Iran, Kuwait, and the

TABLE 8.3: Japan's Exports to the Middle East, 1973–1983 (thousands of U.S. dollars)

Country	1973	1974	1975	1976	1977	1978	1979	1980	1981	1982	1983
Middle East	1,399,830	3,099,077	5,364,919	6,623,005	8,114,031	9,911,396	9,880,930	13,224,051	16,498,301	15,447,787	15,511,946
Egypt	13,618	73,959	212,370	328,917	387,379	400,336	397,036	644,306	795,428	661,093	851,036
Iran	484,170	1,013,556	1,854,296	1,706,560	1,926,416	2,691,082	925,392	1,529,530	1,485,520	934,904	2,819,888
Iraq	49,116	473,540	818,811	625,441	872,159	951,450	1,608,823	2,169,476	3,026,030	2,755,179	631,643
Israel	58,215	88,506	73,156	84,332	88,754	99,295	141,079	108,628	141,967	202,245	266,714
Kuwait	166,746	277,142	367,232	719,367	935,458	774,088	885,501	11,272,938	1,647,924	1,789,937	1,762,555
Lebanon	63,711	94,039	84,045	2,909	56,474	66,130	92,860	191,617	158,272	—	—
Libya	110,089	233,844	239,588	326,592	277,226	353,718	547,106	525,663	1,063,392	284,960	363,047
Oman	12,599	44,739	70,270	83,593	111,052	133,929	191,170	304,225	454,126	460,544	468,468
Saudi Arabia	388,815	676,954	1,350,780	1,888,895	2,342,255	3,254,346	3,828,763	4,855,717	5,876,433	6,621,316	6,686,574
Sudan	28,951	52,772	95,916	63,081	118,454	83,554	76,190	67,687	100,864	77,136	55,000
Syria	23,800	70,060	108,247	157,069	152,515	88,165	141,968	198,390	254,530	167,943	250,273
UAE	—	—	420,208	636,249	845,889	1,015,303	1,045,042	1,355,874	1,493,815	1,492,530	1,356,678

Source: Japan, Ministry of Foreign Affairs, Economic Affairs Bureau, *Statistical Survey of Japan's Economy,* 1975, 1977, 1978, 1980, 1982, 1984.

United Arab Emirates, purchased two-thirds of Japan's total exports to the region. From $388 million worth of Japanese exports purchased in 1973, Saudi Arabia in 1983 purchased over $6.6 billion. According to recent reports, however, Japan's market share in Saudi Arabia, as well as in Kuwait, Bahrain, Qatar, Oman, and the U.A.E., dropped dramatically. Part of the reason for this reduction in Japanese export earnings has been the high value of the Japanese yen. The importation of Japanese products has recently taken a downward turn in Iraq as well. In 1970, Iraq purchased $15.9 million worth of Japanese exports. By 1981, total Japanese sales to Baghdad had multiplied to over $3 billion, but they have plummeted since. While Iraq was Japan's sixth largest customer in the region, by 1984 the value of Japanese sales had dropped to about $800 million. Much of this may be attributed to the damage caused by the Iran-Iraq War, which has resulted in reductions in the level of Iraq's oil exports. Iran, on the other hand, increased its purchases of Japanese exports from $935 million in 1982 to over $2.8 billion in 1983. In 1984, however, Japanese sales to Teheran fell to $1.6 billion and in the first half of 1985 were valued at some $500 million.

Japan's major commodity exports to the Middle East are machinery and equipment. In 1970 Japan had a 9 percent market share of machinery and equipment exports to the Middle East[17] while the U.S. share was 23 percent. By 1982 the Japanese share had increased to 23 percent while that of the U.S. was about 20 percent. In addition, Japan exports metal and metal products, textile goods, and a variety of other products to the region. (See Table 8.4.) Japanese industrial plant exports to the Middle East have reflected the general decline in recent export earnings from the region—from more than $4.6 billion in 1979, industrial plant sales earned $1.7 billion in 1984. Military equipment is the one major commodity that Japan does not export to the Middle East.

OIL DEPENDENCE AND TERMS OF TRADE

Japan's desire to expand export sales to the Middle East is largely the result of the need to finance its substantial energy imports from the region; over 64 percent of Japan's crude oil and refined products came from that region in 1982. In 1983 Japan purchased over 4.1 million barrels of crude oil a day, of which 66 percent or 2.7 million barrels came from the Middle East. (See Table 8.5A and 8.5B) Saudi Arabia was the leading exporter of oil to Japan. (See Table 8.6.)

TABLE 8.4: Exports by Commodity to the Middle East, 1982 (thousands of U.S. dollars)

Commodity Country	Food Stuffs	Raw Materials and Fuels	Textile Goods	Non-Metallic Mineral Products	Other Light Industrial Products	Chemical Goods	Metal Goods	Machinery	Reexport Commodities Transactions Not Classified According To Kind
Total Exports	175,849	20,363	1,208,672	404,641	962,358	188,345	3,033,936	9,867,741	42,335
Bahrain	2,277	161	23,496	2,112	17,844	24,355	34,578	142,347	281
Iran	4,374	6,115	16,045	3,990	14,825	56,117	255,395	431,548	2,136
Iraq	1,663	5,244	126,917	54,269	171,927	32,994	460,943	1,890,193	11,031
Israel	790	2,963	4,794	2,165	18,643	9,733	11,418	143,456	8,284
Jordan	2,343	253	13,216	3,857	20,055	2,722	48,229	158,023	341
Kuwait	11,211	1,305	90,950	146,362	113,094	12,019	320,194	1,092,427	2,376
Lebanon	4,847	71	9,779	3,705	22,011	2,219	6,713	109,680	657
Oman	(Total Value of Exports 460,544; Specific Commodities not Cited								
Qatar	2,369	86	15,061	13,517	19,085	2,120	69,673	225,215	235
Saudi Arabia	125,634	1,990	479,518	145,764	378,906	39,195	1,346,589	4,093,334	10,386
Syria	3,904	583	32,487	1,345	27,363	1,078	7,651	93,430	101
Turkey	—	1	1,955	208	4,561	4,788	84,899	119,026	244
UAE	8,095	1,228	207,895	16,396	10,804	16,227	269,324	866,704	4,857
Yemen Arab Republic	(Total Value of Exports 190,928; Specific Commodities not Cited)								
PDRY	425	255	12,331	—	8,451	1,373	9,661	55,945	399

Source: Japan External Trade Organization, *White Paper on International Trade, Japan 1973,* Tables 57 through 71.

TABLE 8.5A: Origin of Japan's Crude Oil Imports, 1961–1983 (thousands of barrels per day [percent of total imports])

Country/Region	1961	1963	1965	1967	1969	1971	1973
Total Imports	820	1,220	1,745	2,405	3,065	4,615	5,760
U.S.A.	55	65	40	45	35	40	30
	(6.7)	(5.3)	(2.2)	(1.8)	(1.1)	(0.8)	(0.5)
Caribbean	5	25	30	45	85	15	10
	(0.6)	(2.0)	(1.7)	(1.8)	(2.7)	(0.3)	(0.1)
Western Europe	—	—	5	—	—	10	—
			(0.2)			(0.2)	
Middle East	610	920	1,435	2,035	2,650	3,810	4,385
	(74.3)	(75.4)	(82.2)	(84.6)	(86.4)	(82.5)	(76.1)
North Africa	—	—	—	—	5	20	20
					(0.1)	(0.4)	(0.3)
West Africa	—	—	—	—	—	40	110
						(0.8)	(1.9)
East Indies	90	—	—	—	—	—	—
	(10.9)						
Southeast Asia	—	130	140	180	240	645	1,115
		(10.6)	(8.0)	(7.4)	(7.8)	(13.9)	(19.3)
USSR, E. Europe, China	60	65	90	95	45	30	558
	(7)	(5)	(5)	(3.9)	(1.4)	(0.6)	(0.9)
Other Eastern Hemisphere	—	15	5	5	5	5	35
	(3)	(1.2)	(0.2)	(0.2)	(0.1)	(0.1)	(0.6)

Source: Gilbert Jenkins, *Oil Economist's Handbook 1985* (London: Elsevier Applied Science Publ., 1985)

Japan's dependence on Middle East oil has resulted in a continuing negative trade balance with the region, despite the significant growth in Japanese exports to that area in the early 1980s. In 1973, Japan's balance of trade with the Middle East registered a negative $3.2 billion (see Table 8.7). Although Tokyo's overall positive trade balance has expanded considerably in the last decade, its unfavorable balance of trade with the Middle East has also grown. Since peak of the unfavorable balance in 1980 (−$28.9 billion), the terms of trade with the region have improved for Japan, but the negative balance of trade remained substantial, over $16 billion in 1983. In 1984 the trade deficit rose to $23 billion. In 1983 Japan had a favorable trade balance with seven out of the twelve countries listed in Table 8.7. It is only with the major oil-producing states such as Saudi Arabia, the UAE, and Iran, that the magnitude of Japanese

TABLE 8.5B: Origin of Japan's Crude Oil Imports, 1961-1983 (thousands of barrels per day [percent of total imports])

Country/Region	1975	1977	1979	1981	1983
Total Imports	4,945	5,510	5,605	4,460	4,145
U.S.A.	30	60	35	40	105
	(0.6)	(0.5)	(0.6)	(0.8)	(2.5)
Canada	—	—	—	—	5
					(0.1)
Latin America	20	10	10	155	180
	(0.4)	(0.1)	(0.1)	(3.4)	(4.3)
Western Europe	—	—	—	5	—
				(0.0)	
Middle East	3,675	4,095	4,155	3.020	2,750
	(74.3)	(74.3)	(74.1)	(67.7)	(66.3)
North Africa	70	25	15	70	40
	(1.4)	(0.4)	(0.2)	(1.5)	(0.9)
West Africa	70	—	—	20	5
	(1.4)			(0.4)	(0.1)
East/South Africa	—	—	—	5	—
				(0.1)	
South Asia	—	—	10	5	15
			(0.1)	(0.1)	(0.3)
Southeast Asia	885	1,155	1,215	950	780
	(17.8)	(20.9)	(21.6)	(21.3)	(18.8)
Australia	358	45	15	—	30
	(0.7)	(0.8)	(0.2)		(0.7)
USSR, E. Europe, China	(3)	150	150	190	235
	(3)	(3)	(2.6)	(4.2)	(5.6)

Source: Gilbert Jenkins, *Oil Economist's Handbook 1985* (London: Elsevier Applied Science Publ., 1985)

petroleum purchases overwhelms the positive trade balance which, despite the significant decline in recent export earnings, Tokyo maintains with the majority of Middle East states. (See Table 8.8.)

Japan's trade with Israel is a function of its dependence on Arab oil and its desire to increase its trade with the Arab world. Wary of taking any actions that might undermine the potential expansion of Japanese exports, Japan has complied with the Arab boycott of Israel through the lack of anti-boycott legislation and the compliance of Japanese firms with Arab demands to curtail economic relations, especially trade, with Israel. In 1973 the trade balance between Japan and Israel was $138 million (see Tables 8.3 and 8.6). By 1983 the trade balance had grown to almost $455 million;

TABLE 8.6: Japan's Imports from the Middle East, 1973–1983 (thousands of U.S. dollars)

Country	1973	1974	1975	1976	1977	1978	1979	1980	1981	1982	1983
Middle East	4,271,099	13,346,578	166,218,274	17,904,825	19,953,887	19,827,764	28,059,518	42,145,048	39,938,772	35,632,080	31,592,969
Egypt	48,070	168,655	12,383	67,881	78,684	82,829	94,666	141,769	207,688	166,569	257,224
Iran	1,921,643	4,766,182	4,977,849	4,445,077	4,242,932	42,433,623	4,271,331	4,100,950	1,920,062	22,566,883	4,231,432
Iraq	3,422	201,642	395,949	578,603	735,211	776,874	1,815,670	4,339,066	934,065	779,534	141,067
Israel	79,874	65,494	89,429	79,944	97,255	173,029	201,562	277,013	203,618	186,291	188,130
Kuwait	585,347	2,131,949	2,011,705	2,013,211	2,487,553	2,481,850	4,413,767	3,457,571	3,608,616	1,626,571	1,387,415
Lebanon	3,787	3,193	1,779	332	181	5,323	670	436	161	—	—
Libya	34,979	364,006	280,776	206,324	112,043	16,228	100,834	357,897	350,622	46,120	4,869
Oman	151,568	378,069	520,210	682,920	882,964	904,098	1,339,815	1,732,764	2,327,751	1,702,408	2,012,164
Saudi Arabia	1,386,371	5,238,315	6,135,160	7,823,962	8,505,480	8,459,652	12,133,884	19,538,142	21,482,081	20,527,593	15,529,981
Sudan	51,933	27,135	15,701	48,966	57,275	58,056	52,617	56,271	57,366	45,699	46,450
Syria	4,105	1,938	3,322	6,506	6,156	4,294	1,347	2,760	10,745	1,553	1,437
UAE	—	—	1,774,041	2,468,099	2,748,153	2,621,908	3,633,355	8,190,409	9,935,997	7,982,868	7,792,800

Source: Japan, Ministry of Foreign Affairs, Economic Affairs Bureau, *Statistical Survey of Japan's Economy,* 1975, 1977, 1978, 1980, 1982, 1984.

TABLE 8.7: Japan's Balance of Trade With the Middle East, 1973–1983 (thousands of U.S. dollars)

Country	1973	1974	1975	1976	1977	1978	1979	1980	1981	1982	1983
Total Middle East	(3,321,269)	(10,247,467)	(10,853,355)	(11,281,820)	(11,839,856)	(9,916,368)	(18,178,588)	(28,920,997)	(23,440,471)	(20,184,302)	(16,081,029)
Egypt	(34,452)	(94,696)	199,987	261,036	308,695	317,507	302,370	502,537	587,740	494,524	593,812
Iran	(1,437,473)	(3,752,626)	(3,123,553)	(2,741,517)	(2,316,516)	(1,552,541)	(3,345,939)	(2,571,420)	(434,542)	(16,311,979)	(1,411,544)
Iraq	45,694	271,898	422,862	46,838	136,948	174,576	(206,847)	(2,169,590)	2,091,965	1,975,645	490,576
Israel	(21,659)	230,112	(16,273)	4,388	(8,501)	(73,734)	(60,483)	(118,385)	(61,651)	15,954	78,584
Kuwait	(418,601)	(1,854,807)	(1,644,473)	1,293,844	(1,552,095)	(1,707,762)	(3,528,266)	(1,844,633)	(1,960,692)	163,366	375,140
Lebanon	59,924	(90,846)	82,266	2,577	56,293	60,807	92,190	191,181	158,111	—	—
Libya	75,110	(130,162)	(411,888)	120,268	165,183	337,490	446,272	167,766	712,770	238,840	358,178
Oman	(138,969)	(333,330)	(449,940)	(599,327)	(771,192)	(770,169)	(1,148,645)	(14,728,539)	(1,873,625)	11,241,864	(1,543,696)
Saudi Arabia	(997,556)	(4,561,361)	(4,784,350)	(7,635,067)	(6,163,225)	(55,205,306)	(8,305,121)	(14,682,425)	(15,605,648)	(13,906,277)	(8,846,407)
Sudan	(22,982)	25,637	80,215	14,115	61,179	25,498	23,573	11,416	43,498	31,437	8,620
Syria	19,695	68,122	104,925	150,563	146,359	83,871	140,621	195,630	243,785	166,390	248,836
UAE	—	—	(1,353,833)	(1,831,850)	(1,902,264)	(1,606,605)	(2,588,313)	(68,834,535)	(7,342,182)	(6,490,338)	(6,436,122)

Numbers in parentheses indicate a negative trade balance.

Source: Japan, Ministry of Foreign Affairs, Economic Affairs Bureau, *Statistical Survey of Japan's Economy,* 1975, 1977, 1978, 1980, 1982, 1984.

TABLE 8.8: Japan's Imports by Commodity from the Middle East, 1982 (thousands of U.S. dollars)

Commodity Country	Food Stuffs	Raw Materials	Mineral Fuels	Manufactured Goods	Re-imports Commodities Transactions Not Classified According To Kind
Total Exports	44,509	45,472	36,986,603	398,246	38,668
Bahrain	0	0	188	106,528	311
Iran	3,826	4,474	2,555,747	2,665	171
Iraq	1	0	765,434	31	14,067
Israel	9,977	2,344	—	173,842	129
Jordan	—	17,208	—	7	518
Kuwait	2,668	707	1,618,541	416	4,238
Lebanon	19	0	—	18	78
Oman	(Total Value of Imports 1,702,408; Specific Commodities Not Cited)				
Qatar	0	11	1,777,009	2,740	4,016
Saudi Arabia	2,047	763	20,513,566	115	11,102
Syria	—	1,377	—	77	99
Turkey	22,112	15,971	—	2,117	156
UAE	420	2,405	7,868,233	109,515	2,295
Yemen	(Total Value of Imports 1,533; Specific Commodities Not Cited)				
PDRY	1,360	0	16,505	—	578

Source: Japan External Trade Organization, *White Paper on International Trade Japan 1973*, Tables 57 through 71.

Japanese exports to the Jewish state were valued at $266.7 million while sales of Israeli products in Japan earned $188.1 million. Polished diamonds constitute the majority of Japan's imports, with chemicals, fertilizers, and minerals making up a significant portion. Japan's exports to Israel include machinery and transportation, optical, and electrical equipment.[18] Trade relations between Japan and Israel are kept in low profile, making it difficult to determine the extent of Arab influence on Japanese compliance with boycott demands. However, it seems clear that "Japanese uneasiness about the boycott has the effect of discouraging exploration of new markets for Japanese goods in Israel"[19] and this has been particularly true since 1973.

Japan has attempted to lessen its vulnerability to potential oil shocks by intensifying its efforts to reduce oil consumption and to develop alternative sources and suppliers of energy. The Sunshine Project, conceived in 1972 and operating with government funds, seeks to "integrate new, alternate energy technologies with fossil fuels, nuclear energy and other non-petroleum based forms of energy into a total energy system."[20] Work on the project began in 1974 and the focus subsequently was narrowed to three technologies: solar and geothermal energy and coal liquefaction. On October 1, 1980, a semi-governmental organization, the National Energy Development Authority (NEDA), was established to increase and coordinate public and private research.[21]

While oil remains Japan's primary energy source, Tokyo has reduced its consumption and significantly increased its use of both nuclear power and natural gas during the same period (see Table 8.9). Yet despite Japan's efforts to reduce its oil needs and diversify its energy sources, the country's emphasis on economic growth continues to make petroleum products from abroad vital. As noted by Yasuoki Takeuchi, president of the Petroleum Association of Japan, "Petroleum is indispensable for our nation's industry and livelihood, and we in the Japanese petroleum industry have a mission to ensure its stable and secure supply to the nation's economy."[22]

Japan's desire to diversify its oil supplies has led it to purchase crude from sources other than the Middle East, especially Indonesia, China, and Mexico. Yet, despite the fact that in the first quarter of 1984 almost 35 percent of the Japanese oil imports came from countries outside the Middle East, the region remains Japan's dominant supplier.

The degree of Japan's vulnerability because of its dependence on Middle Eastern oil has been reduced by the world oil glut and the consequent reduction in crude oil prices in the 1980s. And the Arab oil-producing states no longer retain as much leverage as they once did. Supply and price constraints, as well as Japan's efforts to diversify its energy sources and suppliers and reduce its vulnerability to future oil shocks, have altered the situation. Notwithstanding the decline in oil's percentage of Japan's total consumption from 66.1 percent in 1980 to 60.3 percent in 1983, Japan remains dependent on oil for its energy requirements—and oil imports from the Middle East make up the largest share. Perhaps more important than actual dependence is Japan's perception of its vulnerability. The 1973 crisis had a profound effect on the Japanese psyche and that fundamental insecurity persists in spite of an overall improvement in the world oil situation. Japan's economic interests in the Middle East are considered both lucrative (in the case of markets for their

TABLE 8.9: Japan's Energy Consumption, 1973–1983 (million of tons)

	1973	1974	1975	1976	1977	1978	1979	1980	1981	1982	1983
Oil											
Japan	269.1	259.9	244.0	253.5	260.4	262.7	265.1	237.7	223.9	207.8	205.8
Total NCW[a]	23,301.0	2,248.8	2,182.9	2,327.3	2,391.9	2,462.0	2,487.8	2,356.2	2,252.5	2,174.9	2,141.0
Percent Japan of NCW	(11.5)	(11.5)	(11.1)	(10.8)	(10.8)	(10.6)	(10.6)	(10.0)	(9.9)	(9.5)	(9.6)
Coal[b]											
Japan	53.7	53.3	54.4	52.5	52.5	46.5	50.4	57.6	63.6	62.0	63.0
Total NCW	799.2	801.4	784.7	829.5	842.3	839.3	909.1	951.2	977.6	983.2	999.0
Percent Japan of NCW	(6.7)	(7.1)	(6.9)	(6.3)	(6.2)	(5.5)	(5.5)	(6.0)	(6.5)	(6.3)	(6.3)
Natural Gas[b]											
Japan	5.3	7.0	7.7	9.3	10.9	15.8	20.3	23.4	24.2	24.7	25.2
Total NCW	818.3	823.6	789.4	819.4	821.4	845.3	892.5	893.1	887.2	857.3	838.7
Percent Japan of NCW	(0.6)	(0.8)	(0.9)	(1.1)	(1.3)	(1.8)	(2.2)	(2.6)	(2.7)	(2.8)	(3.0)
Hydroelectrictiy[b]											
Japan	17.3	18.7	19.1	20.4	17.4	16.8	19.2	20.9	20.3	19.5	19.5
Total NCW	283.1	296.2	305.3	305.9	315.8	339.7	343.6	346.4	351.3	368.5	382.0
Percent Japan of NCW	(6.1)	(6.3)	(6.2)	(6.6)	5.5	(4.9)	(5.5)	6.0	(6.7)	(5.2)	(5.1)
Nuclear Elec.[b]											
Japan	203.0	4.6	5.3	9.0	6.9	12.7	14.9	20.1	21.5	27.0	27.5
Total NCW	45.4	56.6	79.7	95.6	118.4	134.9	135.8	148.1	174.0	189.8	207.0
Percent Japan of NCW	(5.0)	(8.1)	(6.6)	(9.4)	(5.8)	(9.4)	(10.9)	(13.5)	(12.3)	(14.2)	(13.2)

[a]Non-Communist World.

[b]Million Tons of Oil Equivalent.

Source: Gilbert Jenkins, *Oil Economist Handbook 1985,* (London: Elsevier Applied Science Publ., 1985).

exports) and vital to the national interest (in terms of oil imports from the region).

JAPAN AND THE POLITICS OF THE MIDDLE EAST

> Japan has attached great importance to the Middle East as a vital strategic region and as a major supply source of energy.[23]

After the 1973 Arab-Israeli war Japan began to discard its cautious approach to Middle East politics and to adopt an independent approach rather than to follow the basic lines of U.S. policy in the region. In doing so, Tokyo shifted from a policy of relative neutrality to one with an obvious pro-Arab bias, as indicated in various policy statements and actions. Nevertheless Japan does not consider itself anti-Israeli. In defending such actions as the Arafat visit discussed earlier, the government attempts to explain its vision of how an end to the conflict may be achieved:

> From the viewpoint that comprehensive peace should be realized in the Middle East in a peaceful manner, Japan has exerted its efforts to bring about an atmosphere for peaceful solutions by *making close contact with the parties concerned in the conflict.* It was one of these efforts that Prime Minister Suzuki and Foreign Minister Sonada met Mr. Arafat, Chairman of the PLO, during the Chairman's visit to Japan in 1981.[24][Emphasis added]

Japan apparently believes that, in order to bring about a just solution to the Arab-Israeli conflict, it is necessary to deal with all the parties involved. Given this perspective, Japan's closer relations with the Arab states do not necessarily signify that Tokyo has become anti-Israeli and proponents of this view argue that, despite Arab pressure to sever those ties, Japan has retained both diplomatic and economic relations with the Jewish state. Japan has determined that a comprehensive Middle East peace is important to its interests and thus must be pursued more actively, although no substantive Japanese peace efforts have been attempted.

Major disruptions in the Persian Gulf, particularly the Iran-Iraq war, increasingly have posed a threat to Japanese interests and have focused Japan's attention in that sector and lessened it in the Arab-Israeli sector. However, unlike the Arab-Israeli conflict, Japan has carefully avoided alignment with either belligerent in the Gulf conflict. Japan's conduct demonstrates its overriding concern with economic self-interest and reluctance to abandon its policy of neutrality in the Iran-Iraq war. Japanese diplomats have made attempts to reduce the hostilities, but these efforts have not been successful and Japan has not been willing to assume a greater role than that of "communicator" between the two warring nations. Although few Western nations have maintained cordial relations with Iran since 1979, Japan has been able to retain relatively stable links with both Iran and Iraq. Tokyo has made a concerted effort to assure both sides of its neutrality in any potential peacemaking initiative. In late May and early June 1984, a Japanese diplomat shuttled between Baghdad and Teheran to assure each side of Japan's neutral role.

Japan's reluctance to assume a greater political role is due primarily to the fact that Japan receives most its oil from that area. Moreover, while Japan is wary of angering such major oil-exporters as Saudi Arabia, which has sought to have Japan end its purchases of Iranian oil, it also does not wish to antagonize Iran, where, in addition to its oil dependence it has substantial investment in the petrochemical project at Bandar Khomeini. It remains cautious about pursuing policies that have the potential to jeopardize its economic interests. However, with attacks on oil tankers in the Gulf, there has been growing pressure on Japan to relinquish its neutral approach and assume a more active diplomatic role. As other attempts at ending attacks on Gulf shipping, notably those of UN Secretary General Perez de Cuellar, have failed, the pressure on Japan to increase its diplomatic efforts has mounted. On September 26, 1984, Japanese Foreign Minister Shintaro Abe presented a plan to the UN General Assembly that proposed actions to halt the air attacks and limit the fighting. Tokyo's plan called for Iraq to end its use of poison gas, a commitment by both states to allow unhampered navigation in the Gulf, and Iranian permission to allow the dredging and reopening of Iraqi ports and harbors closed since the onset of the war by Iranian air attacks. Given the importance of the latter to Iraq and the significance of the former concession to Iran, Japanese diplomats were optimistic that their initiative could lead to an accord. Japanese efforts were to be attempted in round robin meetings held with Iraqi Deputy Prime Minister Tariq Aziz and Iranian Foreign Minister Ali Akbar Velayati in conjunction with Japanese officials and UN Secretary General Perez de Cuellar. Iran rejected the Japanese plan, however, and Japan maintained the role of communicator rather than mediator, a role that it continued to believe would promote cordial relations with both parties.

Japan's inability to achieve success in its efforts relating to the Iran-Iraq war leads to the questions of whether or not Japan can assume any meaningful political role in the Middle East and of whether it has the necessary qualifications to make a significant contribution to the political affairs of the region. Japan's lack of a real understanding of the varied and complicated perceptions, emotions, and historical subtleties that influence policy in the Middle East is probably the most significant impediment to its playing a responsible and substantial diplomatic role in the region. The Japanese had little contact with or knowledge of the Middle East prior to the mid-twentieth century and before that time little interest was expressed in establishing relations with the region. The contemporary Japanese interest is primarily crisis-motivated: the possibility of conflicts resulting in a cutoff of vital energy supplies or a reduction in export sales or both sustain Japanese interest in the region. As such, Japanese policies tend to change as Japan's perception of threats to its national interests fluctuate. Given the importance that the region is perceived to have for Japanese national interests, Tokyo has become more aware of the area's political problems. However, since relations have been overwhelmingly economic in nature, substantive knowledge or understanding of the Middle East remains scant, and, at least until the 1980s, seemingly little Japanese effort had been made to reduce that ignorance. While economic relations have been pursued for some time, Japan has been rather dilatory in its attempt to better understand the historical, religious, cultural, and political forces that influence the countries of the Middle East.

The results of a national survey conducted in February 1984 suggested: "broadly aware of the Middle East's importance to their country, many Japanese are concerned about conflicts in the region but seem confused and ill-informed about the issues. Majorities are unable to express an opinion on most issues."[25] The Iran-Iraq war was perceived to be the most worrisome problem in the region, with 81 percent of the people surveyed envisioning harm to Japan if the conflict prohibits or restricts oil shipments from the Persian Gulf.[26] However, while those surveyed perceive the importance of oil from the Persian Gulf to Japan, approximately 60 percent of the Japanese polled did not know which superpower was supporting which combatant in the war.[27] It was concluded that on Middle East issues thought to be of little relevance to Japan, Japanese public opinion is "characterized by widespread ignorance and uncertainty."[28] The dispute in Lebanon seems to fall in the latter category. "When asked which Middle Eastern countries presently have troops in Lebanon [in February 1984], most (92 percent) could not name a single country."[29] When asked who they were more sympathetic to in the Arab-

Israeli conflict, 56 percent of Japanese adults polled in 1984 did not express an opinion, and among those with an opinion, 24 percent stated they sympathized more with neither Israel nor the Arab states.[30] Only 27 percent of those surveyed considered the Israeli-Palestinian problem to be the most worrisome of the Middle Eastern issues. And in contrast with their government's statements on the subject, few Japanese viewed the Palestinian question as the essential problem in the Arab-Israeli dispute.

Japan's lack of knowledge of the Middle East is reciprocated by the peoples and regimes of the region. Japan is perceived in the Middle East as having limited importance to the security of the area and ranks considerably below the superpowers and the former colonial powers in that regard. The limited Japanese historical connection and minimal role in providing military and economic assistance have been important factors in conditioning this perspective. Japan is primarily an economic power and its role is seen as limited to that sector. Middle Eastern lack of knowledge of Japan is partly the result of a cultural gap—the language barrier and the lack of historical connections is often manifested in stereotyping and misperception, which in turn impedes the development of closer relations. The peoples of the Middle East admire the Japanese "economic miracle" and most view Japan as a powerful economic giant. Japan has technical skills that most Middle Eastern countries could use, and in that sense Japan is thought to be important to the region. For Middle Easterners, the perception of the Japanese as a pragmatic, business-oriented people reflects the essence of Tokyo's relations in the region.

In addition to the lack of understanding on both sides, Japanese efforts to establish relations beyond the purely pragmatic are hampered by a self-limiting element. In its attempt to distance itself from American actions or policies deemed unpopular in the Arab world, Japan has "stood back" while the United States has borne the brunt of Arab disapproval. However, while Tokyo may often consider Washington's positions as detrimental to its own interests, Japan nevertheless benefits from a strong U.S. presence and U.S. actions in the region that help to maintain a steady flow of oil. Despite those benefits, Japan has demonstrated a reluctance, especially since 1973, to align itself with U.S. policies in the Middle East. This hesitation is largely a function of diverging U.S.-Japan perceptions on their respective national interests in the region. Tokyo has developed a "tunnel vision" approach to the Middle East; oil supplies from the region are perceived as being vital to the national interest and its foreign policy approach is largely dominated by oil considerations. The Japanese accord the highest priority to the maintenance of a steady supply of oil from the Gulf. The results of a 1984 national survey indicate that approximately 7 in 10 Japanese believe it is "at least fairly likely that current problems will lead to a cutoff or severe reduction of oil shipments from the region."[31] It appears that the divergence in American and Japanese priorities has resulted in Japan's attempt to distance itself from U.S. policy in the region. "Oil, the world's most precious commodity since 1973, molded Japan's pro-Arab Middle East strategy and has served as an effective wedge to move the Japanese further away from the U.S. on Middle East issues."[32]

Unlike its policy in other regions of the world, Japan believes that it should not defer to the United States in the Middle East because it sees U.S. policy as too one-sided in favor of Israel to be successful. Given this perception of Washington's unconcealed bias, the Japanese do not foresee much Arab support for a U.S. peace initiative. Until 1973, Japanese policy in the region was largely a reflection of U.S. policy but, since the oil crisis, Tokyo has been concerned about its close connection to the United States and a possible "guilt-by-association." Some Japanese believed that it was their country's close connection with the United States that was the root cause of Japan's being a target country at the start of the oil crisis. Japanese officials appear to believe that their actions since 1973 have demonstrated to the Arab world Tokyo's individuality and distinctiveness from the U.S. approach to the region. While American support of Israel is seen as hindering U.S. initiatives, the Japanese believe that they can make a successful, albeit realistically less significant, contribution toward peace. Tokyo views its ability to offer economic and technical assistance to the Arab nations as well as its oft-stated and pragmatic policy of having no political interest in the region as being its two major advantages in the Middle East.

U.S. concern for regional security is not opposed by the Japanese but neither has Tokyo shown any desire "to share seriously the U.S. sense of urgency regarding the security of energy supplies and to coordinate actions for protecting Western interests in the Persian Gulf."[33] While Middle East stability can only be beneficial to Japan, Japan appears unwilling to share the burden of achieving that peace, the fear that certain policies will anger the Arab oil-producing nations being uppermost in Japanese minds. As a result of those concerns, since 1973 Tokyo has developed a strong Arab "tilt" in its policy regarding the Arab-Israeli conflict. While it has repeatedly pressed for the rights of the Palestinians, Japan has been far less supportive of Israel.

Tokyo's preeminent focus on economic self-interest came into significant conflict with the United States in 1979/80, during the hostage crisis in Iran. Concerned with securing its energy needs and safeguarding its investment at Bandar Khomeini, Tokyo "tried unilaterally to obtain all the oil it could before it had to cooperate with the U.S." in imposing economic sanctions against Iran.[34] Japan's desire to remain neutral in the Iranian crisis led then-U.S. Secretary of State Cyrus Vance to castigate Japanese lack of action as "insensitive." In April 1980, five months after the initial U.S. embargo, Japan joined with the European Economic Community in refusing to purchase Iranian oil. But the Japanese sanctions against Iran were less a result of Tokyo's anger at the hostage situation and more a function of Japanese business and political acumen;[35] the price demanded by Iran was considered too high. In addition, Tokyo was wary of further angering the United States. With the release of the hostages in January 1981, Japan promptly rescinded its sanctions against Iran. By February of that year Tokyo had signed oil-purchasing agreements with both Iran and Iraq.[36]

Despite the lessened Japanese vulnerability to potential oil shocks from the region, its perceived vulnerability, which determines Japan's policy, remains high. In terms of influence, Tokyo has also not progressed significantly since 1973. Despite its occasionally more vocal stance, Japan has taken very few actions. Tokyo's official pleadings with the United States on behalf of the Arabs and the PLO have not endeared Tokyo to Washington, let alone Israel. Japan is not eager to assume a more prominent role and it has been cautious not to overestimate the extent of the role it might play. As one Japanese diplomat observed, "the Saudis perceive us as condescending businessmen begging for oil and in that way act differently towards us than they do towards France and West Germany."

Caught between the United States, its most important ally, and the Arab states, from whom it receives most of its oil supplies, Japan is wary of adopting a stance that would harm its relationship with either. In responding to accusations that Arab oil threats have convinced Japan to become "pro-Arab and anti-Israel," Japanese diplomats quickly note that despite Arab pressure to do so, Tokyo has not broken its relations with the Jewish state. Japan-Israel relations in the period since 1973 may be characterized as normal but not active. They also note that by their support of UNSC Resolution 242, they are advocating Israel's right to live in peace with secure and recognized borders. In recent years there has been an effort to tread carefully the line between adopting positions that might seem to favor the Arabs or Israel. Following Israel's October 1985 attack on PLO headquarters in Tunis, Vice Foreign Minister Kensuke Yanagiya issued a statement that: "The government of Japan deeply regrets and strongly condemns the Israeli violation of Tunisian territory" but also noted that "Japan deplores the recent cycle of violence which has led to the murder of Israelis in Cyprus . . . and this bombing."[37] Japan continues to advocate Israeli negotiations for peace with the PLO.

Japanese officials have defended some actions, such as their maintaining a dialogue with the PLO and diplomatic relations with both Iran and Iraq, as being beneficial for the United States. The Japanese explanation is that by retaining relations with groups or states who may be hostile to the United States, Tokyo can better defend the U.S. position and can act as an information conduit. Tokyo argues that the effect of such acts as the 1981 invitation to Arafat makes the Arabs more respectful of Japanese efforts toward peace. The Japanese contend that while the United States may publicly criticize Japanese actions, it privately appreciates such moves. U.S. officials, they say, are kept informed of Tokyo's actions in or regarding the region and recognize that both Japan and the United States are working toward common goals—those of achieving a comprehensive peace and of reducing Soviet influence in the region.

In numerous official statements the government of Japan "hopes" and "urges" that a just and lasting peace will be achieved in the Middle East. While Japan is certainly not alone in engaging in such political rhetoric, the question remains whether the Japanese will, in fact, do more than just "hope" for peace. Do they really foresee themselves being more than just a bystander in any international peace effort in the Persian Gulf or Arab-Israeli sectors? Humanitarian concerns for a peaceful resolution to the Middle Eastern conflicts do exist in Japan's policy approach to the region. The Japanese make no attempt to deny, however, that economic considerations provide the major impetus for their seeking an end to regional hostilities. Prime Minister Yasuhiro Nakasone has a reputation for being more concerned than most of his predecessors with security and defense-related issues. In numerous public statements he has repeatedly expressed his desire to move Japan toward adopting a more active and responsible international role. As part of the Japanese government's aspiring international role, it has increasingly spoken out on issues pertinent to the Middle East. In an address at the United Nations on September 8, 1984, Japanese Foreign Minister Shintaro Abe spoke of his government's "responsibility to take action in view of the growing expectations among the

Middle Eastern countries that Japan take on a political role commensurate with its economic power." The Japanese argue that Japan has been asked by certain Middle Eastern states to assume a greater role in the area. Their response focuses on the September 1984 Iran-Iraq initiative but notes other, albeit secret, efforts.

Japan faces a dilemma. Despite its political statements, it does not want to become involved in the Middle East's web of political conflicts, which appear to have little chance of being resolved. It does not have the political leverage to influence significantly the major combatants in the region and this is realized by Japanese officials. Tokyo's record of economic success is impressive while its lack of comparable success with diplomatic ventures is equally noteworthy. Tokyo has little experience in dealing with the region's political disputes. Whether Japan intends to become a more significant actor in the region is questionable. Japanese officials reluctantly acknowledge the slowness that has characterized Japan's efforts to close that cultural and historical gap. Japan's view of the Middle East remains largely obscured by that lack of understanding as well as by the concern for oil. Addressing the Japanese Diet on January 24, 1975, then-Prime Minister Miki declared "Japan, heavily dependent on the Middle East oil, naturally has to make careful consideration in framing her Middle East policy."[38] If Japan is to assume a more responsible political role in the region, it will have to broaden its perspective to realize that economic interests, while undeniably important, cannot be the sole consideration shaping Japan's approach to the Middle East.

NOTES

1. Text in the New York *Times* (December 26, 1973), p. 49.

2. Text in *Mainichi* (October 26, 1973) as translated in American Embassy, Tokyo, Political Section, Translation Services Branch, *Daily Summary of Japanese Press* [hereafter *Daily Summary*] (October 30, 1973), p. 13.

3. Text in *Nihon Keizai Shimbun* (November 6, 1973) as translated in *Daily Summary* (November 7, 1973), p. 7.

4. Statement issued by Susumu Nikaido, Chief Cabinet Secretary, in Tokyo on November 22, 1973 (collection of Middle East-related documents compiled by the First Middle East Division of Ministry of Foreign Affairs [hereafter Middle East-related documents], Vol. 1, 1973–1975, p. 55; document supplied by the Embassy of Japan, Washington, D.C.).

5. Yuan-li Wu, *Japan's Search for Oil: A Case Study on Economic Nationalism and International Security* (Stanford, CA: Hoover Institute Press, 1977), p. 5.

6. Michael M. Yoshitsu, *Caught in the Middle East: Japan's Diplomacy in Transition*, (Lexington, MA: Lexington Books, 1984), p. 15.

7. Remarks by H. E. Ambassador Shizuo Saito at the Security Council on the Question of the Middle East on January 14, 1976 (Middle East-related documents, Vol. 2, 1975–1977, p. 40).

8. Henry Scott Stokes, "Japanese agree with PLO on backing Saudi Peace Plan," New York *Times* (October 14, 1981), p. 14.

9. Don Oberdorfer, "Japanese policy of aid to Arabs pays off in oil," Washington *Post* (February 3, 1974), p. 5.

10. William Brooks, "The politics of Japan's foreign aid to the Middle East," in Ronald A. Morse (ed.), *Japan and the Middle East in Alliance Politics* (Washington, D.C.: The Wilson Center, 1985), p. 81–91, esp. Table 1.

11. *Ibid.*, Table 4.

12. Simon Proctor, "Iran," *Middle East Economic Digest, Special Report* (December 1980), p. 47.

13. See Jitsuro Terashima, "The lessons of Mitsui from its experience in Iran," in Morse, *Japan*, p. 93–96.

14. "Mitsui and Company," *Middle East Economic Digest*, Special Report: Japan and the Middle East (December 1985), p. 19.

15. Kathryn Babayan, "Trends in Japanese trade relations with the Middle East," in Morse, *Japan*, pp. 97–109, Table 3.

16. *Middle East Economic Digest*, Special Report (December 1985), page 4.

17. U.S. Congress, Office of Technology Assessment. *Technology Transfer to the Middle East* (Washington, D.C.: September 1984), p. 5.

18. "Sun rises on Japan-Israel trade," *The Israel Economist*, Israel-Asia Trade Special Supplement (November 1983), p. s20.

19. *Ibid.*, p. s21.

20. Jacky Law, "Sunshine project," *Middle East Economic Digest* Special Report: Japan and the Middle East (December 1980), p. 17.

21. *Ibid.*

22. Quoted in *Middle East Economic Digest*, Special Report: Japan and the Middle East (December 1985), p. 24.

23. *Diplomatic Bluebook*, 1982 Edition, Review of Recent Developments in Japan's Foreign Relations (Tokyo: Foreign Press Center, 1982), p. 22.

24. *Ibid.*, p. 58.

25. United States Information Agency, Research Memorandum, "Japanese public opinion on Middle East issues" (Washington, D.C., February 29, 1984), p. 1.

26. *Ibid.*, p. 5.

27. *Ibid.*

28. *Ibid.*, p. 3.

29. *Ibid.*

30. *Ibid.*, p. 4.

31. Ibid., p. 3.

32. Ronald Morse, "Japan's search for an independent foreign policy: An American perspective," (n.p., n.d.), p. 7.

33. *Ibid.*, p. 8.

34. *Ibid.*, p. 9.

35. Yoshitsu, *Caught in the Middle East*, p. 50.

36. *Ibid.*

37. *Middle East Economic Digest* Special Report: Japan and the Middle East (December 1985), p. 4.

38. Address by Foreign Minister Miyazawa to the Diet, January 24, 1975. (Middle East-related documents, Vol. 2, 1975–1977, p. 63).

9
Korea

Bernard Reich and Cheryl Cutler

History records isolated instances of contact between Korea and the Arab world in ancient times and up to the present, but these were sparse and of little continuing value. The difficulty in forging closer links may be attributed to various factors including distance, cultural diversity, the lack of economic complementarity, and the relative isolation of the Koreans from the mainstream of international commerce and intercourse. Differing historical legacies, particularly colonial experiences, contributed to the mutual lack of knowledge or understanding of the religious, ethnic, and historical experiences that undergird contemporary developments in Korea and in the Middle East.

Although the liberation of Korea after World War II might have provided a new opportunity for interaction with the Middle East, the initial postwar years witnessed meager contacts as Korea focused on consolidation of its domestic political system and then on the regional environment. The Korean War was a major factor contributing to South Korea's[1] lack of international activity—it did not have the interests or the resources to play a major role in the Middle East. The states of the Middle East, with the exception of Israel, similarly had little incentive to focus on this relationship, concentrating instead on terminating colonial control, consolidating independence, and dealing with regional issues, particularly the Arab-Israeli conflict.

In the 1950s, Turkey was the sole Middle Eastern state with which Korea maintained full diplomatic relations, largely because of Turkey's role in the Korean War and its close ties with the United States. During this period Korea had no policy of consequence for the Middle East. By the early 1960s Korea's role increased as it began to normalize its diplomatic relations with the Western-oriented Arab monarchies of Jordan, Morocco, and Saudi Arabia, as well as with other states, and various embassies or consulates were established in Seoul. In 1962 Korea formally recognized Israel and in 1969 it permitted the establishment of an Israeli Embassy in Seoul.

By the end of the 1960s Korea began to reassess its position and to take a more active role in the Middle East as well as in other global areas. The increased interest in the Middle East seemed to be foreshadowed by an announcement by the Foreign Minister in August 1970 that Korea supported the implementation of UN Security Council Resolution 242. This did not represent a major substantive change in Korea's policy, but it was significant because the statement was made. Korea continued to maintain ties with Israel for both bilateral reasons and those connected to the Korean-U.S. relationship and no major change in Korea's policy took place until the oil crisis of 1973/74.

ECONOMIC INTEREST AND POLITICAL ACTION

By the early 1970s Korea had begun to emerge as a significant international economic actor, primarily as a consequence of its growing industrial power. At the same time, its dependence on Middle Eastern oil had grown and its vulnerability to changes in access, supply, and price of that oil had become apparent. Changes in the Middle East associated with the October War of 1973 and in Korea's economic situation combined to lead the Korean government to alter its approach to the region and to adopt a position more favorable to the Arab states in the Arab-Israeli conflict. Although Korea continued to be geographically and culturally distant from the Middle East, and involved diplomatically and politically only to a minor extent compared with other powers, in the years following the 1973 oil crisis it developed an interest in the Middle East as a consequence of its oil dependence, its quest for economic development, and changing regional and international economic circumstances. The generation and accumulation by the Arab oil producers of huge amounts of petrodollars, as well as the threat posed by potential Arab oil embargoes, enhanced the significance and influence of the Arab oil-producing states in the international community and made them attractive targets of opportunity for various states seeking to earn petrodollars through the provision of goods and services. Korea inaugurated a major and concerted effort to develop extensive economic contacts and relationships with many of the states of the region.

The oil crisis of 1973 and the concomitant price increases had a significant effect on Korea's economy. The cost of oil rose rapidly, petroleum imports doubled their share of the country's imports, the current account deficit worsened, and the negative trade balance widened. In 1973, 99.7 percent of Korea's crude oil imports came from the Middle East (see Table 9.1). Because it lacked any significant petroleum stockpile and was so dependent on Middle East oil imports, Korea was especially sensitive to accusations that it was "pro-Israel" as these might lead to a reduction in oil supplies.

On December 15, 1973, the Korean government outlined its position toward the Arab-Israeli conflict and the means by which peace should be achieved:

> International disputes should be settled through peaceful negotiations, not by force of arms, and territorial [?"occupation" sic] by force of arms should not be tolerated. Israel should withdraw from the territories it occupied during the 1967 war. The legitimate claim of Palestine [sic] should be respected. The independence and the right to territorial preservation and existence of all states should be recognized and guaranteed.[2]

In substance, Seoul's policy statement was similar to UNSC Resolution 242, but Korea had chosen the Arab interpretation of that statement in that, unlike the resolution, it specifically called for the recognition of the "legitimate claim" of the Palestinian people. Korea's perspective and motivation was clear. In a broadcast on Seoul Radio on December 17 "an informed source" commented:

> In the past, oil supplies to our country dropped considerably because our country was regarded as a neutral nation. On 15 December, however, our government issued a statement outlining its position on Middle East peace negotiations. In it, it declared a pro-Arab foreign policy shift, thus aligning itself as a pro-Arab state. As a result, oil imports are expected to increase notably in the future . . .[3]

The December 15 statement was but one of a number of Korean attempts to gain the goodwill of the Arab oil-producing states. Korean government contributions to the United Nations Relief and Works Agency to aid Palestinian refugees and the establishment of a Korea-Arab association were among the gestures made during the oil crisis. Composed of businessmen, scholars, and researchers, the

TABLE 9.1: Origin of Korea's Crude Oil Imports, 1973–1981 (thousands of metric tons [percent of total imports])

Country/Region	1973	1974	1975	1976	1977	1978	1979	1980	1981
Total Imports	14,070	15,510	15,970	18,300	20,740	22,990	25,040	24,840	24,500
Total Middle East	14,040	15,510	15,970	18,300	20,740	22,990	24,620	23,420	19,730
	(99.7)	(100)	(100)	(100)	(100)	(100)	(98.3)	(94.2)	(80.5)
Iran	540	1130	1760	1970	2140	1670	2020	860	
	(3.8)	(7.2)	(11.0)	(10.7)	(10.3)	(7.2)	(8.0)	(3.4)	
Iraq	1270	470			450		480		
	(9.0)	(3.0)			(2.1)		(1.9)		
Kuwait	4210	4120	8020	8070	6810	7680	8110	6980	5101
	(29.9)	(26.5)	(50.20)	(44.0)	(32.8)	(33.4)	(32.3)	(28.0)	(20.4)
Saudi Arabia	8020	9790	6190	8260	11,340	13,640	14,010	15,580	14,020
	(57.0)	(63.1)	(38.7)	(45.1)	(54.6)	(59.3)	(55.9)	(62.7)	(57.2)
UAE									700
									(2.8)
Total Africa									190
									(0.7)
Total Asia	30						20	110	530
	(0.2)						(0.07)	(0.4)	(2.1)
Total North America							420		
							(1.6)		
Total South America								190	2370
								(0.7)	(9.6)
Not Specified							−20	1120	1680
							(−0.07)	(4.5)	(6.8)

Sources: United Nations, *World Energy Supplies 1973–1978* (New York, 1979); *1979 Yearbook of World Energy Statistics* (New York, 1981); *Energy Statistics Yearbook 1981* (New York, 1984).

goal of the association was to "contribute to promoting friendly relations with Arab countries on the private level."[4] The Korean news agency noted that "the association was established in line with the government policy to win more oil from the Arab countries . . . (and that) although Korea remains neutral in the Arab-Israeli dispute, it suffers seriously from the Arab oil squeeze."[5]

In December 1973 a mission headed by presidential special assistant Choe Kyu-ha, and including several senior Korean officials, visited Saudi Arabia and Kuwait. During their two week visit, the mission met with King Faisal of Saudi Arabia and Amir Al-Sabah of Kuwait. Apparently, those contacts and Korea's other efforts to gain Arab goodwill were successful. Two months after the initiation of the Arab oil embargo, both Saudi Arabia and Kuwait, which together supplied more than 85 percent of Korea's imported crude oil, pledged to lift their restrictions on oil shipments to Seoul.

ECONOMIC RELATIONSHIPS

While Korea has little diplomatic and political interest and power in the Middle East, its economic importance in the region has grown significantly and its activities in the Middle East have become a major element in the Korean economy. The primary focus of Korea's efforts has been to provide goods and services to the Middle East as a means of earning the petrodollars it has expended to secure needed energy (i.e., oil) resources from the region.

Overseas Construction Industry

Korea's primary response to the situation created in the wake of the 1973 oil crisis was to expand the efforts and activities of its overseas construction industry. The decision to penetrate and exploit the Middle East market was to involve economic-commercial and political-diplomatic activity by the private firms directly involved, supported by the government of Korea. This was a logical outgrowth of the already-developed Korean construction industry and the demand in the Middle East for the rapid and efficient execution of substantial public works projects.

The Korean construction industry had developed as a consequence of the devastation caused by the Korean War. It flourished as part of the postwar reconstruction effort and the subsequent rapid expansion and industrialization of the Korean economy when it engaged in infrastructure construction projects. The overseas construction industry (construction activities for foreign clients by Korean domestic contractors, including construction in Korea for foreign clients and foreign joint ventures), which has grown more rapidly than Korean commodity exports, began in 1965 when three Korean construction companies entered the market in Southeast Asia. In 1966 the companies began work in Vietnam and activities were soon expanded to other areas in the Pacific and Asia and a few ventures elsewhere. This expansion primarily was a result of the improved technical and management skills developed by the companies and the strong support and subsidies provided by the Korean government.

Korea first entered the Middle East construction market in 1973, when the Samwhan Corporation secured a $24 million contract for a road construction project in Saudi Arabia, and it increased its activities after the loss of the South Vietnam construction market in 1975 and with the increased number of projects and resources becoming available in the Arab Middle East. Expansion to the UAE, Jordan, and Kuwait took place in 1974, to Bahrain and Iran in 1975, to Qatar and Egypt in 1976, to Iraq, Libya, and the Sudan in 1977, and to Oman and Yemen in 1978. By 1979 Korea had become one of the five major contractors in the Middle East, a significant factor in infrastructure projects and a prime contractor rather than a subcontractor. The states of the Middle East sought rapid and massive development of their infrastructure in housing, roads, power plants, desalting plants, ports, refineries, new cities, university complexes, and related sectors, and Korea was able to provide the necessary labor for these sectors.

The almost immediate success that the Korean construction industry experienced in the Middle East was the result of a number of factors, of which strong and active governmental support was particularly significant. The Korean government's motivation derived from a desire to reduce the deterioration in its balance of payments and the importance it accorded to developing stronger ties with the oil producers. It saw the privately-owned Korean construction companies as a useful complement to diplomatic efforts. To ensure the success of the industry, the government offered such incentives as "low cost loans, loan guarantees and 5-year tax exemptions on earnings from exports of construction materials and equipment," all of which enabled the Korean firms to compete more favorably against their Western counterparts.[6] Korean construction firms also benefited from the fact that they were able to underbid foreign competitors because of lower wage levels in Korea.

> In these situations of tough international bidding on construc-
> tion projects a big comparative advantage for Korea was the
> prevailing low wage rates, reportedly $420 per month for Korean
> worker(s) in the Middle East. The low labor cost enabled
> Koreans to underbid rivals by 10 percent or more. For instance,
> a Korean engineer in Saudi Arabia costs less than 50 percent of
> the cost of an American counterpart.[7]

For their part, Korean construction workers often were eager to
work in the Middle East because their salaries were much higher
than at home.

The Middle Eastern oil producers approved of the Korean
government's willingness to take responsibility for its firms and
they benefited from the lower construction costs. In addition, Korea
was perceived to be a politically stable state which, like the Arab
regimes it hoped to service, was ardently anti-communist. Equally
important, Seoul was geographically distant from the region and
had little interest in becoming involved in the domestic affairs of the
Arab states. The Arab perception of Koreans as hard
workers—"employees live in spartan desert camps, get only two
days off a month and send 80 percent of their wages home"—also
helps explain Korea's success.[8] Professor Ui-Sup Shim has also
argued that a number of "political" factors have aided Korea's efforts in the Arab world:

> Most of the Gulf States are anti-communist, the tie that bound
> the cooperation between Korea and the Gulf States. Further-
> more, Islam has less cultural differences with Oriental culture
> than does Western culture. Another factor which favors Korean
> companies is the 'Arab Boycott of Israel' which adversely affects
> Western corporations, especially USA corporations.[9]

Since its inception, the Korean overseas construction industry
has undergone substantial changes. From 1965 to 1974 the value of
Korean overseas construction contracts rose from $5.6 million to
$260.6 million.[10] In 1975 the amount more than tripled to $812
million. By 1980 overseas construction contracts amounted to more
than $8.2 billion and peaked the following year when they totalled
$13.6 billion.[11] Since 1981 the value of the contracts has dropped to
$13.3 billion in 1982 and $10.4 billion in 1983.[12] The Middle East
comprised only 5.7 percent of Korea's total overseas construction
activity between 1966 and 1973;[13] the major focus at that time was
Southeast Asia. By 1976, however, the Middle East accounted for
97.1 percent of Korea's overseas construction work and remained

at about 95 percent in 1980. In 1981 Korea ranked second in the world in the value of its overseas construction contracts, some 93 percent of which were in the Middle East.[14] In 1982, advances by Southeast Asia, Latin America, and Oceania reduced Korean construction activity in the region to 85 percent of their total overseas contracts.[15]

Seoul's aggressive pursuit of the Middle East construction market has been amply rewarded. Since the initial forays in the region, Korea has won more than $65 billion in construction contracts and holds the largest share of regional construction.[16] Saudi Arabia is Korea's largest single customer, accounting for over $40 billion of the total value of contracts won, and Korea's share of the Saudi market fluctuates between 30 and 50 percent. Libya is Korea's second largest client. In November 1983 Libya awarded the Dong Ah Construction Company a contract worth $3.3 billion, an amount almost equal to the total value of Libya's awards during the period 1973–1981.[17] The "Great Man-made River Project" called for the construction of a 1,900 kilometer waterway and was reportedly "the largest single civil engineering contract ever undertaken by a . . . construction firm in the world."[18] It was estimated that millions of Koreans would be employed, directly and indirectly, and that $672 million worth of Korean-made construction equipment would be sold during the course of the 83-month construction period.[19] In addition to the direct value of the contracts, Korea has benefited from various "spin off" returns. Significant side projects have often accompanied major construction projects and, in turn, generated additional income. Related Korean exports also benefit from such undertakings. Korea's export sales of associated construction materials were valued at $390 million in 1959, $500 million in 1980, $520 million in 1982, and $360 million in 1983.[20]

Receipts from Middle East construction contracts have had a major effect on Korea's trade balance. In 1975 Korea had a negative trade balance with the Middle East of nearly $900 million (See Table 9.2). By 1978 receipts from construction activity in the region comprised almost 66 percent of Korea's total goods and services to the Middle East, which in that year exceeded total crude imports from the area by over $1.3 billion. The effects of the 1979 oil price increase, largely responsible for Korea's negative trade balance with the region in 1980, had almost been alleviated by 1982. In addition, the receipts from overseas construction projects have had a positive contribution to its foreign exchange earnings. In 1976 Korea earned $344 million in foreign exchange from construction projects in the Middle East, which then grew to $1.7 billion in 1978, $1.8 billion in

TABLE 9.2:   Korea's Balance of Trade with the Middle East, 1975-1982 (millions of U.S. dollars)

Year	Total Crude Imports From Middle East	Total Goods and Services to Middle East[1]	Trade Balance
1975	1272	386	-866
1976	1606	1175	431
1977	1960	2516	556
1978	2193	3546	1353
1979	3131	3495	364
1980	5373	3736	-1637
1981	5841[2]	5010	-831
1982	4766[2]	4506	-260

[1]Includes both commodity exports to the Middle East and overseas construction receipts (more than 90% of which are from the Middle East)

[2]Does not include Iran and Iraq

Source: Korea Economic Institute, "Korea's Economy," (August 1983), p. 2.

1980, and $2.1 billion in 1981.[21] The influx of foreign exchange has made a significant contribution to "the improvement of Korea's balance of payments position and rapid economic growth attained by Korea."[22] In 1979 its share of Korea's gross national product (GNP) was 2.7 percent. In 1980 it was responsible for 3.2 percent, 3.3 percent in 1981, 4 percent in 1982, and in 1983, foreign exchange earnings accounted for 3 percent of the Korean GNP.[23]

The construction contracts have also benefited Korean workers. In quantitative terms, the Middle East contracts have provided jobs for workers sent to regional sites as well as for those laborers employed in manufacturing related exports at home. The qualitative benefits include the training skills acquired by Korean workers employed on the foreign sites. In 1982 Korea sent about 220,000 workers overseas. In the following year this figure had been reduced to about 180,000.[24]

While positive benefits have resulted from Korean construction activity in the Middle East, not all of the results have been desirable. The inflow of foreign exchange has caused Korea's money supply to expand, thus having an inflationary effect on domestic prices. A shortage of domestic labor in those sectors of production that are especially labor-intensive has contributed to a rise in the domestic wage level. From 1974 to 1982, wages in the domestic construction industry rose an average of 24 percent a year.[25]

In recent years Korea has found it increasingly difficult to collect payments from some of its Middle Eastern clients—by the end of 1984 Korean construction companies had yet to receive "$1.6 billion for work done in Saudi Arabia, $420 million in Libya and $200 million in Iraq."[26] The failure to pay has led to a loss of earnings and highlights Korea's vulnerability in its relations with the Arab oil-producing states. While Korea's dependence on Middle East oil dropped 21.8 percent between 1980 and 1983, Seoul continued to rely on the region for 74 percent of its oil imports in 1983, although that degree of dependence has continued to decrease since then. A report released by the Korean Ministry of Energy and Resources in May 1985 showed that imports of crude oil from the Middle East fell below 60 percent during the first four months of 1985 with Iran as the largest supplier, accounting for 18.5 percent of total crude oil imports, and Saudi Arabia as the second largest, providing 17 percent of Korea's oil imports.[27] Thus while Korea's dependence on the Middle East for its oil needs has been substantially reduced, the region remains Seoul's largest supplier of oil. Despite significant construction activities, Seoul's dependence on Middle East oil has left it in a weak position in relation to the oil producers. While Korea is largely dependent on oil imports from the Middle East, its Middle East clients have a number of alternatives to the Korean construction companies.

In recent years Korean overseas employment has decreased as has the value of overseas construction contracts. From more than 100 firms during the "boom" period of the late 1970s, the number of overseas Korean contractors had, by 1983, been reduced to just 59.[28] In part, these reductions have occurred because of Korea's heavy dependence on the Middle East, where changing economic circumstances have influenced these trends.

As a country dependent on foreign supplies for its energy requirements, Korea has benefited from the worldwide decline in oil prices in the 1980s, while at the same time it has continued attempting to decrease its consumption of petroleum (see Table 9.3). Between 1978 and 1982 Korea's consumption of petroleum fell 5.5 percent, from 63.5 percent of total energy consumed in 1978 to 58 percent in 1982. Consumption of coal rose by approximately 8 percent during the same period. Seoul has also attempted to diversify its suppliers of crude oil. After Iran and Saudi Arabia, Korea's third and fourth largest suppliers of oil imports are Indonesia and Ecuador. The diversification of both its sources and suppliers of energy has had a positive impact on Korea's economy. However, as a supplier to the region, Korea has suffered from the weakening

TABLE 9.3: Korea's Energy Consumption, 1977–1982 (in 1,000 metric tons equivalent to oil [percent])

	1977	1978	1979	1980	1981	1982
Total	34,371	38,252	43,463	44,115	46,052	45,974
	(100)	(100)	(100)	(100)	(100)	(100)
Coal	9,638	9,894	11,844	13,199	15,243	15,450
	(28.0)	(25.9)	(27.3)	(29.9)	(33.1)	(33.6)
Petroleum	21,250	24,287	27,358	27,034	26,916	26,662
	(61.8)	(63.5)	(62.9)	(61.3)	(58.4)	(58.0)
Hydro	348	452	582	496	677	501
	(1.0)	(1.2)	(1.3)	(1.1)	(1.5)	(1.1)
Nuclear	18	581	788	869	724	944
	(0.1)	(1.5)	(1.8)	(2.0)	(1.6)	(2.1)
Firewood/ Charcoal	3,117	3,038	2,892	2,517	2,492	2,417
	(9.1)	(7.9)	(6.7)	(5.7)	(5.4)	(5.3)

Note: Conversion rate = 10,000 kcal/kg.

Source: Yonhap News Agency, *Korea Annual 1983* (Seoul, July 1983); Ministry of Energy and Resources.

position of the Middle East oil producers. The "soft" oil market has forced the Arab oil-producing nations to cut back on their expenditures, which has included funds spent on public development projects. As oil revenues decrease, even Saudi Arabia has felt the effect of the world oil glut and has postponed or reduced the scale of planned construction projects. Included among the affected projects was a $110 million oil refining plant that was to have been built by five Korean construction firms. As a consequence of the Arab states' reduction in infrastructure development and Korea's desire to compensate for that reduction, new areas of activity have been explored including petrochemical plants, harbor facilities, power plants, salt-to-fresh water distillation plants, railway construction, large-scale tire plants, and gas inter-dependence schemes.[29] The emerging protectionist policies of some of the Arab states have affected the Koreans. Planning for a less "oil-dominated" world, the Saudis and other Arab oil producers have begun to establish construction industries of their own and are reserving much work for them. The Iran-Iraq war has also had a negative effect. As a result of Iranian military actions, Iraq has suffered a sharp drop in oil revenues. Deprived of its much needed oil revenues, Iraq has "cancelled nonstrategic projects and [fallen] behind in payments for ones in progress."[30] Each of these circumstances has contributed to the problems now confronting the Korean construction industry in the Middle East. At the same time internal factors have also contributed to Korea's difficulties.

Korea's competitive pricing—the ability of Korean companies to consistently underbid their rivals because of the low wages received by Korean construction workers—has diminished as Korean wages have increased steadily over the years. Climbing wages combined with growing competition from Indian and Pakistani companies (which have even lower labor costs) have reduced the competitive position of Korean firms. The lack of advanced construction and engineering skills have also begun to hurt Korea's hitherto strong position. Residential construction, road building, and civil engineering have long been the established strength of Korean contractors in the Middle East. The United States, West Germany, and Japan have, in contrast, dominated the region's commercial trade in technology transfers. Now, as many of the oil-producing nations, especially Saudi Arabia, have almost completed their infrastructure construction, many of the new industrial skills required cannot be provided by Korean companies.

Korea's reputation for dedicated and efficient work was a major asset to Korean contractors first entering the Middle East market. Changing economic circumstances and some slipshod workmanship and management have weakened that image. Some Korean companies have been pushed to the edge of bankruptcy, partly as the result of the new economic trends, but also, in part, of their own making. Korean executives concede that "in the rush to get established, some bid dangerously low, then couldn't finish the job and ran out of cash. They acknowledge that some of the workmanship was substandard."[31] Payment disputes between Korean contractors and their Middle East clients are occurring with greater frequency, a situation which does not bode well for the industry's future rebound.

Korea's concentration of its activities in terms of particular countries and specific projects in the Middle East has increased its vulnerability. Saudi Arabia has accounted for more than $40 billion of the total $65 billion that Korea has earned from its construction activities in the Middle East. Such a weighted interest in one country, or in single projects like the Libyan waterway, makes Seoul extremely sensitive to any disturbance in that country or to that project. Associating themselves with a specific political group or politician, a tendency of which the Koreans have been accused, also involves much risk since a political upheaval that finds that particular party or individual in disfavor will obviously not bode well for anyone with whom they have been associated. Such was the case in Iran, where the Korean contractors were supporters of the Shah's regime and when the Shah was deposed, Korea lost a substantial market and has had difficulties in reentering since.

Korea's significant construction activity has made a substantial contribution to the rapid economic growth experienced by Seoul since the mid 1970s. At the same time the type of trade conducted, mainly the temporary export of Korean workers, has significantly increased Korea's visibility and simultaneously increased the pressure on Seoul to adopt a more assertive political stance. The states of the Middle East do not consider Korea to be a significant political actor in the region and Seoul does not aspire to such a role. Yet its relatively substantial economic interests have brought Korea the unpopular burden of political responsibility; while the Arab petroleum-exporting states do not want Korea to attempt to influence their political decisions, they would like Seoul to be more publicly supportive of them.

THE POLITICS OF ECONOMICS

In its involvement in the Middle East, Korea has paid little attention to politics, focusing instead on the economic relationships and the benefits to be derived therefrom. Since the 1973 oil crisis Seoul has actively pursued closer relations with the Arab oil-producing states, although these relations have remained primarily of an economic nature. This emphasis, rather than political interaction, is reflected in Korea's positions on the major political issues of the region.

Korea's political role in the Middle East is affected by two overriding considerations. The first is the realization that it is a minor factor in the political calculus of the region. Second, to a great extent Korea is seen in much of the Arab world as closely linked with the United States and therefore, by extension, as an ally of Israel. Korea has been a minor and primarily late arrival as an economic actor in the Middle East. Its positions and policies have not been considered in the political and diplomatic activities in the region and it has taken no major political-diplomatic actions. Its relationship with the United States has been a major factor in the views held of it by the states of the region and this has led to assumptions about Korean policies in support of U.S. efforts. At the same time, Korea's early links to Israel established a pattern and perception that Korea has worked to alter since the 1973 oil crisis. The Arab world's perception of a Korea-United States-Israel link has been modified by Korean-Middle Eastern economic activity since 1973, but it has not eliminated this perspective. Korean-Israeli relations are maintained at a low profile, but they remain important for both states.

Korea's ability to affect the nature and course of the Arab-Israeli conflict is minimal. Korea therefore has been content (and allowed to remain content) with broad statements of policy rather than becoming involved in specific actions. Other than its public support of UNSC Resolution 242, Seoul has avoided issues pertinent to the Arab-Israeli conflict. It has been (as in its 1973 policy statement) supportive of the rights of the Palestinians and it has increased its donations to and support of Palestinian refugee relief efforts. The PLO maintains close ties with North Korea[32] and that fact, coupled with potential U.S. disapproval, especially in the form of a negative Congressional reaction, has made Seoul wary of increasing its relations with the PLO, which it has refused to recognize. Seoul's willingness to support the Palestinians publicly and financially has not extended to actual material support. Although asked to join the multinational peacekeeping force in Lebanon, Korea chose not to participate. Relations with Israel have been maintained albeit at a less visible level than in earlier years. Seoul maintains no embassy or consulate in Israel and since 1977, the Israeli Ambassador accredited to Korea has resided in Tokyo rather than Seoul, but this was a result of an Israeli decision, based primarily on economic grounds, and does not reflect the nature of the relationship.

While Iran remains a major oil supplier for Korea, diplomatic and other economic ties between Teheran and Seoul have weakened considerably since the Islamic Revolution. Under the Shah's regime Iran was a major customer of Korea. Following the Revolution, Seoul's previous close relationship with the deposed Shah has made it difficult for the Koreans to reenter the Iranian market and this has been compounded by their relationship with the United States. Korea's ties to Iran have not been significantly affected by the Iran-Iraq war. Despite the hostilities, the supply of Iranian oil to Korea has remained relatively unimpeded. Since the Revolution this supplier-client "oil relationship" has constituted the sole basis of interaction between the two nations.

Unlike its once cordial relations with Teheran, South Korea's relationship with Baghdad had been far less amiable prior to the Iran-Iraq war. The lack of ties between Baghdad and Seoul is linked to Iraq's support of the North Korean regime. Since the start of the Iran-Iraq war, Korea has "tilted" more toward the side of Iraq, largely due to the prodding of such Arab states as Jordan and Saudi

Arabia. Iraq has become Korea's third largest customer in the region after Saudi Arabia and Libya. As is evident from the Iranian share of Korean oil imports, Korea's closer relationship with Baghdad has not, so far, impeded its "oil relationship" with Teheran.

A CONCLUDING NOTE

The basis for Korean interest in the Middle East is essentially economic. The supply of oil from the region, the original impetus for Korean interaction, has expanded in the last decade to include a substantial export of Korean construction services. After a tremendous "boom" in the late 1970s, Korean contracts in the Middle East peaked in 1981 and have exhibited a steady decline ever since. In an effort to improve the industry's standing in the Arab markets, the Korean government has set forth a number of measures designed to achieve that objective. The government has stepped up its financial support of the industry by providing, among other things, $1 billion in Korea Export-Import Bank funds annually to those companies involved in overseas construction projects. In addition, the government has arranged takeovers of less efficient construction companies by their healthier, more productive counterparts. In an effort to improve the image of the industry abroad, the government has initiated more stringent requirements that Korean contractors must first meet before they can obtain overseas work. The government has also provided incentives for those firms to develop more advanced technological skills. Under this plan, the government will provide the Korean companies with tax benefits and will require them to use a portion of their overseas contract earnings for technology development. Rising wages of Korean construction workers have resulted in growing competition from certain foreign rivals. To regain their competitive pricing position in terms of labor costs, Korean construction firms will be permitted by the government to employ foreign laborers.

Not all of the Korean construction industry's present difficulties have been of their own making. Declining revenue from oil sales has tightened the once abundant Arab markets, forcing Arab states to cut back expenditures, including funds earmarked for development projects. Korea is seeking to diversify its market into other regions including Southeast Asia, Africa, and Latin America and has already had some success. At the same time, Seoul does not want to dissolve its ties to the still lucrative Middle East market.

Despite a reduction in their oil imports from the region, as the Korean construction interests in the Middle East have expanded, so too has their vulnerability. It would be in Korea's best interest to make every effort not to become embroiled in the Middle East's emotion-laden political disputes. While perhaps eliciting some economic returns, adopting a political role in the region would mostly serve to increase Seoul's vulnerability in the Middle East. Korea must try to resist pressure to "take sides" in regional conflicts.

Korea continues to depend heavily on the Middle East for the health and prosperity of its construction industry and for related sectors of the economy. Despite some successful efforts to diversify into other geographical areas, the Middle East remains the focus of Seoul's overseas activities. In recent years Korea has begun to run into a number of problems with its work in the Arab states. The Arabs increasingly sought barter deals (primarily exchanging oil for contracting services) rather than payment in cash. The Koreans then faced the difficulty of disposing of the oil at a reasonable price to ensure themselves a profit. There has also been the problem posed by the shrinking of the Middle East market. By 1983 Korean companies began to be affected by the various problems encountered in the Middle East. It was estimated that nearly 20 companies had experienced financial difficulties because of overseas financial problems and several had gone bankrupt.

Korea is likely to continue to pursue a policy in the Middle East whose essence remains economic and to avoid politicization of its role—it is unlikely to take a more visible political position beyond seeking expanded diplomatic relationships in the area.

NOTES

1. The discussion focuses on the role of the Republic of Korea (South Korea) in the Middle East and North Africa. Nevertheless, it should be noted that North Korea has become increasingly active in the region although many of its activities have escaped public attention. For basic data on the relationship between North Korea and the Middle East see "Chronology of Relations Between Two Koreas and the Middle East; Part II: North Korea—The Middle East," *Korea & World Affairs* 8, No. 2 (Summer 1984), pp. 420–41.

2. Seoul Domestic Service, December 15, 1973. Text in Foreign Broadcast Information Service, *Daily Report: Asia and Pacific* [hereafter FBIS, *Daily Report*] (December 19, 1973).

3. FBIS, *Daily Report* (December 19, 1973).

4. FBIS, *Daily Report* (December 11, 1973).

5. *Ibid.*

6. Ui-Sup Shim, "Korea's participation in the Middle East construction market: An introduction," *Korean J. Middle East Studies* 4 (1983), p. 89.

7. *Ibid.*, p. 88.

8. John Burgess, "South Korea shakes up its global construction trade," Washington *Post* (October 23, 1984), p. D16.

9. Shim, "Korea's participation," p. 90.

10. Ibid., p. 88.

11. "Korea's Economy," Korea Economic Institute, Vol. 2, No. 8 (August 1983), p. 1.

12. Ibid., p. 1. See also Burgess, "South Korea shakes up," p. D16.

13. R. D. McLaurin and Chung-In Moon, "A precarious balance: Korea and the Middle East," *Korea and World Affairs* (Summer 1984), p. 246.

14. U.S. Congress, Office of Technology Assessment, *Technology Transfer to the Middle East* (Washington, D.C.: OTA-ISC-173, September 1984), p. 476.

15. "Korea's Economy," p. 2.

16. Shim, "Korea's participation," p. 86.

17. Yu Kun-ha, "3.3 bil. Libyan contract boost for Korean industry," The Korea *Herald* (November 10, 1983), p. 7.

18. "Dong Ah Wins $3.3 Bil. Libya Waterway Contract," Korea *Newsreview* (November 12, 1983), p. 14.

19. *Ibid.*

20. Boo Ki-yol, "Koreans building around the world," The Korea *Herald* (July 20, 1984), p. 3.

21. McLaurin and Moon, "A precarious balance," p. 248.

22. Boo Ki-yol, "Koreans building," p. 3.

23. *Ibid.*

24. Shim, "Korea's participation," p. 91.

25. "Korea's Economy," p. 6.

26. A government source quoted in "Saudis shelve Korean contracts," The Korea *Herald* (March 31, 1985), p. 6.

27. "Midwest oil imports fall below 60 percent of national demand," The Korea *Herald* (May 24, 1985), p. 7.

28. Yu Kun-ha, "3.3 bil. Libyan contract," p. 9.

29. "Further Korea-Arab cooperation stressed," The Korea *Herald* (April 3, 1985), p. 6.

30. Burgess, "South Korea shakes up," p. D16.

31. *Ibid.*

32. In a message sent to PLO Chairman Yasser Arafat on November 28, 1985, North Korean President Kim Il-Song expressed his solidarity with "the determined struggle of the Palestinian people" and the "just cause . . . of the Palestinian revolution. I take this opportunity to sincerely wish the Palestine Liberation Organization and the Palestinian people greater progress in their sacred struggle for sovereignty and independence." Text in FBIS, *Daily Report* (November 29, 1985), p. D10.

Suggested Reading

There is a vast literature, of varying quality and in numerous languages, on the Middle East that focuses on virtually all aspects of the subject matter of this book. The following highly selective list is designed to suggest a number of works that amplify the themes discussed in this volume.

GENERAL

L. Carl Brown, *International Politics and the Middle East: Old Rules, Dangerous Game* (Princeton, NJ: Princeton Univ. Press, 1984).

Shahram Chubin, *Security in the Persian Gulf IV: The Role of Outside Powers* (Totowa, NJ: International Institute for Strategic Studies, 1982).

Alvin J. Cottrell (ed.), *The Persian Gulf States: A General Survey* (Baltimore: Johns Hopkins Univ. Press, 1980).

Harry N. Howard, *Turkey, the Straits and U.S. Policy* (Baltimore: Johns Hopkins Univ. Press, 1974).

Chaim Herzog, *The Arab-Israeli Wars: War and Peace in the Middle East from the War of Independence Through Lebanon* (New York: Vintage Books, 1984).

Bruce R. Kuniholm, *The Persian Gulf and United States Policy: A Guide to Issues and References* (Claremont, CA: Regina Books, 1984).

George Lenczowski, *The Middle East in World Affairs*, 4th Ed. (Ithaca and London: Cornell Univ. Press, 1980).

Bernard Lewis, *The Arabs in History* (New York: Harper and Row, 1960).

Robert Litwak, *Security in the Persian Gulf, II: Sources of Interstate Conflict* (Montclair, NJ: The International Institute for Strategic Studies, 1981).

David E. Long and Bernard Reich (ed.), *The Government and Politics of the Middle East and North Africa*, 2nd Ed. (Boulder, CO: Westview Press, 1986).

Alvin Z. Rubinstein (ed.), *The Arab-Israeli Conflict: Perspectives* (New York: Praeger, 1984).

United States

Dean Acheson, *Present at the Creation: My Years in the State Department* (New York: Norton, 1969).

John S. Badeau, *The American Approach to the Arab World* (New York: Harper and Row, 1968).

Zbigniew Brzezinski, *Power and Principle: Memoirs of the National Security Adviser, 1977–1981* (New York: Farrar, Straus, Giroux, 1983).

John C. Campbell, *Defense of the Middle East: Problems of American Policy*, Rev. Ed. (New York: Praeger, 1960).

Jimmy Carter, *Keeping Faith: Memoirs of a President* (Toronto, New York, London, Sydney: Bantam Books, 1982).

John A. DeNovo, *American Interests and Policies in the Middle East, 1900–1939* (Minneapolis, MN: Univ. Minnesota Press, 1963).

Dwight D. Eisenhower, *The White House Years: Waging Peace, 1956–1961* (Garden City, NY: Doubleday, 1965).

David H. Finnie, *Pioneers East: The Early American Experience in the Middle East* (Cambridge, MA: Harvard Univ. Press, 1967).

J. C. Hurewitz, *Middle East Dilemmas: The Background of United States Policy* (New York: Harper, 1953).

Lyndon Baines Johnson, *The Vantage Point: Perspectives of the Presidency, 1963–1969* (New York: Holt, Rinehart, and Winston, 1971).

Henry Kissinger, *White House Years* (Boston and Toronto: Little, Brown, 1979).

Henry Kissinger, *Years of Upheaval* (Boston and Toronto: Little, Brown, 1982).

William R. Polk, *The United States and the Arab World*, 3rd Ed. (Cambridge MA and London, UK: Harvard Univ. Press, 1975).

William B. Quandt, *Decade of Decisions: American Policy Toward the Arab-Israeli Conflict, 1967–1976* (Berkeley, CA: Univ. California Press, 1977).

Bernard Reich, *Quest for Peace: United States-Israel Relations and the Arab-Israeli Conflict* (New Brunswick, NJ: Transaction Books, 1977).

Bernard Reich, *The United States and Israel: Influence in the Special Relationship* (New York: Praeger, 1984).

Mohammed K. Shadid, *The United States and the Palestinians* (London: Croom, Helm, 1981).

E. A. Speiser, *The United States and the Near East*, Rev. Ed. (Cambridge, MA: Harvard Univ. Press, 1950).

Seth P. Tillman, *The United States in the Middle East: Interests and Obstacles* (Bloomington, IN: Indiana Univ. Press, 1982).

Harry S. Truman, *Memoirs: Volume II: Years of Trial and Hope* (Garden City, NY: Doubleday, 1956).

Cyrus Vance, *Hard Choices: Critical Years in America's Foreign Policy* (New York: Simon and Schuster, 1983).

Soviet Union

Anthony Arnold, *Afghanistan: The Soviet Invasion in Perspective* (Stanford, CA: Hoover Institution Press, 1981).

Malumud Ata Alla, *Arab Struggle for Economic Independence*, (Translated by Bernard Isaacs; Moscow: Progress Publishers, 1974).

Alexander J. Bennett, "Arms transfer as an instrument of Soviet policy in the Middle East" *The Middle East Journal* 39 (Autumn 1985), pp. 745–74.

Henry S. Bradsher, *Afghanistan and the Soviet Union* (Durham, NC: Duke Univ. Press, 1983).

Joseph J. Collins, *The Soviet Invasion of Afghanistan: A Study in the Use of Force in Soviet Foreign Policy* (Lexington, MA: Lexington Books, 1985).

Adeed Dawisha and Karen Dawisha (eds.), *The Soviet Union in the Middle East: Policies and Perspectives* (New York: Holmes & Meier, 1982).

Faramarz S. Fatemi, *The U.S.S.R. in Iran: The Background History of Russian and Anglo-American Conflict in Iran, Its Effect on Iranian Nationalism, and the Fall of the Shah* (South Brunswick, NJ and New York: A. S. Barnes & Co., 1980; London: Thomas Yoseloff Ltd., 1980).

Robert O. Freedman, *Soviet Policy Toward the Middle East Since 1970* 3rd. ed. (New York: Praeger, 1982).

Jon D. Glassman, *Arms for the Arabs: The Soviet Union and the War in the Middle East* (Baltimore and London: Johns Hopkins Univ. Press, 1975).

Benson Lee Grayson, *Soviet Intentions and American Options in the Middle East*, National Security Affairs Monograph Series 82-3 (Washington, D.C.: National Defense Univ. Press, 1982).

A. A. Gromyko and B. N. Ponomarev (eds.), *Soviet Foreign Policy: 1917–1980*, 2 vols., 4th ed., revised and enlarged (Translated by David Skvirsky; Moscow: Progress Publishers, 1981).

Fred Halliday, *Soviet Policy in the Arc of Crisis* (Washington, D.C.: Institute for Policy Studies, 1981).

Thomas T. Hammond, *Red Flag Over Afghanistan: The Communist Coup, the Soviet Invasion, and the Consequences* (Boulder, CO: Westview Press, 1984).

Mohamed Heikal, *The Road to Ramadan* (New York: Ballantine Books, 1975).

Mohamed Heikal, *The Sphinx and the Commissar* (New York: Harper & Row, 1978).

Mark V. Kauppi and R. Craig Nation (eds.), *The Soviet Union and the Middle East in the 1980s: Opportunities, Constraints, and Dilemmas* (Lexington, MA: Lexington Books, 1983).

Arthur Jay Klinghoffer, *Israel and the Soviet Union: Alienation or Reconciliation?* (With Judith Apter; Boulder, CO: Westview Press, 1985).

George Lenczowski, *Soviet Advances in the Middle East* (Washington, D.C.: American Enterprise Institute, 1971).

Stephen Page, *The Soviet Union and the Yemens: Influence in Asymmetrical Relationships* (New York: Praeger, 1985).

The Policy of the Soviet Union in the Arab World: A Short Collection of Foreign Policy Documents (Moscow: Progress Publishers, 1975).

Y. M. Primakov, *Anatomy of the Middle East Conflict* (Translated by H. Vladimirsky; Moscow: "Nauka" Publishing House, 1979).

Bernard Reich and Alexander J. Bennett, "Soviet policy and American response in the Middle East" *Journal of East and West Studies* 13 (Fall/Winter 1984), pp. 79–112.

Yaacov Ro'i (ed.), *From Encroachment to Involvement: A Documentary Study of Soviet Policy in the Middle East, 1945–1973* (New York and Toronto: John Wiley & Sons, 1974; Jerusalem: Israel Univ. Press, 1974).

Yaacov Ro'i (ed.), *The Limits to Power: Soviet Policy in the Middle East* (London: Croom Helm, 1979).

Yaacov Ro'i (ed.), *The U.S.S.R. and the Muslim World: Issues in Domestic and Foreign Policy* (Boston and London: George Allen & Unwin, 1984).

Alvin Z. Rubinstein, *Red Star on the Nile: The Soviet-Egyptian Influence Relationship since the June War* (Princeton, NJ: Princeton Univ. Press, 1977).

Alvin Z. Rubinstein, *Soviet Policy Toward Turkey, Iran, and Afghanistan: The Dynamics of Influence* (New York: Praeger, 1982).

Herbert L. Sawyer, *Soviet Perceptions of the Oil Factor in U.S. Foreign Policy: The Middle East-Gulf Region* (Boulder, CO: Westview Press, 1983).

Amnon Sella, *Soviet Political and Military Conduct in the Middle East* (New York: St. Martin's Press, 1981).

Oles M. Smolansky, *The Soviet Union and the Arab East under Khrushchev* (Lewisburg, PA: Bucknell Univ. Press, 1974).

Aryeh Y. Yodfat, *The Soviet Union and the Arabian Peninsula: Soviet Policy Towards the Persian Gulf and Arabia* (London and Canberra: Croom Helm, 1983; New York: St. Martin's Press, 1983).

Aryeh Y. Yodfat, *The Soviet Union and Revolutionary Iran* (London and Canberra: Croom Helm, 1984; New York: St. Martin's Press, 1984).

Europe

David Allen and Alfred Pijpers (eds.), *European Foreign Policy-Making and the Arab-Israeli Conflict* (The Hague: Martinus Nijhoff, 1984).

Salah Al-Shaikhly, *The Euro-Arab Dialogue* (New York: St. Martin's Press, 1983).

Mustapha Benchenane, *Pour un dialogue Euro-Arabe* (Paris: Editions Berger-Levrault, 1983).

Adam M. Garfinkle, *Western Europe's Middle East Diplomacy and the U.S.* (Philadelphia, PA: Foreign Policy Research Institute, 1983).

Rouhollah K. Ramazani, *The Middle East and the European Common Market* (Charlottesville, VA: Univ. Press of Virginia, 1964).

Howard Morely Sachar, *Europe Leaves the Middle East, 1936–1954* (New York: Alfred A. Knopf, 1972).

Ann Williams, *Britain and France in the Middle East and North Africa* (London: Macmillan, 1968).

Great Britain

Jacob Abadi, *Britain's Withdrawal from the Middle East, 1947–1971* (Princeton, NJ: Kingston Press, 1982).

Philip Darby, *British Defence Policy East of Suez, 1947–1968* (London: Oxford Univ. Press for Royal Institute of International Affairs, 1973).

M. A. Fitzsimons, *Empire by Treaty: Britain and the Middle East in the Twentieth Century* (Notre Dame, IN: Univ. Notre Dame Press, 1964).

J. B. Kelly, *Arabia, the Gulf and the West* (London: Weidenfeld and Nicolson, 1980).

J. B. Kelly, *Britain and the Persian Gulf, 1795–1880* (Oxford: Clarendon Press, 1968).

Sir David Lee, *Flight from the Middle East: A History of the RAF in the Arabian Peninsula and Adjacent Territories, 1945–72* (London: HMSO, 1980).

Sir William Luce, "Britain's withdrawal," *Survival* ll, No. 6 (June 1969).

Elizabeth Monroe, *Britain's Moment in the Middle East 1914–71* (London: Chatto and Windus, 1981).

William Roger Louis, *The British Empire in the Middle East 1945–1951* (Oxford: Clarendon Press, 1984).

Sari J. Nasir, *The Arabs and the English* (London: Longman, 1979).

Sinclair Road, "Prospects for trade between Britain and the Arab Gulf," *Arab Gulf Journal* (October 1984).

Royal Institute of International Affairs, *British Interests in the Mediterranean and the Middle East* (New York: Oxford Univ. Press, 1958).

Sarah Searight, *The British in the Middle East* (London and the Hague: Weidenfeld and Nicholson, 1979).

William Wallace, *The Foreign Policy Process in Britain* (London: Royal Institute of International Affairs, 1975).

Keith Wilson (ed.), *Imperialism and Nationalism in the Middle East: The Anglo-Egyptian Experience 1882–1982* (London: Mansell, 1983).

France

Sylvia K. Crosbie, *A Tacit Alliance: France and Israel from Suez to the Six Day War* (Princeton, NJ: Princeton Univ. Press, 1974).

Alfred Grosser, *French Foreign Policy under de Gaulle* (Boston: Little, Brown & Company, 1965).

Stanley Hoffman, "Gaullism by any other name," *Foreign Policy* 57 (Winter 1984/1985), pp. 38–57.

R. J. Knecht, *Francis I* (New York: Cambridge Univ. Press, 1982).

Edward A. Kolodziej, "France and the arms trade," *International Affairs* (London) 56 (January 1980), pp. 54–72.

Edward A. Kolodziej, *French International Policy Under De Gaulle and Pompidou: The Politics of Grandeur* (Ithaca, NY: Cornell Univ. Press, 1974).

Stephen Hemsley Longrigg, *Syria and Lebanon Under French Mandate* (London: Oxford Univ. Press, 1958).

Dominique Moisi, "Mitterand's foreign policy: The limits of continuity," *Foreign Affairs* 60 (Winter 1981/82, pp. 347–57.

Frederick Seager, "New directions in French Middle East policy," *Middle East Review* 14 (Spring/Summer 1982); pp. 49–54.

Tony Smith, *The French Stake in Algeria, 1954–1962* (Ithaca, NY: Cornell Univ. Press, 1978).

John P. Spangnolo, *France & Ottoman Lebanon, 1861–1914*, Middle East Monographs No. 7 (Oxford: St. Anthony's, 1977).

John P. Spangnolo, "French influence in Syria prior to World War I," *The Middle East Journal* 23 (Winter 1969), pp. 45–62.

F. Roy Willis, *The French Paradox: Understanding Contemporary France* (Stanford, CA: Hoover Institution Press, 1982).

Asia

Edward E. Azar, "Soviet and Chinese roles in the Middle East," *Problems of Communism* 28 (May/June 1979), pp. 18–30.

Hashim S. H. Behbehani, *China's Foreign Policy in the Arab World, 1955–1975* (London and Boston: Kegan Paul International, 1981).

Michael Brecher, *Israel, the Korean War and China* (New Brunswick, NJ: Transaction Books, 1974).

Lillian Craig Harris, *China's Foreign Policy Toward the Third World*, Washington Papers No. 112 (New York: Praeger, with The Center for Strategic and International Studies, Georgetown Univ., Washington, D.C., 1985).

Ronald A. Morse (ed.), *Japan and the Middle East in Alliance Politics* (Washington, D.C.: The Wilson Center, 1985).

Yitzhak Shichor, *The Middle East in China's Foreign Policy 1949–1977* (Cambridge, UK: Cambridge Univ. Press, 1979).

Ui-Sup Shim, "Korea's participation in the Middle East construction market: An introduction," *Korean Journal of the Middle East Studies* 4 (1983), pp. 79–95.

Michael M. Yoshitsu, *Caught in the Middle East: Japan's Diplomacy in Transition* (Lexington, MA: Lexington Books, 1984).

Yuan-li Wu, *Japan's Search for Oil: A Case Study on Economic Nationalism and International Security* (Stanford, CA: Hoover Institution Press, 1977).

Index

Meijing Dynasty, 281
Mesopotamia, 181, 182, 183, 184
Mexico, 4, 5, 15, 17, 299
Middle East Association, 204, 218
Miki, Takeo, 287, 308
military assistance, 26, 32, 33, 35, 48, 49, 50, 64, 67, 75, 76, 83, 92, 93, 97, 98–102, 304
Military balance, 18, 23, 30
Mission Civilisatrice, 226
Missouri (Battleship), 25
Mitterrand, Francois, 173, 242–43, 245, 246, 247–52, 253–55, 258, 260–63
Mollet, Guy, 235, 236, 238
Molotov-Ribbentrop negotiations, 111
Mondialisme, French policy of, 237
Montreaux Convention, 21–23, 25, 26
Morocco, 49, 102, 131, 132, 133, 134, 137,138, 139, 140, 141, 153, 156, 158, 160, 161, 181, 279, 311; See also Maghreb and North Africa
Mossadeq, Muhammad, 32
Mubarak, Hosni, 30, 114, 133, 212
Multinational Force and Observers (MFO), 174, 202, 215
Multinational Force in Lebanon (MNF), 46, 86, 88, 94, 95, 174, 175, 205, 212, 215, 323; French Contingent of, 254–55
Murphy, Richard, 91
Musandam Peninsula, 18

Nakasone, Yasuhiro, 287, 307
Napoleon Bonaparte, 228, 237
Napolen, Louis, 230
Nasser, Gamal Abdul, 27–29, 39, 42, 43, 129, 136, 190, 191, 192, 235–36, 273
National Salvation Front, 47
Nationalism, 7, 27–28, 32, See also Arab nationalism
NATO, See North Atlantic Treaty Organization
Neo-Destour Party, 233
Netherlands, 9, 156, 163, 208
Neutral Zone, 5

Nicholas I, 230
Nigeria, 4, 5, 7, 252, 258
Nixon, Richard, 70, 73; Doctrine, 69, 70, 81; "new-initiative" concept, 72; resignation, 74
North Africa, 39, 49, 114, 115, 117, 125, 133, 140, 145, 156, 157, 294–95. See also Maghreb, individual countries
North Atlantic Treaty Organization (NATO), 10, 22, 23–27, 29, 30, 48, 59, 112, 115, 118, 124, 138, 156, 195, 199
North Korea, 323
North Sea, 15, 17, 30
North Yemen. See Yemen, North
Norway, 4, 5, 152
nuclear power, 15, 35, 252, 261, 299–300, 320

OAPEC. See Organization of Arab Petroleum Exporting Countries
OAU. See Organization of African Unity
occupied territories, 8, 40–41, 42, 162, 163, 170, 171, 200, 202, 203, 204, 212, 239, 263, 286, 213
Oceania, 317
OECD. See Organization for Economic Cooperation and Development
October 1917 (Russian) Revolution, 110, 136
October War (1973). See Arab-Israeli Wars, 1973
oil, 3–20, 23, 24, 30, 31–34, 35, 48–51, 72, 75, 91, 92, 157, 160, 162, 163, 164, 165, 167, 168, 175, 176, 177, 239, 244, 245, 269, 275, 281, 282, 283, 284, 285, 287, 288, 292, 294, 298, 299, 302, 303, 304, 305, 306, 308, 311, 312, 313, 314, 315, 316, 317, 318, 319, 320, 321, 322, 323, 324, 325. See also International Energy Agency, oil

About the Editor and Contributors

BERNARD REICH is Professor of Political Science and International Affairs and former Chairman of the Department of Political Science at George Washington University in Washington, D.C. He is the author of numerous books and articles on various aspects of the politics and international relations of the Middle East including *Quest for Peace: United States-Israel Relations and the Arab-Israeli Conflict* (Transaction, 1977), *The United States and Israel: Influence in the Special Relationship* (Praeger, 1984), and *Israel: Land of Tradition and Conflict* (Westview, 1985). He is coeditor of *The Government and Politics of the Middle East and North Africa* (Westview, 1980 and 1986) and *Israel Faces the Future* (Praeger, 1986).

ALEXANDER J. BENNETT has a Ph.D. in political science from the George Washington University where he served as a Graduate Teaching Fellow. His dissertation focused on the Soviet Union and its military supply relationship with the states of the Middle East. He has published several articles on the Soviet role in the Middle East.

PATRICK COQUILLON holds B.A. and M.A. degrees in linguistics as applied to economics from Toulouse in France and an M.A. in Middle Eastern studies from the George Washington University in Washington, D.C. He resides in the Ivory Coast and is involved in the import-export business between Europe, Africa, and the Middle East.

TIMOTHY J. PIRO is a Ph.D. candidate and Graduate Teaching Fellow in the Department of Political Science at George Washington University. He recieved his B.A. from Fordham University where he majored in political science and French literature.

CHERYL CUTLER is a Ph.D. candidate in the Department of Political Science at George Washington University where she is a Graduate Teaching Fellow. She received a B.A. in economics from Brandeis University and an M.A. in Middle Eastern studies from George Washington University. She specializes in the politics and economics of the Middle East and has studied at the Jacob Hiatt Institute in Jerusalem.

ROSEMARY HOLLIS graduated from King's College, London, with an M.A. in war studies. She subsequently did research on Middle Eastern history in London and is completing a Ph.D. in political science with a Middle East specialty at George Washington University where she teaches a course on politics and values. The focus of her research is on the role of Britian in the Middle East. Her publications include an examination of the relationship of the United Nations and Israel and the Reagan administration's peace efforts in the Middle East. Her latest publications focus on conflict and conflict resolution in the Middle East.

GERSHON R. KIEVAL is Adjunct Professor of Political Science at George Washington University. He is the author of *Party Politics in Israel and the Occupied Territories*, coeditor and coauthor of *Israel Faces the Future*, and author of various articles on United States Middle East policy and Israeli politics.

JOHN H. McFADDEN is a retired army officer who spent most of his career dealing with Middle Eastern affairs, including assignments with the Political Military Affairs and the Political Sections of the U.S. Embassy in Ankara, Turkey. He served as Director of Middle East Studies at the John F. Kennedy Institute for Special Warfare and in the Defense Intelligence Agency. He holds a Ph.D. in political science from the George Washington University and has published a number of articles on Middle East politics and on civil violence in Turkey.